Lecture Notes in Business Information Processing 587

Series Editors

LNBIP reports state-of-the-art results in areas related to business information systems and industrial application software development – timely, at a high level, and in both printed and electronic form.

The type of material published includes

- Proceedings (published in time for the respective event)
- Postproceedings (consisting of thoroughly revised and/or extended final papers)
- Other edited monographs (such as, for example, project reports or invited volumes)
- Tutorials (coherently integrated collections of lectures given at advanced courses, seminars, schools, etc.)
- Award-winning or exceptional theses

LNBIP is abstracted/indexed in DBLP, EI and Scopus. LNBIP volumes are also submitted for the inclusion in ISI Proceedings.

Francesca Zerbato · Jelena Zdravkovic ·
Luise Pufahl · Geert Poels · Marite Kirikova
Editors

Intelligent Information Systems

CAiSE 2026 Forum and Doctoral Consortium
Verona, Italy, June 8–12, 2026
Proceedings

Springer

Editors
Francesca Zerbato
Technical University of Eindhoven
Eindhoven, The Netherlands

Jelena Zdravkovic
Stockholm University
Kista, Sweden

Luise Pufahl
Technical University of Munich
Heilbronn, Germany

Geert Poels
University of Ghent
Ghent, Belgium

Marite Kirikova
Riga Technical University
Riga, Latvia

ISSN 1865-1348 ISSN 1865-1356 (electronic)
Lecture Notes in Business Information Processing
ISBN 978-3-032-27996-5 ISBN 978-3-032-27997-2 (eBook)
https://doi.org/10.1007/978-3-032-27997-2

This Springer imprint is published by the registered company Springer Nature Switzerland AG
The registered company address is: Gewerbestrasse 11, 6330 Cham, Switzerland

Preface CAiSE 2026 Forum

The CAiSE conference series is the flagship international venue for information systems engineering, providing a platform for disseminating research results and exchanging experiences from industrial practice. The 38th edition of the CAiSE conference was held in Verona, Italy, June 8–12, 2026. This year, the conference specifically addressed the theme "Rethinking Information System Engineering in a continuously changing information system world," reflecting the need to evolve our theoretical and operational foundations to meet the demands of modern, volatile digital ecosystems.

The CAiSE Forum is an interactive session within the conference for presenting and debating emerging research ideas and software tools. In alignment with the aims and scope of CAiSE 2026, the Forum considered two types of submissions:

- Vision papers that present innovative research projects or emerging problems and areas of interest for the community. These papers articulate novel visions based on preliminary insights.
- Demo papers that describe innovative tools and prototypes developed to implement research results.

The Forum received 21 submissions. Additionally, 13 submissions were redirected to the Forum from the CAiSE main research track and had already undergone the peer review process of the conference. The 21 submissions were each reviewed by three Forum PC members in a single-blind review process. The submissions that achieved the highest consensus on novelty and rigor were accepted for presentation at the Forum. Out of the 21 regular submissions, 10 papers were accepted. In total, 23 papers were presented at the CAiSE 2026 Forum, of which 16 were vision papers, and seven were tool demonstrations.

We would like to thank the authors for their contributions and the reviewers for their commitment to maintaining the quality of the research presented at the CAiSE Forum. We extend our gratitude to the General Chairs, the Program Chairs of the main conference, and the Proceedings Chair for their support in coordinating the Forum organization.

June 2026

Francesca Zerbato
Jelena Zdravkovic

Organization

Chairs

Francesca Zerbato	Technical University of Eindhoven, The Netherlands
Jelena Zdravkovic	Stockholm University, Sweden

Program Committee

Anti Alman	Free University of Bozen-Bolzano, Italy
Steven Alter	University of San Francisco, USA
Yannis Bertrand	Hasselt University, Belgium
Drazen Brdjanin	University of Banja Luka, Bosnia and Herzegovina
Cinzia Cappiello	Politecnico di Milano, Italy
Anouck Chan	Onera, France
Sergio de Cesare	University of Westminster, UK
Sybren de Kinderen	Eindhoven University of Technology, The Netherlands
Djordje Djurica	Vienna University of Economics and Business, Austria
Michael Fellmann	University of Rostock, Germany
Hans-Georg Fill	University of Fribourg, Switzerland
Mohamad Gharib	University of Tartu, Estonia
Jānis Grabis	Riga Technical University, Latvia
Sergio Guerreiro	INESC-ID/University of Lisbon, Portugal
Simon Hacks	Stockholm University, Sweden
Martin Henkel	Stockholm University, Sweden
Christian Janiesch	TU Dortmund, Germany
Jānis Kampars	Riga Technical University, Latvia
Marite Kirikova	Riga Technical University, Latvia
Janne J. Korhonen	Aalto University, Finland
Elena Kornyshova	Conservatoire National des Arts et Métiers, France
Agnes Koschmider	University of Bayreuth, Germany
Lawrence Chung	University of Texas at Dallas, USA
Henrik Leopold	Kühne Logistics University, Germany

Andrea Marrella	Sapienza University of Rome, Italy
Raimundas Matulevičius	University of Tartu, Estonia
Giovanni Meroni	Technical University of Denmark, Denmark
Jose Ignacio Panach Navarrete	Universitat de València, Spain
Oscar Pastor	Universidad Politécnica de Valencia, Spain
Henderik A. Proper	TU Wien, Austria
Manuel Resinas	University of Seville, Spain
Andrey Rivkin	Technical University of Denmark, Denmark
Ben Roelens	Open Universiteit, The Netherlands
Mattia Salnitri	University of Bergamo, Italy
Irene Vanderfeesten	KU Leuven, Belgium
Charlotte Verbruggen	TU Wien, Austria
Manuel Wimmer	Johannes Kepler University Linz, Austria
Karolin Winter	Eindhoven University of Technology, The Netherlands

Additional Reviewers

Marianne Schnellmann
Maximilian Britton
Yorck Zisgen
Quan Huynh

Preface CAiSE 2026 Doctoral Consortium

This volume contains the accepted papers presented at the Doctoral Consortium, held in conjunction with the 38th International Conference on Advanced Information Systems Engineering (CAiSE 2026). The CAiSE 2026 conference took place in Verona, Italy, from June 8 to 12, 2026, under the theme "Rethinking Information System Engineering in a continuously changing information system world". In line with the tradition of the CAiSE conference series, the Doctoral Consortium aimed to attract PhD candidates working on foundations, techniques, tools, and applications in the Information Systems Engineering field. It provided a supportive environment for these candidates to present their research, receive constructive feedback from peers and senior faculty, and engage in discussions tailored to their needs and interests.

The CAiSE 2026 Doctoral Consortium received a total of 15 submissions, of which 8 were accepted for presentation and inclusion in these proceedings. The review process was single-blind, with each submission reviewed by at least two senior researchers from the Doctoral Consortium Mentoring Board. The main evaluation criteria included relevance, originality, significance, technical soundness, accuracy, clarity, and the expected benefits to the PhD candidate from participating in the Doctoral Consortium.

The eight accepted papers cover several topics within the scope of the conference and are structured in three sessions, with two to three papers each. Within the **Process Mining: Supporting Analysis and Use in Practice** session, Zahra Ahmadi's research investigates interactive, context-aware navigation of process models discovered from event data by leveraging contextual information to balance model complexity and interpretability. Antolin Claude's research investigates AI-mediated scaffolding to support hypothesis testing in process mining by simulating complementary analytical roles and improving analytical reasoning. Angela Sekulovska's research examines how different archetypes of process mining setups in organizations influence performance through a mixed-methods approach.

Within the **Requirements Engineering** session, Franziska Hollauf's research introduces methods and algorithms to verify temporal requirements under uncertainty using the concept of agile controllability, Jessica Kollmorgen's research extends the scope of UX evaluation by incorporating user- and context-related prerequisites to improve the interpretability of evaluation results, and Ada Slupczynski's research proposes a knowledge-based and LLM-supported framework to enable more transparent and evidence-based modernization decisions for legacy information systems.

Within the **Data Foundations for Information System Engineering** session, Hosna Hooshyar's research develops ontology-based foundations for object-centric event data, including its conceptualization, extraction from legacy systems, and querying, and Vito Chan's research focuses on integrating geospatial data into business process management to better capture and analyze processes in physical environments.

Participation in the Doctoral Consortium offered PhD candidates the opportunity to receive constructive and personalised feedback from dedicated mentors, to interact with established researchers and practitioners, and to develop a supportive community of peer scholars. Furthermore, participants become eligible to apply for the "CAISE PhD Award" after their thesis has been defended.

We would like to express our gratitude to the CAiSE 2026 General Chairs, Carlo Combi and Hajo Reijers, and the Organizational Team and the Proceedings Chairs for their support. We are also grateful to the members of the Mentoring Board for their invaluable time and expertise in reviewing the submissions and providing guidance to the students. Finally, we thank all the PhD candidates for their contributions and active participation. We are confident that they have a successful career ahead of them.

April 2026

Luise Pufahl
Geert Poels
Marite Kirikova

Organization

Chairs

Marite Kirikova	Riga Technical University, Latvia
Geert Poels	University of Gent, Belgium
Luise Pufahl	Technical University of Munich, Germany

Doctoral Consortium Mentoring Board

Andrea Marrella	Sapienza University of Rome, Italy
Barbara Pernici	Politecnico di Milano, Italy
Ben Roelens	Open Universiteit, The Netherlands
Dominik Bork	TU Wien, Austria
Felix O. Garcia	University of Castilla-La Mancha, Spain
Giovanni Meroni	Technical University of Denmark, Denmark
Han van der Aa	University of Vienna, Austria
Iris Beerepoot	Utrecht University, The Netherlands
Isabelle Wattiau	ESSEC Business School, France
Jānis Grabis	Riga Technical University, Latvia
Janis Stirna	Stockholm University, Sweden
Jana-Rebecca Rehse	University of Mannheim, Switzerland
Jeffrey Parsons	Memorial University of Newfoundland, Canada
Jolita Ralyté	University of Geneva, Switzerland
Mieke Jans	Hasselt University, Belgium
Pnina Soffer	University of Haifa, Israel
Robert Andrei Buchmann	Babeş-Bolyai University of Cluj Napoca, Romania
Sander J. J. Leemans	RWTH Aachen, Germany
Ulrich Frank	Universität Duisburg-Essen, Germany

Contents

CAiSE 2026 Doctoral Consortium - Data Foundation for Information System Engineering

CAiSE 2026 Forum – Vision Papers

Train While You Fight - Technical Requirements for Advanced Distributed Learning Platforms

Simon Hacks(✉)

Stockholm University, Stockholm, Sweden
simon.hacks@dsv.su.se

Abstract. "Train While You Fight" (TWYF) advocates continuous learning during operations, not just before or after. This paper examines the technical requirements that advanced distributed learning (ADL) platforms must meet to support TWYF, and how existing software engineering patterns can fulfill these requirements. We (i) derive challenges from PfPC/NATO documentation and recent practice, (ii) define solution objectives, and (iii) conduct a systematic mapping from challenges to proven patterns. We identify seven technical challenges: interoperability, resilience, multilingual support, data security and privacy, scalability, platform independence, and modularity. We illustrate the patterns with a national use case from the German armed forces.

Keywords: Advanced Distributed Learning · Train While You Fight · Interoperability · Resilience

1 Introduction

For decades, military education and training have been guided by the maxim "train like you fight (TLYF)." [18] In practice, this meant preparing forces in peacetime through exercises and courseware that emulate anticipated operational conditions as closely as possible, with the expectation that well-rehearsed routines would transfer into real missions [32].

However, recent large-scale conflicts, most prominently Russia's war against Ukraine, have demonstrated that tactics, techniques, and technologies evolve so rapidly in contact that static, pre-deployment training is no longer sufficient. New weapon systems, counter-measures, and command-and-control (C2) procedures[1] appear and iterate on timescales of weeks or even days, rendering previously prepared materials partially obsolete. This underscores the need for continuous, adaptive learning during operations [27,32]. Reflecting this, the Partnership for Peace Consortium (PfPC) Advanced Distributed Learning (ADL) Working Group Co-Chair and German ADL Director, Lt. Col. Nickolaus, stresses that

[1] C2 describes the structures, processes, and tools by which commanders direct and coordinate forces [16].

F. Zerbato et al. (Eds.): CAiSE 2026, LNBIP 587, pp. 3–10, 2026.
https://doi.org/10.1007/978-3-032-27997-2_1

sustaining effective training through crisis and war is an operational imperative, with the goal of hardening training establishments against intended targeting during war so that personnel can continue learning while fighting.

Train While You Fight (TWYF) addresses these challenges and is operationalized through four complementary strategies [27,32]: (i) *Lean Principles in Training Design.* (ii) *Mass Customization and Personalized Learning.* (iii) *On-Demand Production of Training Content.* (iv) *Digital Learning Ecosystems.* [1,2,14]. To align with TWYF, classical learning platforms must evolve. Traditional, monolithic Learning Management System (LMS) deployments and coarse-grained course packages struggle with: (a) interoperability across heterogeneous national systems and standards; (b) resilience to cyber/kinetic disruptions and bandwidth constraints; (c) multilingual localization; and (d) user security and privacy in a federated, cross-border environment. Addressing these constraints requires architectural and design choices that go beyond incremental feature additions [2,32].

While technological architectures enable TWYF, it is commanders who operationalize it under pressure. The resilience of training systems depends not only on platforms and networks but on leadership, organizational culture, governance, and institutional readiness to adapt under wartime conditions [27].

In Design Science Research terms, this paper addresses the early phases of problem identification and definition of solution objectives. First, drawing on TWYF-aligned requirements from PfPC/NATO documents and recent practice, we consolidate recurrent technical concerns into a set of design-relevant challenge areas for ADL platforms (Sect. 3). Second, we translate these challenge areas into solution objectives and systematically map them to software engineering patterns that offer reusable implementation principles for addressing them (Sect. 4). The resulting pattern set should therefore be understood not as a finished instantiation, but as a design-oriented knowledge base that informs later DSR phases concerned with artefact design, implementation, and evaluation. We illustrate this prospective application using the *Virtuelle Lernumgebung der Bundeswehr*[2] (VLBw) as an example context for demonstrating how the identified patterns could guide a future platform implementation (Sect. 5).

2 Related Work and Background

A set of recent TWYF-focused contributions provides the operational and governance context for this paper. The PfPC information paper frames TWYF as a coalition imperative, draws lessons from Ukraine, and stresses that training infrastructure must be treated as an intentional military target; it therefore recommends resilient-by-design, standards-based ADL, strict handling of personal data, and interoperability and shareability across partners under denied, degraded, intermittent, and limited conditions [32]. Presnall et al. further elaborate TWYF as a response to rapid operational change, describing "novel strategies" (lean, mass customization, on-demand content, digital ecosystems) and

[2] engl.: Virtual Learning Environment of the German Armed Forces.

highlighting that mature interoperability standards are still underused in multinational sharing; they emphasize decentralized learning networks and governance for classification, licensing, and version control to enable safe reuse [27]. Complementing these, the MCDC guidebook targets commanders with practical tools to sustain training under cyber/kinetic/spectrum pressure, including the DTRMM and MTCC to support continuity, failover, and surge planning across institutions operating at different maturity levels [21].

From a broader ADL perspective, the literature describes a shift from isolated courseware and monolithic LMS deployments toward an integrated learning ecosystem that spans organizations and platforms [26]. Recent work argues that future learning infrastructures require open interoperability frameworks and shared architectural approaches to connect diverse stakeholders and data flows at scale [3,26].

3 Challenges of an Advanced Distributed Learning Platform

Interoperability *Challenge.* ADL platforms must integrate heterogeneous national systems and exchange content across organizational and technical boundaries. Interoperability encompasses syntactic and semantic compatibility, federation of identity and access, and cross-system discovery while respecting classification [2]. *Rationale.* Standards-based interoperability (e.g., SCORM, xAPI, LTI) and cataloging/metadata practices are emphasized [1,14] to enable shareable-by-design content and federated data flows in multinational contexts. Presnall et al. [27] highlight that allies currently underutilize mature e-learning standards and lack systemic mechanisms for discovery and sharing.

Resilience *Challenge.* TWYF platforms must operate under contested, degraded, and denied conditions, including cyber attacks, kinetic disruptions, intermittent power and bandwidth, and loss of central infrastructure.[3] *Rationale.* Training infrastructure becomes an intended target in war and must be survivable, redundant, and recoverable; PACE-style delivery (Primary/Alternate/Contingency/Emergency) and cloud–edge hybrids help ensure continuity [32]. Presnall et al. [27] argue that resilient, decentralized delivery and rapid incorporation of lessons learned are essential for sustaining learning during operations.

Multilingual Support *Challenge.* NATO coalitions operate in many languages. Therefore, contents must be localized and culturally adapted. [23]. *Rationale.* NATO DEEP [23] and PfPC [32] reports foreground multilingual delivery as a condition for intellectual interoperability and rapid uptake at scale, documenting successful translation campaigns and tooling needs for localization and re-use. Presnall et al. [27] explicitly call for "designed-to-share" content with clear licensing, classification, and versioning to support multinational localization and economies of scale.

---

[3] Resilience is not solely technical, but covers multiple layers in an organization, such as human, infrastructure, procedures, and culture.

Data Security and Privacy *Challenge.* Learning systems process sensitive personal data (PII), operational contexts, and classified materials; in wartime, compromise of learner identities or activity data can endanger personnel. *Rationale.* PfPC [32] stresses the heightened risk of personal data misuse by adversaries and recommends minimizing PII, enforcing secure-by-design practices, and carefully managing cross-border sharing. Reach-back intensifies security and privacy demands: ingesting media from mobile devices across organizational boundaries requires strong identity and auditable cross-domain handling, while a 24/7 intake hub must absorb bursty uploads from dispersed units and route them through review and publication pipelines without delaying routine delivery.

Scalability *Challenge.* TWYF requires rapidly scaling throughput to train surges of recruits, re-skill units on new systems, and propagate updates within days. Platforms must elastically scale content delivery, assessment, analytics, and storage across regions while sustaining acceptable latency over constrained links [32]. *Rationale.* Case evidence from Ukraine and NATO exercises points to dramatic fluctuations in training demand and the need for cloud-based elasticity, CDN-style distribution, and edge caches for low-bandwidth theaters [27,32].

Platform Independence *Challenge.* Forces use diverse devices (e.g., desktop, mobile, ruggedized edge), operating systems, and national platforms. *Rationale.* Emphasis on standards targets portability across heterogeneous environments and future components, enabling nations to adopt without rip-and-replace [2]. PfPC [32] advocates using open standards and modular interfaces to avoid siloed national solutions and to facilitate federation, including secure mobile access at the point of need.

Modularity *Challenge.* To keep pace with change, platforms must support modular design, recomposition of curricula, and branching by role, mission, or classification. *Rationale.* Contemporary practices (e.g., microlearning, reusable learning objects) consistently argue for modular content to improve adaptability, reuse, and analytics [14]. Presnall et al. [27] promote mass customization and on-demand production predicated on modular, metadata-rich content and processes.

4 Software Engineering Patterns for an Advanced Distributed Learning Platform

Interoperability The *Adapter Pattern* [12] wraps legacy LMS, simulation, or repository APIs behind uniform interfaces so otherwise incompatible systems can interoperate. The *Service Broker Pattern* decouples clients and services by routing requests through a broker that registers capabilities and mediates calls [11,30]. For cross-module events, *Publish–Subscribe Messaging* enables services to publish updates (e.g., xAPI statements, content changes) and consumers to subscribe without tight coupling [13].

Resilience *Primary–Backup Replication* provides failover by maintaining a hot standby that can take over if the primary fails [5,31]. The *Bulkhead* and *Circuit Breaker* patterns limit cascading failures and enable controlled degradation when dependencies are unstable [19,22]. *Client-side caching and synchronization* supports DDIL continuity by keeping content and progress locally and syncing when connectivity returns [15,25].

Multilingual Support The *Externalized Resources Pattern* moves UI strings and media into resource bundles so new languages can be added easily [17].

Data Security and Privacy *Federated Identity/SSO* delegates authentication to trusted Identity Providers (IdPs) and enables cross-system access without replication [4]. *RBAC* enforces least privilege through role/attribute assignments and supports auditable access control [28]. Centralized *Audit and Intrusion Detection* provides tamper-resistant logs and monitoring [9].

Scalability *Load Balancing* spreads requests across instances to reduce bottlenecks and tail latency [7,20]. *Caching and content distribution* place hot content closer to users to reduce latency and bandwidth use [25]. *Sharding and replication* scale storage and throughput by partitioning learners/content and using replicas where needed [6,8].

Platform Independence A *Wrapper Façade* hides OS/device specifics behind a stable interface to keep clients portable [29]. *Microservices* expose capabilities through technology-agnostic APIs, allowing heterogeneous clients and national systems to integrate [10]. A *Plugin Architecture* adds new adapters via extension points without changing core logic [12,30].

Modularity A *Microkernel* keeps a small core and adds capabilities as plugins for evolution [30]. *Microservices* support independent deployment and targeted scaling of specific functions [10]. *Separation of concerns* keeps presentation, domain logic, and integration/data access distinct to localize change [24].

5 Demonstration

To demonstrate the mapping between challenges and patterns, we use the VLBw as a working example. VLBw is being developed and will be operated on the Bundeswehr private cloud for open and confidential information and assembles a modular ecosystem around a central 2D/3D entry portal, a common learning middleware that integrates functional elements, and a set of core services: LMS, virtual classrooms, a 3D learning environment, authoring and trainer tools, quality-assured document management with workflows, evaluation and exam administration, semantic search with AI-supported recommendations and chatbot, social functions, and a streaming platform. The platform also integrates with systems and training applications, while reusing email, chat, and calendar features from the intranet. Access is differentiated by user groups[4] with integrated registration for linked legacy services.

Interoperability. A pragmatic approach is to let the common learning middleware act as a lightweight service broker and integration layer, using adapters to wrap legacy systems behind uniform APIs, and a small publish–subscribe

[4] (1) members of the German armed forces; (2) non-members of the German armed forces with access to confidential information; (3) non-members of the German armed forces with no access to confidential information.

backbone for cross-module events [12,13,30]. **Resilience** Because disruption is expected, services should be isolated and protected against cascading failures and support DDIL continuity through edge/offline delivery: forward caches/LRS buffering and offline-first clients that synchronize when connectivity returns; the reach-back path should follow the same offline-first and protected design [15,22]. **Multilingual support** Internationalize the platform via externalized resources, and keep content translations aligned with masters through a simple language-pack workflow that preserves shared metadata and blocks publication until required locales are ready [17]. **Data security and privacy** Use federated SSO with RBAC/attributes for coalition access, central auditable logging, and classification/release tags enforced at service boundaries; reach-back requires the same controls plus redaction and guarded cross-domain handling [4,9,28]. **Scalability** Plan for surge with load balancing, edge caching for media and popular content, and scalable data services, using queues where workloads are bursty [7,8]. **Platform independence** Hide device specifics behind a wrapper façade on clients and expose stable microservice APIs on the server so new tools integrate via adapters and plugins without changing core services [10,29]. **Modularity** Keep a small core (portal/middleware) and add capabilities as loosely coupled services/plugins with clear separation of concerns so components can evolve or be replaced incrementally [24,30]. To support commanders in disruption scenarios, the platform should expose a small set of decision hooks and enable PACE-style rerouting and relocation by re-binding endpoints via the broker and pre-positioning content to alternative sites [21].

6 Discussion and Conclusions

This study maps TWYF-related challenges to software engineering patterns. The problem framing relies on publicly available sources; classified details and nation-specific constraints are out of scope, which supports reproducibility but may miss requirements that only appear in protected settings. The consolidation of challenges requires interpretation, so some construct bias is possible despite explicit criteria. We also assume that standards are widely available and consistently implemented, whereas in practice, national profiles, policy restrictions, and classification rules can constrain interoperability and sharing. Finally, the paper focuses on technical design; governance, acquisition, sustainment, and training workforce factors are acknowledged but not assessed.

The mapping is grounded in well-established distributed systems, integration, and security patterns, but it is not exhaustive. Claims that patterns mitigate challenges are supported by the literature rather than by prototypes or controlled comparisons. The VLBw demonstration is illustrative; without implementation, exercises, or user studies, we cannot make empirical claims about effectiveness, effort, or risk reduction, and generalization across nations remains limited. Although developed in a military training context, the identified patterns are transferable to civilian critical infrastructures, which increasingly must be designed for resilience against hybrid disruptions affecting society.

The main insight is that TWYF does not require new technology as much as careful composition of proven patterns. A brokered, event-driven core with federated identity and consistent data tagging supports interoperability and controlled sharing, while edge-aware delivery, modular boundaries, and offline synchronization support continuity and stepwise adoption. Treating training infrastructure as an intentional military target sharpens these priorities and links technical choices to disruption scenarios. Future work should validate the blueprint through prototyping and quantitative evaluation, run cross-national interoperability trials and security assessments, and extend the pattern set toward zero-trust variants and AI-supported content and observability pipelines.

Acknowledgments. I would like to thank Dr. Aaron Presnall and Lt. Col. Michael Nickolaus for their valuable input on this work.

Disclosure of Interests. The author serves as a reserve soldier in the unit overseen by Lt. Col. Michael Nickolaus, which is responsible for the VLBw program. This study was conducted entirely outside that service. The Bundeswehr provided no study-specific funding and had no role in the study design, data collection, analysis, writing, or the decision to publish. Only publicly available and unclassified sources were used.

References

1. ADL Initiative: Scorm 2004, 4th edn. (2004). https://adlnet.gov/scorm/
2. ADL Initiative: Total learning architecture: Overview and reference implementation. Tech. rep., U.S. DoD (2022). https://adlnet.gov/projects/tla/
3. Barr, A.B., Fletcher, J.D., Morrison, J.E.: The advanced distributed learning's total learning architecture: Ida report 2020 (2020). Institute for Defense Analyses
4. Broeder, D., Florio, L., Wartel, R., et al.: Federated identity management for research collaborations (fim4r) - a roadmap for research communities. Tech. rep, CERN, Geneva, Switzerland (2012)
5. Budhiraja, N., Marzullo, K., Schneider, F.B., Toueg, S.: The primary-backup approach. In: Distributed Systems, 2 edn., pp. 199–216. ACM Press / Addison-Wesley (1993)
6. Corbett, J.C.: Spanner: Google's globally-distributed database. In: 10th USENIX Symposium on Operating Systems Design and Implementation, pp. 251–264. USENIX Association (2012)
7. Dean, J., Barroso, L.A.: The tail at scale. Commun. ACM **56**(2), 74–80 (2013)
8. DeCandia, G., et al.: Dynamo: Amazon's highly available key-value store. In: 21st ACM Symposium on Operating Systems Principles, pp. 205–220. ACM (2007)
9. Dougherty, C., Sayre, K., Seacord, R., Svoboda, D., Togashi, K.: Secure design patterns (2009)
10. Dragoni, N., et al.: Microservices: Yesterday, today, and tomorrow. In: Present and Ulterior Software Engineering, pp. 195–216. Springer (2017)
11. Fernandez, E.B., Yoshioka, N.: Two patterns for distributed systems: enterprise service bus (esb) and distributed publish/subscribe. In: 18th Conference on Pattern Languages of Programs, pp. 1–10 (2011)
12. Gamma, E., Helm, R., Johnson, R., Vlissides, J.: Design patterns: elements of reusable object-oriented software, Pearson Deutschland GmbH (1995)

13. Hohpe, G., Woolf, B.: Enterprise Integration Patterns: Designing, Building, and Deploying Messaging Solutions. Addison-Wesley, Boston, MA (2004)
14. IEEE: Experience api (xapi) specification version 2.0 (2022). https://opensource.ieee.org/xapi/xapi-base-standard-documentation
15. Kistler, J.J., Satyanarayanan, M.: Disconnected operation in the Coda file system. ACM Trans. Comput. Syst. **10**(1), 3–25 (1992)
16. Lundberg, J., Hacks, S., Andersson, K.E.: Refinement of a conceptual model of a military c2-system through low-level goal decomposition. In: Practice of Enterprise Modeling Forum. CEUR Workshop Proceedings, vol. 3855. CEUR-WS.org (2024)
17. Mahemoff, M.J., Pozza, L.D.: The planet pattern language for software internationalisation. In: Proceedings of PLoP'99 (1999)
18. McGraw, A.P.: "Train Like you Fight": A Literature Review of Best Practices for Training Marines to Perform in Stressful Combat Situations. North Carolina State University (2023)
19. Mendonça, N.C., Aderaldo, C.M., Cámara, J., Garlan, D.: Model-based analysis of microservice resiliency patterns. In: ICSA. IEEE (2020)
20. Mitzenmacher, M.: The power of two choices in randomized load balancing. IEEE Trans. Parallel Distrib. Syst. **12**(10), 1094–1104 (2001)
21. No Author: Commander's guidebook on sustaining military training in wartime (to be published). Tech. rep., Multinational Capability Development Campaign (2025), draft version 0.5, 15 Oct 2025
22. Nygard, M.T.: Release It!: Design and Deploy Production-Ready Software. The Pragmatic Bookshelf, 2 edn. (2018)
23. Operations Division Defence and Security Cooperation Directorate NATO HQ: Nato deep eacademy: Enhancing distance learning and faculty development (2023). https://www.nato.int/cps/en/natohq/topics_139182.htm
24. Parnas, D.L.: On the criteria to be used in decomposing systems into modules. Commun. ACM **15**(12), 1053–1058 (1972)
25. Pathan, M., Buyya, R.: A taxonomy and survey of content delivery networks. In: Content Delivery Networks, pp. 33–77. Springer (2008)
26. Perisic, A., Perisic, I., Lazic, M., Perisic, B.: The foundation for future education, teaching, training, learning, and performing infrastructure - the open interoperability conceptual framework approach. Heliyon **9**(6), e16836 (2023)
27. Presnall, A., Nickolaus, M., Banks, S.: Train while we fight: Novel strategies for improving education and training. Connections Quarterly J. **24**(1), 59–71 (2024)
28. Sandhu, R.S., Coyne, E.J., Feinstein, H.L., Youman, C.E.: Role-based access control models. IEEE Comput. **29**(2), 38–47 (1996)
29. Schmidt, D.C.: Wrapper facade. In: Pattern Languages of Program Design, vol. 2, Addison-Wesley (1996)
30. Schmidt, D.C., Stal, M., Rohnert, H., Buschmann, F.: Pattern-oriented software architecture, patterns for concurrent and networked objects. John Wiley & Sons (2013)
31. Schneider, F.B.: Implementing fault-tolerant services using the state machine approach: a tutorial. ACM Comput. Surv. **22**(4), 299–319 (1990)
32. Seguin, B., Wagner, R., Pavliuk, O., Mirnenko, V., Thurkettle, P., Presnall, A., Bogdanoski, M.: Training while we fight: Lessons from Ukraine's use of distributed learning in war, Marshall European Center for Security Studies (2023). information Paper

Automated Extraction of Conceptual Representations from Research Articles Using Large Language Models

Jacky Akoka[1], Isabelle Comyn-Wattiau[2](✉), and Cédric du Mouza[1]

[1] CEDRIC-CNAM, 2 Rue Conté, 75003 Paris, France
jacky.akoka@lecnam.net, dumouza@cnam.fr
[2] ESSEC Business School, 3 Av Bernard Hirsch, 95021 Cergy, France
wattiau@essec.edu

Abstract. The growing complexity of academic literature makes it increasingly difficult for researchers to synthesize existing knowledge. This paper presents an automated method to conceptualize design science research articles using large language models (LLMs), helping scholars build their own information systems. Our approach extracts "paths of knowledge contributions" from abstracts and introductions, leveraging an established representation framework. We evaluate four prominent LLMs through a three-step process. Model performance varies, with trade-offs between conciseness, precision, and alignment with researcher-encoded paths, and no single LLM consistently superior. One use case illustrates the method's value for different researcher profiles. Scaling the analysis also reveals opportunities to extend the representation language.

Keywords: Path of knowledge type · large language model (LLM) · AI-assisted academic research · design science research (DSR) · information systems (IS)

1 Introduction

While artificial intelligence (AI) holds significant potential to streamline research tasks, such as standard text synthesis tools, though applicable, remain insufficiently tailored to the nuanced needs of researchers. The challenge lies in designing AI systems that not only facilitate scholarly work but also uphold transparency, reproducibility, and structural rigor. This principle underpins the emerging field of AI-assisted academic research. We propose leveraging generative AI to systematically analyze and synthesize literature, thereby alleviating the cognitive burden on PhD students, reviewers, and researchers. Literature review requires categorization, context-specific analytical framing, and objective-driven synthesis. To assess AI's, particularly LLMs', capacity to assist in these domains, we evaluate in this paper their ability to generate a synthetic representation of an article's research contributions. Capitalizing on an existing representation, our approach frames automatically a paper as a path of knowledge contributions, a structured articulation of its artifact production. When applied to a corpus, the paths of knowledge

F. Zerbato et al. (Eds.): CAiSE 2026, LNBIP 587, pp. 11–19, 2026.
https://doi.org/10.1007/978-3-032-27997-2_2

contributions facilitate classification, characterization, comparison, and even evaluation of the articles. To our knowledge, no structured method currently exists to automatically generate such paths of knowledge types, neither through AI nor alternative techniques. We propose an approach to automatically deduce these paths from paper abstracts and introductions. The research question we address is: *How can we automatically extract the content of a scientific article in terms of its articulated production of artifacts, represented as a path of knowledge contributions, to facilitate the analysis of an information systems paper corpus?*

The rest of this paper is organized as follows. Section 2 briefly reviews the state of the art in AI-assisted scientific literature analysis. Section 3 presents an overview of the research approach. Section 4 details our approach, including its application. Section 5 discusses the results obtained and concludes.

2 AI-Assisted Academic Research - State of the Art

We first synthesize the literature on AI for academic research by activity. Eger et al. [1] review AI's role in academic research, emphasizing idea generation as central to scientific progress. Khalifa & Albadawy [2] highlight AI's transformative impact on data management and analysis, including advanced interpretation, visualization, and dataset curation. Danler et al. conduct an exploratory assessment of the quality and effectiveness of AI tools designed to assist in literature review and analysis [3].

Researchers leverage several techniques for literature review and analysis: citation analysis, natural language processing (NLP), and machine/deep learning. AI-enhanced NLP allows content citation analysis [4]. Ofori-Boateng et al. provide a comprehensive review of techniques used at each stage of systematic reviews [5]. LLMs are increasingly used to streamline literature reviews. Agarwal et al. outline two primary applications: identifying relevant articles and drafting Related Work sects [6]. Additional LLM-based tools, such as Ateia et al.'s system, directly address researchers' queries about article content [7], further supporting summary generation and content analysis.

To our knowledge, no automated analysis of the design science research literature exists, nor is there an approach that automatically extracts the content of a scientific article in terms of an articulated production of artifacts, represented as a graph of knowledge contributions. This article addresses both gaps.

3 Research Approach

Advancements in AI-driven content extraction now enable the automatic processing of textual data. NLP techniques and generative AI, especially LLMs, excel at tasks such as named entity recognition, relation extraction, summarizing research articles, translating content, synthesizing information, and comparing texts. Our objective is to generate a structured synthesis to compare information systems (IS) research articles and obtain a rich representation of a corpus. We adopt the path of knowledge types [8] as our representation. We therefore examine whether LLMs can automate this process.

Akoka et al. define the construct path of knowledge types as a directed graph, with a sequence of labeled nodes (knowledge types) and edges to represent the dynamic contributions of a research paper [8]. Thus, a research paper may be described as a path of knowledge types. Each node in this path is an artifact. The artifact types we consider are: language, metamodel, concept, system design, ontology, taxonomy, framework, architecture, requirement, methodology, guideline, algorithm, method fragment, metric, implemented system, example. For the edges, we used the eleven labels (Table 3) to define the semantics of links between nodes and their successors, as proposed in [8]. As an illustration, the article [8] itself may be represented by the following path:

Concept - constructs for → Language - completed with → Guidelines - applied to → Example.

Nodes and edges labels are *concepts* that provide *constructs* defining a *language* to represent research papers. Completed with some *guidelines*, this language has been *applied to* several exemplar papers. Our proposed approach (Fig. 1) comprises six steps.

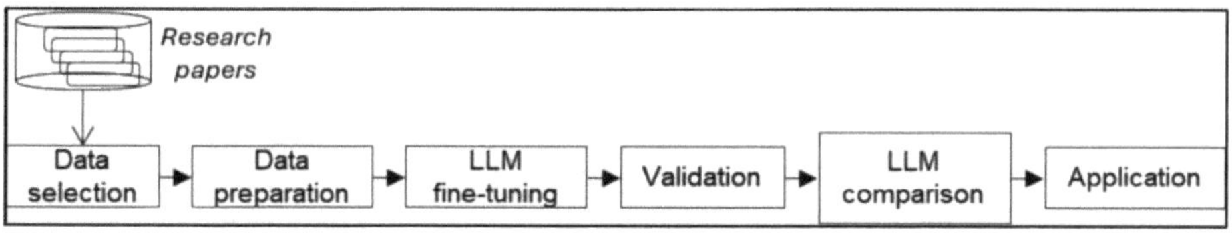

Fig. 1. Research approach.

The first step, **data selection**, identifies a set of research articles for analysis. We aim to analyze IS papers by representing them as paths of knowledge contributions. A dataset of IS articles is required to train the LLMs effectively. We selected relevant and sufficiently rich articles to ensure high training performance.

The second step, **data preparation**, labels articles to train LLMs to extract their path of knowledge representation. To do so, the articles are encoded as paths of knowledge contributions. For example, an article introducing and implementing a query language, applied to an example, yields the path: *language – applied to → example.*

Our encoding process distinguishes two node levels: 1) type level that identifies the artifact category (e.g., language) and, 2) instance level that specifies the artifact's name mentioned in the article (e.g., the name of the query language).

The third step, **LLM fine-tuning**, trains selected LLMs on the annotated data, to learn the correspondence between the textual discourse of articles and their formalized paths of knowledge contributions. Each training instance associates an article (abstract and introduction) to its path. The model progressively acquires an understanding of how textual cues, argumentation patterns, and rhetorical structures map onto the logical organization of scientific knowledge creation.

Step 4 performs a **validation** on an additional set of annotated papers, in order to assess the model's generalization capabilities and to guide the optimization of its parameters. It evaluates how well the model reproduces path structures for articles it has not encountered before. This step provides an ongoing measure of performance stability and prevents overfitting to specific textual or structural patterns.

Step 5 compares the outputs of all LLMs to select the most effective model for the task. It consists of a **comparative analysis of different LLMs** fine-tuned for the task.

This analysis aims to determine which models yield the most accurate, coherent, and interpretable results, and to identify how their performance varies across article types, path structures, and levels of representation. Particular attention is paid to distinguishing models that perform well at the category level, accurately identifying artifact types, from those that demonstrate stronger performance at the instance level, where precision in naming or contextualizing artifacts is required.

Finally, step 6 **applies** the selected model to a new set of articles to generate their representation and interprets the resulting representation related to a specific use case.

4 Step-by-Step Application of the Approach

Data Selection. The training dataset comprised 148 DSR articles sourced from the AIS basket of eleven journals published between 2004 and 2020. We screened the articles in these journals to identify those relevant to the DSR approach, thereby eliminating articles applying qualitative or quantitative methods or those relevant to IS economics.

Data Preparation. Three experts independently coded the 148 articles, then reconciled their results. The derived dataset consists of the original articles and a spreadsheet detailing both type-level and instance-level encodings for each article. These paths served as structured representations of the key concepts and relationships discussed in the articles, providing a ground truth for training the LLMs. The characteristics of the paths produced by the experts are reported in the tables below for comparison with the paths produced by the LLMs. The training inputs for each LLM consisted of the article's abstract and introduction, and the associated expert-defined knowledge paths (type and instance levels). To ensure consistency and focus on relevant relationships, the LLMs were constrained to use the predefined vocabulary of terms. This constraint was critical to maintaining uniformity in the knowledge path predictions across all models.

LLM Fine-Tuning. The training task aims to enable the LLM to learn the correspondence between the textual discourse of articles and their formalized paths of knowledge contributions. Each training instance associates an article with its reference path representation. Four widely used LLMs are fine-tuned for our comparative study: ChatGPT by OpenAI, powered by the GPT-4o Mini model, Claude by Anthropic, employing the Sonnet 4 model, Gemini by Google, leveraging the 2.5 Flash model, and Grok by xAI, utilizing the Grok 3 model. They were fine-tuned on 133 articles out of 148. The central learning objective is to minimize the divergence between the predicted and annotated paths, both in terms of node classification and edge structuring.

Validation. To validate the training process, the remaining test set of 15 articles was used. These articles were processed in the same way, with abstracts, introductions, and expert-defined knowledge paths provided to the LLMs. This validation step assessed the models' ability to map textual content to the correct knowledge paths, confirming the effectiveness of fine-tuning (Table 1). It shows that Experts produce the most synthetic (avg = 2.692) and coherent paths (SD 0.722). ChatGPT generates the longest paths with strong uniformity. Gemini and Grok fall in the middle range, while Claude, though concise, shows the highest variability, indicating less stability.

Table 1. Structural comparison (path length corresponds to the number of nodes).

Model	Average size of path	Variance	Std deviation
Experts	2.692	0.521	0.722
ChatGPT	6.538	0.402	0.634
Grok	4.769	0.331	0.576
Claude	4.000	0.615	0.784
Gemini	5.231	0.485	0.697

Semantically, to compare the generated paths, we use the Dice similarity coefficient which measures the degree of overlap between two sets. It is defined as Dice (A, B) = $2|A \cap B| / (|A| + |B|)$. Compared to Jaccard, it gives more weight to shared elements and is more sensitive to partial matches. We also use the Edit distance. The Dice similarity matrix (Fig. 2a) and the Edit distance matrix (Fig. 2b) indicate that Grok achieves relatively high Dice scores and low Edit distances compared to experts, suggesting strong overlap and minimal divergence in the types used. When these findings are combined with the path length analysis, Grok emerges as the model whose behavior most closely mirrors the expert approach.

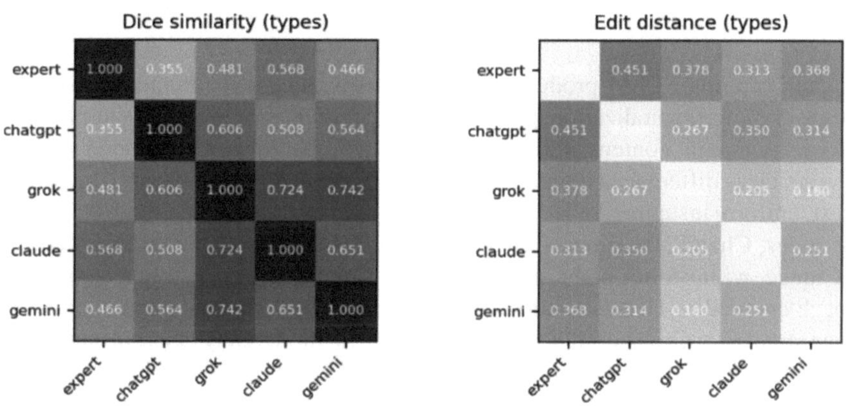

a) b)

Fig. 2. a) Average similarity for types. b) Average distance for types.

LLM Comparison. The trained LLMs were subsequently applied to a new dataset consisting of 35 articles from the CAISE2025 conference. For each article, only the abstract and introduction were provided as inputs, and the LLMs were tasked with predicting the knowledge paths at both the type and instance levels. This testing phase evaluated the models' ability to generalize their training to a new set of academic texts. The comparative results presented in Table 2 highlight substantive differences in the average knowledge-path and instance lengths generated by the four LLMs. The analysis of the path length statistics reveals distinct strategies among the LLMs. ChatGPT consistently generates the longest paths with the lowest standard deviation, signifying a robust, predictable tendency toward maximal detail and completeness. Conversely, Grok produces the shortest paths with high consistency, prioritizing maximal conciseness by focusing solely on the core subject and outcome. Gemini offers a balanced, intermediate level of detail with high predictability. In contrast, Claude, despite having an intermediate average length, exhibits the highest variability (range 3 to 6), suggesting its extraction strategy is highly contextual and less uniform across different input abstracts. This shows that differences in length are not random variations but reflect systematic behavioral characteristics inherent to each LLM.

Table 2. Knowledge-path and instance lengths comparison.

	Knowledge-path			Instance		
Model	Avg length	Variance	Std. Dev.	#avg. words	Variance	Std. Dev.
ChatGPT	6.97	0.27	0.52	3.77	3.30	1.82
Grok	4.37	0.36	0.60	4.58	2.43	1.56
Claude	5.20	1.75	1.32	4.65	27.71	5.26
Gemini	5.74	0.55	0.74	4.97	4.82	2.20

To fairly compare LLM-produced instances, we applied text normalization removing surface variations (capitalization, punctuation, inflections, stop words, boilerplate) while preserving semantic content and technical terminology. Table 2's instance size analysis reveals clear differences aligning with path-length behavior. ChatGPT produces the shortest, uniform instances, reflecting its longest-path strategy. To maintain clarity across many nodes, ChatGPT segments information into smaller units rather than dense content. Claude, with shorter paths, shows extreme variability, suggesting a compensatory approach embedding rich semantic detail in fewer steps. Grok and Gemini adopt intermediate strategies: Grok combines concise paths with moderately dense instances, while Gemini balances medium-length paths with slightly longer instances. These differences highlight how architecture and training shape reasoning strategies: ChatGPT prioritizes structural depth and consistency, Claude emphasizes semantic richness over stability, and Grok and Gemini balance coverage and compactness.

In Table 3, we analyze semantic diversity of edges, revealing significant differences in how models structure semantic links. Claude shows overwhelming reliance on *is applied to*, suggesting a highly pragmatic, direct mapping strategy focused exclusively on linking concepts to applications with minimal elaboration. ChatGPT and Gemini also favor *is applied to*, but balance this with other relations like *provides constructs for* and *is evaluated by formulating*, enriching paths with evaluative and compositional semantics beyond operational mapping. Grok exhibits a distinct strategy, emphasizing structural composition, with *is completed with* dominating at 54.24%, far exceeding other models. Combined with moderate use of *is evaluated by formulating* (10.17%)

Table 3. Edge analysis.

Arcs	ChatGPT	Grok	Claude	Gemini
is applied to	28.00%	27.12%	93.88%	21.69%
is tested with or implemented in	8.00%	6.78%	4.76%	18.67%
is abstracted into	2.50%	0.85%	0.00%	3.01%
provides requirements for	6.50%	0.00%	1.36%	4.22%
provides constructs for	13.00%	0.00%	0.00%	15.66%
is completed with	6.00%	54.24%	0.00%	12.05%
provides theoretical basis for	6.50%	0.00%	0.00%	1.20%
provides practical basis for	11.50%	0.00%	0.00%	0.00%
provides principles for	6.00%	0.85%	0.00%	0.00%
is evaluated by formulating	10.50%	10.17%	0.00%	14.46%
precedes	1.50%	0.00%	0.00%	9.04%

and *is tested with or implemented in* (6.78%), this reflects a bias toward articulating fine-grained conceptual assembly rather than direct application. These distributions reveal divergent philosophies: Claude's near-exclusive application focus contrasts with Grok's compositional emphasis, while ChatGPT and Gemini balance operational and structural relations. These tendencies likely stem from architectural differences: Claude optimized for high-level pragmatic mapping, Grok for structural detail, and ChatGPT/Gemini for hybrid strategies balancing abstraction with elaboration.

Finally, we analyze the types of knowledge (artifacts) that are generated (Table 4). Artifact type distribution reveals distinct LLM strategies in structuring domain knowledge. Grok emphasizes examples, method fragments, and metrics, signaling a granular, component-oriented approach favoring illustrative and measurable elements. Claude and Gemini prioritize conceptual artifacts and methodologies. Claude reinforces this with strong allocation to examples, suggesting theoretical framing supported by illustrative cases. Gemini pairs concept-focus with frameworks and algorithms, indicating bias toward computational and structural clarity. ChatGPT exhibits balanced distribution: concepts, methodology, frameworks, algorithms, and examples, suggesting hybrid strategy integrating conceptual abstraction, procedural guidance, and structural elements. Low-frequency categories (ontology, requirement, taxonomy, language) remain marginal across models (<3%).

Application. A first use case involves applying the approach to a research article to derive its path of knowledge contribution. This can be valuable for reviewers, PhD students, or journal editors seeking to quickly grasp an article's core contributions. Let's consider the article [9]. It leverages the NIS2 Directive, which requires EU Member States to implement risk-management measures to ensure high cybersecurity standards for essential and important entities. The paper demonstrates how NIS2 user stories can evaluate organizational information security levels by extracting legal requirements and mapping them to the goals of six defined personas. Through requirements elicitation,

Table 4. Types of knowledge identified.

Artifact Type	ChatGPT	Grok	Claude	Gemini
Language	1.25%	2.86%	0.55%	0.00%
Metamodel	2.92%	2.14%	0.55%	0.00%
Concept	17.92%	5.71%	20.33%	28.43%
System design	5.83%	0.00%	0.00%	1.02%
Ontology	2.08%	2.86%	1.10%	1.02%
Framework	10.42%	8.57%	6.04%	11.68%
Architecture	2.50%	2.86%	1.10%	1.02%
Requirement	0.83%	2.86%	4.95%	1.52%
Methodology	14.17%	16.43%	16.48%	13.20%
Guideline	4.17%	1.43%	1.65%	1.52%
Algorithm	9.58%	3.57%	8.24%	11.68%
Method fragment	3.33%	9.29%	3.30%	0.00%
Metric	7.08%	10.00%	2.20%	12.18%
Implemented system	6.67%	7.86%	7.69%	3.55%
Example	11.25%	23.57%	25.82%	13.20%
Language	1.25%	2.86%	0.55%	0.00%

the authors derived and validated ten user stories using established security evaluation methods from the literature. These user stories facilitate the adaptation of existing evaluation tools to NIS2 compliance and inform the development of new methods to mitigate administrative overhead. We submitted the paper to our approach. Grok generates the following path of knowledge (the path is described at the instance level with the types of nodes in parentheses):

NIS2-compliant user stories for security level evaluation (requirement) – completed with → six key personas (concept) – completed with → ten user stories (requirement) – applied to → existing security evaluation instruments and methods (methodology).

Thus, our approach provides reviewers with a high-level, artifact-focused overview, enabling rapid assessment of their expertise for reviewing this paper.

5 Conclusion

This article offers three main contributions. First, we introduce an automated approach to extract conceptual representations of DSR articles using LLMs and a controlled vocabulary, demonstrated through several use cases. Second, we compare four LLMs on this task, outlining their respective strengths and limitations. Third, we illustrate one scenario where researchers can benefit from this method. Our findings confirm that LLMs, while capable of capturing structural patterns, remain assistive tools requiring expert validation to ensure reliability and interpretive consistency. The approach is currently limited to design-evaluate DSR articles. Moreover, the training set, drawn from IS journals, may introduce bias. The controlled vocabulary imposes constraints. Finally, the evaluated LLMs exclude newer open models such as Llama.

References

1. Eger, S., et al.: Transforming science with LLMs: A survey on ai-assisted scientific discovery, experimentation, content generation, and evaluation. arXiv preprint (2025). https://arxiv.org/abs/2502.05151
2. Khalifa, M., Albadawy, M.: Using AI in academic writing and research: an essential productivity tool. Comput. Methods Programs Biomed. Update **5**, 100145 (2024)
3. Danler, M., Hackl, W.O., Pfeifer, B.: Quality and effectiveness of AI tools for students and researchers for scientific literature review and analysis. In: dHealth 2024, pp. 203–208 (2024)
4. Ding, Y., Zhang, G., Chambers, T., Song, M., Wang, X., Zhai, C.: Content-based citation analysis: the next generation of citation analysis. J. Assoc. Inf. Sci. Technol. **65**(9), 1820–1833 (2014)
5. Ofori-Boateng, R., Aceves-Martins, M., Wiratunga, N., Moreno-Garcia, C.F.: Towards the automation of systematic reviews using NLP, machine learning, and deep learning: a comprehensive review. Artif. Intell. Rev. **57**(8), 200 (2024)
6. Agarwal, S., et al.: LitLLMs, LLMs for Literature Review: Are we there yet?. (2024). https://arxiv.org/abs/2412.15249
7. Ateia, S., Kruschwitz, U., Scholz, M., Koschmider, A., Almohaishi, M.: LLM-based information extraction to support scientific literature research and publication workflows. In: International Conference on Theory and Practice of Digital Libraries, pp. 90–99. Springer Nature Switzerland, Cham (2025)
8. Akoka, J., Comyn-Wattiau, I., Prat, N., Storey, V.C.: Knowledge contributions in DSR: paths of knowledge types. Decis. Support. Syst. **166**, 113898 (2023)
9. Seeba, M., Valgre, M., Matulevičius, R.: Evaluating organization security: user stories of European Union NIS2 directive. In: CAiSE Proceedings, pp. 57–74. Springer (2025)

Constraint-Aware Pipeline for Generating High-Quality Utterances from OpenAPI Specifications Using LLMs

Vitor Gaboardi dos Santos[1(✉)], Boualem Benatallah[2], and Silvana Togneri MacMahon[1]

[1] Dublin City University, Dublin, Ireland
{vitorgaboardidos.santos,silvana.macmahon}@dcu.ie
[2] Insight Research Ireland Research Centre on Data Analytics, School of Computing, Dublin City University, Dublin, Ireland
boualem.benatallah@dcu.ie

Abstract. The integration of Large Language Models (LLMs) with APIs requires high-quality datasets that link user utterances to valid API calls. However, existing approaches for generating such datasets often overlook important quality attributes, leading to unnatural utterances, limited parameter coverage, and invalid API calls that violate documentation constraints. In this paper, we present a constraint-aware pipeline (CAP) for generating high-quality utterance–API call pairs from OpenAPI Specifications (OAS). CAP explicitly models and incorporates API constraints during generation to ensure constraint adherence, naturalness, and parameter diversity. We generate synthetic datasets using different LLMs and compare CAP against an existing prompting-based pipeline. Experimental results show that CAP improves constraint adherence, parameter coverage and naturalness.

Keywords: LLM · API · Utterances · Chatbots · Constraints

1 Introduction

Large Language Models (LLMs) have shown strong performance in conversational AI, serving as natural language interfaces that fulfil user utterances and enable interaction with services through the integration with tools and APIs [3]. Nevertheless, training or fine-tuning robust models to perform API selection or API calling requires high-quality datasets linking utterances to APIs [4,8].

Recent work has focused on generating utterance-API call pairs using OpenAPI specification (OAS). ToolBench [9] generated utterances with different levels of complexity. Sheng et al. [12] generated datasets to evaluate an LLM's proficiency in using APIs by designing a prompt with guidelines encouraging parameter diversity and natural values for parameters. However, existing work often overlooks different quality attributes of datasets simultaneously, which have shown to impact the performance of tool-using LLMs trained on such data [4].

F. Zerbato et al. (Eds.): CAiSE 2026, LNBIP 587, pp. 20–27, 2026.
https://doi.org/10.1007/978-3-032-27997-2_3

In this paper, we propose a pipeline for generating high-quality datasets of utterance-API call pairs, focusing on three quality attributes: *naturalness*, *parameter diversity*, and *constraint adherence*. *Naturalness* ensures that utterances sound like authentic human requests when talking to chatbots [13]. *Parameter diversity* ensures the generation of utterances with different parameters and their combinations, reflecting distinct user intents [10]. *Constraint adherence* ensures that API calls include parameters that respect constraints imposed by OAS, such as valid values, formats, and dependencies between parameters, making utterances closely aligned with the API method [2,12]. For instance, a "*departureDate*" parameter may require a `YYYY-MM-DD` format and dates only after `2022-01-01`. Failing to address these attributes may result in utterances and API calls that do not generalize to real-world conversations, fail to generalize to parameter combinations, and produce utterances with infeasible API calls [4,12].

In summary, we make the following contributions: (1) we propose a constraint-aware pipeline (CAP) to generate natural and parameter-diverse utterances that adhere to OAS constraints; and (2) we generate datasets using `GPT-4o` and `DeepSeek-V3` with CAP and compare their quality against a pipeline proposed by Sheng et al. [10]. The code, dataset, and results are available on GitHub[1].

2 Constraint-Aware Pipeline for Utterance-API Call Pairs Generation

As summarised in Fig. 1, our pipeline consists of three steps: (1) API parameter constraint extraction; (2) OAS enrichment; and (3) utterance-API call pairs generation.

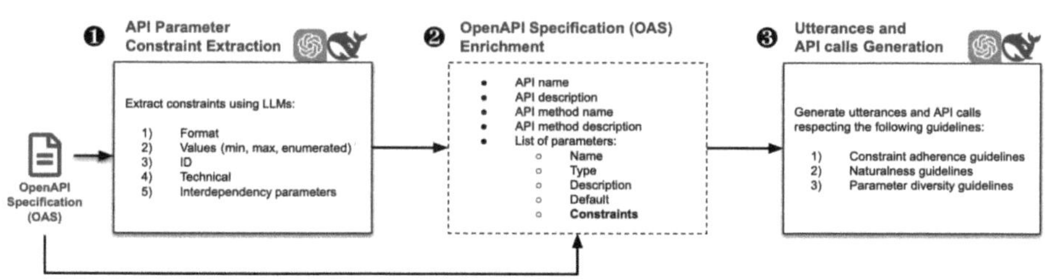

Fig. 1. Pipeline overview for generating constraint adherence, natural, and parameter diverse utterance-API call pairs using LLMs from OpenAPI specifications.

[1] https://github.com/vitorgaboardi/ConstraintAPIBench.

2.1 API Parameter Constraint Extraction

CAP extracts five types of parameter constraints from OAS. We build upon standard constraint definitions from API testing literature [1,5,6], while introducing a Technical constraint to filter non-conversational parameters and enhance the generation of natural utterances. The five constraint types are defined as follows: **(1) Values constraint (VAL)**: Possible values that a parameter can assume. This includes: Maximum (maximum value); minimum (minimum value); and enumerated (a closed set of acceptable values); **(2) Format constraint (FOR)**: Any required input format a parameter must adhere to in an API call, such as IATA airport code (e.g., `MAD` for Madrid) or ISO currency code (e.g., `USD` for US dollar); **(3) ID constraint**: Boolean value that is `True` if the parameter represents an identifier (ID) (e.g., `message_id`, `gameId`, `hotelIds`). **(4) Technical constraint (TEC)**: Boolean value that is `True` if the parameter is primarily used by developers rather than end users for creating API calls or formatting pages (e.g., parameters such as page number, page size, offset, access token, API key). Parameters used by users that affects sorting or limits the output must be `False` (e.g., sort, limit, orderBy, sortBy). (5) **Interdependency constraints (IDP)**: Describes dependencies between parameters. We use six constraints presented in Martin et al. [5]. They refer to a set of parameters and include constraints where: (5.1) the presence of one parameter requires the presence of another parameter (e.g., if startDate is provided, endDate must be included); (5.2) one or more parameters must be included in the API call (e.g., at least one contact method, such as email or phone, must be provided); (5.3) one and only one parameter must be included in the API call (e.g., either username or email must be provided in an authentication API); (5.4) either all or none parameters must be included in the API call (e.g., latitude and longitude must be included only together); (5.5) zero or one parameter can be present in the API call (e.g., at most one discount method, such as promoCode or discountId, can be provided); (5.6) parameters are related by arithmetic constraints (e.g., minPrice must be less than maxPrice).

To ensure that the LLM can identify constraints even when they are not mentioned in parameter descriptions, we provide to the LLM the API name, API description, API method name, API method description, and a list of all parameters with their name, type, description, default value, and whether it is required or not. Finally, we include one example of a flight search API method with ten parameters that illustrate at least one instance of each constraint type.

2.2 OpenAPI Specification (OAS) Enrichment

CAP enriches an original OAS in two ways to provide a more complete representation of API parameter constraints. First, a "constraint" field is added to each API parameter description in the enriched OAS, listing all constraints extracted in the previous step. Making constraints explicit in the OAS offers a well-structured reference that supports the generation of utterance-API call pairs with better constraint adherence. Second, parameters where the "technical" constraint was `True` are removed in the enriched OAS. These parameters typically represent control configurations intended for developers, making it unnatural to include them in utterances. For instance, a user would not normally say mention "api key" information.

2.3 Utterance-API Call Pairs Generation

CAP generates utterance-API call pairs by prompting LLMs with the enriched OAS, which explicitly details parameter constraints. The pipeline guides the generation process using structured rules designed to ensure constraint adherence, naturalness, and parameter diversity.

Constraint Adherence. We proposed four rules to ensure constraint adherence: (1) required parameters must be included in all generated utterance-API call pairs; (2) values must conform to range limits and respect the enumerated set of values; (3) the parameter values in the API call must conform to the format constraint; and (4) the combination of parameters must respect any interdependency constraints. The generated utterance-API call pairs will closely align with the corresponding API method if the LLM adheres to these rules, which likely reduces API calling errors.

Naturalness. We proposed five rules to ensure naturalness: (1) omit the API name from utterances, unless it corresponds to a well known consumer brand (e.g., Spotify, YouTube, Booking.com), rather than a generic API (e.g., Movies API, Converter API).(2) do not use general placeholders such as "this URL" or "this name"; (3) every parameter value in the API call must be inferable from the utterance; (4) do not include parameter values in the utterance with a format the user would not normally say. For instance, users say city names instead of latitude and longitude coordinates; (5) if the "ID" constraint is True, do not generate artificial IDs, but generate values representing what the ID refers to. IDs are commonly used to reference resources and are not known by users.

Parameter Diversity. We proposed five rules to promote parameter diversity: (1) include each optional parameter at least once across generated utterances, unless the number of optional parameters is too large for the number of utterances requested. This promotes parameter coverage while avoiding overloaded requests; (2) use different combinations of optional parameters across utterances. This reflects the many intents users might express a request. For instance, a movie search API might be called with parameters such (title, year) or (title, genre); (3) cycle through allowed values for any parameter that includes the "enumerated" constraint; and (4) avoid repeating parameter values across utterances. Rules (3) and (4) aim to ensure a rich set of parameter values.

3 Experiments

We designed experiments that assess the quality of generated utterances.

3.1 Dataset Generation

OAS Dataset. We selected a subset of 237 APIs (1,044 methods) from ToolBench [9] to generate utterance-API call pairs. From each of the 49 categories, we selected the 5 most popular APIs based on the *popularity score* provided by RapidAPI. We applied three filtering criteria to select APIs: (1) each method must include at least one parameter; (2) API descriptions must contain at least five words; and (3) the number of methods must not exceed 30. These criteria were designed to ensure that parameter constraints can be extracted, to keep the dataset size manageable and to maintain a balanced distribution of APIs. Nevertheless, this design choice affects only evaluation, not the applicability of CAP, which can be applied to large industrial APIs with hundreds of operations.

Data Generation Pipelines. We generated 10 utterance-API call pairs per API method using two pipelines: (1) our proposed **constraint-aware pipeline (CAP)**, which implements the design principles described in Sect. 2; and (2) the **description-based pipeline (DBP)**, based on Sheng et al. [10]. We selected DBP because it has instructions that align with our goals: promoting naturalness, covering all parameters, and requiring parameter inclusion.

Models. We used `GPT-4o` and `DeepSeek-V3` models to generate utterance-API call pairs. We set the temperature to 0.0 for reproducibility.

3.2 Evaluation Metrics

We evaluate the quality of generated utterances across three dimensions: naturalness, parameter diversity, and constraint adherence. We report metrics on a sample of 50 randomly selected APIs, which led to 237 API methods.

Naturalness. We evaluate naturalness using two LLMs as judges: Llama-3.1-70B and GPT-4.1. Recent studies have shown that LLM-based evaluations have high correlation with human judgments when evaluating text quality attributes [7]. We provide LLMs with a definition of naturalness, examples of utterances, and ask the LLM if each utterance is 'natural' or 'unnatural', reporting the number of utterances labelled as 'natural'.

Parameter Diversity. We measure parameter diversity using two metrics: Parameter Coverage (**PC**), which represents the proportion of an API method's parameters used across generated utterances, and Parameter Combination Coverage (**PCC**), which represents the diversity of parameter combinations in generated API calls by counting unique parameter combinations per method. Higher PCC values indicate broad intent coverage.

Constraint Adherence. We measure constraint adherence by counting violations using an automated checker. It validates generated parameter values against ground truth constraints (manually annotated from the OAS) for three types: (1) Values (VAL): Checks if values fall within numeric ranges or belong to enumerated sets. (2) Format (FOR): Uses regular expressions to verify string patterns. (3) Interdependency (IDP): Evaluates logical conditions between parameters. A violation occurs when any check fails. We focus on these types because they evaluate whether values respect API requirements, while ID and technical constraints guide parameter inclusion during generation.

3.3 Results

We compare quality performance in terms of naturalness, parameter diversity, and constraint adherence between generation pipelines and LLMs.

Naturalness. We found that **CAP generated more natural utterances than DBP for both LLMs, and DeepSeek-V3 created more natural utterances than GPT-4o.** Table 1 shows the number of utterances judged as natural from Llama-3.1-70B (`NAT-LL3.1`) and GPT-4.1 (`NAT-GPT4.1`) as well as the Cohen's κ inter-rater agreement coefficient [11] between these two models.

Table 1. Naturalness comparison between DBP and CAP across different LLMs. Values show the percentage of utterances labeled as natural.

Model	Prompt	NAT-LLA3.1	NAT-GPT4.1	Cohen's κ
GPT-4o	DBP	1,080 (50.7%)	991 (46.5%)	80.2%
	CAP	1,384 (67.1%)	1,293 (62.7%)	75.4%
DeepSeek-V3	DBP	967 (44.3%)	930 (42.6%)	80.5%
	CAP	1,479 (67.5%)	1,526 (69.6%)	75.1%

CAP improved naturalness by 16.4% for GPT-4o and by 23.1% for DeepSeek-V3 in the NAT-LLA3.1 evaluation, demonstrating that CAP consistently guides LLMs towards more natural generation. Through CAP, DeepSeek-V3 achieved higher naturalness than GPT-4o (69.7% vs. 62.8%) according to NAT-GPT4.1, indicating that CAP has a stronger positive impact on naturalness for DeepSeek-V3. While NAT-GPT4.1 showed lower scores overall (suggesting stricter criteria), the relative ranking remained consistent. Furthermore, GPT-4o with CAP generated the natural utterance *Can you suggest some songs similar to 'Shape of You' by Ed Sheeran?* while DBP generated the unnatural *Find similar songs to the one identified by key 987654321*, referencing the song by ID.

To validate the LLM-as-a-judge evaluation, we randomly sampled 100 utterances per configuration (400 total) and had one author manually label each as "natural" or "unnatural." We computed Cohen's κ for each configuration, achieving substantial inter-rater agreement: $\kappa = 0.70 \pm 0.07$ (vs. GPT-4.1) and $\kappa = 0.66 \pm 0.06$ (vs. Llama-3.1-70B). These results support the use of LLM judges for naturalness evaluation, despite some misclassifications.

Parameter Diversity. We found that **CAP achieved higher parameter coverage than DBP for both models. CAP also produced more unique parameter combinations with GPT-4o, while DeepSeek-V3 produced fewer parameter combinations.** Table 2 shows the parameter coverage (PC), parameter combination coverage (PCC) and total parameters (TP).

Table 2. Parameter diversity results using DBP and CAP across different LLMs.

Model	Prompt	PC	PCC	TP
`GPT-4o`	DBP	0.9092	373	592
	CAP	0.9823	416	545
`DeepSeek-V3`	DBP	0.9140	416	592
	CAP	0.9733	376	499

CAP improved parameter coverage for GPT-4o from 90.92% to 98.23%. CAP also increased unique parameter combinations from 373 to 416 despite reducing the total parameter pool from 592 to 545 (47 fewer technical parameters). For DeepSeek-V3, CAP achieved higher parameter coverage than DBP (97.33% vs. 91.40%), but decreased parameter combination coverage from 416 to 376. This reduction is mainly due to the decrease in the total parameter pool from 592 to 499 (93 fewer technical parameters were filtered by CAP), limiting the number of possible parameter combinations.

Constraint Adherence. We found that **CAP reduced constraint violations for both models compared to DBP, and GPT-4o produced fewer violations than DeepSeek-V3**. Table 3 reports constraint violations in terms of Values (VAL), Format (FOR), and Interdependency (IDP) constraints. Results are reported across the same set of 50 evaluation APIs.

Table 3. Constraint violations count using DBP and CAP across different LLMs. Lower values indicate better constraint adherence.

Model	Prompt	VAL	FOR	IDP	Total
`GPT-4o`	DBP	10	49	7	66
	CAP	2	21	4	27
`DeepSeek-V3`	DBP	26	59	6	91
	CAP	19	34	0	53

CAP reduced total violations by 59% for GPT-4o (66 to 27) and by 42% for DeepSeek-V3 (91 to 53), demonstrating that constraint-aware generation improves API compliance. The largest improvements came from FOR violations, which decreased from 49 to 21 for GPT-4o and from 59 to 34 for DeepSeek-V3. CAP also eliminated all IDP violations for DeepSeek-V3 (0 vs. 6 with DBP), although GPT-4o still had minimal violations under both conditions.

This paper presented a constraint-aware pipeline for generating high-quality utterances from OAS using LLMs. Our approach models different constraint types and demonstrated improved constraint adherence, naturalness, and parameter diversity, indicating the potential of constraint-aware generation for building reliable API-grounded language interfaces. Future work will focus on extending the framework to additional constraint categories, evaluating more LLMs and pipelines, and fine-tune LLMs using the generated data.

Acknowledgments. This publication has emanated from research conducted with the financial support of Taighde Éireann-Research Ireland under Grants No. 18/CRT/6223 and SFI/12/RC/2289_P2.

References

1. Alonso, J.C., Martin-Lopez, A., Segura, S., Bavota, G., Ruiz-Cortés, A.: Satori: Static test oracle generation for rest apis (2025). arXiv preprint
2. Alonso, J.C., Martin-Lopez, A., Segura, S., Garcia, J.M., Ruiz-Cortes, A.: Arte: automated generation of realistic test inputs for web apis. IEEE Trans. Software Eng. **49**(1) (2022)
3. Dam, S.K., Hong, C.S., Qiao, Y., Zhang, C.: A complete survey on llm-based ai chatbots (2024). arXiv preprint
4. Iskander, S., Tolmach, S., Shapira, O., Cohen, N., Karnin, Z.: Quality matters: Evaluating synthetic data for tool-using LLMs. In: Proceedings of the 2024 Conference on Empirical Methods in Natural Language Processing, pp. 4958–4976, Miami, Florida, USA (2024)
5. Martin-Lopez, A., Segura, S., Ruiz-Cortés, A.: A catalogue of inter-parameter dependencies in restful web apis. In: Service-Oriented Computing: 17th International Conference, ICSOC 2019, Springer, Toulouse, France (2019)
6. Martin-Lopez, A., Segura, S., Ruiz-Cortés, A.: Restest: Black-box constraint-based testing of restful web apis. In: Service-Oriented Computing: 18th International Conference, ICSOC 2020, Dubai, United Arab Emirates. Springer (2020)
7. Murugadoss, B., Poelitz, C., Drosos, I., Le, V., McKenna, N., Negreanu, C.S., Parnin, C., Sarkar, A.: Evaluating the evaluator: Measuring llms' adherence to task evaluation instructions. Proceedings of the AAAI Conference on Artificial Intelligence 39(18), pp. 19589–19597 (2025)
8. Patil, S.G., Zhang, T., Wang, X., Gonzalez, J.E.: Gorilla: large language model connected with massive apis. In: Advances in Neural Information Processing Systems, vol. 37, pp. 126544–126565 (2024)
9. Qin, Y., et al.: Toolllm: facilitating large language models to master 16000+ real-world apis. arXiv preprint arXiv:2307.16789 (2023)
10. Sheng, Y., Gandhe, S., Kanagal, B., Edmonds, N., Fisher, Z., Tata, S., Selvan, A.: Measuring an llm's proficiency at using apis: a query generation strategy. In: Proceedings of the 30th ACM SIGKDD Conference on Knowledge Discovery and Data Mining, pp. 5680–5689. KDD '24, New York, NY, USA (2024)
11. Sun, S.: Meta-analysis of cohen's kappa. Health Serv. Outcomes Res. Method. **11**(3), 145–163 (2011)
12. Wang, S., Jean, S., Sengupta, S., Gung, J., Pappas, N., Zhang, Y.: Measuring and mitigating constraint violations of in-context learning for utterance-to-API semantic parsing. In: Findings of the Association for Computational Linguistics, pp. 7196–7207, Singapore (2023)
13. Yaghoub-Zadeh-Fard, M.A., Benatallah, B., Casati, F., Barukh, M.C., Zamanirad, S.: User utterance acquisition for training task-oriented bots: a review of challenges, techniques and opportunities. IEEE Internet Comput. **24**(3) (2020)

A Case Study of eXplainable AI in Smart Agriculture. Lessons Learned for Information Systems Engineers

Rima Grati[1], Najla Fattouch[2], Khouloud Boukadi[2], Francesca De Luzi[3(✉)], Massimo Mecella[3], and Ahmed Seffah[1]

[1] College of Technological Innovation, Zayed University, Dubai, UAE
{rima.grati,ahmed.seffah}@zu.ac.ae
[2] Faculty of Economics and Management, University of Sfax, Sfax, Tunisia
khouloud.boukadi@fsegs.usf.tn
[3] Sapienza Università di Roma, DIAG, Rome, Italy
{luzi,mecella}@diag.uniroma1.it

Abstract. While Vision-Language Models (VLMs) show promise in smart agriculture, they often function as black boxes, lacking the domain-specific transparency needed for farmer trust. Current models suffer from hallucinations or fail to provide actionable context. This paper addresses these limitations by proposing a novel integration of the BLIP-2 multimodal model with the Olive Leaf Disease Ontology. Following design science principles, our approach grounds AI-generated explanations in a structured knowledge graph to ensure semantic consistency. Results demonstrate that combining VLMs with ontologies effectively eliminates hallucinations and provides transparent, practically valuable insights into disease causes and treatments for agricultural decision support.

Keywords: Vision–language models · eXplainable AI · Ontologies · Knowledge graphs · Sustainable agriculture

1 Introduction

In recent years, advances in machine learning (ML) and deep learning (DL) have offered promising solutions for early plant disease detection through image-based analysis [8]. Convolutional neural networks (CNNs), transformers, and vision language models have demonstrated high predictive accuracy in classifying diseased versus healthy leaves [9,14]. Despite these achievements, most existing studies have primarily focused on improving prediction performance, often overlooking the interpretability of the results for end users (e.g., farmers and agronomists). Interpretability, however, is not merely an academic concern; it is essential for the practical adoption of *intelligent information systems.*

This case focuses on that explainability gap and explores how it can be addressed through a domain-dependent approach tailored to the realities of smart agriculture, by also abstracting and providing insights to practitioners

F. Zerbato et al. (Eds.): CAiSE 2026, LNBIP 587, pp. 28–36, 2026.
https://doi.org/10.1007/978-3-032-27997-2_4

and information systems engineers. The situation faced by practitioners in olive cultivation is marked by rising environmental variability, stringent sustainability standards, and a pressing need for timely and precise disease management. Olive production is increasingly threatened by plant diseases that affect both yield and quality. Among these, olive leaf diseases, such as olive leaf spot (*Spilocaea oleagina*) and other foliar pathogens, represent a major risk factor due to their direct impact on photosynthetic activity and long-term tree vitality [3]. eXplainable AI (XAI) approaches, therefore, play a critical role in bridging the gap between complex ML models and actionable agricultural insights.

The action taken involved the design and implementation of BLIP-OLIVE[1], a framework designed to enhance explainability in olive leaf disease diagnosis. In the first phase, *Expert-Enriched Multimodal Fine-Tuning of BLIP-2*, we extend baseline vision-language models by incorporating domain expert knowledge into the fine-tuning process, thereby improving the semantic alignment between image representations and textual descriptions. In the second phase, *Ontology Integration with BLIP-2 for Knowledge-Grounded Reasoning*, we anchor the outputs to a structured ontology named OLDO (Olive Leaf Disease Ontology). This ontology-driven integration enables consistent interpretation, disambiguation, and reasoning over agricultural knowledge. By combining enriched multimodal embeddings with ontology-based constraints, BLIP-OLIVE advances not only the accuracy of semantic retrieval and explanation but also ensures transparent, knowledge-grounded decision support.

The context of this case is particularly relevant, as the olive tree represents one of the most emblematic and economically significant crops in the Mediterranean basin. Beyond its cultural heritage, olive cultivation makes a substantial contribution to sustainable agriculture in the region, supporting rural livelihoods, maintaining biodiversity, and ensuring resilience in semi-arid environments [13]. Olive oil production, in particular, plays a central role in the global agri-food sector, with the Mediterranean countries accounting for more than 90% of the world's output [4]. The case provides a concrete example of how intelligent information systems might impact sustainability and other goals such as responsible production and consumption provided by initiatives such as COP30[2]. Insights derived from the case are abstracted and provided as engineering knowldege for researchers and practitioners.

The rest of the paper is organized consistently with the structure proposed by vom Brocke and Mendling [19] for case studies, so as to guide the reader through the problem addressed (Sect. 2), the actions taken (Sect. 3), the results obtained (Sect. 4), and the lessons learned in the artifact design process (Sect. 5).

---

[1] The BLIP-OLIVE's code is available at https://github.com/optim762-prog/olive_leaf_disease_description.

[2] Cf. https://cop30.br/en/about-cop30/sustainability.

2 Situation Faced and State-of-the-Art

Olive leaf diseases pose significant threats to olive production and long-term crop sustainability. Recent advances in Artificial Intelligence (AI), particularly deep learning (DL), have enabled accurate image-based detection and classification of olive diseases. Convolutional Neural Networks (CNNs), hybrid CNN–LSTM models, transformer-based architectures, and lightweight feature extraction pipelines have all demonstrated high predictive performance on curated datasets [1,6,9,12,14,16]. However, most existing approaches primarily optimize classification accuracy, offering limited support for explainability. When explanations are provided, they typically rely on visual attribution techniques such as Grad-CAM [14], which highlight image regions influencing predictions. While useful for identifying salient areas, these methods do not provide semantic insight into symptoms, causes, environmental conditions, or recommended treatments. As a result, they fall short of supporting actionable decision-making for farmers and agronomists. More broadly, recent research in eXplainable AI (XAI) has explored concept-based explanations and knowledge-grounded approaches to link model predictions to human-understandable abstractions. Nevertheless, ontology-driven reasoning remains largely unexplored in the specific context of olive disease diagnosis. Existing systems rarely integrate structured agricultural knowledge or environmental validation mechanisms, and many are not released in reproducible or reusable forms suitable for integration into information systems.

This gap motivates the need for a domain-grounded, neurosymbolic approach that combines multimodal learning with formal knowledge representation to deliver explanations that are not only technically transparent but also semantically meaningful and operationally useful in smart agriculture settings.

3 Action Taken

We adopted a design science research approach [7], developing and evaluating an artifact for domain-grounded explainability in smart agriculture. The implementation is publicly available to ensure reproducibility. BLIP-OLIVE is a two-phase neurosymbolic framework that integrates multimodal learning with formal knowledge modeling. The framework consists of two complementary phases which are presented in detail in the following.

Phase I: Expert-Enriched Multimodal Fine-Tuning of BLIP-2. Phase I adapts BLIP-2 [10] to the olive disease domain through expert-enriched fine-tuning. The goal is to align visual features of olive leaves with structured textual descriptions capturing symptoms, causes, and remedies. We constructed a multimodal dataset of 300 annotated olive leaf images, each encoded in JSON format with fields `image_path`, `disease_name`, `symptoms`, `causes`, and `remedy`. Textual information was validated and enriched in collaboration with domain experts from the Olive Association in Sfax. The model was fine-tuned by updating domain-relevant layers while preserving general visual representations, enabling adaptation to olive-specific patterns without losing pre-trained knowledge. This process improved the semantic coherence between image content and generated disease descriptions, forming the basis for explainable image-to-text generation in olive pathology.

Phase II: Ontology Integration with BLIP-2. In Phase II, the fine-tuned model is integrated with OLDO to enable knowledge-grounded reasoning and semantic validation. This coupling transforms the predictive model into an explainable information system by anchoring generated captions to formally defined domain concepts and relations.

OLDO Construction Using the NeOn Methodology. OLDO was developed following the NeOn methodology [18], using competency-driven modeling and expert interviews with agronomists and plant pathology specialists. The ontology captures diseases, symptoms, causal agents, environmental conditions, and treatments related to olive leaf disorders. To ensure semantic interoperability, OLDO reuses and aligns with established ontologies, including the Plant Ontology (anatomy), ENVO (environmental conditions), the Plant Stress Ontology (disease hierarchy), and NCBITAXON (pathogens). Alignment was achieved through superclass mapping, terminology harmonization, and synonym management (e.g., "peacock spot" vs. "olive leaf spot"), and validated through reasoner-based consistency checks. The ontology defines core relations linking symptoms to diseases, diseases to etiological agents, and diseases to treatments, as well as environmental conditions that favor or trigger specific disorders. This structure enables traceable diagnostic and prescriptive reasoning.

Ontology Mapping & Reasoning Engine. The reasoning pipeline (Algorithm 1) maps BLIP-2 generated captions to OLDO concepts to construct a domain-specific Knowledge Graph (KG). This pipeline follows methodological directions that have shown the effectiveness of combining LLMs and KGs for improving complex inference and linguistic interpretation tasks [2]. Semantic similarity measures align extracted symptoms with ontology concepts, mitigating linguistic variability. If alignment fails, the prediction is re-evaluated. When alignment succeeds, environmental metadata is retrieved and validated against ontology-encoded causal rules (SWRL), an example is depicted in Fig. 1. Inconsistencies trigger re-evaluation; otherwise, the caption is enriched with ontology-grounded explanations, linking symptoms, causes, and recommended treatments in a semantically coherent manner.

```
OLDO:WarmTemperature(?tCond) ^ OLDO:HighHumidity(?hCond) ^ OLDO:hasTemperatureValue(?tCond, ?tVal) ^
OLDO:hasHumidityValue(?hCond, ?hVal) ^ hasDurationDays(?tCond, ?tDur) ^ hasDurationDays(?hCond, ?hDur) ^
swrlb:greaterThanOrEqual(?tVal, 15) ^ swrlb:lessThanOrEqual(?tVal, 25) ^ swrlb:greaterThanOrEqual(?hVal, 70) ^
swrlb:greaterThanOrEqual(?tDur, 10) ^ swrlb:greaterThanOrEqual(?hDur, 10) -> affectsDisorder(?tCond, Peacockspot1)
```

Fig. 1. An example of a SWRL rule for Peacock Spot disease.

Algorithm 1 Knowledge-Grounded Olive Leaf Disease Explainability Pipeline

Require: BLIP-2 Caption C, $\tau = 0.5$
Ensure: Olive Leaf Disease Detection Result or Knowledge-Grounded Explainability Caption

```
Extract disease candidate d and symptom set S_C from C
Construct Knowledge Graph KG = {disease, symptoms, affectedDisorder, treatment} using OLDO ontology
Apply BERT-based semantic comparison between S_C and S_KG (symptoms from KG)
if Similarity score < τ then
   Call Olive Leaf Disease Detection Model again (re-evaluation step)
else
   Extract Date t from C
   Query OpenWeather API using t to obtain environmental data W
   Apply SWRL rules: check consistency between disease environmental conditions in KG and W
   if Correspondence = 0 (False) then
      Call Olive Leaf Disease Detection Model again (re-evaluation step)
   else
      Enrich caption C using KG (augment with knowledge-grounded explanation)
   end if
end if
return Final enriched caption or re-predicted disease
```

4 Results Achieved

The fine-tuning of the BLIP-2 model was conducted on a CUDA-enabled GPU server, which enabled efficient model training and scaling with augmented data. Fine-tuning was performed using the PyTorch framework, with Hugging Face Transformers providing access to pretrained BLIP-2 weights and optimization pipelines. Pandas[3] was employed for handling JSON data, Pillow[4] for image pre-processing and augmentation, and the Evaluate[5] library for metric computation. Initial trials with partial fine-tuning and LoRA adaptation demonstrated limited effectiveness, producing generic outputs with weak image–text alignment. To address this, full fine-tuning was adopted, updating both the vision encoder and text decoder. This strategy allowed the model to adapt more effectively to the agricultural context and to generate domain-relevant disease descriptions. The experimental dataset consisted of 300 curated image–text pairs, each describing plant diseases with their causes, symptoms, and remedies. To mitigate the limited sample size, augmentation techniques were applied, including horizontal, vertical, and combined flips. This expanded the dataset to 1 196 image–text pairs, while the same training settings were retained for consistency.

[3] Cf. https://pandas.pydata.org/.
[4] Cf. https://github.com/python-pillow/Pillow.
[5] Cf. https://github.com/huggingface/evaluate.

Model performance was evaluated using BERTScore [20], ROUGE-L [11], and BLEU [15], which together provide complementary perspectives on semantic similarity, content fidelity, and lexical precision. The results obtained with and without augmentation are presented in Table 1.

Table 1. Experimental results for BLIP-2 fine-tuning with and without augmentation.

Setting	Samples	Train Loss	BERTScore	ROUGE-L	BLEU
Without augmentation	300	0.4751	0.8431	0.3150	0.0221
With augmentation	1196	0.0281	0.9539	0.7215	0.7092

The results clearly demonstrate that augmentation significantly improved the model's descriptive accuracy and stability. Training loss was reduced by an order of magnitude, while all evaluation metrics increased substantially. In particular, BLEU rose from 0.02 to 0.71, highlighting a major improvement in lexical precision. These findings confirm the importance of data augmentation in enabling robust domain-specific fine-tuning of vision–language models.

We conducted a controlled user study to assess the *feasibility* of BLIP-OLIVE, involving five employees (two agronomists, two farmers, and one production manager) from Caprigliano[6]. Participants evaluated explanations generated by baseline BLIP-2 and by BLIP-OLIVE across six representative disease cases along three dimensions: *(i)* clarity (is the explanation understandable?); *(ii)* actionability (does it suggest clear actions?) and *(iii)* trustworthiness (does it appear reliable and consistent with domain knowledge?). Ratings were collected using a 5-point Likert scale. Overall, ontology-grounded explanations were consistently preferred, being perceived as clearer, more actionable, and better aligned with domain knowledge than the baseline outputs. These results provide initial evidence of the practical usefulness of integrating formal knowledge grounding into multimodal explainable systems for smart agriculture.

5 Lessons Learned and Concluding Remarks

This case study allow the derive some lessons learned, which we abstract here and provide the added value for information systems engineers.

- Explainability in specific domains (such as smart agriculture) cannot rely on generic XAI techniques alone. While visual tools such as heatmaps offer a first hint of where a disease might appear, they fall short of answering the questions that matter most to domain experts, e.g., for farmers: *What is the disease? Why is it happening? And what should I do now?*. We learned that effective explainability means for domain practitioners to be able to interpret model outputs to their specific knowledge (agronomic in our case), and not just provide suggestions to identified image regions.

[6] Cf. https://www.caprigliano.com/.

- Integration of an ontology fundamentally changed how explanations were perceived. In our case, once symptoms, causes, and treatments were expressed through OLDO's structured concepts, users began to recognize the system as an *agricultural assistant* rather than a black box. This showed us that domain-grounded explanations generate *trust* because they speak the language of practitioners—diseases, humidity conditions, fungal agents, and concrete actions they can take in the field. Therefore the construction of domain-specific ontologies is the effective tool to be layered on top of machine learning techniques (even if applied to image processing) in order to provide explainability.
- User involvement and evaluation reminded us that farmers and agronomists value clarity over complexity. They preferred concise, actionable narratives enriched with treatments and causal links, rather than abstract descriptions. The success of BLIP-OLIVE therefore lies not only in its technical accuracy but in its ability to translate multimodal AI into meaningful, trustworthy recommendations. This call for the development of user-centered XAI methodologies, to be defined and validated in more cases.
- Notably, adopting knowledge representation techniques is a part of AI, even if currently neglected in some trends in favor of ML/DNNs/LLMs – black box approaches. What is called neurosymbolic AI is indeed to intersection of ML with knowledge representation, and this case study supports the argument that this is one of the viable approaches to build XAI for practitioners.
- Concretely, achieving XAI requires a lot of effort, as knowledge modeling and injecting it into existing ML techniques is error-prone, iterative, user-centered, and requires a lot of effort and multi-disciplinary competencies. This has been argued several times, but trying effectively is the best approaches to be fully convinced of it. It would be interesting to develop estimation approaches that can guide projects' implementation in order to properly allocate time and resources.

We are currently working on the assessment of the *effectiveness* of explanations generated by different XAI methods—Grad-CAM [17], Grad-CAM++, LIME [5], and SHAP, applied to olive leaf disease classification and detection. It combines quantitative scales and open-ended questions to assess dimensions such as clarity, relevance, usefulness, trustworthiness, and overall usefulness. We plan to ask participants to rate how well each explanation highlights the diseased regions, promotes understanding. More generally, our future work is exactly in the direction outline above, i.e., how to devise a general framework and methodology for a user-centered XAI based on neurosymbolic techniques, to be validated in several cases. We have access to smart agriculture, Industry 4.0 and Public Administrations and Government contexts, and we aim at using those for our scientific validation purposes.

Acknowledgments. The work has been partly supported by the EU Projects GAINAfrica (ID 101298559).

References

1. Al-khateeb, S.N.: An AI-based framework for olive disease identification using SqueezeNet, artificial neural networks, and support vector machines. In: 2024 IEEE 30th International Conference on Telecommunications (ICT), pp. 01–05. IEEE (2024)
2. Bianchini, F., Calamo, M., De Luzi, F., Macrì, M., Mecella, M.: Enhancing complex linguistic tasks resolution through fine-tuning LLMs, RAG and knowledge graphs. In: International Conference on Advanced Information Systems Engineering, pp. 147–155. Springer (2024)
3. Buonaurio, R., Almadi, L., Famiani, F., Moretti, C., Agosteo, G.E., Schena, L.: Olive leaf spot caused by venturia oleaginea: an updated review. Front. Plant Sci. **13**, 1061136 (2023)
4. FAO: Olive and olive oil statistics, Food and Agriculture Organization of the United Nations (2020)
5. Guo, X.: LIME: a method for low-light image enhancement. In: Proceedings of the 24th ACM International Conference on Multimedia, pp. 87–91 (2016)
6. Hamdaoui, H., Zarrouk, Y., Kouddane, N.E., Hsana, Y., AL Kaddouri, H., Chkird, F.: A deep learning-based model for efficient olive leaf disease classification. In: International Conference on Electronic Engineering and Renewable Energy Systems, pp. 477–487. Springer (2024)
7. Johannesson, P., Perjons, E.: An Introduction to Design Science. Springer (2014). https://doi.org/10.1007/978-3-319-10632-8
8. Kamilaris, A., Prenafeta-Boldú, F.X.: Deep learning in agriculture: a survey. Comput. Electron. Agric. **147**, 70–90 (2018)
9. Kareem, M.R.: Image analysis and detection of olive leaf diseases using recurrent neural networks. Al-Mustansiriyah J. Sci. **35**(1), 60–65 (2024)
10. Li, J., Li, D., Savarese, S., Hoi, S.: BLIP-2: bootstrapping language-image pre-training with frozen image encoders and large language models. In: Proceedings of the 40th International Conference on Machine Learning. ICML'23. JMLR.org (2023)
11. Lin, C.Y., Och, F.: Looking for a few good metrics: ROUGE and its evaluation. In: NTCIR workshop, pp. 1–8 (2004)
12. Mahmood, M.A., Alsalem, K.: Olive leaf disease detection via wavelet transform and feature fusion of pre-trained deep learning models. Comput. Materials Continua **78**(3) (2024)
13. Muhie, S.H.: Novel approaches and practices to sustainable agriculture. J. Agric. Food Res. **10**, 100446 (2022)
14. Pacal, I., Kilicarslan, S., Ozdemir, B., Deveci, M., Kadry, S.: Efficient and autonomous detection of olive leaf diseases using AI-enhanced MetaFormer. Artif. Intell. Rev. **58**(10), 303 (2025)
15. Papineni, K., Roukos, S., Ward, T., Zhu, W.J.: BLEU: a method for automatic evaluation of machine translation. In: Proceedings of the 40th annual meeting of the Association for Computational Linguistics, pp. 311–318 (2002)
16. Rahman, F., Raghatate, K.S.: Smart agriculture: Predicting diseases in olive using deep learning algorithms. In: SHS Web of Conferences. vol. 216, p. 01009. EDP Sciences (2025)
17. Selvaraju, R.R., Das, A., Vedantam, R., Cogswell, M., Parikh, D., Batra, D.: Grad-CAM: Why did you say that? arXiv preprint (2016). arXiv:1611.07450

18. Suárez-Figueroa, M.C., Gómez-Pérez, A., Fernández-López, M.: The NeOn methodology for ontology engineering. In: Ontology Engineering in a Networked World, pp. 9–34. Springer (2011)
19. Vom Brocke, J., Mendling, J.: Business process management cases. Springer (2018)
20. Zhang, T., Kishore, V., Wu, F., Weinberger, K.Q., Artzi, Y.: Bertscore: evaluating text generation with BERT (2019). arXiv:1904.09675 arXiv preprint

ProvenanceTrace: Atomic Claim Verification Across Financial and Open-Domain AI Systems

Krati Saxena[1(✉)], Bhaskarjit Sarmah[1], and Stefano Pasquali[2]

[1] Domyn, Gurugram, India
{krati.saxena,bhaskarjit.sarmah}@domyn.com
[2] Domyn, New York, USA
stefano.pasquali@domyn.com
https://www.domyn.com/

Abstract. Enterprise use of Large Language Models (LLMs) is expanding rapidly, but high-stakes deployment in enterprise information systems (EIS), especially in domains like finance, remains constrained by auditability and accountability requirements. Existing provenance systems are mostly document-level, leaving claim-level evidence gaps that increase review effort and governance risk. In this vision paper, we present **ProvenanceTrace** as an enterprise integration framework that decomposes outputs into atomic claims and links each claim to evidence (or flags it unsupported) through retrieval and verification. We present preliminary proof-of-concept (PoC) evidence intended to validate architectural feasibility and integration viability in both a financial agentic system and open-domain question answering. These early results suggest that claim-level provenance can operate across heterogeneous workflows, improve audit readiness through evidence links per claim, and support architectures integrated with governance, risk, and compliance processes.

Keywords: Provenance Tracing · Claim Verification · Finance AI · LLM Auditability · Trustworthy AI

1 Introduction

Large Language Models (LLMs) are increasingly embedded in enterprise information systems (EIS) that support regulated reporting, compliance, and decision workflows in finance. From an Information Systems Engineering (ISE) perspective, this shifts the problem from model performance to governance of socio-technical decision processes: enterprises must demonstrate accountability, traceability, and control across models, data assets, and operational systems. Yet today's RAG citations and system logs provide document-level traceability, not verification of the specific statements that drive action. This gap is material in finance, where regulations such as the EU AI Act, GDPR Article 22, and MiFID IIrequire auditable and accountable automation.

F. Zerbato et al. (Eds.): CAiSE 2026, LNBIP 587, pp. 37–45, 2026.
https://doi.org/10.1007/978-3-032-27997-2_5

Related work has advanced several pieces of the problem, including orchestration traces, lineage modeling, and fact-checking attribution [1,3–6,11]. However, these strands are often disconnected in enterprise practice: lineage is captured without claim-level grounding, or claim checks are performed without workflow-level accountability integration. To address this gap, we position **ProvenanceTrace** as an enterprise integration blueprint that decomposes outputs into *atomic claims* and links each claim to supporting evidence (or marks it unsupported), so provenance can operate as an ISE capability embedded in governance workflows through provenance-ready architectures, service-level controls, and governance, risk and compliance integration.

We provide an initial PoC to demonstrate feasibility and to anchor a research agenda for operationalization in real organizations. The contributions are as follows:

- **Enterprise integration of claim-level provenance:** We show how atomic claim traceability supports accountability and governance in enterprise use.
- **Financial-domain application blueprint:** We present an end to end framework that decomposes outputs into claims and links them to evidence.
- **Early feasibility signals:** We report proof of concept results in a financial agentic workflow and open domain QA to motivate an ISE evaluation agenda.

2 Related Works

Agentic AI systems require richer provenance than traditional pipelines. Recent provenance frameworks capture workflow execution well, including prompts, tool calls, and reasoning traces [11,13], and reliability-oriented governance metrics for finance [9]. Earlier lineage systems such as PROV-IO+ and yProv [1,4] improve reproducibility and interoperability, but they are not designed for atomic claim verification. As a result, most provenance approaches remain strong on process tracking but weak on claim-level auditability, which is central in regulated enterprise settings.

In parallel, claim verification and attribution methods have advanced retrieval-grounded checking and fine-grained citation alignment. Representative work includes RAGE for retrieval-linked verification [10], OLMoTrace for span-level attribution [6], and SelfCite for sentence-level citation calibration [2]; long-form and agentic factuality pipelines further improve robustness [12]. However, these methods are often evaluated as stand-alone fact-checking components rather than integrated with enterprise provenance infrastructure. ProvenanceTrace focuses on that integration point, not on claim verification itself: it unifies claim-centric verification with workflow-aware provenance so evidence, lineage, and accountability remain connected across financial agentic systems and open-domain question answering.

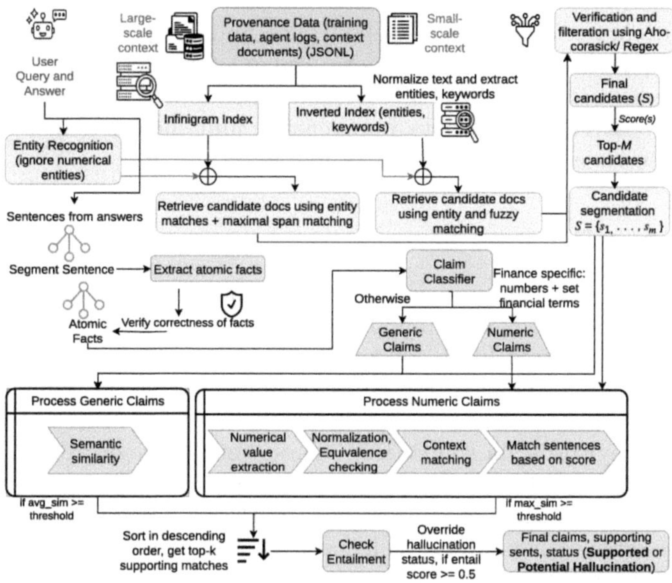

Fig. 1. Overview of ProvenanceTrace. Red, yellow and green components corresponds to *Data Layer*, *Index and Retrieval Layer* and *Claim Verification Layer*, respectively. (Color figure online)

3 Why Claim-Level Provenance Matters

Atomic-claim traceability turns AI outputs into accountable decision inputs by treating each claim as a verifiable unit with a status, linked evidence, and ownership. This enables organizations to justify approvals and audit why a decision was accepted, escalated, or blocked. The need is especially acute as faster, more autonomous AI workflows increase the risk that unsupported statements propagate into reports or customer-facing actions. We evaluate this idea in both financial agentic workflows and open-domain question answering, showing that claim-level accountability is useful across high-stakes and general-purpose settings.

4 Methodology

We propose ProvenanceTrace as a three-layer, enterprise-ready method for claim-level provenance, combining practical NLP components with governance-oriented design; Fig. 1 summarizes the framework.

4.1 Data Layer

The *Data Layer* stores all source information needed to reconstruct provenance. In agentic AI workflows, this includes data fetched, generated, or referenced during execution, reasoning steps, tool outputs, and decision logs. In non-agentic LLM systems, it comprises the corpora and context documents used during inference. We use a standardized JSONL format so inputs from different sources are consistent: each line represents a provenance unit such as a document chunk, a tool response, or a workflow step with metadata.

4.2 Index and Retrieval Layer

This layer enables efficient retrieval through indexing optimized for dataset scale and computational constraints. For large corpora we use scalable substring indexing with Infini-gram [6,7]; for smaller repositories we use a conventional inverted index over normalized text. We normalize text (lowercasing and whitespace cleanup) and extract named entities using SpaCy's NER[1]; if entities are sparse, we add keywords via KeyBERT[2]. These entities/keywords act as anchors in the index, making retrieval fast and transparent to reviewers.

For each claim, we extract anchors from both the user query and the model answer, then retrieve candidate evidence from the chosen index. With Infini-gram, we use maximal matching spans to find strong substrings across large corpora; with the inverted index, we use exact matches and light fuzzy matching for abbreviations or typos. We also verify that anchors actually appear in the retrieved text (e.g., via Aho-Corasick or regex checks) to reduce false positives. We score the candidates using a simple blend of Jaccard overlap, syntactic similarity, and semantic similarity (e.g., SBERT[3]), then rank them to produce a small, reviewable evidence set for each claim. This ranked evidence set is the supporting evidence used to verify the atomic claims in the next layer.

4.3 Claim Verification Layer

The *Claim Verification Layer* turns model output into an *auditable set of atomic claims* with a corresponding evidence trail, so each claim can be supported, flagged for review, or blocked based on enterprise policy. It performs three steps that keep the method understandable while still audit-ready.

Claim Extraction. Model responses often bundle multiple assertions in one sentence. For example, "In Q4 2025, the company reported revenue of USD 4.2B and net income of USD 0.8B" contains two atomic claims: "The company reported revenue of USD 4.2B in Q4 2025" and "The company reported net income of USD 0.8B in Q4 2025". We split responses into sentences and extract minimal, self-contained claims that can be verified independently. We use a lightweight two-stage generation and verification process: first generate candidate claims with a fixed enterprise LLM to reduce operational variance, then validate each claim against the source sentence to ensure clarity and atomicity.

[1] https://spacy.io/usage/linguistic-features#named-entities.
[2] https://github.com/MaartenGr/KeyBERT.
[3] https://sbert.net/.

We remove the duplicates and keep track of claim positions for traceability. Parallely, we normalize, de-duplicate and segment the candidates obtained from the retrieval layer above.

Policy-Driven Routing and Alignment. To support reliable decisions and auditability in EIS workflows, ProvenanceTrace routes claims through different verification paths based on policy: generic text claims follow a semantic support check against source evidence, while numeric or finance-critical claims go through stricter validation. For numeric claims, the system standardizes number formats and structured representations (e.g., key–value records), then checks value, unit, and scale consistency before assigning support. The final claim–evidence alignment combines structural match, domain terminology, and contextual meaning to produce a reviewable decision trail. Finally, any claims initially flagged as unsupported or potential hallucinations undergo a definitive entailment analysis using a specialized language model, ensuring that all synthesized outputs maintain the strict factual integrity required for enterprise deployment.

5 Evaluation: Initial Feasibility Evidence

In this paper, we focus on reporting implemented proof-of-concept results (retrieval quality, hallucination routing behavior, and runtime/stability) across two representative settings to assess feasibility rather than benchmark leadership.

Financial Agentic Veracity (FAV): This use-case evaluates provenance tracing in a realistic enterprise financial workflow where a central orchestrator coordinates 8 specialized agents (web searchers, data scrapers, summarizers, extractors, analysts, and advisors) to turn market information into investment recommendations; in practice, this reflects how organizations combine multiple services before a decision is issued. For a query such as "Should I buy this stock based on its P/E ratio and recent earnings?", agents gather market/public evidence, synthesize findings, extract structured facts, and produce advice, while agent logs act as data-layer artifacts for auditability. Provenance on agentic data is especially important because final outputs are composed from multiple intermediate tool calls and transformations, so accountability requires tracing both the final claim and the execution path that produced it. The dataset combines templated financial queries with curated ticker symbols across Technology and Financial sectors, covering investment decisions, market analysis, and portfolio management; we run 420 unique prompts twice (840 total runs).

Open-Domain Wikipedia Fact Audit (OWFA): This use-case uses the "allenai/olmo-mix-1124" Wikipedia dataset[4] as a trusted reference and includes questions such as "In what year did World War II begin?" and "Which organization is responsible for the Nobel Prize?" We run 241 prompts three times each (723 total runs). Beyond the finance-specific case, this open-domain evaluation provides preliminary indications that the same architecture can be applied to larger, heterogeneous corpora common in enterprise environments.

[4] https://huggingface.co/datasets/allenai/olmo-mix-1124/viewer/wiki.

Evaluation Metrics: We evaluate ProvenanceTrace on three enterprise-relevant feasibility dimensions: retrieval accuracy, hallucination detection, and operational robustness. Retrieval is measured by Hit@5 (at least one supporting source in the top five), average first-relevant rank, and full rank distributions, using an LLM judge for supportiveness; hallucination detection checks claim support via semantic similarity and LLM-based entailment, reporting score distributions, means, and hallucination counts. For scalable PoC evaluation at high claim volume, we use Domyn-Small[5] (temperature = 0.0) with fixed prompts for Hit@5 and support labeling (released for reproducibility[6]), and assess robustness through end-to-end runtime plus stability (coefficient of variation) over answer length, fact counts, and support labels across runs. This submission reports preliminary feasibility evidence and does not yet include comparative baselines, component ablations, human calibration studies, or sensitivity analysis over key thresholds.

5.1 Results

Table 1. Consolidated Results for FAV and OWFA Experiments

Category	Metric	FAV	OWFA
Retrieval	Hit@5 Success Rate (%)	91.3	72.7
Retrieval	Mean Rank (Successful Hits)	1.4	1.7
Hallucination	Total Claims Evaluated	23,093	3,082
Hallucination	Supported Rate (%)	87.4	69.6
Hallucination	Hallucination Rate (%)	12.6	30.4
Efficiency/Stability	Mean Runtime (s)	84.71	161.03
Efficiency/Stability	Answer Length CV	~0.4 (moderate)	~0.2 (lower)
Efficiency/Stability	Fact Count CV	~0.4 (moderate)	~0.8–1.2 (broad)
Efficiency/Stability	Support Rate CV	near zero	~1.0 (broad)

Hit@5 Analysis: As shown in Table 1, the stronger FAV retrieval results are expected in this PoC by design, not a weakness in high-stakes assurance. The FAV pipeline includes domain-specific financial normalization and numeric consistency checks, which improve matching for structured enterprise evidence. OWFA, in contrast, uses a more generic semantic verification setup over heterogeneous open-domain content, where lexical and contextual variation naturally introduces more misses. For information systems, this demonstrates that claim-level provenance can be tuned to domain risk and data characteristics: adding

[5] https://www.domyn.com/language-models.

[6] https://github.com/kratisaxena-domyn/ProvenanceTrace_Assets.

domain-grounded controls (especially numeric checks) improves audit performance while preserving the same core provenance architecture.

Hallucination Detection Analysis: As shown in Table 1, FAV has lower hallucination rates and higher support rates because its evidence space is smaller and tighter with agent data and logs, making the top-M set (here $M = 5$) more likely to contain directly supporting evidence. This aligns with the higher Hit@5 in FAV. OWFA uses a much larger and noisier Wikipedia space, where top-M candidates are often only partially relevant, reducing Hit@5 and support rates. For information systems, this is expected in the current PoC design and indicates clear improvements: adaptively increase M and improve candidate selection to better capture relevant evidence spans. Statistical separation remains strong in both settings: similarity and entailment distinguish supported from unsupported claims with p-values below 0.0001 in t-tests and Mann–Whitney tests.

General Analysis and Runtime Insights: System efficiency and stability show clear domain differences. In FAV, mean runtime is 84.71 s and is tightly clustered, with most cost coming from multi-agent orchestration. In OWFA, mean runtime rises to 161.03 s, driven mainly by hallucination scoring and consistency alignment over large, unstructured Wikipedia evidence. Coefficient of variation analysis reinforces this contrast. In FAV, answer length and fact count vary moderately, while support rate CV stays near zero, indicating stable verification consistency. In OWFA, constrained prompts reduce answer-length variation, but heterogeneous evidence causes broader spread in fact count and support rate. The broader OWFA CV spread is statistically significant (p-value < 0.01) and reflects greater extraction and claim-support variability.

ProvenanceTrace, as a focused proof-of-concept for enterprise and financial-domain use of atomic claim-level provenance, prioritizes architecture feasibility over exhaustive benchmark comparison. We leave direct baseline and attribution comparisons (e.g., BM25+cross-encoder [8], OLMoTrace [6], and SelfCite [2]) to future integration studies.

6 Discussion

In this vision paper, we present ProvenanceTrace as a practical step toward provenance-ready enterprise systems. Instead of treating an LLM response as a single opaque output, it treats each atomic claim as an auditable unit linked to concrete evidence. This shift is important because organizations do not govern answers in aggregate; they govern decisions, controls, and accountability at claim level.

This is especially relevant in the current AI landscape, where LLMs are moving from assistive drafting to workflow participation in reporting, compliance, and customer-facing operations. In these settings, document-level citations are often insufficient for sign-off, escalation, and post-hoc audit. Claim-level provenance fills this gap by connecting generated statements to evidence in a form that can be used by risk, compliance, and audit functions.

For organizations, adoption can be incremental rather than disruptive. A practical rollout path is to start in one high-value workflow, define provenance

SLAs (coverage, latency, escalation), and embed verification checkpoints into existing processes. The PoC results suggest that the architecture can be adapted to structured enterprise contexts and broader domains with appropriate retrieval controls and review policies.

Open challenges remain, but they are now concrete engineering and governance tasks rather than abstract trust concerns. Next steps are to complement LLM-based judging with calibrated human review under explicit policies, add retrieval and attribution baselines, and report clearer quality measures for claim extraction and atomicity. We will also specify dataset and prompting protocols more explicitly, deepen numeric-verification details for unit/scale/currency edge cases, and formalize governance integration through standards-aligned provenance mappings and escalation schemas. These steps strengthen external validity while preserving the paper's vision focus on provenance-ready enterprise architectures.

Disclosure of Interests. The authors have no competing interests.

References

1. Abedin, B., Meske, C., Junglas, I., Rabhi, F., Motahari-Nezhad, H.R.: Designing and managing human-ai interactions. Inf. Syst. Front. **24**(3), 691–697 (2022)
2. Chuang, Y.S., et al.: Selfcite: self-supervised alignment for context attribution in large language models. ArXiv abs/2502.09604 (2025). https://api.semanticscholar.org/CorpusID:276317486
3. CrewAI Inc.: Crewai: a multi-agent automation framework (2024). https://www.crewai.com/. Accessed 14 Nov 2025
4. Han, R., Zheng, M., Byna, S., Tang, H., Dong, B., Dai, D., Chen, Y., Kim, D., Hassoun, J., Thorsley, D.: PROV-IO++: a cross-platform provenance framework for scientific data on HPC systems. IEEE Trans. Parallel Distrib. Syst. **35**(5), 844–861 (2024)
5. LangChain Inc.: Langchain: a platform for reliable agents (2025). https://www.langchain.com/. Accessed 14 Nov 2025
6. Liu, J., et al.: Olmotrace: tracing language model outputs back to trillions of training tokens (2025). arXiv:2504.07096 arXiv preprint
7. Liu, J., Min, S., Zettlemoyer, L., Choi, Y., Hajishirzi, H.: Infini-gram: Scaling unbounded n-gram language models to a trillion tokens (2024). arXiv:2401.17377 arXiv preprint
8. Lu, M., Chen, C., Eickhoff, C.: Pathway to relevance: How cross-encoders implement a semantic variant of bm25 (2025). https://arxiv.org/abs/2502.04645
9. Raza, S., Sapkota, R., Karkee, M., Emmanouilidis, C.: Trism for agentic AI: a review of trust, risk, and security management in LLM-based agentic multi-agent systems (2025). arXiv:2506.04133 arXiv preprint
10. Rorseth, J., Godfrey, P., Golab, L., Srivastava, D., Szlichta, J.: Towards explainability in retrieval-augmented LLMs. In: 2024 IEEE 40th International Conference on Data Engineering (ICDE), pp. 5669–5670. IEEE (2024)
11. Souza, R., et al.: Prov-agent: unified provenance for tracking AI agent interactions in agentic workflows. In: 2025 IEEE International Conference on eScience (eScience), pp. 467–473. IEEE (2025)

12. Wei, J., Yang, C., Song, X., Lu, Y., Hu, N., Huang, J., Tran, D., Peng, D., Liu, R., Huang, D., et al.: Long-form factuality in large language models. Adv. Neural. Inf. Process. Syst. **37**, 80756–80827 (2024)
13. Yao, S., Zhao, J., Yu, D., Du, N., Shafran, I., Narasimhan, K.R., Cao, Y.: React: synergizing reasoning and acting in language models. In: The Eleventh International Conference on Learning Representations (2022)

Towards a FAIR Data Management Framework for Ontology-Driven Explainable Machine Learning

Donika Xhani[1(✉)], João Luiz Rebelo Moreira[2], Marten van Sinderen[2], Luís Ferreira Pires[2], Giancarlo Guizzardi[2], and Marcos R. Machado[1]

[1] FEBIS Group, BMS Faculty, University of Twente, Enschede, The Netherlands
{d.xhani,m.r.machado}@utwente.nl

[2] SCS Group, EEMCS Faculty, University of Twente, Enschede, The Netherlands
{j.luizrebelomoreira,m.j.vansinderen,l.ferreirapires,g.guizzardi}@utwente.nl

Abstract. Data is a valuable asset for any business to remain competitive and agile. Many companies rely on Artificial Intelligence (AI) to improve their processes, products and services. However, most of the time, data is stored in silo applications, which are usually not interoperable, and data scientists struggle to understand the semantics or to interpret the results of AI solutions over this data. The Findable, Accessible, Interoperable, and Reusable (FAIR) principles offer a key approach for improving data management by providing guidelines that enhance data understandability. When combined with eXplainable Artificial Intelligence (XAI) techniques, the FAIR principles can increase understanding by enhancing transparency and building trust. This paper presents a contribution towards a framework designed to improve data management and enable XAI within organizations. It also presents a set of Reference Architecture (RA) viewpoints that illustrate how to implement the framework in practice, outlining the necessary processes and supporting tools. The framework and RA were implemented and validated in a manufacturing company whose main goals were to improve data management and develop transparent, explainable Machine Learning (ML) models.

Keywords: Data Management · FAIR Principles · Explainable ML · Reference Architecture · Ontology

1 Introduction

Data management involves collecting, storing, and using data efficiently, securely, and cost-effectively. As one of a company's most valuable assets, data can drive marketing, operational improvements, and cost savings to boost profits. Yet, many organizations struggle with fragmented data silos, inconsistent datasets, and weak semantics. Poor data management has major implications, as 66% of organizations state that at least half of their enterprise data remains unused or ambiguous [1], and data scientists spend up to 80% of their time on data cleaning

F. Zerbato et al. (Eds.): CAiSE 2026, LNBIP 587, pp. 46–53, 2026.
https://doi.org/10.1007/978-3-032-27997-2_6

and preparation [2]. The FAIR principles (Findable, Accessible, Interoperable, and Reusable) provide guidance for better data management by ensuring that data can be understood and reused by both humans and machines [3], creating opportunities for improved interoperability, reuse, and business value [4].

Due to their effectiveness in learning and performing tasks, Artificial Intelligence (AI) and particularly Machine Learning (ML) are being widely used by companies. However, most of these models are considered black box models because they are opaque and do not provide any explanation on why or how the algorithm achieved that result [5]. This issue is addressed by eXplainable Artificial Intelligence (XAI)[1], which refers to methods and techniques that aim to make ML models transparent, interpretable, or comprehensible to humans [6]. The XAI approaches are classified into two categories, namely: (1) ante-hoc approach, which embed explainability during model design and (2) post-hoc approach which applies semantic resources to the trained black-box ML model. Despite these advances, organizations still face challenges in implementing FAIR principles and ensuring ML outputs are understandable to non-experts.

This paper presents a contribution towards a framework for improving data management and enabling XAI, and provides Reference Architecture (RA) viewpoints that can serve as guidelines for implementing the framework, showcasing the needed processes and tools. The combination of XAI, FAIR and ontology topics into an approach is novel and needed because it enables transparent, trustworthy AI that can be seamlessly integrated, audited, and reused across complex data ecosystems. The framework was applied in a manufacturing company, resulting in two key artifacts: a domain ontology and the eXplainable Machine Learning Pipeline Ontology (XMLPO) [7]. The produced artifacts were evaluated through an expert opinion assessment involving company stakeholders.

This paper is structured as follows: Sect. 2 provides background information on FAIR principles and related work. Section 3 introduces the framework. Section 4 presents the RA viewpoints. Section 5 describes the implementation of the framework and initial validation results. Section 6 discusses the contributions, limitations and future work.

2 Background and Related Work

The FAIRness level of a database indicates how many of the FAIR principles have been implemented or complied with [8], and it can be measured by using FAIR metrics or by using FAIR assessment tools. FAIR metrics can be developed using templates [9], which aim to create clear, measurable and universal metrics. This template focuses on the creation of FAIR metrics for machines as measuring FAIRness to humans is more subjective. A method for qualitatively assessing perceived FAIRness to humans[2] is the usage of open questions, which aim to assess how and to what extent principles are implemented. For example, the 18

[1] Throughout this paper, the terms XAI or Explainable ML are used interchangeably.
[2] In this paper, FAIRness to humans refers solely to making data FAIR to human users, and it does not relate to ethical or social notions of fairness.

questions proposed by [10] evaluate FAIRness from the perspective of users or stakeholders (e.g., how data were accessed or whether metadata were available).

According to the I1 Interoperability principle of FAIR, data and metadata should be described using a formal, accessible, shared, and broadly applicable language for knowledge representation [3]. Semantic Interoperability (SI) is the ability of systems to exchange and interpret information based on shared, explicit meanings grounded in clear ontological commitments, allowing machines to combine and reason over data [11]. This is achieved through formally defined ontologies grounded in ontological foundations such as the Unified Foundational Ontology (UFO), with OntoUML as an example of an modeling language [12].

As highlighted by our systematic literature review on the role of SI and XAI [13], SI tools (e.g., ontologies) can actively enhance XAI by providing structured, ontology-based domain knowledge that supports clearer, more transparent, and context-aware explanations. Ontologies play a role both in interoperability and in explaining. Several studies demonstrated this by combining ontologies with ML or XAI techniques, for example, OnML [14], OntoXAI [15], to provide richer, more meaningful semantic explanations.

3 Framework Design

Based on a literature review [13], we identified the need for a framework to improve the FAIRness of the data and enable explainable ML. The framework assesses the current FAIRness level, aligns it with the stakeholder goals, and guides improvements towards the desired state with improved data management and explainable ML (Fig. 1). It consists of four phases and is cyclic rather than strictly sequential, allowing iteration or parallel execution when needed.

Phase 1 evaluates current data practices by assessing FAIRness through metrics for machine compliance and stakeholder interviews, identifying implemented

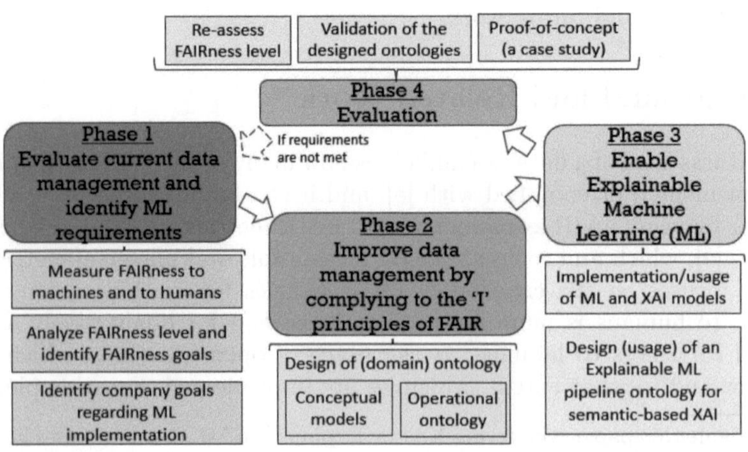

Fig. 1. FAIR Data Management Process for Explainable Machine Learning.

principles and remaining gaps. Because interoperability is often the main bottleneck in practice, limiting data integration, automation, and reuse, Phase 2 targets compliance with the Interoperability principle by designing a domain ontology that defines concepts and relationships unless there are existing ontologies that can be reused or integrated. Phase 3 focuses on enabling explainable ML, where the designed ontologies aid in improving the semantic clarity and transparency of the ML pipeline. Phase 4 evaluates outcomes by reassessing FAIRness, conducting a proof of concept, and validating ontologies using reasoning tools, qualitative evaluation with experts and/or SPARQL queries. If requirements are not met, the process iterates for further refinement.

4 FAIR-Based Reference Architecture for XAI

Implementing the proposed framework (Fig. 1) can be challenging, as stakeholders may find it difficult to identify and execute the necessary business processes or the needed tools. To support this, we provide RA viewpoints in the ArchiMate language, a standard for enterprise architecture modeling [16]. Labels such as EmployeeA, DatasetA, etc., are used only for illustration; in practice, the number, type, and naming of entities may vary.

Figure 2 illustrates the first phase of the framework, highlighting the main activities using the business process element from ArchiMate and their connections to information structures, software applications, and stakeholders. The phase begins with assessing machine-perceived FAIRness using FAIR metrics. It then evaluates human-perceived FAIRness through structured interviews, making it important to schedule interviews with company employees and analyze their feedback. Finally, existing ML models are examined by mapping current implementations and gathering requirements for future ML/AI use.

Figure 3 presents the set of processes involved in designing a domain ontology using the SABiO methodology [17], which offers a systematic approach to ontology development. This phase comprises four main processes and highlights

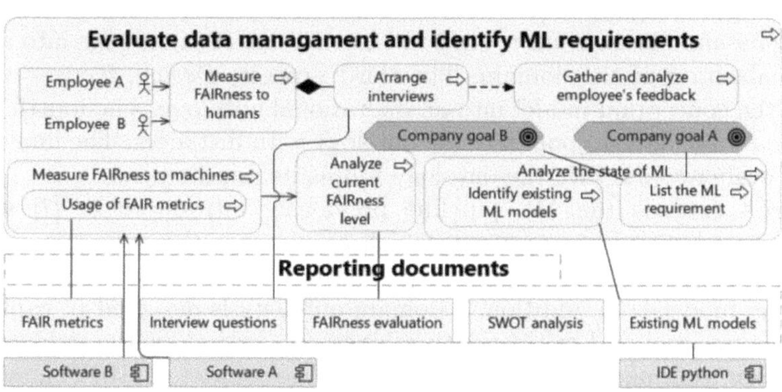

Fig. 2. Reference Architecture Viewpoint for Implementing Phase 1 of the Framework.

example tools and languages that can support design and implementation. These examples are illustrative rather than prescriptive. For instance, OntoUML is an ontology-driven conceptual language grounded in UFO [12], while gUFO[3] offers a lightweight OWL implementation. Python with RDFLib can support ontology instantiation and data integration. Other tools may also be suitable, but the figure shows a coherent set commonly aligned with SABiO's structure.

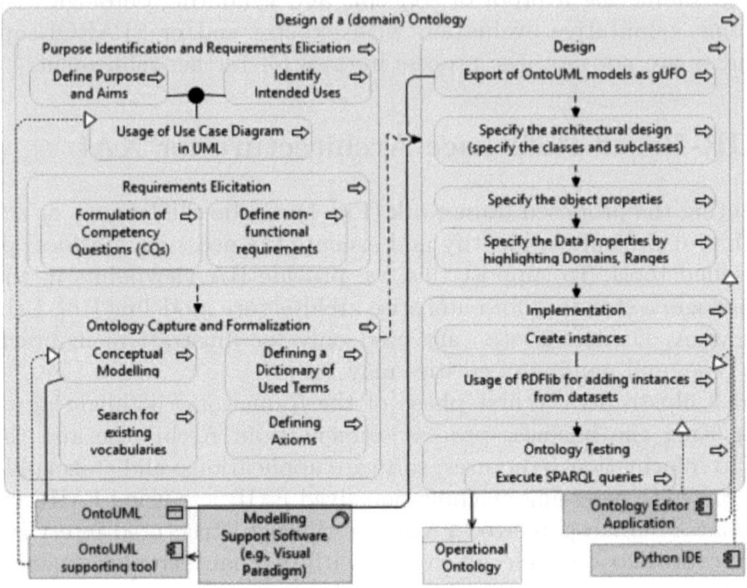

Fig. 3. Reference Architecture Viewpoint for Implementing Phase 2 of the Framework.

The first process, *Purpose Identification and Requirements Elicitation*, focuses on defining the ontology's purpose, identifying its intended uses and users, and specifying the requirements it must satisfy. The second process, *Ontology Capture and Formalization*, aims to translate the requirements into an initial conceptualization of the domain. The third process, *Design*, focuses on transforming the conceptual model into an operational ontology. The fourth process, *Implementation*, aims to populate the ontology with instances. The final process, *Testing*, evaluates whether the ontology fulfills its requirements.

Figure 4 extends the ML pipeline previously introduced in [7] with the semantic-based post-hoc approach, which emphasizes the usage of ontologies. Here, the XMLPO ontology is used to represent pipeline components (e.g., preprocessing, models). In addition, a domain ontology is designed to capture feature semantics and real-world relationships (e.g., causal or hierarchical dependencies). For example, in a battery manufacturing context, XMLPO may contain

[3] https://nemo-ufes.github.io/gufo/.

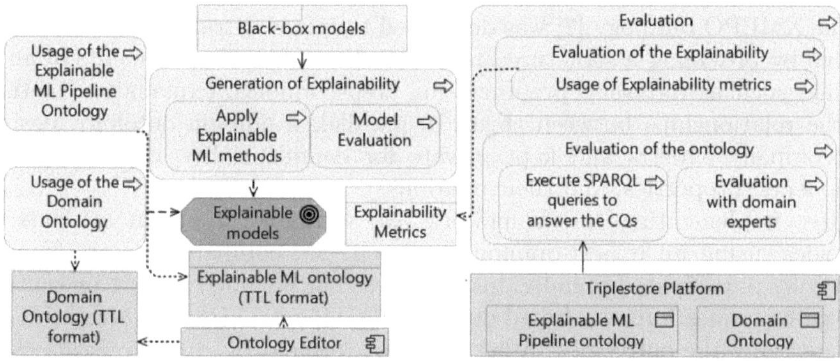

Fig. 4. RA Viewpoint for Following a Semantic-based Post-hoc Approach in ML.

a feature such as *BatteryTemperature*, while the domain ontology encodes that high battery temperature accelerates chemical reactions and may reduce battery lifespan.

Next, XAI methods (e.g., LIME, SHAP) are applied to the trained black-box models to produce interpretable outputs. The domain ontology plays an important role in interpreting these outputs. For example, while SHAP model shows the feature importance or influence of specific feature, it does not explain why a feature behaves in a certain way. Finally, evaluation validates both the explanations and the ontologies, with expert review ensuring semantic correctness.

5 Framework Implementation and Validation

By following the guidelines provided by the reference architecture viewpoints, we have implemented the framework in a manufacturing company. All supplementary materials, such as the RA viewpoints, FAIRness assessment and validation are available on GitHub[4]. Although the framework recommends assessing FAIR implementation through both machine-perceived and human-perceived FAIRness, a metric-based evaluation was not feasible in this case. The company's infrastructure did not support the verification with FAIR metrics, and essential metadata could not be accessed. We therefore focused exclusively on human-perceived FAIRness, using interviews and a short questionnaire.

We conducted five interviews and distributed a questionnaire. To support participants without an IT background, we provided brief definitions of key terms and clarified questions when needed. Results indicate no full compliance with any FAIR principle, though partial compliance exists for some sub-principles, such as minimal metadata (F2), authenticated access (A1), and use of industry standards (R1.3). These reflect implications of stakeholder responses rather than full satisfaction of the principles.

[4] https://github.com/DonikaXhani/FAIR-data-management-framework.

The XMLPO ontology [7] was developed to increase transparency of the ML pipeline by providing a structured representation of the key elements of an ML pipeline, such as datasets, preprocessing steps, models, explanation methods, and the relationships between them. In parallel, a domain ontology, designed with company experts and kept private for confidentiality, captures product components, properties, and their relations.

After implementing the framework, we validated its main artifacts, the ontologies, using an expert-opinion approach. Six company experts from different roles participated in individual sessions that included a short presentation followed by a questionnaire based on the UTAUT model [18]. Although UTAUT evaluates only the ontologies rather than the framework, positive feedback still provides indirect validation, as these artifacts are key outputs of the framework. Experts highlighted that ontologies improve data management, interoperability, and understanding of data relationships, and suggested they could become a best practice if centrally adopted. However, some expressed concerns about organization-wide implementation and relevance to their roles, reflecting both recognition of benefits and uncertainty about adoption effort.

6 Final Remarks

This paper presents a contribution to a framework for FAIR data management for explainable Machine Learning, comprising four phases. To support its adoption, we provide Reference Architecture viewpoints modeled in ArchiMate, illustrating key activities and involved stakeholders and systems. The framework and RA were implemented and validated in a manufacturing company.

Although the framework recommends evaluating FAIRness through metrics (machine-perceived) and interviews (human-perceived), this project relied solely on interviews. FAIR metrics could not be applied due to the company's restrictive infrastructure, which limited access to key information, and the project's one-year timeframe. Furthermore, this work focused solely on implementing the Interoperability principle, aligned with stakeholder goals and requirements. However, the implementation of additional FAIR principles may also be necessary, and future work could therefore extend the framework to address them.

While the current implementation provides initial evidence of the framework's practicality, a key limitation is the lack of full-scale, multi-organizational validation, which remains an important direction for future work. We also recognize that the expert opinion involved only six experts, which may introduce validity threats and limit generalizability. Future work could strengthen external validity by applying and evaluating the framework in other domains.

References

1. Google Cloud: Data and AI Trends Report (2024). https://services.google.com/fh/files/misc/data_ai_trends_report.pdf, Accessed 18 Nov 2025
2. Forbes: From Pipelines To Profit: Data Engineering's Impact On Expansion. https://www.forbes.com/councils/forbestechcouncil/2025/05/29/from-pipelines-to-profit-data-engineerings-impact-on-expansion/, Accessed 26 Feb 2026
3. Wilkinson, M., et al.: The FAIR guiding principles for scientific data management and stewardship. Sci Data. **3**(1), 160018 (2016)
4. van Vlijmen, H., Mons, A., Waalkens, A., Franke, W., Baak, A., Ruiter, G., et al.: The Need of Industry to Go FAIR. Data Intell. **2**(1–2), 276–84 (2020)
5. Yang, G., Ye, Q., Xia, J.: Unbox the black-box for the medical explainable AI via multi-modal and multi-centre data fusion: a mini-review, two showcases and beyond. Inform. Fusion **1**(77), 29–52 (2022)
6. Seeliger, A., Pfaff, M., Krcmar, H.: Semantic web technologies for explainable machine learning models: a literature review. In: PROFILES/SEMEX@ ISWC, 27 Oct, vol. 2465, pp. 1-6 (2019)
7. Xhani, D., Moreira, J.L., van Sinderen, M.J., Pires, L.F.: XMLPO: an ontology for explainable machine learning pipeline. In 14th International Conference on Formal Ontology in Information System, FOIS 2024, pp. 193-206 (2024). IOS
8. Feijoó, M.P.P., Jardim, R., da Cruz, S.M.S., Campos, M.L.M.: Evaluating FAIRness of genomic databases. In: ER 2020. LNCS, vol. 12584, pp. 128–137. Springer, Cham (2020). https://doi.org/10.1007/978-3-030-65847-2_12
9. Wilkinson, M.D., Sansone, S.A., Schultes, E., Doorn, P., Bonino da Silva Santos, L.O., Dumontier, M.: A design framework and exemplar metrics for FAIRness. Sci Data **5**(1), 180118 (2018)
10. Bishop, B.W., Hank, C.: Measuring FAIR principles to inform fitness for use. Int. J. Digit. Curation **13**(1), 35–46 (2018)
11. Guizzardi, G.: Ontology, Ontologies and the "I" of FAIR. Data Intell. **2**(1–2), 181–191 (2020)
12. Guizzardi, G., Botti Benevides, A., Fonseca, C.M., Porello, D., Almeida, J.P., Prince, S.T.: UFO: Unified foundational ontology. Appl. Ontol. **17**(1), 167–210 (2022)
13. Xhani, D., Sedrakyan, G., Gavai, A., Guizzardi, R., van Hillegersberg, J.: The role and applications of semantic interoperability tools and eXplainable AI in the development of smart food systems: findings from a systematic literature review. Intell. Syst. Appli. **27**, 200547 (2025)
14. Ayranci, P., Lai, P., Phan, N., Hu, H., Kolinowski, A., Newman, D., et al.: OnML: an ontology-based approach for interpretable machine learning. J. Comb. Optim. **44**(1), 770–93 (2022)
15. Sharma, S., Jain, S.: OntoXAI: a semantic web rule language approach for explainable artificial intelligence. Cluster Comput. **27**(10), 14951–75 (2024)
16. The Open Group. ArchiMate®3.0. 1 Specification. Van Haren Publishing(2017). https://pubs.opengroup.org/architecture/archimate31-doc/toc.html, Accessed 26 Feb 2026
17. Falbo, R.A.: SABiO: systematic approach for building ontologies. In: Proc. 1st Joint Workshop ONTO.COM / ODISE, vol. 1301 of CEUR Workshop Proceedings, pp. 1-14. CEUR-WS.org (2014)
18. Venkatesh, V., Morris, M.G., Davis, G.B., Davis, F.D.: User acceptance of information technology: toward a unified view. MIS Q. **27**(3), 425–78 (2003)

Towards Explaining Process Variants with Examples

Carlos Capitán-Agudo[1,2(✉)], Claudio Di Ciccio[3], Cristina Cabanillas[1,2], and Manuel Resinas[1,2]

[1] SCORE Lab, Universidad de Sevilla, Seville, Spain
{cristinacabanillas,resinas,c.diciccio}@us.es
[2] I3US Institute, Universidad de Sevilla, Seville, Spain
ccagudo@us.es
[3] Utrecht University, Utrecht, The Netherlands

Abstract. Understanding how and why business processes unfold differently across subsets of cases, commonly referred to as *process variants*, is essential to identifying improvement opportunities. Existing approaches to process variant analysis largely depend on machine learning models that classify cases into variants and then use model explanations to highlight the features driving such classifications. Prior user studies in artificial intelligence have shown that these model explanations can be complemented through the selection of *natural examples* that better capture these differences. Thus, process variant analysis can be enriched by elevating the explanation from highlighting features that better describe their differences to selecting the cases containing these features. Inspired by prior work in process variant analysis, we propose a framework that extracts, quantifies, and leverages declarative behavioral rules to identify these cases. Particularly, we identify two types: cases that are representative of the process variants (prototypes) alongside cases that shore up their frontiers (boundary cases), as means to complement existing process variant approaches.

Keywords: Process mining · Variant analysis · Explainability · Natural example · Declarative specifications · Explainable Artificial Intelligence

1 Introduction and Motivation

Information systems are central to the execution of business processes, as they capture their operational behavior through large-scale event logs. An event log consists of cases, each representing a process case described as an ordered sequence of events. Every event typically records the activity performed, its completion timestamp, and the corresponding case identifier; further attributes, such as the resource involved or associated costs, may also be included. Process mining techniques leverage these logs to discover actual process executions, assess performance, and analyze behavioral patterns.

F. Zerbato et al. (Eds.): CAiSE 2026, LNBIP 587, pp. 54–62, 2026.
https://doi.org/10.1007/978-3-032-27997-2_7

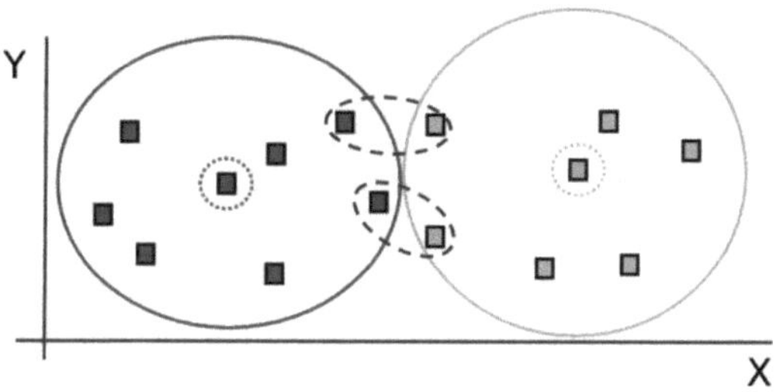

Fig. 1. Bidimensional representation of case examples for two process variants (yellow and red). Solid circles denote decision boundaries, squares represent cases, dashed circles highlight prototypes, and the squares within the purple dashed ovals indicate boundary case pairs. X and Y are feature projections. (Color figure online)

Recently, increasing attention has been directed toward understanding differences among specific subsets of cases, commonly referred to as *process variants* [13]. These encompass cases that share a distinguishing characteristic, such as a specific outcome or attribute value, that sets them apart from the rest of process executions. For example, consider an event log related to the management of traffic fines with activities such as 'Send Fine', 'Payment', or 'Appeal to Judge'. Process variants could be defined according to whether the payment is completed on time or with a delay. Analyzing differences between these variants can show the causes of delays (e.g., offenders appealing the fine instead of paying it directly).

To identify differences between process variants, some approaches use machine learning (ML) techniques to extract sets of rules that explain the distinguishing features [1,5]. These rules are typically expressed in an "if X then Y" format, where X is a logical combination of features, and Y indicates a specific process variant. For instance, in the traffic fine scenario, a possible rule might be: *"If 'Appeal to Judge' occurs in a case, then it belongs to the delayed process variant"*.

However, although these rules already provide useful information, they are not the only way differences between process variants can be explained. For instance, user studies in the field of explainable artificial intelligence (XAI) have shown that this format of explanation can be complemented with examples [11]. *Example-based explainability methods* uses real or artificially generated samples to illustrate model behavior and reasoning [10].

Aligned with these ideas, in this vision paper, we call for elevating real cases from passive data points to first-class explanatory artifacts. Rather than asking only which features distinguish variants, we propose asking: Which concrete executions best demonstrate these differences? This shift reframes variant explanation as a principled example selection problem. Following a similar approach as prior work in variant analysis [13], we envision a framework in which a machine learning model predicts the process variant of a case based on execution data. This model structures the behavioral landscape of cases, enabling the systematic identification of informative examples. Particularly, we consider two complementary explanatory constructs. First, we introduce *prototypes*, i.e., cases that are maximally representative of a variant and embody its characteristic behavioral patterns. Secondly, we introduce *boundary cases*, i.e., correctly classified cases that lie near the decision frontier. These cases expose the limits of process variants (see Fig. 1), that differ in small behavioral deviations alter classification, revealing subtle distinctions. These constructs provide an example-centered perspective to process variants analysis that broadens the explanatory foundations of process variant analysis and complements existing rules-only approaches. Furthermore, this work opens a new empirical and methodological agenda including questions such as: How should representativeness and proximity be defined in behavioral spaces derived from event logs? How can process mining tools integrate abstract rules and concrete cases into coherent explanatory workflows?

The remainder of this paper is organized as follows. Section 2 presents the background and related work. Section 3 details the envisioned framework. Section 4 draws the conclusions from this paper.

2 Background and Related Work

We divide the background and related work into the following three areas.

2.1 Process Variant Analysis

In recent years, many approaches have been proposed for analyzing process variants. A survey on this topic recommends classifying these approaches according to how they explain the differences between variants [13].

Some approaches extract interpretable differences (e.g., rule sets) that highlight distinguishing characteristics of each variant. Several rely on statistical techniques to identify such rules [2,12]. For example, Taymouri et al. [12] detect statistical differences in control flow and performance dimensions between two variants. Other approaches use ML to discover discriminative differences (e.g., rule sets) by assigning a class label to each case based on a specific criterion (e.g., whether the case deviates from an expected process) [13]. For instance, Bose and van der Aalst [1] encode cases as feature vectors by extracting features related to both individual activities (e.g., repetitions of activity A) and their sequences (e.g., how often activity A is immediately followed by B). Using these vectors they apply association rules and decision tree algorithms to generate conditional statements that describe each variant. Different works have extended this idea by enhancing case encodings. For example, Di Francescomarino et al. [5] use declarative encodings of cases, involving features related to activity occurrences and attribute values. They describe the declarative behavior using DECLARE rules and encode them based on their activation results.

Prior research has shown that these rule-based explanations can be complemented with examples [11]. *Artificial example methods* have been adapted to explain ML models trained on event log data for tasks such as predictive process monitoring [8]. This consists in altering a case to change the model prediction, the changes are the explanations. Complementary to them, *natural example methods* have not been explored in process variant analysis.

2.2 Natural Example-Based Explainability Methods

Natural example-based explainability methods use samples from a dataset to explain a particular class or the dataset as a whole [10]. These methods can be categorized according to the type of insight the examples provide. Two categories are particularly relevant in this context. The first comprises approaches for retrieving *prototypes*, which are representative instances of a dataset. The representativeness of the prototypes depends on their purpose. One common use is to provide *post-hoc interpretability* of ML models. In a classification task, a prototype is a sample exhibiting the most important features for a specific class of the dataset. Some approaches for retrieving prototypes have been developed in process mining as well. Mohammadreza et al. [6] define an approach to improve the process discovery using prototypes. The purpose of our approach is different since we focus on explainability methods. Closer to our work, Grigore et al. [7] define a framework to analyze process variants including prototypes. The cases are encoded at activity and event levels. By contrast, our framework encoding relies on DECLARE, and we complement prototype-based explanations with boundary cases to better understand the differences between process variants.

The second category includes approaches that provide *natural counterfactual examples*, which reveal the boundaries between the class samples by highlighting feature differences that lead to the model predictions. Given a sample S, a natural counterfactual is the closest existing sample in the dataset for which the ML model produces a different prediction [10]. To illustrate this, consider a binary classification problem where the task is to predict a loan approval. Consider that a sample that is predicted as "not approved". Its natural counterfactual would be the closest instance in the data that is predicted as "approved". Together, the natural sample and the natural counterfactual form a pair of cases, each one belonging to a different process variant. This pair is particularly effective in revealing the boundaries between variants [10].

2.3 Declarative Behavioral Rules and Measures

Declarative behavioral rules are an effective means to train ML models for process variant prediction [5]. These rules describe permissible order relationships between activities without prescribing the full, end-to-end linearization of the execution order [4]. A widely used language to define such rules is DECLARE [9], which offers rule templates to express temporal relations between activities. For example, the DECLARE rule RESPONSE(A, B) indicates that whenever activity A occurs, activity B must eventually follow. Each occurrence of A in a case is a rule *activation*. Once the rule is activated, if B eventually occurs, RESPONSE(A, B) is *fulfilled*, otherwise it is *violated*.

Different measures can be computed to assess the extent to which a case satisfies a DECLARE rule [3]. A commonly used measure is *confidence*, defined as the ratio of fulfilments over activations, with values ranging from 0 to 1 if an activation occurs in the case. For instance, consider the case $\langle A, B, A, B, C, A\rangle$ and the rule RESPONSE(A, B). The activation A occurs 3 times. The first two lead to fulfilment (B follows A), the third one does not, then confidence is $\frac{2}{3}$.

3 Envisioned Framework

Figure 2 shows our envisioned framework for obtaining a set of *natural examples* that highlight differences between process variants. It assumes that the event log has already been partitioned into variants. To illustrate it, consider a travel declaration process with three variants (*accepted*, *denied*, and *partially accepted*) composed of activities such as *Request Travel Budget* (*RTB*), *Send Declaration* (*SD*), *Travel* (*T*), *Reject* (*R*) and *receive Payment* (*P*). Our approach receives the travel declaration log and its variants, and returns two types of samples that explain the differences between them: (i) prototypes and (ii) boundary cases, near the decision frontier.

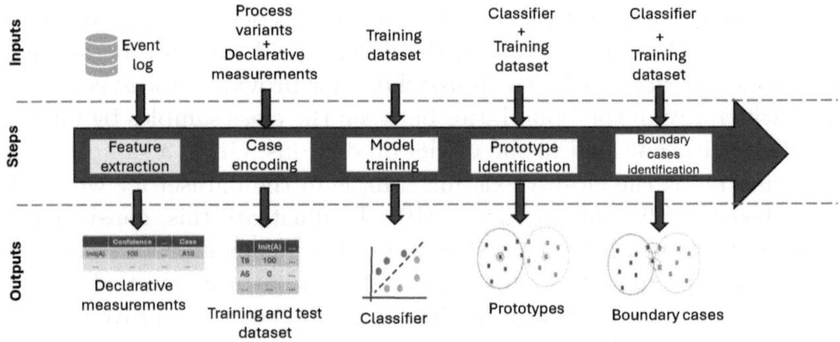

Fig. 2. Overview of our framework. Inputs highlighted in green are given as an external parameter, and outputs highlighted in purple are the final outcomes. (Color figure online)

Step 1: Feature Extraction. The first step involves the extraction of features that represent each case in the input log. In this paper, we focus on control-flow-based features because they can be retrieved from any event logs as they constitute the expected minimal information provision, i.e., a multi-set of event sequences labeled by activity names. Specifically, we use features derived from declarative behavioral rules, given the strong predictive performance shown in prior work [5]. Each case is thus described by the confidence values of all DECLARE rules mined from the log. Those values can be obtained using known techniques in declarative process discovery [4]. If a rule is not activated in a case, the value is set to *none*. Suppose, e.g., that the travel declaration log contains cases $c_1 = \langle T, P \rangle$, $c_2 = \langle T, SD \rangle$, and $c_3 = \langle RTB, R \rangle$. The rule RESPONSE$(T, P)$ has a confidence of 1 for c_1 (fulfilled), 0 for c_2 (violated), and *none* for c_3 (no T occurs).

Step 2: Case Encoding. In this step, we encode each case of the input log as a vector, where each feature obtained in the previous step corresponds to a dimension. The resulting vectors are assembled into a matrix X, in which rows represent cases and columns correspond to features. Each entry in X stores the *confidence* value of a feature for a given case. Table 1 shows an excerpt based on the example cases. We also build a vector Y containing the process variant associated to each case. Finally, X and Y are randomly split into training (X_{train},Y_{train}) and test sets (X_{test},Y_{test}), preserving the process variants' distribution.

Step 3: Model Training. In this step, we train an ML classifier using X_{train} and Y_{train}. We define our classifier as a model M that predicts the probability that a case c belongs to each process variant of a log L based on its feature vector. Once trained, M can determine the variant of unseen cases using their DECLARE-rule measures. Importantly, we require that classifiers are well-calibrated and output probability distributions over all variants rather than a single predicted label.

Step 4: Prototype Identification. After training the classifier, we identify a prototype for each variant using X_{train}, following standard practice [10]. The prototype of a variant V is defined as the training case c that maximizes the predicted probability of belonging to V. This case captures the most characteristic features of the variant while remaining most distinct from the others. For example, let the *accepted* variant's prototype be $c_{\text{acc}} = \langle RTB, T, SD, P \rangle$, and the *denied* variant's prototype be $c_{\text{den}} = \langle SD, T, RTB, R \rangle$. Comparing these cases reveals distinct behavioral patterns. In the *accepted* variant's prototype, T follows RTB, SD follows T, and the case concludes with P, reflecting a compliant execution that leads to approval. By contrast, in the *denied* case, SD precedes T, T precedes RTB, no payment is recorded, and the case ends with R. These differences are reflected in the RESPONSE(RTB, T) and RESPONSE(T, SD) DECLARE rules, which hold in the *accepted* prototype but not in the *denied* one.

Step 5: Boundary Case Identification. After identifying the prototype of each variant, we search for *boundary cases*, i.e., pairs of cases from different

Table 1. An excerpt of a matrix containing feature vectors of cases

	RESPONSE(T, SD)	RESPONSE(RTB, R)	...
c_1	1	*none*	...
c_2	0	*none*	...
c_3	*none*	1	...
...	...	...	...

process variants that lie near the decision frontier. These pairs expose subtle behavioral differences that can explain why a case belongs to one particular variant rather than another [10]. They can be identified by searching for cases whose probability to belong to two specific process variants are as close as possible. The identification of *boundary cases* may not be feasible for all the process variants in an event log, due to the scarcity of cases that have similar features yet belong to different classes [10]. In this case, artificial example-methods are needed to obtain them.

For example, in the travel declaration process, let the following cases be the boundary cases of *accepted-denied*: $c_{\text{acc-bound}} = \langle RTB, T, SD, R, SD, P\rangle$, and $c_{\text{den-bound}} = \langle SD, T, RTB, R, SD, R\rangle$. They reveal that a rejection can occur in accepted cases, because some errors occur when processing the declaration, but the final output is the acceptance of the case after sending the declaration.

3.1 Conceptual Demonstration

To illustrate our framework, we consider the Road Traffic Fines log. Each case starts with the creation of a fine, including an amount. A penalty is added if it is not made within a required period. Offenders may appeal the fine to a judge or prefecture. If no payment is made, a collection agency is involved. Völzer et al. [14] classify these cases into four distinct outcomes: (i) *fully paid*: the fine is paid, including expenses and penalties, (ii) *dismissed*: the fine is waived due to a successful appeal, (iii) *collected*: an agency is assigned to collect the unpaid amount, (iv) *unresolved*: the fine is neither fully paid, dismissed, or collected.

We consider each of the above as a process variant. In this scenario, prototypes would look like the ones displayed in Table 2 (left). These prototypes convey class characteristics intuitively. For example, *fully paid* prototype reflects that *Payment* activity (*PYM*) is what distinguishes this class from others. Additionally, a boundary case pair would look like Table 2 (right), presenting subtle differences by starting similarly, but further unfolding differently.

Table 2. Prototypes and boundary case examples. Activity names are abbreviated: *CF*: Create Fine; *SF*: Send Fine; *IF*: Insert Fine Notification; *AP*: Add Penalty; *PYM*: Payment; *ID*: Insert Date Appeal to Prefecture; *SA*: Send Appeal to Prefecture; *AJ*: Appeal to Judge; *SC*: Send for Credit Collection.

Variant	Prototype
Collected	⟨ *CF, SF, IF, AP, SC* ⟩
Dismissed	⟨ *CF, SF, IF, AP, AJ* ⟩
Fully paid	⟨ *CF, PYM* ⟩
Unresolved	⟨ *CF, SF* ⟩

Variant	Boundary case
Fully paid	⟨ *CF, SF, IF, ID, SA, AP, PYM* ⟩
Unresolved	⟨ *CF, SF, ID, SA, IF, AP, PYM* ⟩

4 Conclusion

As the process mining field matures, the question of how insights are communicated and understood by analysts becomes increasingly central. Explanation is not merely a by-product of analysis; it is a problem by itself. In the context of process variant analysis, explanations have largely focused on abstract feature characterizations, usually through rules. In this paper, we argue for broadening this perspective by elevating real cases to first-class explanatory artifacts.

By conceptualizing explanation as an example selection problem, we introduce prototypes and boundary cases as complementary constructs for making variant differences tangible and behaviorally grounded. This expands the explanatory toolkit to include example selection alongside rules and measures, opening a new avenue for designing process analytics that are not only accurate, but also more meaningful to human decision-makers.

This vision raises concrete research questions to be addressed in future work about whether model-guided examples enable analysts to recognize variant membership more effectively, how different types of examples support reasoning, and how example-based explanations interact with formal abstractions like rules. Addressing these questions requires not only algorithmic development, but also controlled user studies and interaction design, bringing explanation research in process mining closer to human-centered evaluation practices.

Acknowledgments. This work is part of the projects PID2021-126227NB-C21, PID2022-140221NB-I00, and PID2024-156482NB-I00 funded by MICIU/AEI/10.13039/501100011033 FEDER/UE; and VII PPIT-2025 of the University of Seville. C. Capitán-Agudo is supported by the Spanish Ministry of Education under the FPU national plan (FPU21/03631).

References

1. Bose, R.J.C., van der Aalst, W.M.P.: Discovering signature patterns from event logs. In: CIDM, pp. 111–118 (2013)
2. Cecconi, A., Augusto, A., Di Ciccio, C.: Detection of statistically significant differences between process variants through declarative rules. In: BPM Forum, pp. 73–91 (2021)
3. Cecconi, A., De Giacomo, G., Di Ciccio, C., Maggi, F.M., Mendling, J.: Measuring the interestingness of temporal logic behavioral specifications in process mining. Inf. Syst. **107**, 101920 (2022)
4. Di Ciccio, C., Montali, M.: Declarative process specifications: reasoning, discovery, monitoring. In: Process Mining Handbook, pp. 108–152. Springer (2022). https://doi.org/10.1007/978-3-031-08848-3_4
5. Di Francescomarino, C., Donadello, I., Ghidini, C., Maggi, F.M., Puura, J.: Business process deviance mining with sequential and declarative patterns. Bus. Inf. Syst. Eng. **67**, 877–894 (2025)
6. Fani Sani, M., Boltenhagen, M., van der Aalst, W.M.P.: Prototype selection using clustering and conformance metrics for process discovery. In: BPM Workshops, pp. 281–294 (2020)

7. Grigore, I.M., Marques Tavares, G., Pasquadibisceglie, V., Seidl, T., Barbon Junior, S.: Towards trace variant explainability. In: ADBIS, pp. 95–110 (2026)
8. Hundogan, O., Lu, X., Du, Y., Reijers, H.A.: Created: generating viable counterfactual sequences for predictive process analytics. CAiSE, pp. 541–557 (2023)
9. Pesic, M., Schonenberg, H., van der Aalst, W.M.P.: DECLARE: full support for loosely-structured processes. In: EDOC, pp. 287–287 (2007)
10. Poché, A., Hervier, L., Bakkay, M.C.: Natural example-based explainability: a survey. In: XAI World Conference, pp. 24–47 (2023)
11. Rabold, J., Siebers, M., Schmid, U.: Generating contrastive explanations for inductive logic programming based on a near miss approach. Mach. Learn. **111**, 1799–1820 (2022)
12. Taymouri, F., La Rosa, M., Carmona, J.: Business process variant analysis based on mutual fingerprints of event logs. CAiSE, pp. 299–318 (2020)
13. Taymouri, F., La Rosa, M., Dumas, M., Maggi, F.M.: Business process variant analysis: survey and classification. Knowl. Based Syst. **211**, 106557 (2021)
14. Völzer, H., Zerbato, F., Sulzer, T., Weber, B.: A fresh approach to analyze process outcomes. In: ICPM, pp. 97–104 (2023)

OntoLLM: A Framework for Trustworthy LLM Pipelines

Ada Bagozi, Devis Bianchini, Massimiliano Garda, Michele Melchiori, and Anisa Rula(✉)

University of Brescia, Brescia, Italy
{ada.bagozi,devis.bianchini,massimiliano.garda, michele.melchiori,anisa.rula}@unibs.it

Abstract. Enterprise information systems increasingly rely on LLM-based pipelines, yet they offer no systematic guarantees on the consistency of generated outputs with domain knowledge, constraint compliance, or execution provenance. This paper presents *OntoLLM*, a conceptual framework that structures LLM-based pipelines as governed and traceable processes through three layers: a *Conceptual Layer* grounding execution in ontologies and constraints; a *Procedural Layer* defining step types, executors, templates and trust requirements; and a *Monitoring and Trust Layer* assessing trust requirements at each execution step. We illustrate its potential through two representative scenarios, namely knowledge graph creation and personalised recommendation, showing how the architecture is conceived to enforce trust requirements at each step of an LLM-based pipeline. OntoLLM is positioned as a conceptual foundation for engineering trustworthy and semantically governed LLM pipelines.

Keywords: LLM-based Systems · Information Systems Engineering · Ontologies and Semantics · Trustworthy AI · Constraint Validation

1 Introduction

Large Language Models (LLMs) are increasingly integrated into information systems to support natural language interaction and knowledge-intensive tasks. However, despite their expressive power, LLMs remain unconstrained generative models: they lack semantic grounding, may violate domain constraints and provide limited support for provenance or accountability [8]. These limitations are especially problematic in domains requiring explainability and auditability.

Retrieval-Augmented Generation (RAG) mitigates some issues through context injection [5], but existing RAG pipelines are operational rather than methodological: they do not prescribe how ontologies, constraints, provenance rules or trust requirements should be embedded into the lifecycle of LLM-based pipelines. As a result, systems often exhibit unpredictable behaviour, silent constraint violations and partially grounded explanations, and provide no systematic basis for monitoring or certification.

F. Zerbato et al. (Eds.): CAiSE 2026, LNBIP 587, pp. 63–71, 2026.
https://doi.org/10.1007/978-3-032-27997-2_8

Problem Statement. There is currently no general framework for designing LLM-based pipelines as governed, traceable processes that integrate domain semantics, constraint validation and trust monitoring throughout execution. What is missing is an architecture that (i) treats symbolic assets and LLM operations as interoperable components, (ii) provides explicit execution semantics for pipeline steps, and (iii) embeds trust assessment mechanisms directly into the operational lifecycle.

Approach and Contributions. We propose *OntoLLM*, a trust-oriented framework for hybrid symbolic–LLM pipelines consisting of: (i) a *Conceptual Layer* of ontologies, mappings and constraints; (ii) a *Procedural Layer* with step types and operational profiles specifying executors, templates and trust requirements; and (iii) a *Monitoring and Trust Layer* assessing each execution step and classifying it as *success*, *warning* or *failure* according to trust requirement fulfilment. The framework, currently at a conceptual stage, makes three contributions: (1) a unified architecture integrating ontologies, constraints, provenance and trust indicators for governed LLM-based pipelines; (2) a conceptual pipeline model with explicit executors, templates and trust requirements per step, grounded in PROV-O for provenance and adopting SHACL as the constraint validation formalism; (3) illustrative application in two scenarios, namely knowledge graph creation and personalised recommendation, outlining the potential of end-to-end trust enforcement in heterogeneous LLM-based pipelines.

The rest of the paper presents the pipeline design (Sect. 2), the illustrative applications (Sect. 3), related work (Sect. 4), and conclusion (Sect. 5).

2 Pipeline Design

Figure 1 illustrates the OntoLLM architecture. At the bottom, heterogeneous *Data Sources* feed into the *Conceptual Layer*, which structures domain knowledge through an ontology, declarative mappings and SHACL constraints, producing an ontology-consistent Knowledge Graph (KG). The *Procedural Layer* orchestrates pipeline execution as a sequence of typed steps. Each step is executed by an *executor*, a human, an LLM, or a rule engine, which is the agent responsible for producing the step's output. When the executor is an LLM, its behaviour is governed by a *behavioural template*: a structured prompt schema that constrains the LLM's output space to ontology-aligned responses. Each step also carries a set of *trust requirements* specifying what must be checked at execution time. The *Monitoring and Trust Layer* operates across all steps: as each step completes, it evaluates provenance records, constraint reports and the consistency of outputs with ontology terms against the declared trust requirements, classifying the outcome as *success*, *warning* or *failure*. Critical failures halt the pipeline; warnings propagate and may trigger human oversight. Together, the three layers enforce a clean separation between domain knowledge, execution logic and governance, keeping OntoLLM technology-agnostic. In the following, we formalise each layer in turn.

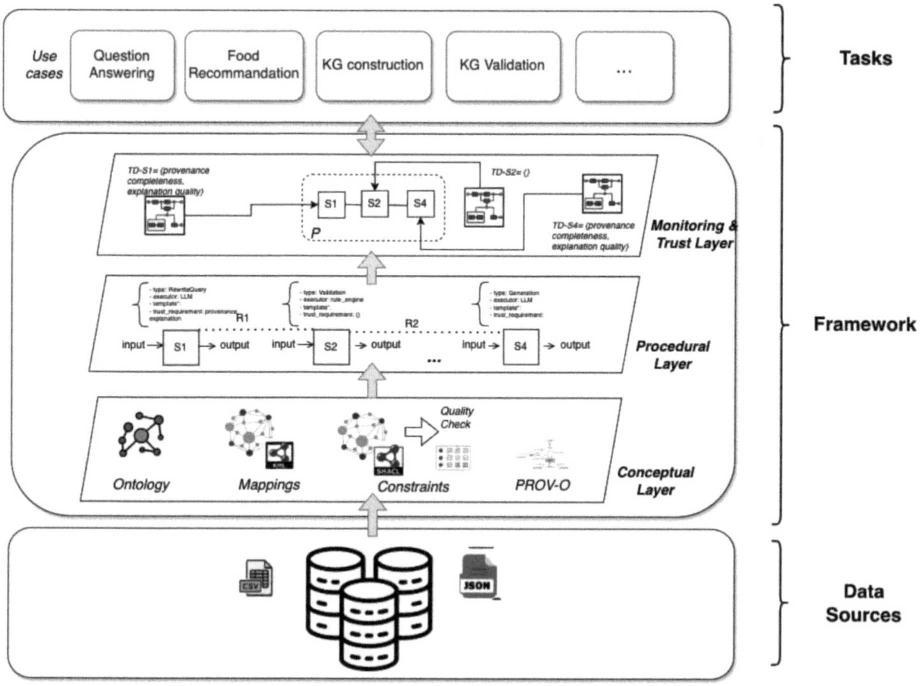

Fig. 1. Overview of the OntoLLM architecture integrating conceptual, procedural and monitoring layers for LLM-based pipelines.

2.1 Conceptual Layer

Formally, the Conceptual Layer is represented as a tuple $\mathcal{C} = \langle \mathcal{O}, \mu, \Delta, \text{PROV-O} \rangle$, where:

- **Ontologies** ($\mathcal{O}$): domain classes, relations and axioms enabling consistent interpretation of user queries, data sources and generated responses.
- **Semantic Mappings** (μ): declarative mapping rules (e.g., RML/R2RML) transforming source data into RDF graphs, materialising the core Knowledge Graph (KG).
- **Constraints** (Δ): SHACL shapes specifying admissible states and domain constraints, ensuring correctness of mapped data, semantic validity of retrieved evidence, and consistency of LLM-generated outputs with domain restrictions.
- **Provenance Schema** (PROV-O): vocabulary recording execution traces describing which agent performed each step, which entities were used or generated, and temporal metadata.

These artefacts serve as inputs to procedural steps but do not determine execution logic. All operational behaviour is defined in the Procedural Layer.

2.2 Procedural Layer

The Procedural Layer, denoted with $\mathcal{P}$, operationalises the conceptual artefacts defined in $\mathcal{C}$. Formally: $\mathcal{P} = \langle S, R \rangle$, where S represents the pipeline steps and $R \subseteq S \times S$ is a partial order describing execution dependencies. Each step instance $s_i \in S$ is defined as:

$$s_i = \langle T, \{inputs\}, \{outputs\}, OP \rangle$$

where T is a step type (Table 1), *inputs* and *outputs* are the consumed and produced artefacts, and OP is the operational profile:

$$OP(s) = \{E, \tau, TR\}$$

composed of:

- E: executor function assigning each step to a *human*, an *LLM*, or a *rule-engine* ($E : S \rightarrow$ {human, LLM, rule-engine}).
- τ: behavioural templates constraining LLM executors (e.g., rewriting, semantic chunking, justification templates), reducing variance and mitigating hallucinations. It is optional, since it is applied only when the executor is an LLM.
- TR: trust requirements specifying what must be checked at execution time, including provenance logging, constraint validation, explanation generation, human oversight, and retrieval completeness.

Table 1 summarises the reusable step types available in an OntoLLM pipeline. The same step type may appear multiple times with different operational profiles; for example, *Semantic Creation* can be instantiated both as a deterministic mapping-based step and as an LLM-based enrichment step, each with different executors and trust requirements.

2.3 Monitoring and Trust Layer

The Monitoring and Trust Layer is designed to evaluate whether each step satisfies its declared trust requirements. When a step s_i completes, it emits execution outputs, provenance assertions, validation reports, retrieved evidence, or generated content that form the basis for trust assessment. Formally:

$$\mathcal{M} = \langle TD, Eval \rangle$$

where TD is a finite set of trust dimensions, including constraint compliance, provenance completeness, explanation quality, retrieval relevance, hallucination rate and human oversight, and $Eval(s_i)$ is intended to classify the step outcome as *success*, *warning* or *failure* based on the dimensions activated for $TR(s_i)$.

Critical violations, such as missing mandatory provenance or unsafe constraint violations, are designed to yield *failure* and halt the pipeline; non-critical deviations would yield *warning* and may trigger human oversight. The precise operationalisation of each trust dimension metric is domain-dependent and constitutes a key direction for future work. By grounding monitoring directly in the trust requirements specified in the Procedural Layer, $\mathcal{M}$ is conceived to integrate governance into pipeline execution rather than adding it as a post-hoc process.

Table 1. General catalogue of step types. Each step type is technology-agnostic; its execution depends on the operational profile $\text{OP} = \{E, \tau, TR\}$ defined in the Procedural Layer.

Step Type	Description
Ontology Engineering	Design or extension of domain ontology (manual, semi-automatic, or LLM-assisted).
Semantic Creation	Generation of ontology-aligned representations from heterogeneous sources (mapping-based or LLM-assisted).
Semantic Indexing	Indexing of semantic units for retrieval (embeddings, symbolic signatures, or rule-based clustering).
Constraint Validation	Application of domain/structural rules (e.g., SHACL), optionally combined with LLM-based explanation.
Context Conditioning	Integration of user profiles, preferences or contextual information into queries or prompts.
Query Rewriting	Rewriting of user requests into ontology-aligned form (rule engine, LLM, or human).
Retrieval	Extraction of relevant information from KG or vector store using symbolic, vector, or hybrid techniques.
Response / Rec. Generation	Generation of responses or recommendations from validated evidence and contextual information.
Explanation Generation	Construction of grounded explanations or justifications from retrieved evidence.
Provenance Recording	Generation of PROV-O traces documenting each activity, its inputs, outputs and associated agents.

3 Illustrative Applications

We illustrate OntoLLM by outlining its instantiation in two LLM-based pipelines: (i) knowledge graph (KG) creation and (ii) personalised recommendation as shown in Table 2. Both share the same Conceptual Layer artefacts: the FoCOSA ontology[1], modelling nutrients, sustainability and health concepts [2]; RML/YARRRML mapping rules transforming structured sources into RDF; and SHACL shapes expressing dietary and nutritional constraints. The two pipelines differ only in their selection of step types and operational profiles. Rather than a comparative evaluation, these scenarios are intended to illustrate how OntoLLM's architecture would structure design-time decisions and runtime oversight in heterogeneous settings.

[1] https://dbwis.gitlab.io/focosa/.

Table 2. Pipeline instantiations and intended monitoring outcomes.

Step	Executor	Trust Requirements	Intended Outcome
Use Case 1—Knowledge Graph Creation			
S1-1	rule-engine	provenance_completeness, structural_validity	Triples conform to $\mathcal{O}$ ⇒ *success*.
S1-2	LLM + enrichment template	grounding, hallucination_prevention, provenance_completeness	Grounded output ⇒ *success*; gaps ⇒ *warning*; hallucinations ⇒ *failure*.
S1-3	rule-engine	constraint_compliance	No violation ⇒ *success*; critical violation ⇒ *failure* (halts).
S1-4	rule-engine	provenance_completeness	Complete bundle ⇒ *success*.
Use Case 2—Personalised Recommendation			
S2-1	LLM + parsing template	grounding, provenance_completeness	Ontology-aligned slots ⇒ *success*; unresolved entities ⇒ *failure*.
S2-2	LLM + rewriting template	grounding, hallucination_prevention, provenance_completeness	Only ontology terms ⇒ *success*; invented classes ⇒ *failure*.
S2-3	rule-engine	retrieval_relevance	Results match filters ⇒ *success*; off-target ⇒ *warning*.
S2-4	LLM + explanation template	grounding, hallucination_prevention, provenance_completeness	Grounded in KG facts ⇒ *success*; unsupported claims ⇒ *failure*.
S2-5	rule-engine	provenance_completeness	Complete bundle ⇒ *success*.

3.1 KG Creation Pipeline

The KG creation pipeline instantiates four step types. *S1-1* (Semantic Creation) is intended to materialise RDF triples from heterogeneous sources using mapping rules, fully delegated to a rule engine, illustrating how OntoLLM would assign schema-driven tasks to deterministic executors rather than LLMs, with trust requirements limited to provenance completeness and structural validity. *S1-2* (Semantic Creation) introduces the first LLM-based operation: enrichment templates are designed to constrain the LLM to produce labels and descriptions consistent with the ontology, with grounding, hallucination prevention, and provenance completeness as mandatory trust requirements. *S1-3* (Constraint Validation) is designed to apply SHACL shapes against Δ; critical violations would immediately classify the step as *failure* and halt the pipeline, acting as a mandatory checkpoint that blocks pipeline execution upon critical constraint violations. Finally, *S1-4* (Provenance Recording) is intended to consolidate all execution traces into a unified PROV-O bundle, closing the process with full traceability.

3.2 Personalised Recommendation Pipeline

The recommendation pipeline instantiates five step types, illustrating three distinct LLM uses: extraction (*S2-1* Context Conditioning), rewriting (*S2-2* Query Rewriting) and explanation (*S2-4* Explanation Generation). *S2-1* and *S2-2* are designed to transform a free-form user request into an ontology-aligned semantic query; their operational profiles would impose grounding and hallucination-prevention requirements, making these steps the most sensitive to LLM variability. *S2-3* (Retrieval) would operate deterministically via SPARQL, separating LLM behaviour from rule-based retrieval and introducing *retrieval_relevance* as a structural trust requirement. *S2-4* is intended to generate user-facing explanations constrained by templates to reference only verified KG facts. *S2-5* would consolidate traces from all preceding steps into a unified PROV-O bundle, enabling full reconstruction of how each recommendation was derived.

3.3 Discussion

The two scenarios jointly illustrate the potential of OntoLLM's governance approach across heterogeneous pipelines. The KG creation scenario shows how semantic ingestion, enrichment and constraint validation could be orchestrated with inspectable provenance traces. The recommendation scenario highlights trust requirements arising in user-facing LLM pipelines, where grounding, hallucination prevention and retrieval relevance jointly shape the validity of outputs. Together, they suggest four complementary properties that OntoLLM is designed to provide: (a) robustness of semantic data processing and constraint validation; (b) systematic governance of LLM behaviour through templates and trust checks; (c) predictable interaction between deterministic and LLM-driven steps; and (d) end-to-end provenance consolidation across distinct executors.

4 Related Work

LLMs, RAG and Knowledge Grounding. LLMs excel in text-intensive tasks [8] yet their outputs often lack domain grounding. Approaches combining LLMs with structured knowledge [12], including KG-enhanced recommendation [9], ontology-driven tasks [7], and KG-based fine-tuning [3], improve grounding but do not provide *end-to-end trust enforcement* across multi-step pipelines.

Hybrid AI and KG Ecosystems. Hybrid architectures combining rules, constraints and KG reasoning have shown benefits in explainability and error prevention [4]. Work on KG ecosystems treats constraint and provenance propagation as lifecycle properties [6]. OntoLLM aligns with both views but extends them by designing trust requirements to be specified explicitly and assessed stepwise within an execution pipeline.

Transparency and Requirements Engineering. System-level analyses reveal pervasive gaps in metadata and evaluation transparency for LLMs [10]. Empirical studies in requirements engineering confirm that LLMs frequently violate structural constraints unless guided by explicit knowledge representations [1,11], supporting the grounding and constraint checks that OntoLLM integrates into its operational profiles.

Positioning. Three gaps persist across these lines: (i) LLMs produce unsupported content without explicit checks; (ii) provenance, constraints and trust requirements are not jointly enforced inside a single pipeline; (iii) no existing approach operationalises trust requirements across multi-step LLM executions. OntoLLM is positioned to address these three gaps within a unified framework, representing a step towards systematic, standards-aligned trust enforcement in LLM-based information systems.

5 Conclusion and Future Work

This paper presented OntoLLM, a conceptual framework for engineering trust-aware LLM pipelines through the integration of semantic artefacts, reusable step types and stepwise trust monitoring. The proposed separation between domain knowledge, execution logic and governance is designed to enable heterogeneous executors to operate within an auditable and transparent process. The two illustrative scenarios outlined how operational profiles, grounding checks, constraint validation and provenance consolidation are intended to enforce trust at runtime and prevent the propagation of unsafe outputs across data-centric and user-facing pipelines. The framework is currently at a conceptual stage; full implementation and empirical validation against baseline approaches are planned as immediate next steps.

Future work will extend the monitoring layer with additional trust dimensions (e.g., fairness, drift detection), develop adaptive strategies that automatically adjust operational profiles when trust thresholds are not met, and investigate the automated derivation of templates from domain specifications to reduce per-domain engineering effort.

References

1. Alter, S.: AI-Based requirements analysis assistant that applies explicit knowledge and includes humans in the loop. In: Krogstie, J., Rinderle-Ma, S., Kappel, G., Proper, H.A. (eds.) 37th CAiSE 2025. LNCS, vol. 15701, pp. 20–36 (2025). https://doi.org/10.1007/978-3-031-94569-4_2
2. Bagozi, A., Bianchini, D., Garda, M., Melchiori, M., Rula, A.: Ontology-enhanced rag for a personalised and sustainable food advisory system. In: DKE, p. 102579 (2026)
3. Baldazzi, T., Bellomarini, L., Ceri, S., Colombo, A., Gentili, A., Sallinger, E.: Fine-tuning large enterprise language models via ontological reasoning. In: 7th RuleML+RR. LNCS, vol. 14244, pp. 86–94. Springer (2023). https://doi.org/10.1007/978-3-031-45072-3_6

4. Chudasama, Y., Huang, H., Purohit, D., Vidal, M.: Toward interpretable hybrid AI: integrating knowledge graphs and symbolic reasoning in medicine. IEEE Access **13**, 39489–39509 (2025)
5. Gao, Y., et al.: Retrieval-augmented generation for large language models: A survey. CoRR abs/ arXiv:2312.10997 (2023)
6. Geisler, S., et al.: From genesis to maturity: managing knowledge graph ecosystems through life cycles. VLDB **18**(5), 1390–1397 (2025)
7. Giglou, H.B., D'Souza, J., Auer, S.: Llms4ol: large language models for ontology learning. In: Payne, T.R., et al. (eds.) ISWC, pp. 408–427 (2023)
8. Li, J., Tang, T., Zhao, W.X., Nie, J., Wen, J.: Pre-trained language models for text generation: a survey. ACM Comput. Surv. **56**(9), 230:1–230:39 (2024)
9. Pan, S., Luo, L., Wang, Y., Chen, C., Wang, J., Wu, X.: Unifying large language models and knowledge graphs: a roadmap. In: DKE (7) (2024)
10. Pierri, F., et al.: A Conceptual map for exploring the landscape of large language models. IEEE Access **13** (2025)
11. Reinhartz-Berger, I., Ali, S.J., Bork, D.: Leveraging LLMs for domain modeling: the impact of granularity and strategy on quality. In: 37th International CAiSE 2025. LNCS, vol. 15701, pp. 3–19. Springer (2025). https://doi.org/10.1007/978-3-031-94569-4_1
12. Sequeda, J., Allemang, D., Jacob, B.: Knowledge graphs as a source of trust for llm-powered enterprise question answering. J. Web Semant. **85**, 100858 (2025)

Towards Human-AI Collaborative Cybersecurity Compliance Assessment

Jonathan Christof Orth[1], Alessandro Palma[1](✉), and Marco Angelini[2]

[1] Sapienza University of Rome, Rome, Italy
orth.2065023@studenti.uniroma1.it, palma@diag.uniroma1.it
[2] Link Campus University, Rome, Italy
m.angelini@unilink.it

Abstract. Achieving accountable and consistent cybersecurity compliance requires balancing automation and human judgment. Current approaches focus mainly on technical enforcement, overlooking the procedural dimension that shapes security operations. We envision an audit support system that integrates technical and process compliance with AI-driven recommendations under human oversight. By formalizing requirements from international standards and leveraging process trace alignment with generative models, we propose an approach that aims to transform compliance auditing into a continuous, explainable, and adaptive activity.

Keywords: Cybersecurity Governance · Compliance Management · Audit Automation · Security Standards

1 Introduction

Organizations increasingly depend on security processes to protect assets and demonstrate compliance with recognized standards and regulations. Compliance is often approached primarily as a technical activity, focused on configurations or access control, which offers only a partial view of conformity [14]. In practice, cyber protection is enacted through processes [22], and compliance must extend to how these processes are designed, executed, and maintained. Assessing compliance remains challenging: standards are intentionally broad to ensure applicability [20], while contextual factors – such as domain-specific constraints in critical sectors like healthcare – complicate interpretation. Manual auditing can be costly, subjective, and inconsistent [4], and integrating procedural and technical evidence introduces further complexity [17]. Recent directions include Process Mining [21] and AI-driven analysis [1] to offer opportunities to capture the actual execution of security activities and generate insights from diverse compliance evidence. Yet, these techniques often lack integration and actionable guidance [3,16]. We envision a human-centered, AI-augmented approach that unifies technical and procedural compliance to enable continuous, explainable, and adaptive auditing. This perspective highlights key challenges and formalizes

F. Zerbato et al. (Eds.): CAiSE 2026, LNBIP 587, pp. 72–80, 2026.
https://doi.org/10.1007/978-3-032-27997-2_9

heterogeneous requirements to ensure interpretability and balance automation with expert oversight. This marks the path toward a next-generation compliance paradigm for cybersecurity governance.

2 Requirement Collection and Elicitation

Methodology. To operationalize the system design, we collected and formalized compliance requirements for the IM process, chosen as a representative security governance process with well-established international standards. We consider international standards for IM, i.e., ISO/IEC 27035 [9], NIST SP 800-61 [13], COBIT CMM [6], and ITIL-IM [10], supplemented by compliance management standards [7,8]. Because these standards often provide only high-level operational guidance, we complement them with insights from recent research on IM and compliance assessment.

To do so, three people (P1, P2, and P3) participated in the requirement collection. All are security governance experts, with P2 and P3 specializing in process management and compliance assessment. In the first phase, P1 extracted requirements by manually reviewing the security standards. The goal was to identify the key operations auditors must perform during IM auditing. P1 used the stated paragraph structure of security standards to derive high-level auditor functions. The experts first defined the scope of the collection by filtering out irrelevant paragraphs using keywords such as *Compliance*, *Process*, *Procedure*, *Performance*, *Management*, and *KPIs*. Redundant requirements across standards were consolidated. P2 then refined these requirements into system-level requirements. A set of 21 requirements resulted from this phase.

In the second phase, P1 collected additional requirements from scientific literature. Relevant papers were identified through searches in scientific databases (IEEE Xplore, ACM Digital Library, Springer, Elsevier Scopus, and Google Scholar) using keywords related to IM, compliance, process mining, conformance checking, systems, and literature reviews. Papers were screened based on abstracts, and additional references were included when relevant. The extracted requirements were categorized as either *design* or *compliance*. As with the first phase, P2 refined the resulting set. A set of 17 requirements resulted from this second phase.

This approach ensures that requirements from standards and research are clearly defined, independent, and non-overlapping. P3 reviewed all collected requirements to remove redundancies, merge similar items, and ensure consistent terminology. This led to 15 requirements. The three experts discussed each requirement, formally defining its scope –i.e., the system component responsible for it– and supported personas –i.e., the expertise needed to perform the requirement. P1 and P2 translated functional requirements (what operators must be able to do) into system requirements (what the system must provide), with final review by P3.

Requirement Analysis. Table 1 summarizes the fifteen requirements categorized into four main scopes –i.e., *Performance*, *Recommendation*, *Compliance*,

Table 1. Requirements and their supporting references.

ID	Scope	Requirement	COBIT	ISO 37301	NIST SP-800-61	ISO 27035-1	ISO 27035-2	ISO 19011	[19]	[15]	[16]	[12]	[11]	[5]
REQ1	Performance	The operator shall be able to timely identify and analyze the main process errors using predefined metrics	✓	✓	✓									
REQ2	Performance	The operator shall be able to identify and analyze procedure and impact metrics of incidents	✓											
REQ3	Performance	The operator shall be able to identify the temporal compliance development and areas of concern	✓		✓									
REQ4	Performance	The operator shall be able to track compliance progresses							✓					
REQ5	Performance	The operator shall be able to analyze assessment parameters of process KPIs								✓	✓			
REQ6	Performance	The operator shall be able to identify missing escalation steps when proper response times are exceeded				✓	✓							
REQ7	Recommendation	The operator shall be capable of prioritizing issues based on impact on compliance										✓		
REQ8	Recommendation	The operator shall be able to analyze non-compliance to identify patterns and trends									✓	✓		
REQ9	Recommendation	The operator shall be able to use checklist for security controls that can be adapted process compliance needs											✓	
REQ10	Recommendation	The operator shall be able to compare reports to identify improvement opportunities							✓					
REQ11	Compliance	The operator shall be able to analyze the organization's policy against a reference model	✓											
REQ12	Compliance	The operator shall be able to control or correct incident traces to predict the overall compliance	✓	✓	✓									
REQ13	Compliance	The operator shall be able to include third-party security controls into the custom checklist	✓											✓
REQ14	Documentation	The operator shall be able to produce an assessment report from analysis and evaluation of process compliance		✓		✓	✓	✓	✓					
REQ15	Documentation	The operator shall be able to check if information is complete, correct, consistent and current										✓		

and *Documentation.* Performance refers to the efficiency of the security process in implementing compliance; recommendations refer to the insights the auditor may gain to improve compliance; compliance refers to the measurement and assessment of technical and process compliance; documentation refers to the production of formalized reports and documents. The requirements reveal the alignment and complementarity between established frameworks (e.g., COBIT, ISO 27035, ISO 37301, NIST SP 800-61) and academic research in defining the critical functions required for assessing security process compliance. The research papers provide more details about their actual realization. Standards mainly provide procedural and governance-oriented requirements (e.g., REQ1, REQ6, REQ11, REQ12, REQ14), emphasizing traceability, documentation quality, and adherence to escalation and response timelines. Research contributions complement these with data-driven and adaptive mechanisms for compliance evaluation (e.g., REQ4, REQ5, REQ8, REQ10, REQ15). Together, they balance formal compliance checking with analytical capabilities.

Six performance requirements (REQ1-REQ6) call for systems that analyze process metrics, reveal bottlenecks and trends, and support operators and incident handlers in detecting, classifying, and responding to incidents in real-time. They mainly support *operators* and *incident handlers*, who classify and respond to incidents in real time.

Recommendation requirements (REQ7-REQ10) highlight the proactive side of compliance auditing. They call for systems that prioritize issues, detect recurring patterns, and suggest targeted improvements. Features such as adaptive checklists (REQ9) and report comparison (REQ10) help refine audit outcomes and support iterative reporting as new evidence emerges. They mainly assist *process analysts* and *technical operators*, who implement security controls to improve compliance.

Compliance requirements (REQ11-REQ13) stress the alignment of organizational policies and control sets with established reference models. REQ13, in particular, addresses incorporating third-party controls into customized checklists, crucial in multi-stakeholder contexts where incidents span organizational boundaries. Since security processes involve multiple roles with distinct responsibilities, these requirements call for a flexible compliance model that integrates heterogeneous control sources while remaining consistent with formal standards. They support *compliance officers*, *risk managers*, and *process owners*, who oversee policy alignment with external standards.

Documentation requirements (REQ14-REQ15) emphasize accurate, consistent, and auditable reporting as the outcome of the assessment process. Automatically generating evidence-based reports (REQ14) and validating the integrity of recorded information (REQ15) directly support system automation, while ensuring traceability and reproducibility for internal reviews and external certifications. They concern *auditors* and *reporting officers*, who produce verifiable evidence and formal audit reports.

A relevant finding is that mapping requirements to expertise profiles shows the system must support multiple user personas with different goals and abstraction levels. Operators need real-time performance metrics and process visibility; auditors and analysts require pattern detection, prioritization, and recommendations; compliance managers focus on alignment with reference frameworks and cross-organizational traceability; and reporters and decision-makers rely on automated, reliable documentation for accountability and certification. Thus, an effective compliance-auditing system must combine process measurement and monitoring, intelligent recommendations, standards-aligned verification, and automated, verifiable documentation.

3 A Vision for AI-Augmented Compliance Auditing

Figure 1 reports the envisioned architecture for AI-augmented compliance auditing, organized into three conceptual layers that together address the requirements identified in Sect. 2. This architecture represents a general approach that can be instantiated with different technologies, standards, and organizational contexts.

At the input level, security controls and compliance configurations define what should be assessed and under which conditions, including time windows, thresholds, and preferred compliance metrics (REQ2, REQ3, REQ5). Security controls describe the expected policies, procedures, and organizational measures, and their coverage can be qualitatively or quantitatively assessed. While these are technical inputs, from the process side, incident management logs capture how incidents unfold over time, and reference process models encode the expected behavior prescribed by standards and internal policies. Together, these inputs enable a unified view that spans both technical and procedural dimensions of compliance (REQ1, REQ11).

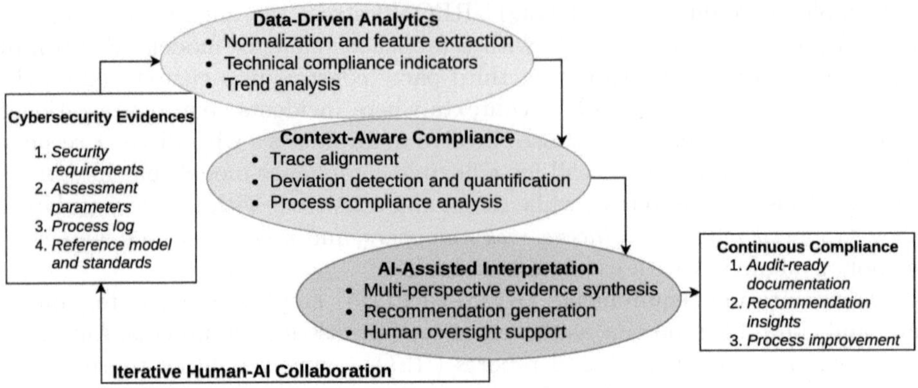

Fig. 1. Overview of Human-AI collaboration for compliance auditing.

The first layer, **Data-driven Compliance Analytics**, focuses on transforming raw technical and process data into interpretable indicators. Heterogeneous incident logs and configuration data are harmonized into a common schema, enriched with domain-specific attributes, and aggregated into metrics such as SLA adherence, incident resolution times, distributions of open and closed incidents, and coverage of security controls over selected periods [14]. This layer supports high-level monitoring and trend analysis (REQ2, REQ3, REQ5), including one- and two-dimensional views over incident populations and time (REQ4, REQ6). It provides the quantitative backbone for subsequent reasoning, ensuring that large-scale, heterogeneous evidence can be consistently analyzed.

The second layer, **Context-aware Process Compliance**, integrates process mining and trace alignment techniques to relate observed behavior to normative models. Building on the idea of context-aware trace alignment [1], this layer uses cost models that can be tailored by security experts to reflect the severity and operational relevance of deviations at different points in the process. This enables conformance analyses that identify where deviations occur, while also quantifying their impact with respect to specific requirements (REQ8, REQ11, REQ12, REQ13). These conformance results become first-class evidence in the compliance assessment, exposing patterns of non-compliance and bottlenecks in incident handling.

The third layer, **AI-assisted Interpretation and Recommendation**, synthesizes the outputs of the previous layers into human-readable insights and guidance. Here, analytic and generative techniques combine technical metrics, process deviations, and contextual parameters to produce recommendations, remediation actions, and explicit indications of uncertainty or data insufficiency. Recommendations can highlight non-compliant areas, draw attention to salient metrics, or suggest potential remediation paths (REQ7, REQ8, REQ9). At the same time, the layer signals when available evidence is insufficient to support reliable conclusions, reinforcing trust and transparency in AI-augmented assessments (REQ7, REQ10, REQ15). This layer is inherently human-in-the-loop: different roles, such as managers and responders, receive views tailored to their informational needs and can validate, refine, or override machine-generated suggestions (REQ1, REQ4, REQ10).

Finally, a reporting and governance perspective cuts across these layers. Compliance evidence, metrics, and recommendations are structured into audit-ready artifacts aligned with established standards, such as ISO/IEC 37301, and organized at the level of individual security controls (REQ13, REQ14, REQ15). Reports combine automated insights with human-provided evidence and rationales, supporting both partial, iterative assessments and final audit outcomes. This supports continuous cycles in which insights feed back into the configuration of controls, process redesign, and future assessments, realizing a vision of compliance as an ongoing, adaptive activity rather than a one-off audit.

In summary, the three-layer architecture articulates how requirements can guide the design of future AI-augmented compliance solutions: from scalable analytics, through context-sensitive process conformance, to human-centered interpretation and reporting, all within an iterative, governance-aware compliance ecosystem.

4 Challenges and Opportunities

The three-layer architecture outlined in Sect. 3 opens a series of technical and organizational challenges, but also highlights concrete opportunities for advancing AI-augmented compliance auditing aligned with the identified requirements.

Challenge 1: *Formalizing heterogeneous compliance evidence.* A first challenge lies in systematically representing heterogeneous inputs, including security controls, process logs, reference models, and compliance configurations, in a way that is both machine-interpretable and faithful to regulatory intent (REQ1, REQ2, REQ11). Security standards are deliberately broad and context-dependent, while operational data are noisy, incomplete, and distributed across systems. This raises questions about how to design shared schemas, ontologies, and mapping mechanisms that can capture nuanced obligations and link them to observable events and metrics. At the same time, there is an opportunity to reuse and extend existing modeling efforts from process mining to build reusable libraries of compliance patterns and indicators, making the data-driven analytics layer more portable across organizations and domains (REQ3, REQ5, REQ6).

Challenge 2: *Defining context-sensitive metrics.* The envisioned data-driven analytics and process conformance layers rely on quantitative metrics like fitness scores, SLA violations, and deviation costs to summarize complex behavior (REQ2, REQ3, REQ8, REQ13). Designing metrics that are robust to assessment variance, comparable across contexts, and meaningful to both auditors and operators remains an open problem. Context-aware alignment introduces flexible cost models but also requires principled methods to elicit, validate, and evolve these models with domain experts. This presents an opportunity to explore interactive metric design, where experts can iteratively shape and calibrate cost functions and thresholds, and to investigate how uncertainty and confidence measures can be integrated into compliance indicators (REQ7, REQ9, REQ15).

Challenge 3: *Balancing automation and human oversight.* The AI-assisted interpretation layer raises research questions about the role of automation in compliance decision-making (REQ1, REQ4, REQ7, REQ10). Fully delegating assessments to AI is undesirable from a governance and accountability perspective, yet overloading humans with low-level outputs risks undermining the benefits of automation. Designing effective human-in-the-loop patterns and deciding where oversight is mandatory – e.g., how explanations are presented, and how disagreements between human and machine judgments are resolved – is a major challenge and opportunity as recent works demonstrate [2,18]. Conversely, there is an opportunity to turn compliance checks into richer socio-technical workflows, where human expertise is amplified rather than replaced, and where the system explicitly learns from human corrections and feedback over time (REQ9, REQ10, REQ15).

Challenge 4: *Ensuring explainability and trust in AI-generated insights.* Generative and analytic models can synthesize complex evidence into recommendations and remediation actions, but their usefulness hinges on transparency and trust (REQ7, REQ10, REQ14). Compliance officers need to understand why a particular area is flagged as non-compliant, which data support this conclusion, and how sensitive the result is to modeling assumptions or missing information. Providing multi-level explanations, ranging from high-level summaries for managers to detailed evidence trails for auditors, while avoiding information overload, is non-trivial. This opens research on explanation interfaces tailored to compliance, including mechanisms to explicitly surface data insufficiencies, model limitations, and alternative scenarios (REQ13, REQ15).

Challenge 5: *Integrating reporting into continuous governance cycles.* Embedding the architecture within real-world governance processes introduces challenges around integration with existing audit practices, regulatory expectations, and organizational decision-making (REQ13, REQ14, REQ15). Traditional reporting is often static and episodic, while the proposed approach promotes continuous, iterative assessment. Organizations must reconcile these modes, deciding how AI-augmented insights feed into formal audit reports, management reviews, and process redesign. At the same time, this integration offers an opportunity to reposition compliance from a reactive, checklist-driven activity to a continuous, intelligence-driven capability that informs strategic risk management and process improvement. Thus, audit reports become not only evidence of past conformity, but also instruments for shaping future security governance.

Overall, these challenges and opportunities delineate a research agenda for AI-augmented compliance: one that spans formal representation, metric design, human-AI interaction, explainable recommendation, and governance integration. Addressing them is key to realizing the vision of scalable, adaptive, and trustworthy compliance ecosystems.

5 Conclusions

This paper outlined a vision for AI-augmented compliance auditing that rethinks how technical and procedural evidence can be combined into continuous, explainable, and human-centered assessment workflows. Building on requirements REQ1–REQ15, we proposed a three-layer approach that couples data-driven analytics, context-aware process conformance, and AI-assisted interpretation and reporting, with the goal of moving beyond static, checklist-based audits toward adaptive compliance ecosystems grounded in international standards and organizational practice. Rather than prescribing a single concrete system, this vision emphasizes design principles: formalizing heterogeneous compliance requirements and evidence, embedding context sensitivity into conformance assessment, and ensuring that automated recommendations remain accountable, transparent, and subject to expert oversight. In doing so, it highlights how emerging techniques such as process mining, context-aware trace alignment, and generative models can serve as building blocks for future compliance support tools, while keeping humans firmly in the decision loop. Several challenges remain open, including robust cost model and metric design, scalable integration with existing governance processes, and the development of interaction mechanisms that make AI-generated insights trustworthy and actionable for diverse stakeholders. Future work will operationalize this vision, explore advanced visual and interactive interfaces for compliance exploration, and refine context and constraint modeling to strengthen the fidelity and reliability of AI-augmented compliance assessments.

Acknowledgments. This work was funded by the Chips JU project Resilient Trust of the EU's Horizon Europe research and innovation programme under Grant agreement No. 101112282, and by the project SERICS (PE00000014) under the MUR National Recovery and Resilience Plan funded by the European Union - NextGenerationEU.

References

1. Acitelli, G., Angelini, M., Bonomi, S., Maggi, F.M., Marrella, A., Palma, A.: Context-aware trace alignment with automated planning. In: 2022 4th International Conference on Process Mining (ICPM), pp. 104–111 (2022)
2. Alzboon, M.S., Bader, A.F., Abuashour, A., Alqaraleh, M.K., Zaqaibeh, B., Al-Batah, M.: The two sides of ai in cybersecurity: opportunities and challenges. In: 2023 International Conference on Intelligent Computing and Next Generation Networks, pp. 1–9 (2023)
3. Boltenhagen, M., Chatain, T., Carmona, J.: A discounted cost function for fast alignments of business processes. In: International Conference on Business Process Management, pp. 252–269. Springer (2021). https://doi.org/10.1007/978-3-030-85469-0_17
4. Carmona, J., van Dongen, B., Solti, A., Weidlich, M.: Conformance Checking. Springer, Switzerland (2018). https://doi.org/10.1007/978-3-319-99414-7

5. Felderer, M., Haisjackl, C., Breu, R., Motz, J.: Integrating manual and automatic risk assessment for risk-based testing. In: Software Quality. Process Automation in Software Development, vol. 94, pp. 159–180. Springer, Berlin Heidelberg (2012). https://doi.org/10.1007/978-3-642-27213-4_11
6. Institute, I.G.: CobiT 4.1: Framework, control objectives, management guidelines, maturity models. IT Governance Institute, Rolling Meadows (2007)
7. ISO 19600:2014 (E): Compliance management systems — Guidelines (2014)
8. ISO 37301:2021 (E): Compliance management systems — Requirements with guidance for use. Standard, ISO, Geneva, CH (Mar 2021)
9. Part 1: Principles of incident management; part 2: guidelines to plan and prepare for incident response (2013). ISO/IEC 27035:2013 (E) part 3: Guidelines for ICT incident response operations
10. ITILv4: Information Technology Infrastructure Library, Standard, Axelos, UK (2019)
11. Jamil, S., Aeiker, J., Crow, D.: Auditing is key. IEEE Ind. Appl. Mag. **16**(1), 47–56 (2010)
12. Masiello, I., Mohseni, Z., Palma, F., Nordmark, S., Augustsson, H., Rundquist, R.: A current overview of the use of learning analytics dashboards. Educ. Sci. **14**(1) (2024)
13. National Institute of Standards and Technology: NIST special publication 800-61, revision 2, computer security incident handling guide (2021-04-23 2021)
14. Palma, A., Acitelli, G., Marrella, A., Bonomi, S., Angelini, M.: A compliance assessment system for incident management process. Comput. Secur. **146**, 104070 (2024)
15. Palma, A., Angelini, M.: Visually supporting the assessment of the incident management process. Eurograph. Assoc. (2024). https://doi.org/10.2312/eurova.20241116
16. Palma, A., Angelini, M.: IMPAVID: enhancing incident management process compliance assessment with visual analytics. Comput. Graph., 104243 (2025). https://doi.org/10.1016/j.cag.2025.104243
17. Palma, A., Sorrentino, A., Bonomi, S.: How to assess measurement capabilities of a security monitoring infrastructure and plan investment through a graph-based approach. Expert Syst. Appl. **262**, 125623 (2025)
18. Sammarone, T., Angelini, M.: A human-ai assisted methodology for the generation of a cybersecurity controls library. In: 2025 IEEE International Conference on Cyber Humanities (IEEE-CH), pp. 1–7 (2025)
19. Schufrin, M., Lücke-Tieke, H., Kohlhammer, J.: Visual firewall log analysis - at the border between analytical and appealing. In: 2022 IEEE Symposium on Visualization for Cyber Security (VizSec), pp. 1–11. IEEE, Oklahoma City, OK, USA (2022)
20. Siponen, M., Willison, R.: Information security management standards: problems and solutions. Inf. Manage. **46**(5), 267–270 (2009)
21. Van Der Aalst, W.: Process mining: discovery, conformance and enhancement of business processes, vol. 136 (2011). https://doi.org/10.1007/978-3-642-19345-3
22. Von Solms, R., Van Niekerk, J.: From information security to cyber security. Comput. Secur. **38**, 97–102 (2013)

Detecting and Explaining Temporal Behavioral Deviations in Business Process Simulation Models

Mei Wang(✉), Karolin Winter, Quang-Vinh Dang, and Remco Dijkman

Department of Industrial Engineering and Innovation Sciences, Eindhoven University of Technology, Eindhoven, The Netherlands
{m.wang2,k.m.winter,q.v.dang,r.m.dijkman}@tue.nl

Abstract. Business process simulation aims to reproduce real process behavior to support analysis and decision-making. In order to enhance simulation quality, detecting and explaining behavioral deviations between simulation and reality is crucial. Most existing techniques for detecting deviations focus either on the control-flow perspective or quantify overall deviation at the behavioral outcome level, for example, by comparing the cycle time distributions of simulated and real event logs. These approaches focus only on deviation magnitude and lack mechanisms to explain deviations through the lens of simulation input drivers, making it impossible to determine which inputs cause the deviations. Therefore, we propose a deviation detection and explanation approach that employs a classifier to identify temporal behavioral deviations between simulation and reality and uncovers how simulation inputs related to arrival times, processing times, and resources lead to the observed deviations. Empirical evaluations show deviations as well as the simulation inputs responsible for them can be detected, enabling a shift from measuring deviations to understanding their underlying causes and supporting data-driven simulation model calibration.

Keywords: Business process simulation · Temporal behavioral deviations · Simulation model assessment

1 Introduction

Business process simulation (BPS) is widely used in organizational research as an effective tool for analyzing process performance to support decision making [1]. With the growing availability of event logs, simulation inputs (e.g., activity processing times) are increasingly derived from data using process mining techniques [2], reducing the need for manual parameter specification. This increasing automation also raises the need to assess how well simulation models reproduce real process behavior. Significant progress has been made in control-flow analysis and in evaluating whether a model represents activity sequences and logical dependencies [10]. However, temporal behavior modeling is often simplified [9], limiting the ability of simulation models to capture real temporal dynamics.

F. Zerbato et al. (Eds.): CAiSE 2026, LNBIP 587, pp. 81–89, 2026.
https://doi.org/10.1007/978-3-032-27997-2_10

Related Work. Among existing methods for assessing simulation behavior, classification-based techniques are most closely related to our approach, which aim to detect deviations by learning to distinguish real traces from simulated ones. Meneghello et al. [11] investigate this idea with control-flow and basic temporal attributes, and Vinci et al. [14] use similar ideas for control-flow model repair. These works demonstrate that classification can expose discrepancies, yet their temporal coverage remains narrow, offering limited explanatory insight into why deviations arise. Chapela-Campa et al. [3] propose a multi-perspective framework combining sequence based metrics with temporal distribution distances. While this framework offers structured metrics, its reliance on aggregated distances overlooks local temporal patterns and provides limited parameter refinement guidance. Ozdemir et al. [13] introduce a utility-based evaluation view centered on downstream predictive performance. This broadens the evaluation space, but still does not connect performance differences to concrete simulation model modifications. Overall, existing research advances the simulation model construction and evaluation, but still lacks an explicit connection between temporal deviations and input assumptions that require adjustment.

Contribution. We present an approach that detects deviations by distinguishing real and simulated cases, verifies whether those deviations are reflected in performance outcomes, and explains detected deviations by attributing them to simulation input parameters. For simulated logs generated from mined BPS models, the approach complements established control-flow assessment methods.

2 Preliminaries

Let A be a finite set of activities, C a finite set of case identifiers, $\mathbb{T} \subseteq \mathbb{R}$ the time domain, and R a finite set of resources. An *event* is a tuple $e = (c(e), a(e), t_s(e), t_c(e), r(e))$, where $c(e) \in C$ is the case identifier, $a(e) \in A$ the executed activity, $t_s(e), t_c(e) \in \mathbb{T}$ the start and completion timestamps with $t_s(e) \leq t_c(e)$, and $r(e) \in R$ the executing resource (optional). The finite set of events is denoted by E. A *trace* σ_c is a finite event sequence ordered by ascending completion timestamps, representing one process execution (case). We denote the set of all traces over E by E^*. A trace is typically written as $\sigma_c = \langle e_1, e_2, \ldots, e_n \rangle$, where $e_i \in E$ for all i and $t_c(e_1) \leq t_c(e_2) \leq \cdots \leq t_c(e_n)$. An *event log* is then defined as a multiset of traces, $L \in \mathcal{B}(E^*)$. When clear from context, we write c instead of $c(e)$ and similarly for other symbols.

Let $e \in E$ be an event with its corresponding start and end timestamps $t_s, t_c \in \mathbb{T}$. The *processing time of the event* is defined as $\text{pt}(e) = t_c - t_s$. For case c, we define arrival time $A_c = \min\{t_s(e) \mid e \in \sigma_c\}$, completion time $C_c = \max\{t_c(e) \mid e \in \sigma_c\}$, and cycle time $CT(c) = C_c - A_c$. Let c_i and c_{i+1} be two consecutive cases in an event log, ordered in ascending order of A_c. Their inter-arrival time is given as $IAT(c_i, c_{i+1}) = A_{c_{i+1}} - A_{c_i}$.

3 Temporal Behavioral Deviation Assessment Approach

Figure 1 illustrates our approach for assessing temporal behavioral deviations between real and simulated logs generated by a mined BPS model. The approach has two phases: *detection* of case-level temporal deviations and *explanation* through attribution to simulation input parameters.

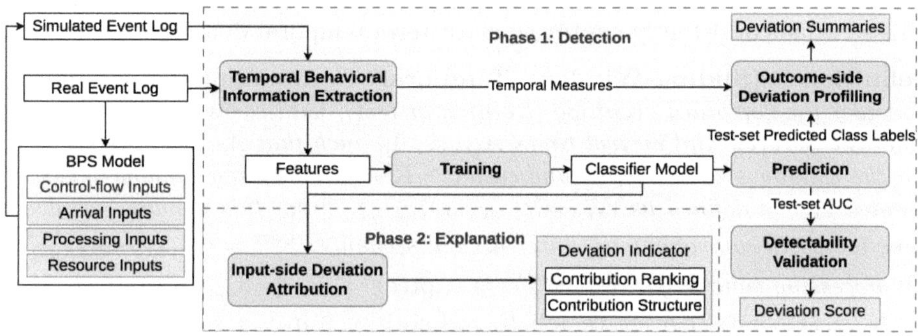

Fig. 1. Overview of Temporal Behavioral Deviation Assessment Approach.

3.1 Phase 1: Detection

With input-side features corresponding to the three highlighted BPS inputs, we evaluate detectability by measuring how well a classifier distinguishes real from simulated cases. We then verify performance by comparing cycle-time summaries across predicted groups. The outputs are the deviation score, deviation summaries, and a trained classifier for subsequent explanation.

Temporal Behavioral Information Extraction. As stated in Sect. 2, each event log contains a case identifier, an activity name, start and completion timestamps, and optionally a resource. For comparison, we use a real log L^{real} and a simulated log L^{sim}, and set $n = \min(|L^{\mathrm{real}}|, |L^{\mathrm{sim}}|)$. We retain the first n cases of each log and sort them by arrival time. Given a split ratio $\eta \in (0, 1)$, the first $\lfloor \eta n \rfloor$ cases form the training set and the remaining cases the test set. For a single split, the training set is used only to learn the classifier, while the test set is reserved for evaluating detectability and generating explanations. We keep time-order splitting instead of random cross-validation, because window features depend on preceding cases and random folds leak future context. As recommended in interpretable machine learning [12], model explanations should not be computed on training data, ensuring that the attributions reflect generalizable behavior rather than overfitting. Then we construct the training and test logs by concatenating the real and simulated cases included in that split, because both groups are represented in one feature space, allowing the classifier to measure how separable real and simulated cases are. To build input-side temporal features, we use three input aspects: arrival, processing, and resource. As highlighted in prior work on BPS, these aspects represent the core simulation input parameters beyond the control-flow structure, covering case arrivals, activity processing times, and resources [1]. In order to reflect short term dynamics, we introduce a sliding window $\mathcal{W}(c)$ for a case c. This sliding window captures temporal context instead of relying only on global distribution comparisons. The window size is a proportion $\rho \in (0,1)$ of the total case count, which allows the window to scale with the dataset while consistently capturing short term temporal dynamics.

Definition 1 (Sliding-Window Temporal Component Constructor). *Consider the combined event log (training or test), with cases ordered by arrival time as $c_1, \ldots, c_n$ and arrival times $A_1, \ldots, A_n$ such that $A_i \leq A_j$ for all $i < j$. For the window size $K = \lfloor \rho n \rfloor$ and each $i \geq K+1$, the sliding window of case c_i, denoted $\mathcal{W}_i$, is defined as $\mathcal{W}_i = \langle c_{i-K}, \ldots, c_{i-1} \rangle$. From this window, we derive three temporal components: i) inter-arrival sequence: $S_i^{\text{arr}} = \big\langle A_{j+1} - A_j \big\rangle_{j=i-K}^{i-2}$ ii) processing-time sequence: $S_{i,t}^{\text{proc}} = \big\langle \text{pt}(e) \;\big|\; e \in \sigma_{c_j},\ a(e) = t,\ j = i-K, \ldots, i-1 \big\rangle$ iii) resource set: $R_i = \big\{ r(e) \mid e \in \sigma_{c_j},\ j = i-K, \ldots, i-1 \big\}$ For brevity, in single-task processes we omit the task index and write S_i^{proc}.*

For illustration, if the training log has $n = 1000$ cases and $\rho = 0.2$, then $K = \lfloor \rho n \rfloor = 200$. Each case c_i with $i > K$ uses the 200 most recent preceding cases as temporal context to construct S_i^{arr}, S_i^{proc}, and R_i. From these sequences, we extract the features and measures used in training and evaluation.

Definition 2 (Temporal Information Extractor). *Given sliding-window temporal components, let $\mathcal{F} = \{\text{Q50}, \text{Q3} - \text{Q1}, \text{P95/P50}\}$ denote the summary operators. The input-side temporal feature vector of case c_i is*

$$\mathbf{x}_{c_i} = \Big(\{f(S_{c_i}^{\text{arr}})\}_{f \in \mathcal{F}},\ \{f(S_{c_i}^{\text{proc}})\}_{f \in \mathcal{F}},\ |R_{c_i}| \Big).$$

The outcome-side temporal measure is the cycle time $z_c = CT(c_i)$, which is used solely for evaluation rather than training. Each case receives a label $y_i \in \{0,1\}$ indicating whether it originates from the real log (0) or from the simulated log (1). The extractor outputs the triplet $(\mathbf{x}_i, z_i, y_i)$. We write $\mathcal{J} = \{1, \ldots, d\}$ for the index set of all input-side temporal features.

Model Training, Prediction. The previous step yields a dataset via train/test splitting and temporal feature extraction. We then train a deviation detection model to predict whether each case originates from the simulated or the real log.

Definition 3 (Deviation Detection Model). *A deviation detection model is a binary classifier, defined as a function $f : \mathbb{R}^d \to [0,1]$, which maps an input-side feature vector $\mathbf{x}_c$ to the estimated probability that the case originates from the simulated event log $(y_c = 1)$.*

Detectability Validation. The model f is trained on the $\mathcal{D}_{\text{train}}$, using only the input-side feature vectors and the labels of the classes. For each test-set case, the model outputs a probability $p_c = f(\mathbf{x}_c)$ interpreted as the estimated likelihood that the case originates from the simulated log. For any threshold $\tau \in [0,1]$, the corresponding true positive rate and false positive rate are $\text{TPR}(\tau) = \Pr(\hat{y}_c = 1 \mid y_c = 1)$, $\text{FPR}(\tau) = \Pr(\hat{y}_c = 1 \mid y_c = 0)$. The ROC curve is the set of points $\{(\text{FPR}(\tau), \text{TPR}(\tau)) \mid \tau \in [0,1]\}$. A predicted label is obtained as $\hat{y}_c = \mathbb{I}[\,p_c \geq \tau^*\,]$, where τ^* denotes the threshold that maximizes the Youden index, corresponding to the point on the ROC curve farthest from the diagonal chance line [7]. We define a deviation score capturing deviations based on τ^*.

Definition 4 (Deviation Score). *Let AUC_{test} denote the area under the ROC curve (AUC) on the test set; the deviation score is* $\text{DS} = 2{\cdot}\max(AUC_{\text{test}} - 0.5, 0)$, *where larger values indicate stronger temporal distinguishability.*

Outcome-Side Deviation Profiling. Outcome-side deviation profiling examines how the outcome-side measure z_c differs across predicted classes. Test-set cases are grouped based on their predicted label: $\mathcal{D}_{\text{test},g} = \{(\mathbf{x}_c, z_c, y_c) \in \mathcal{D}_{\text{test}} : \hat{y}_c = g\}$, $g \in \{0,1\}$. For each group, the outcome measure z_c (e.g., cycle time) is summarized using standard descriptive statistics (e.g., mean, median, minimum, maximum). These summaries, denoted by ODT_g, form the outcome-side deviation profile $\text{ODT} = (\text{ODT}_1, \text{ODT}_0)$. Detected deviations are verified through summary comparisons between predicted simulated and predicted real groups.

3.2 Phase 2: Explanation

The explanation phase aims to attribute the detected deviation to specific simulation input parameters. It relies on the classifier from the detection phase, features derived from the event logs, and Shapley Additive Explanations (SHAP) values [4]. We first compare deviations across input aspects through an *inter-aspect contribution ranking*, since this reveals which aspects are most influential. We further analyze how contributions are distributed within each aspect by constructing an intra-aspect contribution structure to support model calibration.

Input-Side Deviation Attribution. In the explanation phase, features are grouped into the same three simulation input aspects to quantify and compare their contributions to the detected deviation. SHAP is adopted as its additive attributions allow consistent aggregation from features to aspects. For each test-set case c and each input-side feature indexed by $j \in \mathcal{J}$, the SHAP value $\phi_{c,j}$ quantifies the contribution of feature j for case c to the classifier output. We use the absolute attribution $m_{c,j} = |\phi_{c,j}|$ and its mean value $\bar{m}_j = \frac{1}{|\mathcal{D}_{\text{test}}|}\sum_{c \in \mathcal{D}_{\text{test}}} m_{c,j}$, reflecting how strongly feature j contributes to the deviation. For each simulation-related input aspect, we take the top-k features by mean attribution and use their average attribution as the aspect contribution score.

Definition 5 (Inter-Aspect Contribution Ranking). *For each temporal aspect (arrival, processing, resource), let J^k_{arr}, J^k_{proc}, and J^k_{res} denote the index* *sets of the k features within the arrival, processing, and resource aspects, respectively, with the largest mean attributions* $\bar{m}_j$*. The contribution score per aspect is defined as* $D_{\mathrm{arr}}^{\mathrm{SHAP}} = \frac{1}{k}\sum_{j\in J_{\mathrm{arr}}^k} \bar{m}_j$, $D_{\mathrm{proc}}^{\mathrm{SHAP}} = \frac{1}{k}\sum_{j\in J_{\mathrm{proc}}^k} \bar{m}_j$, $D_{\mathrm{res}}^{\mathrm{SHAP}} = \frac{1}{k}\sum_{j\in J_{\mathrm{res}}^k} \bar{m}_j$*. These three scores form the inter-aspect contribution ranking.*

To reveal the internal deviation structure within each temporal aspect, we apply Principal Component Analysis (PCA) to the feature subset of each aspect and examine the aligned first principal component based on absolute SHAP attributions. We align each loading sign with the simulated-real feature mean difference, because PCA component signs are arbitrary [8].

Definition 6 (Intra-Aspect Contribution Structure). *Let* ℓ_j *denote the loading of feature j in the first principal component computed from the absolute SHAP attributions of the features in the aspect. Let* Δ_j *be the difference in the mean value of feature j between simulated and real cases. The deviation-oriented loading for the feature is* $\tilde{\ell}_j = s_j \ell_j$*, where* $s_j = \mathrm{sign}(\Delta_j)$*. The vector of all* $\tilde{\ell}_j$ *represents the intra-aspect contribution structure.*

Definition 7 (Input-Side Deviation Indicator). *Let* $D_{\mathrm{arr}}^{\mathrm{SHAP}}$, $D_{\mathrm{proc}}^{\mathrm{SHAP}}$*, and* $D_{\mathrm{res}}^{\mathrm{SHAP}}$ *denote the inter-aspect contribution scores of the arrival, processing, and resource aspects, respectively, and let* $\tilde{\ell}_j$ *denote the deviation-oriented loadings from the intra-aspect contribution structure. The input-side deviation indicator jointly summarizes the relative contributions of the three temporal aspects and the internal deviation structure within each aspect, is defined as the pair*

$$\mathrm{IDT} = \left(\{D_{\mathrm{arr}}^{\mathrm{SHAP}}, D_{\mathrm{proc}}^{\mathrm{SHAP}}, D_{\mathrm{res}}^{\mathrm{SHAP}}\}, \{\tilde{\ell}_j\}_{j\in\mathcal{J}}\right).$$

For example, if the arrival aspect has the largest mean attributions, then $D_{\mathrm{arr}}^{\mathrm{SHAP}}$ exceeds $D_{\mathrm{proc}}^{\mathrm{SHAP}}$ and $D_{\mathrm{res}}^{\mathrm{SHAP}}$. If the aligned first principal component within arrival places the largest deviation-oriented loading on an inter-arrival variation feature, the IDT identifies arrival as the dominant contributor.

4 Evaluation

The proposed temporal behavioral deviation assessment approach is evaluated on synthetic and real-world event logs, using CatBoost as the default classifier to support more stable feature attribution. This section reports the key findings. Further details are provided in the supplementary material.[1]

Synthetic Event Log Evaluation. The synthetic evaluation examines whether known model manipulations can be detected and explained by our approach. We use a single-activity ground-truth model and manipulate arrival time, processing time, and resource parameters, both individually and jointly, to determine

[1] https://github.com/m-wang-research/detecting-and-explaining-temporal-behavioral-deviations-in-business-process-simulation-models.

whether those manipulations can be correctly detected and explained by the approach. We generate configurations by varying parameters and use manipulations to refer to those variations across arrival ($S_{\mathrm{A}*}$), processing ($S_{\mathrm{P}*}$), resource ($S_{\mathrm{R}*}$), and joint settings at multiple levels (S_{AR}, S_{AP}). S_{BASE} matches the ground-truth configuration, so stochastic variation is not expected to be identified as deviation. Each configuration is simulated for 10 independent runs and evaluated with 70/30 splits, following the procedure in Sect. 3. Figure 2(a) presents the deviation scores across configurations. At S_{BASE}, the score is close to 0, indicating separation close to random guessing, which is expected for the baseline configuration. Manipulated configurations are consistently and clearly above this baseline, indicating detectable deviation from the baseline. Compared with distance-based metrics, the deviation score remains more discriminative and stable across manipulated configurations, which is related to our method's ability to capture temporal patterns. Predicted real/simulated groups remain separated in cycle-time profiles, and larger gaps under stronger manipulations indicate responsiveness to manipulation strength. Figure 2(b) reports aspect contribution scores for the same configurations, where color encoding distinguishes arrival, processing, and resource aspects and hatched bars mark manipulated aspects, which are typically ranked high. Within each aspect, direction signs and dominant feature groups remain stable, indicating consistent input mechanisms under manipulations.

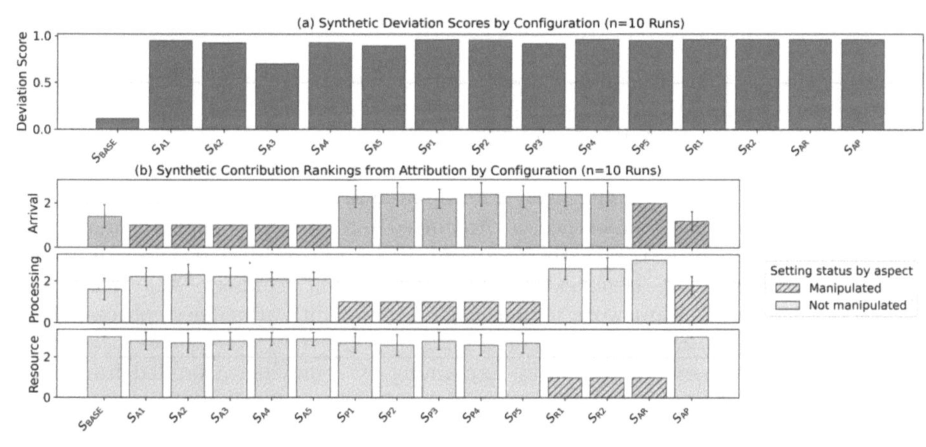

Fig. 2. Synthetic Deviation Scores and Aspect Attribution by Configuration.

Real-world Event Log Evaluation. In the real-world evaluation, we test how well simulated logs from established implementations [3] reproduce temporal behavior on two real-world datasets [5,6]. Across simulation configurations on both datasets, real/simulated groups stay separated in cycle-time profiles, showing that differences in temporal behavior reproduction are detectable. Stable rankings and intra-aspect structures provide reproducible guidance on where to adjust simulation input parameters, which is essential for calibration in practice.

5 Conclusion

Business process simulation plays an important role in process analysis and decision making, which makes reliable simulation model assessment essential. This paper presented a two-phase approach for detecting and explaining temporal behavioral deviations in business process simulation models, addressing the limitation of distance-based temporal assessment that often fails to capture temporal context and offers limited refinement guidance for simulation model calibration. Synthetic results show effective detection and correct attribution to simulation input aspects, and real-world results indicate practical value for identifying temporal mismatches. Future work will extend beyond temporal deviations to other perspectives, such as resource behavior deviations, and integrate explanation outputs into iterative calibration loops.

Acknowledgements. The research leading up to this project is supported by the Dutch government under the NXTGEN Hightech project.

References

1. van der Aalst, W.M.: Business process simulation revisited. In: Workshop on Enterprise and Organizational Modeling and Simulation, pp. 1–14. Springer (2010). https://doi.org/10.1007/978-3-642-15723-3_1
2. Camargo, M., Dumas, M., González-Rojas, O.: Learning accurate business process simulation models from event logs via automated process discovery and deep learning. In: International Conference on Advanced Information Systems Engineering, pp. 55–71. Springer (2022). https://doi.org/10.1007/978-3-031-07472-1_4
3. Chapela-Campa, D., Benchekroun, I., Baron, O., Dumas, M., Krass, D., Senderovich, A.: A framework for measuring the quality of business process simulation models. Inf. Syst. **127**, 102447 (2025)
4. Covert, I., Lundberg, S., Lee, S.I.: Explaining by removing: a unified framework for model explanation. J. Mach. Learn. Res. **22**(209), 1–90 (2021)
5. van Dongen, B.: BPI challenge 2012 (2012). https://doi.org/10.4121/uuid:3926db30-f712-4394-aebc-75976070e91f
6. van Dongen, B.: BPI challenge 2017 (2017). https://doi.org/10.4121/uuid:5f3067df-f10b-45da-b98b-86ae4c7a310b
7. Hajian-Tilaki, K.: The choice of methods in determining the optimal cut-off value for quantitative diagnostic test evaluation. Stat. Methods Med. Res. **27**(8), 2374–2383 (2018)
8. Jolliffe, I.T., Cadima, J.: Principal component analysis: a review and recent developments. Philos. Trans. Royal Soc. A: Math. Phys. Eng. Sci. **374**(2065), 20150202 (2016)

9. Kirchdorfer, L., Özdemir, K., Kusenic, S., van der Aa, H., Stuckenschmidt, H.: A divide-and-conquer approach for modeling arrival times in business process simulation. In: International Conference on Business Process Management, pp. 325–342. Springer (2025). https://doi.org/10.1007/978-3-032-02867-9_20
10. Mannhardt, F.: Multi-perspective process mining. In: 16th International Conference on Business Process Management (BPM 2018), pp. 41–45. CEUR-WS. org (2018)
11. Meneghello, F., Fracca, C., de Leoni, M., Asnicar, F., Turco, A.: A framework to improve the accuracy of process simulation models. In: International Conference on Research Challenges in Information Science, pp. 142–158. Springer (2022). https://doi.org/10.1007/978-3-031-05760-1_9
12. Molnar, C.: Interpretable machine learning. Lulu.com (2020)
13. Özdemir, K., Kirchdorfer, L., Elyasi, K.A., Aa, H.v.d., Stuckenschmidt, H.: Rethinking business process simulation: a utility-based evaluation framework. In: International Conference on Business Process Management, pp. 128–144. Springer (2025). https://doi.org/10.1007/978-3-032-02929-4_8
14. Vinci, F., de Leoni, M.: Balancing fitness and precision in process model repair: framework formalization, assessment, and benefits for simulation. Process Sci. **2**(1), 3 (2025)

A Method for Process Model Matching with LLMs

Francesca Zampino[1], Laura Genga[2], Antonella Longo[1(✉)], Marco Salvatore Zappatore[1], and Remco Dijkman[2]

[1] University of Salento, Lecce, Italy
{francesca.zampino,antonella.longo,marcosalvatore.zappatore}@unisalento.it
[2] Eindhoven University of Technology, Eindhoven, The Netherlands
{l.genga,R.M.Dijkman}@tue.nl

Abstract. Process model matching is widely recognized as a key challenge in business process management, as existing techniques often struggle to capture semantic and contextual variability across models. In this paper, we investigate the use of large language models to address this challenge. Although several recent studies explored the potential of these models in various BPM tasks, to the best of our knowledge this is the first study to apply them to process model matching. We propose a Llama 3-based method that leverages structured prompting and a self-critique refinement stage to enhance semantic reasoning and robustness in process matching. The method is evaluated on three benchmark datasets and compared against both traditional embedding-based and pre-LLM techniques. Across all datasets, our method consistently outperforms baselines, achieving higher F1-score, with improvements of up to 15%.

Keywords: PM Matching · LLMs · Business Process Management

1 Introduction

Organizations rely on large collections of process models that evolve over time, making accurate activity matching critical for reuse and integration [7]. *Process model matching* is the task of mapping process activities from one model to another. We focus on 1:1 correspondences, the most commonly addressed in the literature [2]. Existing approaches often struggle with accurately identifying correspondences, especially when domain-specific terms or synonyms not covered by standard dictionaries are involved. To address this issue, here we propose a method based on Large Language Models (LLMs) that leverages prompt-driven reasoning to match activities accurately. LLMs can infer semantic equivalence and relational meaning directly from activity labels, capturing nuances beyond lexical similarity. Recent works highlight their potential for semantic and structural reasoning in model matching [1,13], though their application to process model matching remains largely unexplored. Motivated by these insights, our method combines structured prompts, semantic reasoning, and iterative self-critique, without relying on external ontologies. We evaluate it on extended

F. Zerbato et al. (Eds.): CAiSE 2026, LNBIP 587, pp. 90–97, 2026.
https://doi.org/10.1007/978-3-032-27997-2_11

benchmark datasets from the Process Model Matching Contest 2015 [4,9], which we further extended with additional matched examples.

The paper is organized as follows: Sect. 2 reviews related work, Sect. 3 describes the method, Sect. 4 outlines the evaluation, and Sect. 5 discusses the main insights and outlines the conclusions.

2 Related Work

According to Ali et al. [2], existing Process Model Matching techniques can be categorized into three main categories. **Lexical methods** rely on textual similarity metrics, such as Levenshtein distance [14], Dice similarity [3], and Jaccard or Cosine similarity with TF-IDF [10,12]. These methods perform well when labels are consistent, but they struggle with paraphrases, domain-specific terminology, or subtle semantic differences. **Structural methods** exploit the topology of process models (e.g., sequences, or gateways) to improve alignment robustness. Dijkman et al. [6,7] introduced graph-based matching algorithms that formalize model comparison as a graph isomorphism task and define quantitative similarity metrics. While these methods improve structural reasoning, their effectiveness remains limited when models differ in granularity and when label matching is challenging. **Semantic and hybrid methods** combine ontologies, probabilistic reasoning, or machine-learned heuristics to capture deeper relationships between tasks. These approaches improve matching under high semantic variation but often require significant manual effort [11]. Some studies have explored leveraging LLMs for model alignment tasks for relational schema elements (e.g., classes or relations). Ahmed et al. [1] proposed SMATCH-M-LLM, a GPT-4–based method with an iterative prompting strategy that outperformed traditional and hybrid baselines. Parciak et al. [13] uses LLMs to reason over both semantic content and structural relationships, with iterative prompting further improving alignment accuracy. These approaches, however, are not tailored to the process domain. In a preliminary study, we applied Llama3 to 1:1 process model matching [15]. While promising, this first attempt remains preliminary, and, to our knowledge, no other prior work has applied LLMs specifically to process model matching.

3 Method

Our pipeline includes two main phases. First, input models are parsed to extract activities and corresponding labels, then BPMN, PNML and XML files are allowed in the current pipeline. The extracted components are then given as input to LLM prompts. The design and refinement of the prompts follow a reproducible framework grounded in the Prompt Patterns proposed by [8], further enhanced by the structured prompt engineering methodology introduced by [5]. This combined method conceptualizes prompt engineering as an iterative optimization process that transforms task requirements into structured, role-conditioned instructions optimized for LLM reasoning. Our work adopts the

```
prompt = f"""
# Role
You are a BPMN process analysis expert specializing in model alignment and similarity.
# Task
Compare two BPMN models ({name_1} and {name_2}) and identify 1:1 correspondences between components.
Then perform self-critique and produce final metrics.
Input:
Model 1:
{chr(10).join(tasks1)}
Model 2:
{chr(10).join(tasks2)}
# Procedure
1) Compute global similarity score (cosine similarity).
2) Identify all 1:1 mappings, classifying as:
   - VB (Verbatim): labels identical or almost identical.
   - MC (Modified Copy): labels differ but semantics match.
   - HR (High Revision): labels substantially differ or one subsumes the other.
3) Output mappings grouped by category (VB → MC → HR) with 1-2 line justification each.
4) Perform self-critique using:
5) - Lexical Overlap: mapping based on superficial label similarity, tasks not actually corresponding.
   - Scope Mismatch: tasks related but belong to different process phases or contexts.
   - Overgeneralization: semantically distinct tasks merged into one broader mapping.
   - Ambiguity: vague or unclear labels lead to multiple possible interpretations.
6) Conclude with metrics: -(i)Total tasks per model, (ii)Counts + % of VB/MC/HR
   - Ambiguous, duplicated, or missing tasks
# Expected Output
A) Initial mappings
B) Self-critique and revised mappings
C) Final metrics and global similarity
# Example
"Record Payment" -> "Record Payment" (identical)
"Approve Order" -> "Approve Purchase Order" (semantically same, labels differ)
# Verification
- Check VB/MC/HR consistency
- Re-evaluate ambiguous mappings
- Refine similarity and categories if needed
- Ensure final outputs are coherent and justified
Execute all steps in order and return structured analysis in English.
"""
```

Fig. 1. Structure of the Chain-of-Thought prompting strategy.

main categories of the Prompt Canvas framework—Scope, Task, Context, Procedure, Role, Output, and Termination—as sequential design steps adapted to the process model matching scenario. We design two prompt strategies, suitable for scenarios with and without a *ground truth* (i.e., a set of correctly matched activities), respectively. The first prompt is the **Chain-of-Thought Prompt**(CoT), shown in Fig. 1. The *scope* is to compare two models and identify potential correspondences; the *context* provides domain-specific information and semantic constraints; and the *role* of the LLM is "Expert in Business Process Modeling and Semantic Alignment." The prompt defines a structured procedure for measuring 1:1 correspondences in a machine-readable format ("Task A" → "Task B"). The matches are further classified as "VB", "MC", or "HR" (steps 1–3 of the prompt) [2]. The matching is performed in an unsupervised setting, i.e., without using any labeled. If the ground truth is available, we enable the "self-critique" component of the prompt (steps 4–6), to perform a self-critique step to identify potential errors or inconsistencies, explain the reasons for these errors and reconsider the initial decisions. The identified errors are then used in the second prompt (which is used only in a supervised scenario).

The **Error-Guided** (EG) prompt refines correspondences by leveraging detected error patterns from prior iterations (Fig. 2). The scope remains to gener-

```
prompt = f"""
# === ERROR-GUIDED BPMN MAPPING ===
# Role
You are a Business Process Modeling expert specializing in semantic alignment, process simi
and iterative refinement.
# Input Data
Previous Mapping CSV (from the initial Chain-of-Thought run):
{initial_mapping_csv}
{initial Self-critique}

# Task
Using the previous mapping CSV and the detected error patterns as the base:
1) Detect and classify errors in the previous mappings:
   - False Positives (mapping exists but not in ground truth)
   - False Negatives (mapping missing but present in ground truth)
   - Category errors (VB vs MC vs HR)
2) Derive refinement rules from detected error patterns
3) Apply these refinement rules to generate **revised mappings**.
4) Provide a **short justification (1-2 lines)** for each revised mapping.
5) Identify ambiguous, duplicated, or potentially missing tasks.
# Output Format
Return structured, machine-readable output:
A) Revised mappings (VB → MC → HR), in the format:
   "Task Model 1" -> "Task Model 2" [VB/MC/HR]
   Justification: ...
B) Self-critique: list detected errors, ambiguities, and how refinement rules were applied.
C) Final metrics:
   - Total tasks in each model
   - Count and percentage of VB, MC, HR
   - Ambiguous / duplicated / missing tasks
   - Global similarity score based on semantic similarity of mapped tasks
```

Fig. 2. Error-Guided Prompt structure.

ate activity correspondences, while the context is enriched with recurring error patterns to guide refinement. The role remains a semantic matching expert. The procedure guides the production of refined correspondences in a structured, machine-readable format, with examples integrated to support consistency of reasoning. The Error-Guided Prompt benefits from the information on errors detected by CoT. By incorporating these error patterns, the model can recognize and avoid recurring mistakes, improving mapping accuracy. Overall, the method establishes a structured reasoning protocol that integrates interpretability with iterative refinement to generate accurate semantic correspondences between process models. The implementation is publicly available in our repository.

4 Evaluation

We evaluate the proposed LLM-based process model matching in three stages. Stage I applies the CoT prompt in an unsupervised setting, without any self-critique. The results are compared against an embedding-based baseline. Stage II assesses the use of the self-critique to refine the output. Stage III applies the EG Prompt on held-out test sets to assess generalization on unseen data. We compute the F1 score for the matched pairs. Furthermore, we compute the recall for the VB, MC, and HR categories. All experiments used Llama 3 with low temperature (0.2), top-p 0.9, maximum output length 2048, three few-shot exemplars, and a deterministic JSON-like response format.

Dataset Preparation. We employed and extended the benchmark datasets from the Process Model Matching Contest 2015, namely University Admission (UA), Birth Registration (BR), and Asset Management (AM). UA (BPMN) and BR (Petri Nets) were enriched with three variants per model to test 1:1 comparisons, injecting controlled differences such as reordering of gateways and lanes. In total, the datasets comprise 36 UA, 18 BR, and 36 AM models. We applied an 80/20 split to each dataset to obtain training and test model sets.

4.1 Results Stage I - Initial Prompt Evaluation

In this section, the unsupervised part of the CoT prompt is applied to the training data to evaluate mapping performance. As baselines, we re-implemented the GloVe approach, an embedding-based method which obtained the best results in the comparative study by Ali et al. [2]. Table 1 shows the obtained results, including the mean F1 scores and their corresponding variances. Llama 3 outperforms GloVe across all datasets in terms of F1 score. For UA and AM datasets, Llama 3 scores best in MC and HR correspondences, while VB mappings results are perfect for both methods. However, GloVe performs better for the MC and HR categories on the BR dataset.

Table 1. Llama vs. GloVe Process Model Matching on Training Sets

	University Admission		Asset Management		Birth Registration	
Metric	Llama	GloVe [2]	Llama	GloVe [2]	Llama	GloVe [2]
F1	0.82 ± 0.03	0.54 ± 0.05	0.58 ± 0.05	0.56 ± 0.04	0.66 ± 0.04	0.59 ± 0.05
VB	1.00 ± 0.00	1.00 ± 0.00	1.00 ± 0.00	1.00 ± 0.00	1.00 ± 0.00	1.00 ± 0.00
MC	0.67 ± 0.06	0.53 ± 0.05	0.90 ± 0.03	0.68 ± 0.06	0.50 ± 0.06	0.55 ± 0.05
HR	0.45 ± 0.05	0.43 ± 0.04	0.77 ± 0.04	0.61 ± 0.05	0.40 ± 0.05	0.47 ± 0.04

4.2 Results Stage II - Error Detection and Self-critique

In this stage, the self-critique mechanism is applied to the training data to assess the model's ability to detect errors in its own mappings. Four main error categories are identified. **Lexical overlap** refers to mappings which rely excessively on lexical similarity, without considering their semantic. For example, "Immatriculate" and "Matriculate" were incorrectly mapped because of their near-identical wording, although they refer to distinct phases of the admission process. **Scope mismatch** occurs when mapping activities from different process phases or roles. For instance, "Wait for results" was incorrectly matched with "Check if bachelor is sufficient", because the model failed to distinguish between actions performed by the institution or by the applicant. **Overgeneralization** occurs when semantically distinct actions are collapsed into broader matches. For instance, "Wait for results" is incorrectly mapped to "Immatriculate", as the LLM generalized both

Table 2. Error Detection and Self-Correction of Llama 3 on Train Data

Dataset	Error Type	Errors Detected	True Errors	Corrected	F1-score
UA	Lexical overlap	72	70	68	0.97 ± 0.01
	Scope Mismatch	59	58	55	0.95 ± 0.02
	Overgeneralization	56	54	52	0.96 ± 0.02
	Ambiguity	26	18	18	0.64 ± 0.04
AM	Lexical overlap	5	4	4	0.73 ± 0.03
	Scope Mismatch	27	20	20	0.73 ± 0.03
	Overgeneralization	19	18	14	0.77 ± 0.03
	Ambiguity	9	5	5	0.53 ± 0.05
BR	Lexical overlap	12	11	10	0.70 ± 0.03
	Scope Mismatch	22	15	15	0.65 ± 0.04
	Overgeneralization	13	12	10	0.82 ± 0.02
	Ambiguity	26	20	20	0.74 ± 0.03

under the notion of "admission progress,". **Ambiguity** is caused by underspecified labels leading to inconsistent alignments. For example, the task "Process application" was ambiguously phrased, and the LLM matched it alternately to "Verify documents" or "Record admission decision". Table 2 summarizes detected errors, highlighting true errors and corrections after self-critique. The model correctly identifies the majority of errors, with true positives close to ground-truth totals, even though Ambiguity remains challenging (F1 0.53–0.64). Overall, the results demonstrate strong error detection, supporting the self-critique process and enabling improvements in subsequent Error-Guided prompting.

4.3 Results Stage III - Generalization Assessment

At this stage, we compare the performance of CoT and EG prompts on test datasets. For the EG prompt, we leverage the results obtained by the self-critique of CoT on the training data. This allows us to assess the capability of the EG Prompt to leverage mistakes made in previously seen process models on unseen samples. Table 3 presents the results.

The EG prompt overall leads to significant improvements of F1-scores across datasets and correspondence categories, with increases ranging from 5% to 15%. VB mappings remain perfect in both approaches, as expected. The greatest improvements are realized in the MC and HR mappings, which present more challenging correspondences. The only exception is the MC category for the AM dataset, where EG obtains results slightly lower (but close to) than the CoT. Overall, the EG prompt outperforms bot CoT and GloVe. The results highlight that leveraging error patterns identified during training enables the model to avoid common misalignments on unseen test data.

Table 3. Test Performance: Chain-of-Thought vs Error-Guided Prompt

Dataset	Model	F1-score	VB	MC	HR
UA	Chain-of-Thought	0.72 ± 0.03	1.00	0.73	0.52
	Error-Guided Prompt	0.82 ± 0.02	1.00	0.80	0.62
	GloVe	0.67 ± 0.04	1.00	0.43	0.23
AM	Chain-of-Thought	0.74 ± 0.03	1.00	0.78	0.74
	Error-Guided Prompt	0.81 ± 0.02	1.00	0.76	0.78
	GloVe	0.57 ± 0.04	1.00	0.52	0.32
BR	Chain-of-Thought	0.71 ± 0.03	1.00	0.78	0.63
	Error-Guided Prompt	0.81 ± 0.02	1.00	0.90	0.67
	GloVe	0.65 ± 0.04	1.00	0.35	0.25

5 Discussion and Conclusion

This study represents a first step in exploring LLM-based process model matching. The results demonstrate that the proposed pipeline method effectively captures 1:1 correspondences in process models. The approach improves mappings in more challenging cases where activity labels differ but remain semantically equivalent, while maintaining perfect performance when activity labels are identical. The use of the self-critique strategy provides interpretable outputs and allows the model to generalize learned error patterns to unseen datasets, enhancing its robustness to common matching issues such as overgeneralization and scope mismatches. Overall, this work illustrates the potential of LLMs as flexible reasoning agents for process model matching, offering a robust alternative to traditional similarity-based methods. Nevertheless, the approach has some limitations. It is currently tailored to BPMN, Petri Net, and XML models, and extending it to other languages or domains would require prompt adaptation. When activity labels are very similar or differ only slightly, embedding-based approaches like GloVe generally yield more consistent correspondences, while Llama may overgeneralize. The method is sensitive to prompt phrasing and configuration. Future work will explore more complex correspondence types (e.g., N:M mappings) and incorporate additional process perspectives, such as control-flow and resource information, to further enhance matching performance.

References

1. Ahmed, N., Kwok, H.C., Hamdaqa, M., Assunção, W.K.G.: SMATCH-M-LLM: semantic similarity in metamodel matching with large language models. In: Proceedings of the 2025 Mining Software Repositories(MSR) Conference. IEEE (2025)
2. Ali, M., Shahzad, K., Muzaffar, S.I., Malik, M.K.: Deep analysis of process model matching techniques. IEEE Access **8**, 99239–99253 (2020). https://doi.org/10.1109/ACCESS.2020.2997097

3. Bell, D., et al.: Candace. Dice similarity coefficient (2020). https://doi.org/10.53347/rID-75056
4. Cayoglu, U., Dijkman, R., Dumas, M., Fettke, P.: The Process Model Matching Contest 2013. Business Process Management Workshops, pp. 442–463. Springer (2014). https://doi.org/10.1007/978-3-642-03848-8_5
5. Chen, Z., He, Z., Zhu, Q., Liu, S.: Unleashing the potential of prompt engineering for large language models: a comprehensive review. arXiv preprint arXiv:2310.14735 (2023)
6. Dijkman, R., Dumas, M., García-Bañuelos, L.: Graph matching algorithms for business process model similarity search. In: LNCS 5701, pp. 48-63. Springer, Heidelberg (2009). https://doi.org/10.1007/978-3-642-03848-8_5
7. Dijkman, R., Dumas, M., Van Dongen, B., Käärik, R., Mendling, J.: Similarity of business process models: metrics and evaluation. Inf. Syst. **36**(2), 498–516 (2011)
8. Hewing, L., Leinhos, L.: The prompt canvas: a literature-based practitioner guide for creating effective prompts in large language models. arXiv preprint arXiv:2412.05127 (2024)
9. Kolb, J., et al.: In: The Process Model Matching Contest 2015. In: Enterprise Modelling and Information Systems Architectures. Lecture Notes in Informatics (LNI), pp. 127–140. Gesellschaft für Informatik, Bonn (2015)
10. Kotu, V., Deshpande, B.: Chapter 4: Classification. 2nd edn. In: Data Science, pp. 65–163. Morgan Kaufman (2019). https://doi.org/10.1016/B978-0-12-814761-0.00004-6
11. Rudwan, M.S.M., Fonou-Dombeu, J.V.: Hybridizing fuzzy string matching and machine learning for improved ontology alignment. Future Internet **15**(7), 229 (2023). https://doi.org/10.3390/fi15070229
12. Steck, H., Ekanadham, C., Kallus, N.: Is cosine-similarity of embeddings really about similarity? In: Companion Proceedings of the ACM Web Conference 2024, pp. 887–890. Association for Computing Machinery (2024). https://doi.org/10.1145/3589335.3651526
13. Parciak, M., Vandevoort, B., Neven, F., Peeters, L., Vansummeren, S.: Schema matching with large language models: an experimental study. ArXiv pre-print arXiv:2407.11852v1 (2024)
14. Po, D.: Similarity based information retrieval using levenshtein distance algorithm. Int. J. Adv. Sci. Res. Eng. **06**, 06–17 (2020). https://doi.org/10.31695/IJASRE.2020.33780
15. Zampino, F., Longo, A.: Exploring business process model similarity with LLMs. In: Grabis, J., Wautelet, Y. (eds) *Advanced Information Systems Engineering Workshops*, CAiSE 2025, LNBI, vol. 556. Springer, Cham (2025). https://doi.org/10.1007/978-3-031-94931-9-20

Capturing Processes in Probabilistic Timed Automata

Harry H. Beyel[1(✉)], Maximilian Prokop[2,3], Jan Křetínský[2,3], Giuseppe De Giacomo[4], and Wil M. P. van der Aalst[1]

[1] RWTH Aachen University, Aachen, Germany
{beyel,wvdaalst}@pads.rwth-aachen.de
[2] Masaryk University, Munich, Czech Republic
prokopm@in.tum.de, jan.kretinsky@tum.de
[3] Technical University of Munich, Munich, Germany
[4] University of Oxford, Oxford, UK
giuseppe.degiacomo@cs.ox.ac.uk

Abstract. Event logs record how business processes execute, yet most discovery techniques (i) treat time only as an ordering device, (ii) filter infrequent but potentially desirable behavior, and (iii) yield static models that cannot express uncertainty or partial control over actions. We propose a process-discovery framework that constructs Probabilistic Timed Automata (PTA) from state-aware logs enriched with multi-perspective information such as resources and case attributes. The framework (i) transforms events into state-action-time traces, (ii) derives PTA whose transitions encode empirical probabilities and time-dependent behavior via configurable time bins, and (iii) distinguishes controllable from uncontrollable actions so that external decisions are modeled as stochastic choices. The resulting models can be analyzed with existing PTA model checkers to answer time-bounded and probabilistic reachability queries.

Keywords: Stochastic Process Mining · Process Discovery · Process Enhancement · Probabilistic Timed Automata · Model-Checking

1 Introduction

Process mining [1] analyzes event logs extracted from information systems. In *process discovery* [3], such logs are used to discover process models that explain the observed behavior. Most discovery approaches focus on control flow and treat time as an ordering device, without distinguishing early from late executions even when timing affects available options and success probabilities (e.g., early vs. late treatment). They filter infrequent behavior to simplify models, thereby risking the removal of rare but desirable variants. Moreover, the resulting models have limited stochastic expressiveness: existing stochastic Petri net based approaches [2,5] do not capture how sojourn times influence probabilities, and assumptions such as exponential firing times may not reflect real executions.

F. Zerbato et al. (Eds.): CAiSE 2026, LNBIP 587, pp. 98–106, 2026.
https://doi.org/10.1007/978-3-032-27997-2_12

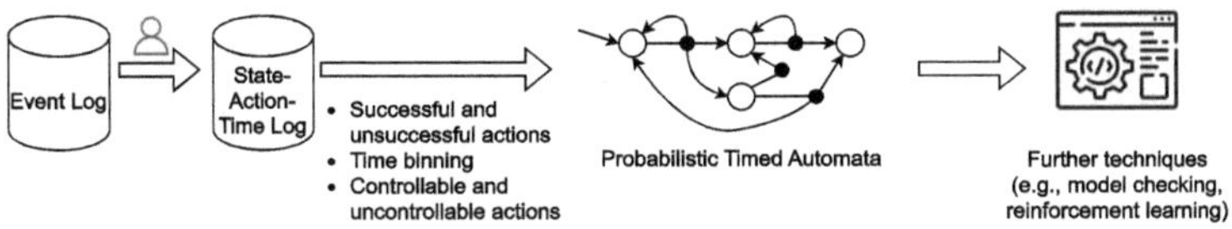

Fig. 1. Overview of the proposed framework.

Other formalisms only address parts of the problem. Markov Decision Processes (MDPs) do not model sojourn times; Semi-Markov Decision Processes (SMDPs) capture time but are difficult to analyze with model checkers; Timed Automata (TA) focus on temporal constraints but usually assume deterministic action effects. Moreover, real processes involve external actors, so assuming full control over all actions is unrealistic and can yield misleading verification results. Business process simulation [7] and predictive process mining [8] provide estimates based on sampling or black-box models, but not formal quantitative guarantees.

To overcome these issues, we provide a framework (see Fig. 1) that constructs Probabilistic Timed Automata (PTA) from multi-perspective execution data, explicitly preserving rare and time-dependent behavior and enabling model checking. Starting from an event log, a user defines a state abstraction that maps events to multi-perspective states, yielding a state-action-time log. From this log, we derive PTA whose edges encode empirical transition probabilities and time-dependent behavior via configurable time bins, and we distinguish *controllable* from *uncontrollable* actions so that external decisions are modeled as stochastic choices. The resulting PTA can be analyzed using existing tools such as PRISM [11], enabling time-bounded probabilistic reachability queries that quantify the likelihood of reaching desirable or undesirable states under different assumptions about control over actions.

2 Related Work

Process discovery techniques [3] focus on the control-flow perspective, and time is typically incorporated after model discovery, e.g., by aligning logs and models to detect bottlenecks [1], which prevents capturing how different sojourn times affect branching probabilities. Declarative approaches with temporal bounds [12, 14] do encode timing, but yield large sets of rules that are hard to interpret as a single model and are not directly linked to quantitative model checking.

Several approaches learn stochastic or timed models from execution data. MDP-based discovery [15] preserves probabilistic choices and rare behavior but disregards sojourn times and assumes that all actions are fully controllable. SMDP-based learning [10] associates sojourn-time distributions with actions but still assumes full control and yields models that are harder to analyze with existing model checkers. Techniques for inferring Timed Automata from logs [6, 13] infer temporal guards and invariants but typically assume deterministic action effects and full controllability, and they do not provide stochastic semantics over alternative outcomes (e.g., success vs. failure of a treatment).

Formalisms that distinguish between decisions of a controller and an environment, e.g., [16], explicitly model controllable versus uncontrollable choices, but are not learned from data and do not combine probabilistic branching with time in the way required for probabilistic model checking over discovered process models. In contrast, our approach constructs PTA directly from state-aware, multi-perspective logs, encodes time-binned empirical probabilities, and explicitly models controllable and uncontrollable actions, enabling the verification of quantitative, time-bounded properties with existing PTA model checkers.

Table 1. Example event log.

Event	Case	Activity	Resource	Available Resources	...	Timestamp
e_1	1	Initial Assessment (a)	Sam	Jack, Sam	...	10:00
e_2	1	Successful Approval (b)	Daniel	Daniel, Max, Angela	...	10:00
e_3	2	Initial Assessment (a)	Sam	Jack, Sam	...	11:00
e_4	2	Successful Approval (b)	Max	Daniel, Max, Angela	...	11:00
e_5	3	Initial Assessment (a)	Sam	Jack, Sam	...	12:00
e_6	3	Successful Approval (b)	Angela	Daniel, Max, Angela	...	12:15
e_7	4	Initial Assessment (a)	Sam	Jack, Sam	...	13:00
e_8	4	Successful Approval (b)	Eva	Eva	...	13:15
e_9	5	Initial Assessment (a)	Sam	Jack, Sam	...	14:00
e_{10}	5	Termination Decision (d)	Eva	Eva	...	14:15
e_{11}	6	Termination Decision (d)	Sam	Jack, Sam	...	15:00

3 Preliminaries

Given a set X, we write $B(X)$ for the set of all multisets over X, and X^* for the set of all finite sequences over X. For a sequence $\sigma = \langle \sigma_1, \ldots, \sigma_n \rangle \in X^*$, we write $|\sigma| = n$ for its length and $\sigma \cdot \sigma'$ for concatenation. A discrete probability distribution over a countable set Q is a function $\mu : Q \to [0,1]$ such that $\sum_{q \in Q} \mu(q) = 1$. We write $\text{Dist}(Q)$ for the set of all such distributions.

Definition 1 (Event Log). *$\mathcal{U}_{ev}$ is the universe of events, $\mathcal{U}_{att}$ the universe of attribute names, and U_{val} the universe of attribute values, with $\{case, act, time\} \subseteq U_{att}$. For each $e \in U_{ev}$ and $an \in U_{att}$, the attribute function $\pi_{an} : U_{ev} \to U_{val}$ returns the value of attribute an. We assume that timestamps have been preprocessed so that $\pi_{time}(e)$ is a natural number for all e. A* trace *is a finite sequence $\sigma = \langle e_1, \ldots, e_n \rangle \in U_{ev}^*$ such that, for all $1 \leq i < n$, $\pi_{case}(e_i) = \pi_{case}(e_{i+1})$ and $\pi_{time}(e_i) < \pi_{time}(e_{i+1})$. An* event log *is a multiset $L \in B(U_{ev}^*)$ of traces such that traces do not share events, i.e., for any two distinct traces $\sigma, \sigma' \in L$ we have $\{e \mid e \in \sigma\} \cap \{e \mid e \in \sigma'\} = \emptyset$.*

Definition 2 (State-Action-Time Log). *Let S be a set of* states *and A a set of* actions. *A* state-action-time trace *is a finite sequence* $\sigma = \langle(s_1, a_1, t_1), \ldots, (s_{|\sigma|}, a_{|\sigma|}, t_{|\sigma|})\rangle \in (S \times A \times \mathcal{U}_{time})^*$ *such that, for all* $1 \leq i < |\sigma|$, *we have* $t_i < t_{i+1}$. *A* state-action-time log *is a multiset* $L \in B((S \times A \times \mathcal{U}_{time})^*)$ *of such traces.*

We use one-clock PTA to capture real-time and stochastic behavior [4]. A PTA is a finite-state automaton equipped with a clock, where each transition has a guard on the clock and a probability distribution over target locations. Clock constraints over clock x, $CC(x)$, are generated by the grammar $\mathcal{X} ::= \mathsf{tt} \mid x \leq d \mid c \leq x \mid \mathcal{X} \wedge \mathcal{X}$, where $c, d \in \mathbb{N}$.

Definition 3 (Probabilistic Timed Automata). *A (one-clock)* probabilistic timed automaton *(PTA) is a tuple* $P = (Loc, \ell_0, x, Act, inv, prob)$ *where Loc is a finite set of locations,* $\ell_0 \in Loc$ *is the initial location, x is the (single) clock, Act is a finite set of actions,* $inv : Loc \to CC(x)$ *assigns a clock invariant to each location, and* $prob \subseteq Loc \times Act \times CC(x) \times \mathrm{Dist}(Loc)$ *is a finite set of probabilistic edges. A tuple* $(\ell, a, g, p) \in prob$ *is a probabilistic edge, where ℓ is the source location, a an action, g a guard, and p a distribution over Loc. For any ℓ' with* $p(\ell') > 0$, *the transition from ℓ to ℓ' resets the clock x to 0.*

4 Capturing Processes in PTA

4.1 From Event Logs to State-Action-Time Logs

To derive a state-action-time log, the user defines a *state abstraction* $\#_s : \mathcal{U}_{ev} \to S$ that maps each event to a state. This function may depend on multiple attributes (e.g., activity, resources, case attributes), enabling multi-perspective states beyond purely control-flow states.

Definition 4 (Event Log to State-Action-Time Log). *Let* $L \subseteq \mathcal{U}_{ev}^*$ *be an event log, S be a finite set of states, and A a finite set of actions. Let* $\#_s : \mathcal{U}_{ev} \to S$ *be a state abstraction function and let* $s_{start}, s_{success}, s_{fail} \notin S$, $start, end \notin A$. *For* $\sigma = \langle e_1, \ldots, e_{|\sigma|}\rangle \in L$, *we obtain its projection* $\gamma(\sigma) = \langle(\#_s(e_1), \pi_{act}(e_1), \pi_{time}(e_1)), \ldots, (\#_s(e_{|\sigma|}), \pi_{act}(e_{|\sigma|}), \pi_{time}(e_{|\sigma|}))\rangle \in (S \times A \times \mathcal{U}_{time})^*$. *Next, we prepend an artificial start and append an artificial end. To decide whether a trace is* successful *or* unsuccessful, *we use a user-defined function* $outcome : (S \times A \times \mathcal{U}_{time})^* \to \{success, fail\}$, *which inspects the entire projected trace. Hence, we define* $s^{out}(\gamma(\sigma)) = \begin{cases} s_{success}, & \text{if } outcome(\gamma(\sigma)) = success, \\ s_{fail}, & \text{otherwise.} \end{cases}$ *The resulting* state-action-time trace *is* $\hat{\gamma}(\sigma) = \langle(s_{start}, start, \pi_{time}(e_1))\rangle \cdot \gamma(\sigma) \cdot \langle(s^{out}(\gamma(\sigma)), end, \pi_{time}(e_{|\sigma|}))\rangle$. *The* state-action-time log *associated with L is the multiset* $L' = [\,\hat{\gamma}(\sigma) \mid \sigma \in L\,]$.

In our example (see Table 1), the state abstraction groups events by the performing resource together with the set of available resources, yielding states $s_0, \ldots, s_3$. For illustration, we may define *outcome* to classify traces as successful whenever the last activity is *Successful Approval (b)* and as unsuccessful whenever it is *Termination Decision (d)*. The first state-action-time trace is $\langle(s_{start}, start, 10{:}00), (s_0, a, 10{:}00), (s_1, b, 10{:}00), (s_{success}, end, 10{:}00)\rangle$.

4.2 PTA Construction with Time Bins and Controllability

We collect counts of transitions between states, refined by actions and time bins. Time bins are (user-defined) non-overlapping intervals over observed sojourn times to distinguish "early" and "late" executions of an action. We partition actions into *controllable* actions, chosen by the process owner, and *uncontrollable* actions, triggered by external parties. Controllability information comes from domain experts, e.g., by distinguishing internal vs. external actors. Controllable actions can fire directly under guards derived from the time bins, while uncontrollable actions are executed via two auxiliary locations: a selection location $s^{pre,a}$ for each uncontrollable action a (where a time bin is drawn from the empirical distribution) and a waiting location $s^{pre,a,I}$ per bin.

Definition 5 (PTA with Time Bins and Controllability). *Let $\mathcal{I}$ be a set of non-overlapping intervals, i.e., for $I, J \in \mathcal{I}, I \neq J, I = [l_I, u_I], J = [l_J, u_J], u_I < l_J$ or $u_J < l_I$. Let A_{uncon} be the set of uncontrollable actions and A_{con} the set of controllable actions such that $A_{uncon} \cap A_{con} = \emptyset$ and $A_{uncon} \cup A_{con} = A$. Let $L \in \mathcal{B}((S \times A \times \mathcal{U}_{time})^*)$ be a state-action-time log of sequences $\sigma = \langle (s_1, a_1, t_1), \ldots, (s_{|\sigma|}, a_{|\sigma|}, t_{|\sigma|}) \rangle$. We define $N_s = |\{(\sigma, i) \mid \sigma \in L, 1 \leq i < |\sigma|, s_i = s\}|$, $N_{s,a} = |\{(\sigma, i) \mid \sigma \in L, 1 \leq i < |\sigma|, s_i = s, a_i = a\}|$, $N_s^{uncon} = \sum_{a \in A_{uncon}} N_{s,a}$, $N_{s,a,I} = |\{(\sigma, i) \mid \sigma \in L, 1 \leq i < |\sigma|, s_i = s, a_i = a, t_{i+1} - t_i \in I\}|$, and $N_{s,a,s',I} = |\{(\sigma, i) \mid \sigma \in L, 1 \leq i < |\sigma|, s_i = s, a_i = a, s_{i+1} = s', t_{i+1} - t_i \in I\}|$. Moreover, we define auxiliary locations for uncontrollable actions:*

- *$S_{pre} = \{s^{pre,a} \mid s \in S, a \in A_{uncon}, N_{s,a} > 0\}$ being locations before executing an uncontrollable action from a state s and*
- *$S_{preI} = \{s^{pre,a,I} \mid s \in S, a \in A_{uncon}, I \in \mathcal{I}, N_{s,a,I} > 0\}$ being locations designed for waiting before executing an uncontrollable action.*

A PTA $P = (Loc, \ell_0, x, Act, inv, prob)$ created by a log is defined as:

- *$Loc = S \cup S_{pre} \cup S_{preI}$, $l_0 = s_{start}$, x is the single clock, $Act = A_{uncon} \cup A_{con} \cup \{wait, \tau\}$ with artificial auxiliary actions,*
- *For $\ell \in Loc$, we define two additional invariants, one for the auxiliary selection state and one for the waiting state*

$$inv(\ell) = \begin{cases} x \leq \max\{u_I \mid a \in A_{con}, I \in \mathcal{I}, N_{\ell,a,I} > 0\}, & \text{if } \ell \in S, N_s > 0 \\ x \leq 0, & \text{if } \ell \in S_{pre} \\ x \leq u_I, & \text{if } \ell \in S_{preI} \\ \text{tt}, & \text{if } \ell \in S, N_s = 0 \end{cases}$$

- *Executing waiting will lead to the auxiliary selection state: $\mu_s^{wait}(s') = \frac{N_{s,a}}{N_s^{uncon}}$, if $s' = s^{pre,a}$ for some $a \in A_{uncon}$ with $N_{s,a} > 0$,*
- *Reaching a waiting state is based on how many data points are in the interval: $\mu_{s,a}^{toBin}(s') = \frac{N_{s,a,I}}{\sum_{J \in \mathcal{I}} N_{s,a,J}}$, if $s' = s^{pre,a,I}, \sum_{J \in \mathcal{I}} N_{s,a,J} > 0$*
- *For probabilistic time binning: $\mu_{s,a,I}^{\tau}(s') = \frac{N_{s,a,s',I}}{N_{s,a,I}}$, if $N_{s,a,I} > 0$*

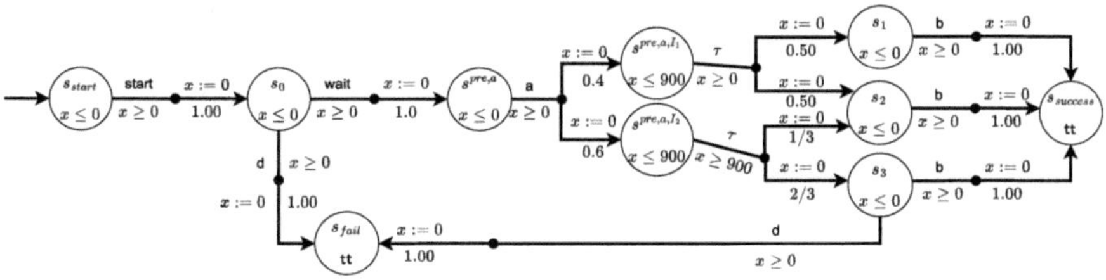

Fig. 2. PTA highlighting the shift of control.

- *For controllable actions:* $\mu_{s,a,I}(s') = \frac{N_{s,a,s',I}}{N_{s,a,I}}$*, if* $N_{s,a,I} > 0$
- *Edges which always reset the clock* x *to* 0*:*
  - $prob^{wait} = \{(s, wait, x \geq 0, \mu_s^{wait}) \mid s \in S, N_s^{uncon} > 0\}$,
  - $prob^{pre,a} = \{(s^{pre,a}, a, x \leq 0, \mu_{s,a}^{toBin}) \mid s^{pre,a} \in S_{pre}, a \in A_{uncon}\}$,
  - $prob^{pre,a,I} = \{(s^{pre,a,I}, \tau, l_I \leq x \leq u_I, \mu_{s,a,I}^{\tau}) \mid s^{pre,a,I} \in S_{preI}\}$,
  - $prob^{s,a,I} = \{(s, a, l_I \leq x \leq u_I, \mu_{s,a,I}) \mid s \in S, a \in A_{con}, I \in \mathcal{I}, N_{s,a,I} > 0\}$,
  - $prob = prob^{wait} \cup prob^{pre,a} \cup prob^{pre,a,I} \cup prob^{s,a,I}$.

An example PTA based on the log shown in Table 1 is presented in Fig. 2. States are process states, the artificial start, success, and failure states. Process states are pairs of (executing resource, available resources) observed at each process step. Concretely, s_0 corresponds to Sam acting from the pool {Jack, Sam}, s_1 to Daniel acting from {Daniel, Max, Angela}, s_2 to either Max or Angela acting from that same pool, and s_3 to Eva acting from {Eva}. From these states, controllable actions can be taken directly with time-binned probabilities derived from the log. If the process owner chooses to *wait*, control is handed to the environment, which selects the next uncontrollable action with probability proportional to its empirical frequency from the current state. The PTA transitions to the corresponding selection location $s^{pre,a}$, and from there to a waiting state $s^{pre,a,I}$ chosen according to the distribution of sojourn times across intervals. From s_0, the log contains five transitions: cases 1 and 2 execute the next step quickly, while cases 3, 4, and 5 each take 15 minutes. This yields the 0.4/0.6 split between the fast and slow time bins on the edge from $s^{pre,a}$. After the clock advances within $s^{pre,a,I}$, the PTA transitions to the next state with probabilities matching the observed outcomes in that bin. For fast execution of a, the next state is s_1 or s_2 with equal probability 0.5. For slow execution of a, two of the three executions lead to s_3 and one to s_2. Because the intervals in $\mathcal{I}$ are non-overlapping, at most one edge for a given action and state is enabled.

If $A_{uncon} = \emptyset$, then $S_{pre} = S_{preI} = \emptyset$ and no *wait* or τ edges are present, yielding a *time-binned PTA* in which all actions are controllable. If $\mathcal{I}$ contains a single interval, we obtain a *simple PTA* without explicit time binning.

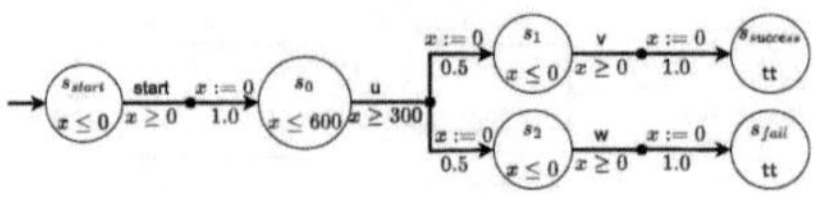

(a) PTA with no time binning.

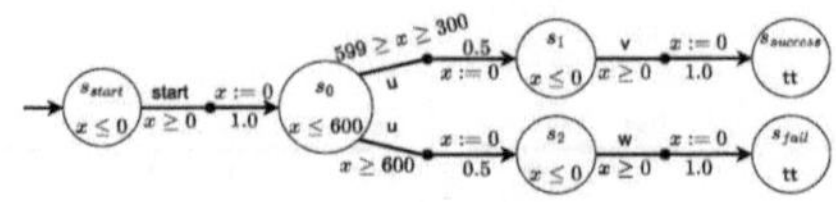

(b) PTA with time binning.

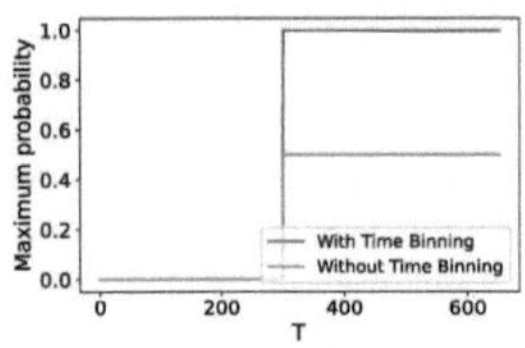

(c) Maximum probabilities of reaching $s_{success}$ by time T for the PTAs in Figures 3a and 3b.

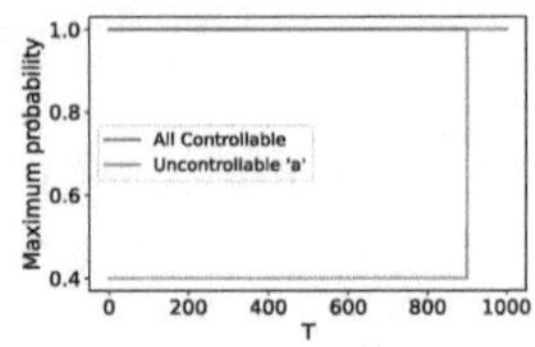

(d) Maximum probabilities of reaching $s_{success}$ by time T for the PTAs in Figures 2 and 3e.

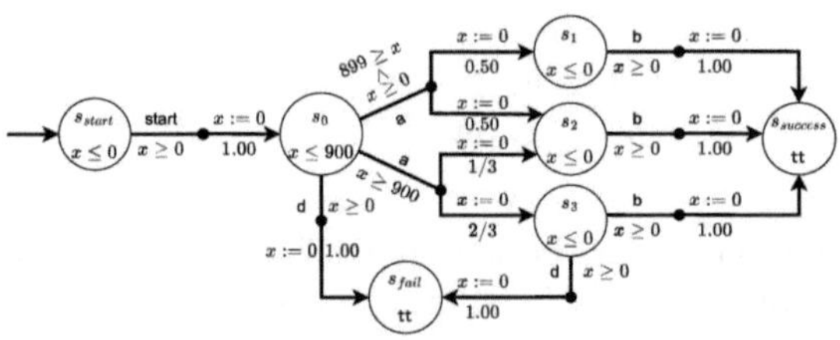

(e) Time-binned PTA with full control over actions.

Fig. 3. Overview of qualitative experiments.

5 Evaluation

5.1 Qualitative Evaluation

We focus on time-bounded probabilistic reachability properties. In a real-world setting, one wants to assess the likelihood of successful completion of the process as a function of the process instance's runtime. To show the impact of our different modeling approaches, i.e., uncontrollable actions and time binning, we consider different PTAs. For each PTA, we compute the maximum probability of reaching $s_{success}$ within time bound T, expressed in PCTL [9], $P_{\max=?}[\mathbf{F}^{\leq T}\, s_{success}]$. Figures 3a and 3b are PTAs illustrating the effect of time binning. Figure 3e is a fully controllable variant of Fig. 2. Consider the plot in Fig. 3c. Without time binning, the maximum probability of reaching a successful outcome is 50 %. However, only a late execution results in failure, whereas an earlier execution always succeeds. With time binning, the model captures that firing early achieves success with probability 1, so the maximum reachable probability rises to 1. Figure 3d illustrates that when action a becomes uncon-

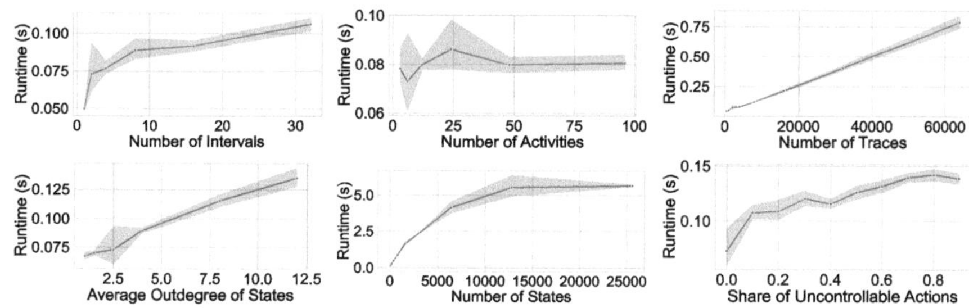

Fig. 4. Runtime for varying parameters. The y-axis scales differ across subplots.

trollable, the maximum success probability at the beginning is lower because the waiting time for a is governed by the empirical distribution.

5.2 Quantitative Evaluation

Our approach is implemented in Python and publicly available[1]. We investigate the runtime of the PTA construction by varying characteristics of the state-action-time log and user parameters one at a time. The baseline configuration uses 2,000 traces, with an average length of 10, 6 activities, 20 states, an average outdegree of 2.5, no uncontrollable actions, and 2 time intervals. For each setting, we generated 10 synthetic logs and measured the end-to-end time to read the log, build the PTA, and export it to the input format of PRISM [11] on a Windows 11 machine (16 GB RAM, Intel i7-1165G7 @ 2.80GHz). Results are shown in Fig. 4. Runtime increases with the number of intervals, traces, states, the average outdegree, and the fraction of uncontrollable actions. The number of distinct activities has only a modest effect. Overall, PTA generation is efficient.

6 Conclusion

Our framework constructs PTA from multi-perspective logs using time-binning and explicit controllability information, thereby preserving rare behavior and enabling quantitative, time-bounded model checking. The process owner can choose which controllable action to execute and within which time bin. Choices between uncontrollable actions and their timing are derived from empirical distributions. Our proof-of-concept implementation shows that different PTA configurations provide complementary views on time-dependent and stochastic behavior and that PTA generation scales to realistic log sizes. Current limitations include reliance on a user-defined success/failure criterion, which transfers modeling burden to the analyst, and the potential for state-space explosion, which we plan to address through state-merging and abstraction techniques.

[1] https://gitlab.com/live-lab/software/cabumm.

Acknowledgments. This work was partially supported by a scholarship from the German Academic Exchange Service (DAAD) and the UKRI Erlangen AI Hub on Mathematical and Computational Foundations of AI (No. EP/Y028872/1).

References

1. van der Aalst, W.M.P.: Process Mining - Data Science in Action, Second Edition. Springer (2016)
2. van der Aalst, W.M.P., Leemans, S.J.J.: Learning generalized stochastic petri nets from event data. In: Principles of Verification: Cycling the Probabilistic Landscape, pp. 3–17. Springer (2024)
3. Augusto, A., et al.: Automated discovery of process models from event logs: Review and benchmark. IEEE Trans. Knowl. Data Eng. **31**(4), 686–705 (2019)
4. Beauquier, D.: On probabilistic timed automata. Theor. Comput. Sci. **292**(1), 65–84 (2003)
5. Burke, A., Leemans, S.J.J., Wynn, M.T.: Discovering stochastic process models by reduction and abstraction. In: Buchs, D., Carmona, J. (eds.) PETRI NETS 2021. LNCS, vol. 12734, pp. 312–336. Springer, Cham (2021). https://doi.org/10.1007/978-3-030-76983-3_16
6. Cornanguer, L., Largouët, C., Rozé, L., Termier, A.: TAG: learning timed automata from logs. In: AAAI, pp. 3949–3958. AAAI Press (2022)
7. Dumas, M., Rosa, M.L., Mendling, J., Reijers, H.A.: Fundamentals of Business Process Management, Second Edition. Springer (2018). https://doi.org/10.1007/978-3-662-56509-4
8. Francescomarino, C.D., Ghidini, C.: Predictive process monitoring. In: Process Mining Handbook, pp. 320–346. Springer (2022). https://doi.org/10.1007/978-3-031-08848-3_10
9. Hansson, H., Jonsson, B.: A logic for reasoning about time and reliability. Formal Aspects Comput. **6**(5), 512–535 (1994)
10. Hundogan, O.A., Verhoef, B.J., Theeven, P., Reijers, H.A., Lu, X.: Reinforcement learning for optimizing responses in care processes. Data Knowl. Eng. **157**, 102412 (2025)
11. Kwiatkowska, M., Norman, G., Parker, D.: PRISM 4.0: verification of probabilistic real-time systems. In: Gopalakrishnan, G., Qadeer, S. (eds.) CAV 2011. LNCS, vol. 6806, pp. 585–591. Springer, Heidelberg (2011). https://doi.org/10.1007/978-3-642-22110-1_47
12. Maggi, F.M., Westergaard, M.: Using timed automata for a Priori warnings and planning for timed declarative process models. Int. J. Cooperative Inf. Syst. **23**(1) (2014)
13. Pastore, F., Micucci, D., Mariani, L.: Timed k-tail: automatic inference of timed automata. In: ICST, pp. 401–411. IEEE Computer Society (2017)
14. Schönig, S., Di Ciccio, C., Maggi, F.M., Mendling, J.: Discovery of multi-perspective declarative process models. In: Sheng, Q.Z., Stroulia, E., Tata, S., Bhiri, S. (eds.) ICSOC 2016. LNCS, vol. 9936, pp. 87–103. Springer, Cham (2016). https://doi.org/10.1007/978-3-319-46295-0_6
15. Verhoef, B.J., Lu, X.: Using reinforcement learning to optimize responses in care processes: a case study on aggression incidents. In: BPM Workshops, pp. 57–69. Springer (2023). https://doi.org/10.1007/978-3-031-50974-2_5
16. Zavatteri, M., Viganò, L.: Conditional simple temporal networks with uncertainty and decisions. Theor. Comput. Sci. **797**, 77–101 (2019)

Detecting Dynamic Relationships in Object-Centric Event Logs

Alessandro Gianola[1(✉)], Zeeshan Hameed[2], Marco Montali[2], Anjo Seidel[3], Mathias Weske[3], and Sarah Winkler[2]

[1] INESC-ID/Instituto Superior Técnico, Universidade de Lisboa, Lisbon, Portugal
alessandro.gianola@tecnico.ulisboa.pt
[2] Free University of Bozen-Bolzano, Bozen-Bolzano, Italy
{hameed,montali,winkler}@inf.unibz.it
[3] Hasso Plattner Institute, University of Potsdam, Potsdam, Germany
{anjo.seidel,mathias.weske}@hpi.de

Abstract. Object-centric process mining examines how processes interact with multiple co-evolving objects, and has gained great interest in recent years. However, object-centric event logs (OCELs) leave object relationships underspecified in several respects, especially if relationships are dynamic, i.e., they change over time. In this paper, we identify and formally define for the first time assumptions that allow to represent and manipulate dynamic relationships in OCELs in a semantically unambiguous way. We evaluate existing logs to show that our assumptions are often satisfied, ensuring full transparency of relationship semantics.

Keywords: Business Process Management · Dynamically Changing Relations · Synchronization

1 Introduction

Process mining aims to extract actionable insights from the execution data recorded by information systems [17]. By analyzing event logs, it seeks to reconstruct the actual behavior of operational processes and reason about performance, deviations, and conformance. While traditional process mining assumes that events refer to a single case notion, modern information systems store data about multiple interacting process instances that share co-evolving objects [15]. This has motivated the development of object-centric process mining, which studies processes that simultaneously evolve several interrelated objects of different types. Executions are recorded using the standard OCEL format (object-centric event logs [8]), where each event may reference multiple objects.

A variety of modeling formalisms has been proposed to represent object-centric processes: object-centric Petri nets (OCPN) [18] extend classical Petri nets to handle multiple object types. OCPNs are relatively simple and amenable to discovery, but known to be underspecified as they cannot track object identities and relationships [16]. More expressive formalisms capturing some form

F. Zerbato et al. (Eds.): CAiSE 2026, LNBIP 587, pp. 107–116, 2026.
https://doi.org/10.1007/978-3-032-27997-2_13

of synchronization include synchronous proclets [5], COA-nets [9,10], object-centric process trees [19], and object-centric Petri nets with identifiers (OPIDs) [11]. While these formalisms can enforce synchronization semantics, they almost exclusively focus on *stable* object relationships that remain unmodified over time.

The current literature thus almost entirely leaves out the important case where relationships dynamically change over time, despite the fact that such relationships are ubiquitous in real life processes: for example, a package might be moved from one truck to another, the destination address of a shipment can be dynamically updated, or the content of an order can change. Some attempts in this respect have been made in the context of conformance checking [11,12].

This shortcoming in current research is largely due to the fact that OCEL, as well as the standard of object-centric event data (OCED) [7], neither relate object relationships with events, nor with time. In this paper, we illustrate the resulting ambiguity by a number of examples. We then identify and formally define for the first time assumptions regarding how to log in an OCEL object-centric event data with dynamically changing relationships in an unambiguous way, with minimal additional domain knowledge. By evaluating available OCELs, we show that these assumptions are indeed respected to a great extent.

2 OCELs and Dynamic Relationships

Contemporary object-centric event data representations [8] lack an explicitly defined semantics regarding the way events impact the evolution of object-to-object relationships—that is, which are the temporal intervals in which links between objects hold. For clarity, we use *relationship* at the type level, and *link* at the instance level. eg., the type-level information that "an order contains items" constitutes a relationship, while the fact that "order o_1 contains item i_2" indicates a link. Such relationships are in the literature almost always assumed to be *rigid* (or *stable*), that is, once established, a link never ceases to exist [3,6,14].

In this paper we call a *dynamic many-to-one* relationship between a many-type μ and a one-type σ a relationship in which at every point in time, every object of type μ is linked to at most one object of type σ. In contrast, in *many-to-many* relationships between types μ and σ, an object of type μ can at some point be linked to many objects of type σ and vice versa. In the sequel, *many-to-one* relationships are always supposed to be dynamic.

The goal of this section is to provide a minimally intrusive mechanism to unambiguously view how an OCEL tracks the evolution of links of relationships. Here "minimally intrusive" means that we want to limit, as much as possible, the number of assumptions made, and the additional domain knowledge needed.

For completeness, we recall the notion of object-centric event logs [18]:

Definition 1. *Given sets of object types Σ, activities $\mathcal{A}$, and timestamps $\mathbb{T}$, an* object-centric event log *(OCEL) is a tuple $L = (E, \mathcal{O}, \pi_{act}, \pi_{obj}, \pi_{time})$ where: (i) E is a set of events; (ii) $\mathcal{O}$ is a set of object identifiers typed by the function* *ot*: $\mathcal{O} \rightarrow \Sigma$; *(iii) the functions* $\pi_{act}: E \rightarrow \mathcal{A}$, $\pi_{obj}: E \rightarrow \mathcal{P}(\mathcal{O})$, *and* $\pi_{time}: E \rightarrow \mathbb{T}$, *mapping each event to an activity, a set of objects, and a timestamp.*

First and foremost, there are two possible ways of interpreting events in an OCEL, as illustrated by the following example.

Example 1. Consider the situation where an order o_1 is created with items i_1 and i_2, then i_2 gets removed from o_1, and later i_3 is added. Depending on how object participation in events is interpreted, this can be expressed in two ways.

Table 1. An order management OCEL with parameter semantics.

event	activity	order	items
$\#_1$	create order	o_1	i_1, i_2
$\#_2$	reduce order	o_1	i_2
$\#_3$	add to order	o_1	i_3

In what we call the *parameter semantics*, objects denote the actual parameters of the activity referred by the event. An OCEL could thus look like Table 1. Note that each event is associated with the objects to which the respective activity applies. The current state after each event, in particular regarding which links are established resp. removed, remains however implicit. On the other hand, one can adopt a so-called *snapshot semantics*, where the objects listed in each event do not represent parameters, but provide instead a snapshot of the new state (e.g., the new state of an order) *after* the respective activity, making the existing links explicit. This would yield the following log in Table 2. Note how in event $\#_2$, the associated item is i_1, i.e., the *remaining* item in o_1 – witnessing that the set of active links for the order-item relationship consists only of (o_1, i_1). This is in contrast to the table above, where event $\#_2$ is associated with i_2, the item *to which the removal operation is applied.*

Table 2. An order management OCEL with snapshot semantics.

event	activity	order	items
$\#_1$	create order	o_1	i_1, i_2
$\#_2$	reduce order	o_1	i_1
$\#_3$	add to order	o_1	i_1, i_3

When adopting parameter semantics, it is impossible to reconstruct from an OCEL alone which links hold at a given point in time: additional transactional domain knowledge on the updates semantics of activities is needed [4]. Indeed, even though this is left implicit, existing approaches typically adopt the snapshot semantics [6]. We hence follow the next assumption.

Assumption 1. *Events are recorded under the snapshot semantics, that is, listing which objects are related as an effect of the event.*

However, the next example shows that even under the snapshot semantics, there is inherent ambiguity in the way OCELs capture changing relationships.

Example 2. Consider a process where employees handle orders in Table 3, and events recording two order creations followed by a change of the handling employee. From the co-participation of orders and employees to the same event, we can only infer that there exists a relationship between some of their instances, but we do not know with which multiplicity constraints. This extra-knowledge is essential: If the relationship is many-to-many, then we may infer from the OCEL that order o_1 is linked to both employees p_1 and p_2 after $\#_6$. If instead the relationship is many-to-one – more specifically, every employee can handle multiple orders, but every order is handled by one and only one employee – then we must instead infer that o_1 was initially linked to p_1, and upon $\#_6$ it changed its link to p_2. This witnesses that the relationship is a *dynamic* one-to-many relationship instead of a rigid many-to-many relationship: over time the same order can be linked to distinct employees but in every instant to only one.

Table 3. An order handling OCEL with orders and employees.

event	activity	order	employee
$\#_4$	create order	o_1	p_1
$\#_5$	create order	o_2	p_1
$\#_6$	change order manager	o_1	p_2

Example 2 shows that some minimal domain knowledge is needed regarding the multiplicity of relationships. In addition, many-to-many relationships are known to make it difficult to properly handle synchronization of related objects, as noted in [2,5]. As pointed out in [5], synchronization can be handled naturally by reification of every many-to-many relationship into a pair of many-to-one relationships with a newly introduced object type in between. We thus assume that such reification was done in a preprocessing step. Moreover, since a one-to-one relationship can be represented as two many-to-one relationships, we restrict ourselves in the sequel to many-to-one relationships, which directly support synchronization. We also assume that relationships exist only between distinct types, since OCEL cannot distinguish objects of the same type with different roles.

Assumption 2. *We assume that domain knowledge is provided, indicating which pairs of distinct object types are connected by a many-to-one relationship.*

In a many-to-one relationship, we refer to the "one" side as the parent, and to the "many" side as the child, and when referring to a many-to-one relationship from the "one" side, we call it a one-to-many relationship. We do not enforce mandatory participation on either side. Even when assuming snapshot semantics, Example 1 and 2 show that the reconstruction of links after an event may depend on whether the event primarily operates on the parent or on the child endpoint of a one-to-many relationship. In Example 1, events primarily operate on the *order* type, i.e., the parent side of the one-to-many relationship with *item*. To unambiguously trace how the relationship evolves after an event that operates on both orders and items, it needs to list the set of items to which the order is linked in that instant. For example, when o_1 occurs with i_1 in $\#_2$, this implies that the item set i_1, i_2 linked to o_1 in $\#_1$ is replaced: link (o_1, i_1) is kept, while (o_1, i_2) removed.

Also in Example 2, events primarily operate on the *order* type. However, there *order* corresponds to the child side of the many-to-one relationship with *employee*. Differently from the previous case, now every event that operates on both an order and an employee with primary focus on the order, indicates to which (parent) employee that order gets linked. Hence, *other* orders that the same employee handles are out of scope, and not mentioned. For example, the fact that employee p_1 handles a second order o_2 according to event $\#_4$ does *not* mean that p_1 does no longer handle order o_1 i.e., $\#_4$ does not delete the link between p_1 and o_1 established by $\#_1$.

Table 4. The combined order management OCEL with snapshot semantics.

	activity	order	item	employee
$\#_1$	create order	o_1	i_1, i_2	p_1
$\#_2$	reduce order	o_1	i_1	
$\#_3$	add to order	o_1	i_1, i_3	
$\#_4$	create order	o_2	i_4, i_5	p_1
$\#_5$	wrap item		i_4	
$\#_6$	change order manager	o_1		p_2
$\#_7$	ship order	o_1	i_1, i_3	
$\#_8$	ship order	o_2	i_4, i_5	

This shows that the snapshot semantics must be further clarified: in the first case, the active links for an order to its items can be reconstructed from the current event alone, while in the second case the active links for an employee to its orders require to also consider previous events. These two ways of operating over links correspond to the classical alternative to maintain links from the many or the one side of the relationship. One may be tempted to impose that only one of the two conventions should be adopted in an OCEL. However, this cannot be done when events operate over three or more object types, as illustrated next. Consider the OCEL in Table 4 obtained by merging those in Example 1 and 2. Now orders are at once linked to the contained items and the employees that handle them. To properly interpret which active links exist after an event, we need to know the primary object type (which we call *reference type*) for each activity. In the OCEL here, this is *order* for all events except wrap item, which can only have reference type *item*. Given these reference types and the multiplicity of all relationships, one can reconstruct the active links after each event. Notice that for events of type create order, we need to consider that the order-to-item relationship is treated from the parent side (thus enumerating the set of items to which the mentioned order is linked), while the order-to-employee one is treated from the child side (thus only indicating what is the current employee to which the mentioned order is linked).

Generalizing the observations in Table 4 we get to the following assumptions.

Assumption 3. *Every activity has one object type as its* reference type, *and every event has exactly one object of the reference type of its activity. We call this object the* reference object.

Assumption 4. *Let* $e = (a, O_e)$ *be an event in the log with activity* a *and object set* O_e, *and* t_{ref} *the reference type of* a. *For every object* $o \in O_e$ *that has an object type* t *that is by the domain knowledge in a relationship with* t_{ref}, *either (a)* (t_{ref}, t) *is a many-to-one relationship,* o *is the only object in* O_e *of type* t, *and* o *is the only object currently in relationship with the reference object; or (b)* (t_{ref}, t) *is a one-to-many relationship and the subset of* O_e *with type* t *are all objects of type* t *currently in relationship with the reference object.*

These conventions clarify the confusion in Table 4: if for all activities except wrap item, we choose the reference type *order*, each event mentions only one object of its reference type, so Assumption 3 holds. As the relationship *order – item* is one-to-many, when activities with reference type *order* refer to sets of items, these are *all* items currently in the order (Assumption 4 b). On the other hand, as *order – employee* is many-to-one, if activity create order with reference type *order* mentions employee p_1, this is the parent of the relationship, and an event mentioning another order o_2 with p_1 does not delete the link between o_1 and p_1; however, when in event #6 the order o_1 occurs with another employee p_2, we assume that the link (o_1, p_1) gets deleted (Assumption 4a).

A last point of attention pertains to a "locality" principle for activities: when an event occurs, what is the scope of the changes its corresponding activity can induce? Intuitively, one may expect that this scope contains only links of the reference object. However, to ensure that children in a one-to-many relationship have only one parent at a time, (implicit) parent updates may be required, which may break this locality principle, as witnessed by the following example.

Example 3. Consider the following OCEL in Table 5 recording teams of multiple employees, with a many-to-one relationship *employee – team*, so that an employee can be a member of only one team (reference types are underlined).

Table 5. An OCEL capturing the management of employees and teams.

	activity	team	empl.
$\#_1$	create team	t_1	p_1, p_2
$\#_2$	create team	t_2	p_3, p_4
$\#_3$	add employee to team	t_2	p_2
$\#_4$	create team	t_3	p_1, p_3

According to Assumptions 3 and 4, after $\#_3$ all of p_2, p_3, p_4 belong to team t_2 (note that the reference type of $\#_3$ is *employee*). However, p_2 is at this point already a member of team t_1. Therefore, to maintain the multiplicity constraints of the many-to-one relationship, we need to conclude that the relationship (t_1, p_2) is implicitly deleted by $\#_3$. A similar problem occurs in $\#_4$, where employees p_1 and p_3 are added to a team, even if they are already a member of another one: also here an implicit deletion would be required to maintain the one-to-many relationship. However, while the implicit deletion in $\#_3$ pertains to the former parent of the reference object, the implicit deletions needed in $\#_4$ pertain to (former) parents of children of the reference object. So the latter case violates the locality principle.

Example 3 shows that if the locality principle is desired, it must be enforced as an additional assumption to prohibit implicit deletions as in $\#_4$ of Ex. 3:

Assumption 5. *Each event only modifies links that involve its reference object.*

3 Evaluation

To evaluate the practicality of our interpretation of OCELs, we check the five assumptions presented in Sect. 2 as much as possible against publicly available event logs[1]. The evaluation of Assumption 1 on snapshot semantics requires domain knowledge, and is hence not possible from event logs alone. However, according to the textual descriptions of the considered logs, no information contradicting the snapshot semantics was found. Assumption 2 requires cardinalities of relationships to be provided. Again, for a reliable interpretation domain knowledge is required. However, assuming the log to be sufficiently complete, similar as required by Armstrong relations in database theory [1], by counting co-occurrences of objects in events, an educated guess can be made. The respective relationship counts for one-to-one (oo), many-to-one (mo), and many-to-many (mm) are listed in Table 6, for both static relationships and dynamic relationship candidates. For static relationships, co-occurrences were counted across the entire log [14]; for the dynamic case, we only counted objects co-occurring in the same events. The differences between these two counts show that dynamic relations are in fact quite common. Next, for Assumption 3 we verify whether every

[1] The evaluation script in https://github.com/bytekid/dynamic-relationships was applied to OCELs from https://www.ocel-standard.org/event-logs.

Table 6. The assumptions evaluated on publicly available OCELs.

OCEL	$\#\Sigma$	static	dynamic	Assumpt. 3			Assumpt. 5
		oo/mo/mm	oo/mo/mm			rt	
Logistics	7	0/3/6	6/1/3	14/14	(100%)	846	100%
Order Man.	6	0/5/8	3/7/3	11/11	(100%)	1296	82%
P2P	7	2/6/1	3/5/1	10/10	(100%)	128	92%
Angular Github	2	0/0/1	0/0/1	16/67	(24%)	–	–
Hinge Production	12	3/19/10	29/3/0	11/11	(100%)	746496	99%
AoE	30	0/69/66	62/60/13	851/851	(100%)	$> 10^{370}$	$\geq$68%
LRMS-O2C	9	1/9/1	10/1/0	20/22	(91%)	–	–
LRMS-P2P	6	0/0/8	7/1/0	12/12	(100%)	432	95%
LRMS-Hiring	6	0/4/4	7/1/0	24/24	(100%)	3072	97%
LRMS-Hospital	8	0/4/5	9/0/0	9/9	(100%)	288	100%
Bundestag	44	0/0/31	7/16/8	95/148	(64%)	–	–
Inventory Man.	7	0/7/10	17/0/0	30/30	(100%)	$\approx 10^{18}$	100%

event type has a candidate for a reference type, i.e., an object type of which in every event of this type exactly one object occurs. In Table 6, entries of the form x/y indicate that for x out of y event types reference types could be identified, and the respective percentage. We also give the number of possible combinations of reference types (rt). In absence of domain knowledge on the update semantics of events, Assumption 4 provides an interpretation of changing relationships but cannot be seen as violated or respected from the log alone. Finally, for Assumption 5, for OCELs where possible reference types were identified earlier, we consider the detected dynamic many-to-one and one-to-one relationships to check whether events only modify links that involve their reference objects. The ratios of events satisfying this assumption are listed in the last column of Table 6, for the combination of reference types where this value is highest (for AoE not all combinations could be checked due to their vast number, though).

4 Related Work

So far, virtually all mining/analysis approaches dealing with OCELs support explicit relationships between objects [3], or implicit relationships established when they co-participate to the same event [6]. However, such relationships are almost always assumed to be stable. In [13], temporal object type models (TOTeM) are mined from OCELs, but the dynamics in these models consider temporal existence windows of objects while their relationships are considered stable: a relationship is simply supposed to exist in all time instants where both objects exist. In [19] instead, *temporal implications* are proposed as one form of dynamic relationship. This notion captures that for a certain timespan, a fixed set of objects of a certain type is linked to only one set of objects of another type. This implicitly assumes snapshot semantics (Assumption 1), as the linked objects are supposed to be those that occurred together in an event. Moreover, temporal implications are a rather restricted form of dynamic relationships, e.g. orders with a growing set of products cannot be modeled, as sets of objects are only compared wrt. equality. Temporal implications basically require stable relationships for a fixed block-structured sub-process;

5 Conclusions

We identified key assumptions to uniquely reconstruct the evolution of dynamic relationships from an input OCEL, given additional minimal domain knowledge on the cardinalities of object type relationships. The evaluation of OCELs showed that these assumptions are indeed often satisfied. In future work, these assumptions can be valuable to discover process models that explicitly capture and enforce the evolution of dynamic relationships, as well as to shape the representation of object relationships in future versions of OCED [7].

Acknowledgments. This work was partially supported by the NextGenerationEU FAIR PE0000013 project MAIPM (CUPC63C22000770006). This work was also partly supported by Portuguese national funds through FundaÃğÃčo para a CiÃłncia e a Tecnologia, I.P. (FCT) under projects UID/50021/2025 (https://doi.org/10.54499/UID/50021/2025) and UID/PRR/50021/2025 (https://doi.org/10.54499/UID/PRR/50021/2025).

References

1. Armstrong, W.W.: Dependency structures of data base relationships. In: Proc. IFIP Congress (1974)
2. Artale, A., Kovtunova, A., Montali, M., van der Aalst, W.M.P.: Modeling and reasoning over declarative data-aware processes with object-centric behavioral constraints. In: Hildebrandt, T., van Dongen, B.F., Röglinger, M., Mendling, J. (eds.) BPM 2019. LNCS, vol. 11675, pp. 139–156. Springer, Cham (2019). https://doi.org/10.1007/978-3-030-26619-6_11
3. Berti, A.: OCEL (Object-Centric Event Log) 2.0 Specification (2024)
4. Chaki, R., Calvanese, D., Montali, M.: Generation of timelines from event knowledge graphs using domain knowledge. In: Proc. 24th CISIM. LNCS, vol. 15927, pp. 275–289. (2025). https://doi.org/10.1007/978-3-032-02406-0_20
5. Fahland, D.: Describing behavior of processes with many-to-many interactions. In: Donatelli, S., Haar, S. (eds.) PETRI NETS 2019. LNCS, vol. 11522, pp. 3–24. Springer, Cham (2019). https://doi.org/10.1007/978-3-030-21571-2_1
6. Fahland, D.: Process mining over multiple behavioral dimensions with event knowledge graphs. In: van der Aalst, W.M.P., Carmona, J. (eds.) Process Mining Handbook. LNBIP, vol. 448. Springer, Cham (2022). https://doi.org/10.1007/978-3-031-08848-3_9
7. Fahland, D., Montali, M., et al.: Towards a simple and extensible standard for object-centric event data (OCED) - core model, design space, and lessons learned. CoRR abs/ arXiv:2410.14495 (2024)

8. Ghahfarokhi, A.F., Park, G., Berti, A., van der Aalst, W.M.P.: OCEL: a standard for object-centric event logs. In: Bellatreche, L., et al. (eds.) ADBIS 2021. CCIS, vol. 1450, pp. 169–175. Springer, Cham (2021). https://doi.org/10.1007/978-3-030-85082-1_16
9. Ghilardi, S., Gianola, A., Montali, M., Rivkin, A.: Petri nets with parameterised data. In: Fahland, D., Ghidini, C., Becker, J., Dumas, M. (eds.) BPM 2020. LNCS, vol. 12168, pp. 55–74. Springer, Cham (2020). https://doi.org/10.1007/978-3-030-58666-9_4
10. Ghilardi, S., Gianola, A., Montali, M., Rivkin, A.: Petri net-based object-centric processes with read-only data. Inf. Syst. **107**, 102011 (2022)
11. Gianola, A., Montali, M., Winkler, S.: Object-Centric Conformance Alignments with Synchronization. In: Proc. 36th CAiSE. LNCS, vol. 14663, pp. 3–19. (2024). https://doi.org/10.1007/978-3-031-61057-8_1
12. Gianola, A., Montali, M., Winkler, S.: Object-centric processes with structured data and exact synchronization - formal modelling and conformance checking. In: Proc. 37th CAiSE. LNCS, vol. 15702, pp. 185–202. Springer (2025). https://doi.org/10.1007/978-3-031-94571-7_11
13. Liss, L., Adams, J.N., van der Aalst, W.M.P.: TOTeM: Temporal Object Type Model for Object-Centric Process Mining. In: Proc. BPM Forum. pp. 107–123. Springer (2024). https://doi.org/10.1007/978-3-031-70418-5_7
14. Seidel, A., Winkler, S., Gianola, A., Montali, M., Weske, M.: To bind or not to bind? Discovering stable relationships in object-centric processes. In: Proc. 44th ER. LNCS, vol. 16189, pp. 223–241 (2025). https://doi.org/10.1007/978-3-032-08623-5_12
15. Aalst, W.M.P.: Object-centric process mining: dealing with divergence and convergence in event data. In: Ölveczky, P.C., Salaün, G. (eds.) SEFM 2019. LNCS, vol. 11724, pp. 3–25. Springer, Cham (2019). https://doi.org/10.1007/978-3-030-30446-1_1
16. van der Aalst, W.M.P.: Toward more realistic simulation models using object-centric process mining. In: Proc. 37th ECMS, pp. 5–13 (2023)
17. van der Aalst, W., et al.: Process mining manifesto. In: Daniel, F., Barkaoui, K., Dustdar, S. (eds.) BPM 2011. LNBIP, vol. 99, pp. 169–194. Springer, Heidelberg (2012). https://doi.org/10.1007/978-3-642-28108-2_19
18. van der Aalst, W.M.P., Berti, A.: Discovering Object-centric Petri Nets. Fund. Inform. **175**(1–4), 1–40 (2020)
19. van Detten, J.N., Schumacher, P., Leemans, S.: Modeling and discovering dynamic identity relations in object-centric process mining. In: Proc. 7th ICPM (2025)

Towards Ontology-Guided Data Augmentation: The Case of Entity Resolution

Federico Scafoglieri[1(✉)], Michela Papandrea[2], and Tiziano Leidi[2]

[1] Sapienza University of Rome, Rome, Italy
scafoglieri@diag.uniroma1.it

[2] University of Applied Sciences and Arts of Southern Switzerland (SUPSI), Manno, Switzerland
{michela.papandrea,tiziano.leidi}@supsi.ch

Abstract. Data Augmentation (DA) is a technique that expands limited training sets with synthetic examples. Knowledge Graphs (KGs) represent entities and their relationships in a structured, graph-based form. Entity Resolution (ER) identifies entities that refer to the same real-world individual. Ontologies provide formal schemas that specify rules and constraints over KG data. While DA is well established in other fields, its adoption in KG tasks remains limited, its application to KG ER is essentially absent, and ontology-guided counterparts remain entirely unexplored. We address these first two gaps with LUFFY, a framework that produces new synthetic training examples for KG ER, a task where labeled data is notoriously scarce. LUFFY combines structural replication with attribute value generation through a fine-tuned pre-trained language model (BART) that interpolates in latent space. Experiments on five benchmarks, using the state-of-the-art ER model BERT-INT, show that LUFFY consistently improves ER performance, with the strongest gains in low-resource regimes. We then outline a vision for ontology-guided augmentation for KG ER, with a first validation showing that even simple ontological constraints already improve quality.

Keywords: Data Augmentation · Knowledge Graphs · Entity Resolution · Ontologies · Pretrained Language Models

1 Introduction

When labeled data for a supervised model is scarce, Data Augmentation (DA) [13] offers a principled solution: producing new artificial training examples that enrich the original dataset without requiring any additional annotation. The approach has become indispensable in computer vision and natural language processing, where it consistently boosts model robustness and generalization capabilities.

Code, data, supplementary material: https://github.com/Scafooo/DAKGEA.

F. Zerbato et al. (Eds.): CAiSE 2026, LNBIP 587, pp. 117–126, 2026.
https://doi.org/10.1007/978-3-032-27997-2_14

Knowledge Graphs (KGs) [7] formalize domains of interest in a graph-based structure, concretely defined as collections of triples. They are central to applications such as question answering, recommendation, data integration [10], and reasoning, and are often paired with formal ontologies that specify rules and constraints over the data. Since KGs are typically constructed independently by different organizations, they inevitably contain overlapping yet heterogeneous descriptions of the same real-world individuals, often with different schemas, naming conventions, and surface forms. The task of identifying such duplicates is known as Entity Resolution (ER) [2,4,5,18], also called Entity Alignment or Instance Matching; solving it is a prerequisite for integrating complementary knowledge. Yet ER is inherently low-resource: obtaining labeled correspondences (seed alignments) is costly and time-consuming, so severely limiting the generalization of learning-based models, making it a natural candidate for DA.

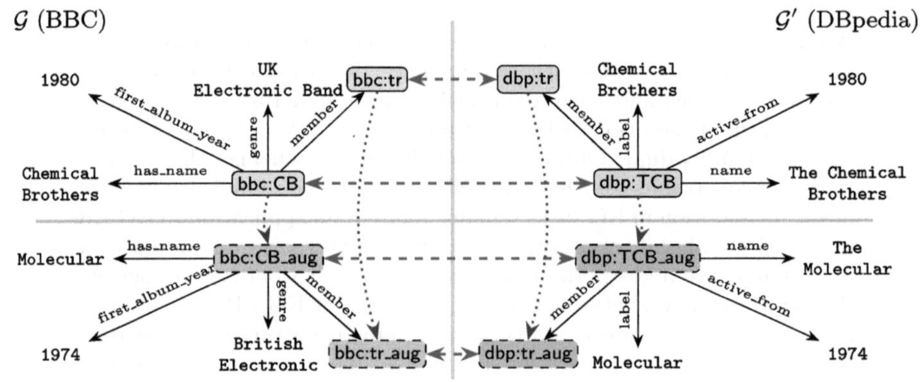

Fig. 1. Original aligned entities (above) and synthetic counterparts (below).

Figure 1 illustrates concretely what DA for KG ER entails and what makes it challenging. Consider two KGs about the music domain: $\mathcal{G}$ (BBC, left) and $\mathcal{G}'$ (DBpedia, right). Above the yellow line, the entities bbc:CB and dbp:TCB are known to represent the same real-world individual, "The Chemical Brothers", and form a seed alignment (red dashed arrow). Each entity carries its own attributes (has_name, first_album_year, genre in $\mathcal{G}$; name, active_from, label in $\mathcal{G}'$) and relations to other entities (member), expressed through different predicates and different literal values, a typical and pervasive source of heterogeneity.

Below the yellow line, a possible DA outcome: a synthetic pair bbc:CB_aug and dbp:TCB_aug. These artificial entities mirror the structural logic of the originals but with generated attribute values, such as `Molecular` as name and `1974` as year. Each pair enriches the training set at no annotation cost. Yet without semantic guards, the generator may yield inconsistencies such as a first_album_year preceding active_from. Bridging this gap is the role we envision for ontologies.

Three nested gaps emerge when we consider applying DA to KGs and ER:

G1. DA for KGs is understudied: despite its maturity in other areas, DA has still received comparatively little attention in the KG community.
G2. DA for KG ER is essentially absent: little attention has been specifically devoted to generating new synthetic training data tailored to KG ER.
G3. Ontology-based DA for KG ER is entirely untouched: no augmentation strategy leverages ontological knowledge to guide or validate generation.

Related Work. DA is mature in NLP [6], where techniques such as mixup [19] and back-translation are standard. For KGs, recent work applies DA to embedding and completion [17] tasks, but not to ER. The closest work to ours is Rotom [12], which augments flat tabular records for entity matching without addressing graph structure, relational context, or ontological constraints [9]. To our knowledge, no prior work jointly addresses all three aforementioned aspects.

Contributions. We address the three aforementioned gaps as follows:

1. We present LUFFY, a DA framework that addresses the lack of DA for KGs (**G1**) and for KG ER in particular (**G2**), combining structural replication with BART-based [11] latent-space interpolation for attribute generation.
2. We provide preliminary empirical evidence on five benchmarks showing consistent improvements, with the strongest gains in low-resource regimes.
3. We address the unexplored role of ontological knowledge in DA for KG ER (**G3**) by articulating a vision and offering an initial empirical validation.

2 Background

A KG is a collection of triples (s, p, o) where $s \in \mathsf{E}$ is a subject entity, $p \in \mathsf{P}$ a predicate, and o an object. We distinguish *relation triples* (s, p, o) with $o \in \mathsf{E}$, and *attribute triples* (s, p, o) with $o \in \mathsf{L}$ (a literal value). For instance, in Fig. 1, (bbc:CB, member, bbc:tr) is a relation triple, while (dbp:TCB, name, `The Chemical Brothers`) is an attribute triple. Real-world KGs are often paired with formal ontologies (OWL, RDFS) and their shape constraints (e.g., SHACL [9]), which declare rules from datatype restrictions to complex domain axioms.

ER is typically formulated over two KGs $\mathcal{G}$ and $\mathcal{G}'$ with entity sets E_1 and E_2, and seeks to identify equivalent entity pairs. A ground truth $\Omega \subseteq \mathsf{E}_1 \times \mathsf{E}_2$ contains all valid matches; a subset $S \subset \Omega$ (seed alignment) serves as training signal. DA produces an augmented set $S' = S \cup S_{aug}$, where S_{aug} contains synthetically generated pairs, aiming to improve the overall ER model's performance.

Pre-trained Language Models (PLMs) such as BERT [3] and BART [11] learn rich representations of natural language text by training on large corpora. BART combines a bidirectional encoder, which maps an input sequence to hidden states $\mathbf{h} = \text{Enc}(x)$, with an autoregressive decoder that reconstructs text via $\text{Dec}(\mathbf{h})$. This structure allows conditional generation and direct manipulation of the hidden-state space, making it well-suited for latent-space interpolation.

3 The Luffy Framework

The core idea behind LUFFY is to exploit the natural variation between aligned entities: the different surface forms of each matched attribute act as interpolation anchors in a fine-tuned language model's latent space, yielding new plausible values that, combined with structural replication, produce complete synthetic entity pairs faithful to the original distribution. To realize this in practice, we identify four key properties that a DA strategy for KG ER should satisfy:

(P1) Structural consistency: synthetic entities must faithfully reproduce the graph structure of the originals—same predicates, same relation patterns—so that the ER model sees realistic and coherent neighbourhood contexts.

(P2) Alignment preservation: every synthetic entity on one side must have a meaningful and aligned counterpart on the other, i.e., the two sides must genuinely describe the same individual, forming a valid training pair.

(P3) Semantic plausibility: generated attribute values must be coherent with the predicate semantics (e.g., a name must resemble a plausible name).

(P4) Diversity without distribution shift: synthetic data should introduce enough variety to improve generalization, yet remain close enough to the original distribution to avoid misleading the downstream ER model.

LUFFY addresses these through a four-stage pipeline (Fig. 2): *attribute matching*, *Set KG construction*, *training tasks*, and *BFS-based mixup generation*.

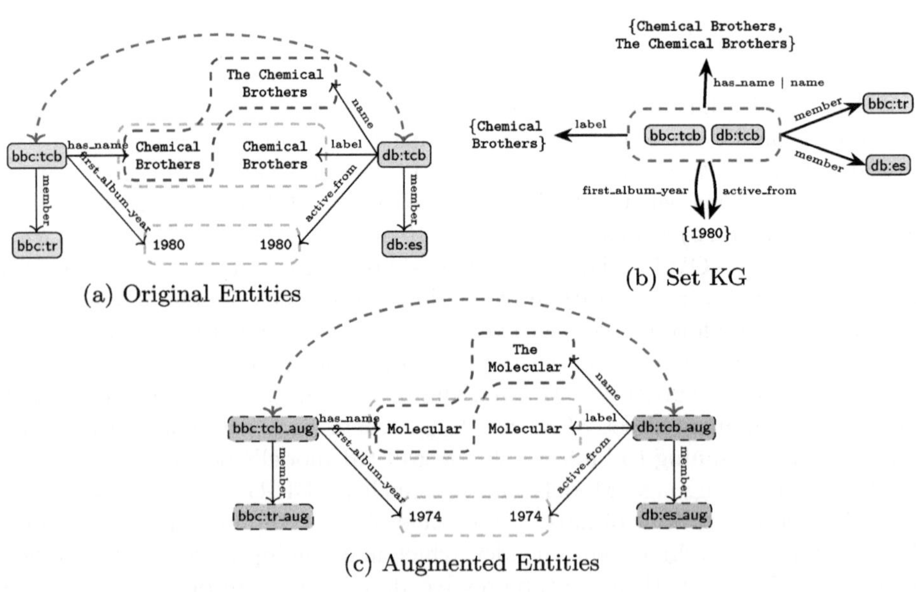

Fig. 2. (a) Original aligned entities with attribute matching. (b) Set KG merges aligned pairs. (c) Augmented entities with interpolated values.

Attribute Matching. Since the two KGs describe the same domain with potentially different schemas, we first identify which attribute predicates refer to the same underlying semantic property (e.g., has_name ↔ name in Fig. 2). Formally, we compute an attribute predicate alignment $\mathcal{A}_P \subseteq \mathsf{P}_1^a \times \mathsf{P}_2^a$, where P_i^a denotes the predicates appearing in attribute triples of each KG $\mathcal{G}_i$, by combining name similarity (sentence-transformer [14] cosine similarity over names) and value similarity (type compatibility, token overlap, statistical proximity). A pair (p_1, p_2) is included only when the combined score exceeds a given threshold.

Set Knowledge Graph. Once predicate correspondences are known, we construct a unified *Set KG* $\mathcal{G}_S$ (Fig. 2b), which serves two roles: defining the structural template for synthetic entities and collecting alternative surface forms that feed fine-tuning and interpolation. For each aligned pair $(e_1, e_2) \in S$, a *set node* $\hat{e} = \langle e_1, e_2 \rangle$ merges both entities. Matched predicates are collapsed into a single edge with merged literals (e.g., has_name | name maps to {`Chemical Brothers`, `The Chemical Brothers`}). Entities reached through relations but lacking an alignment counterpart are included as singleton set nodes, retaining their original predicates and values. This structural inheritance ensures **(P1)**, while the merged value sets lay the ground for **(P3)** and **(P4)**.

Training Tasks. With the Set KG in place, the next step is to train the generative model on the surface-form variation it encodes. To generate plausible attribute values, the language model must first learn the style and distribution of each predicate type. We fine-tune BART [11] on tasks derived from $\mathcal{G}_S$. Every training example prepends a canonical token $\tau(p)$ that identifies the predicate type (e.g., `[HAS_NAME]` for both has_name and name), so that matched predicates from the two KGs are treated uniformly. For each aligned value pair (v_1, v_2), we create examples from three task types: *Identity* ($\tau(p) \oplus v \rightarrow \tau(p) \oplus v$), which anchors the latent space; *Denoising* ($\tau(p) \oplus \tilde{v} \rightarrow \tau(p) \oplus v$, where $\tilde{v}$ applies character- and token-level perturbations), which adds noise robustness; and *Cross-mapping* ($\tau(p) \oplus v_1 \rightarrow \tau(p) \oplus v_2$ and vice versa), which bridges both surface forms. Together, these tasks ensure **(P2)** and **(P3)**.

Augmentation via BFS and Mixup. The fine-tuned model and the Set KG together enable the final stage: generating synthetic aligned pairs (Fig. 2c). Once the model is fine-tuned, we generate new entities by traversing the Set KG. Given a desired augmentation ratio a $= |S_{aug}|/|S|$, the process samples set nodes from $\mathcal{G}_S$ as starting points and, from each, performs a breadth-first traversal up to depth $d_{\max}$. The BFS ensures that when an entity is augmented, its relational neighbours are augmented as well, preserving local graph coherence. To maintain structural isomorphism with the original Set KG, already-generated synthetic entities and their interpolated attribute values are cached and reused whenever the same set node is reached from different traversals. For each visited set node $\hat{e}$, we generate synthetic counterparts by interpolating [19] the alternative surface forms collected in $\hat{e}$ through BART's latent space. For singletons, stochastic decoding ensures that even self-interpolation produces a plausible variation:

$$\mathbf{h}_1 = \text{Enc}(\tau(p) \oplus v_1), \quad \mathbf{h}_2 = \text{Enc}(\tau(p) \oplus v_2)$$
$$\mathbf{h}'_1 = (1-\lambda)\cdot \mathbf{h}_1 + \lambda \cdot \mathbf{h}_2, \quad \mathbf{h}'_2 = \lambda \cdot \mathbf{h}_1 + (1-\lambda)\cdot \mathbf{h}_2$$

where $\lambda \in [0, 0.5]$ controls how much each output is influenced by the opposite side. Decoding yields $v'_1 = \text{Dec}(\mathbf{h}'_1)$ and $v'_2 = \text{Dec}(\mathbf{h}'_2)$: two distinct values, each still anchored to its original, ensuring diversity while avoiding distribution shift **(P4)**. Because generation occurs in the latent space of the fine-tuned model, the outputs remain semantically plausible **(P3)**. The generated entities, together with their triples, are added to their respective KGs, and the new alignment pairs are appended to the seed, yielding the augmented training set $S' = S \cup S_{aug}$.

4 Experimental Evaluation

We evaluate LUFFY on five ER benchmarks from the OpenEA framework [15] using BERT-INT [16] as ER model. The benchmarks span different domains and levels of heterogeneity: BBC-DB aligns BBC music entities with DBpedia; D_W_15K_V1/V2 align 15K entities between DBpedia and Wikidata (V1 sparser, V2 denser); ICEWS-WIKI and ICEWS-YAGO [8] align a temporal event KG with Wikidata and YAGO respectively, featuring high heterogeneity. Following standard OpenEA settings, each dataset is split into training (20%), validation (10%), and test (70%). We set the interpolation weight $\lambda = 0.4$ and BFS depth $d_{\max} = 2$, and use the BERT-INT hyperparameters from the original paper. We report Hits@1, Hits@10, and MRR as standard evaluation metrics.

To assess how augmentation interacts with data scarcity, we vary both the *reduction ratio* $\mathrm{r} \in \{0.1, \ldots, 1.0\}$ (fraction of training alignments retained) and the augmentation ratio a, yielding 100 configurations per dataset. To aggregate results with greater emphasis on low-resource regimes, we introduce **LEAR** (**L**ow-resource **E**ffectiveness of **A**ugmentation **R**atio), a scarcity-weighted mean:

$$\text{LEAR}(\mathrm{a}) = \frac{\sum_{i=1}^{n} w(\mathrm{r}_i)\cdot \Delta(\mathrm{r}_i, \mathrm{a})}{\sum_{i=1}^{n} w(\mathrm{r}_i)}$$

where $P(\mathrm{r}, \mathrm{a})$ denotes the evaluation metric score (e.g., Hits@1) achieved at reduction ratio r and augmentation ratio a, $\Delta(\mathrm{r}, \mathrm{a}) = P_{\text{aug}}(\mathrm{r}, \mathrm{a}) - P_{\text{base}}(\mathrm{r})$ is the absolute performance gap between the augmented and non-augmented baseline models, and $w(\mathrm{r}) = 1/\mathrm{r}$ ensures that low-resource regimes, where gains are expected to be largest, dominate the overall average. Concretely, a LEAR of +0.174 on H@1 means that, weighting scarce-data regimes more heavily, LUFFY consistently improves H@1 by 17.4% points on average over the strong baseline, confirming the low-resource advantage of LUFFY over all tested regimes (Fig. 3).

LEAR scores (Table 1) are consistently positive, with strongest gains on ICEWS-WIKI (+.195 H@1) and BBC-DB (+.174 H@1); the more modest H@10 gains on ICEWS-YAGO suggest that for dense datasets augmentation refines top-1 precision rather than broadening recall. For brevity, we focus the detailed analysis on BBC-DB; full results for all datasets are in the companion repository.

(a) LEAR scores (mean ± std)

Dataset	H@1	H@10	MRR
BBC-DB	+.174±.02	+.063±.02	+.134±.11
D-W-15K V1	+.019±.02	+.033±.07	+.023±.05
D-W-15K V2	+.186±.02	+.175±.05	+.181±.05
ICEWS-WIKI	+.195±.01	+.211±.02	+.199±.02
ICEWS-YAGO	+.113±.01	+.071±.01	+.100±.01

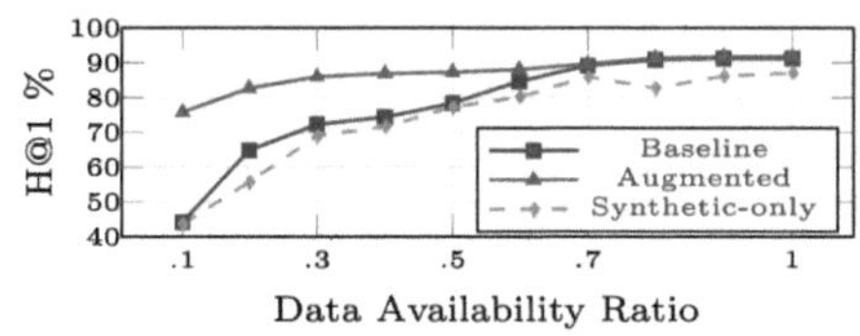

(b) BBC-DB detailed analysis (H@1, best a). Rel = Synth/Orig.

r	Augmentation Base	Aug	Δ	Synthetic-only Orig	Synth	Rel
0.1	44.2	**75.8**	+31.7	44.2	43.7	99%
0.2	64.8	**82.7**	+18.0	64.8	55.7	86%
0.3	72.3	**86.0**	+13.7	72.3	69.0	95%
0.4	74.4	**86.9**	+12.4	74.4	71.6	96%
0.5	78.4	**87.3**	+8.9	78.4	77.3	99%
0.6	84.7	**88.1**	+3.4	84.7	80.2	95%
0.7	89.2	**89.7**	+0.5	89.2	86.0	96%
0.8	90.9	**91.4**	+0.5	90.9	82.8	91%
0.9	91.3	**91.8**	+0.5	91.3	86.2	94%
1.0	91.3	**91.8**	+0.5	91.3	87.1	95%

Fig. 3. (a) LEAR scores and BBC-DB H@1 trend. (b) BBC-DB breakdown at the best augmentation ratio per r. Rel = Synth/Orig.

The BBC-DB breakdown (Table 1) shows gains up to +32.3pp at r = 0.1, gradually decreasing as more real data becomes available—as expected, since Luffy's primary contribution is in low-resource regimes where labeled data is scarce and the marginal value of each synthetic pair is highest. With only 30% of the data, the augmented model already reaches 87.7% H@1, comparable to the full-data baseline (91.3%). The modest gains at r = 1.0 (+0.5pp) confirm that Luffy does not introduce noise even when real data is abundant. The model trained *exclusively* on synthetic data achieves 84–97% of the baseline, confirming that the synthetic pairs generated by Luffy capture genuine alignment signal.

An ablation confirms that fine-tuning is the core mechanism: removing it drops H@1 to 31–53%, as the generator produces fluent but misaligned attributes. Removing structural consistency also hurts (∼5–10pp), confirming that both components provide essential complementary contributions.

All experiments ran on an AMD Ryzen 9 7950X with an NVIDIA RTX 4090. Augmentation scales linearly: BBC-DB takes 8 ± 2 min at r = 0.1 and 142 ± 15 min at r = 1.0, with fine-tuning dominating the cost.

5 Towards Ontology-Guided Augmentation

The results in Sect. 4 show that Luffy already yields substantial improvements on plain KGs. Yet real-world KGs are seldom plain: formal ontologies and SHACL shapes impose constraints that the current pipeline does not exploit [10]. We argue that these constraints can govern generation at two complementary levels: *intra-graph*, validating the internal consistency of each synthetic KG, and *inter-graph*, enforcing value coherence across the synthetic aligned entity pair.

At the intra-graph level, ontological rules restrict the space of valid generations. Datatype ranges ensure that numerical properties receive plausible values; class-level knowledge implies that entities of a given type share characteristic structural patterns, so that type-aware generation can produce more realistic synthetic entities. SHACL shapes can express all such constraints declaratively.

At the inter-graph level, the Set KG $\mathcal{G}_S$ already merges matched predicates into unified set nodes; ontological constraints can extend this by enforcing value coherence across the synthetic pair. When an attribute is present in one KG but absent in the other, the alignment guides cross-graph completion: the missing information is transferred and adapted by the PLM to match the target KG's conventions, thus effectively bridging latent cross-graph schema heterogeneity.

Beyond validation, ontological knowledge can also guide *what* to augment. Rather than selecting seed entities at random, the system can prioritize entities whose type, structure, or attribute coverage makes them most informative for the ER model. For instance, entities that belong to underrepresented classes, or pairs with asymmetric attribute coverage, are prime augmentation candidates.

A natural question is what should happen when a generated value violates a constraint. The simplest strategy is rejection and regeneration. A more refined approach is repair, where the value is adjusted to satisfy the constraint. Drawing from the database literature on inconsistency management [1], one can seek the minimal repair that restores conformance while preserving as much of the generated content as possible. The choice depends on the constraint type.

As an initial validation, we implemented a set of simple SHACL shapes on BBC-DB enforcing datatype validity and coherence between correlated attributes. Listing 1 shows a representative shape grounded in the predicates of Fig. 1: it constrains bbc:first_album_year to a valid integer range and enforces that it does not precede dbo:active_from—catching exactly the inconsistency illustrated in the introduction. Any generated triple violating a constraint is discarded, acting as a rejection filter over the PLM output.

Listing 1.1. SHACL shape grounded in the BBC-DB predicates of Fig. 1.

```
[] a sh:NodeShape ;
  sh:targetSubjectsOf bbc:first_album_year ;
  sh:property [
    sh:path bbc:first_album_year ;
    sh:datatype xsd:integer ;
    sh:minInclusive 1900 ; sh:maxInclusive 2025 ] ;
  sh:sparql [
    sh:message "first_album_year must not precede active_from" ;
    sh:select """
      SELECT $this WHERE {
        $this bbc:first_album_year ?y1 .
        $this dbo:active_from      ?y2 .
        FILTER (?y1 < ?y2) }""" ] .
```

Even this minimal intervention yields a +0.03–0.05pp improvement in H@1 over unconstrained generation, suggesting that ontological enforcement can measurably improve quality and that a tighter integration into the generation process is a promising research direction.

6 Conclusion

This paper introduced LUFFY, showing that DA for KG ER is both feasible and effective, particularly in the low-resource regimes that characterize real-world deployments. Beyond ER, the results point to a more general observation: while instance data changes as organizations update their KGs, the ontological constraints that govern it remain comparatively stable. This asymmetry makes ontologies a natural anchor for governing synthetic data generation—a perspective relevant to any continuously evolving information system. Future work will deepen ontology-guided augmentation, using conformance as reward signal for fine-tuning, and evaluate generalizability across different ER architectures.

Acknowledgment. Federico Maria Scafoglieri was supported by the Swiss National Science Foundation (SNSF) under grant number IZSEZ0_238320.

References

1. Bertossi, L.: Database repairing and consistent query answering. Synth. Lectures n Data Manag. **3**(5) (2011)
2. Christophides, V., Efthymiou, V., Palpanas, T., Papadakis, G., Stefanidis, K.: An overview of end-to-end entity resolution for big data. ACM Comput. Surv. (CSUR) **53**(6), 1–42 (2020)
3. Devlin, J., Chang, M.W., Lee, K., Toutanova, K.: BERT: pre-training of deep bidirectional transformers for language understanding. In: Proceedings of NAACL-HLT, pp. 4171–4186 (2019)
4. Fagin, R., Kolaitis, P.G., Lembo, D., Popa, L., Scafoglieri, F.: A framework for combining entity resolution and query answering in knowledge bases. In: Proceedings of KR (2023)
5. Fagin, R., Kolaitis, P.G., Lembo, D., Popa, L., Scafoglieri, F.: Combining entity resolution and query answering in ontologies: a formal conceptual framework. In: Italian Symposium on Advanced Database Systems (2024)
6. Feng, S.Y., et al.: A survey of data augmentation approaches for NLP. arXiv preprint arXiv:2105.03075 (2021)
7. Hogan, A., et al.: Knowledge graphs. ACM Comput. Surv. **54**(4) (2021)
8. Jiang, X., et al.: Rethinking GNN-based entity alignment on heterogeneous knowledge graphs: new datasets and a new method. CoRR (2023)
9. Knublauch, H., Kontokostas, D.: Shapes constraint language (SHACL). W3C Recommendation, World Wide Web Consortium (W3C) (2017)
10. Lembo, D., Lenzerini, M., Poggi, A., Scafoglieri, F.M.: Enriching ontology-based data management with multidimensional modeling. In: Bork, D., Lukyanenko, R., Sadiq, S., Bellatreche, L., Pastor, O. (eds.) ER 2025. LNCS, vol. 16189, pp. 106–124. Springer, Cham (2025). https://doi.org/10.1007/978-3-032-08623-5_6
11. Lewis, M., et al.: BART: denoising sequence-to-sequence pre-training for natural language generation, translation, and comprehension. In: Proceedings of ACL (2020)
12. Miao, Z., Li, Y., Wang, X.: Rotom: a meta-learned data augmentation framework for entity matching, data cleaning, text classification, and beyond. In: Proceedings of SIGMOD (2021)
13. Mumuni, A., Mumuni, F.: Data augmentation: a comprehensive survey of modern approaches. Array **16** (2022)
14. Reimers, N., Gurevych, I.: Sentence-BERT: Sentence embeddings using Siamese BERT-networks. In: Proceedings of EMNLP-IJCNLP (2019)

15. Sun, Z., Hu, W., Zhang, Q., Qu, Y.: A benchmarking study of embedding-based entity alignment for knowledge graphs. Proc. VLDB Endow. **13**(11) (2020)
16. Tang, X., Zhang, J., Chen, B., Yang, Y., Chen, H., Li, C.: BERT-int: a BERT-based interaction model for knowledge graph alignment. Interactions **100** (2020)
17. Yao, Y., Zhang, Z., Xu, Y., Li, C.: Data augmentation for few-shot knowledge graph completion from hierarchical perspective. In: Proceedings of COLING (2022)
18. Zeng, K., Li, C., Hou, L., Li, J., Feng, L.: A comprehensive survey of entity alignment for knowledge graphs. AI Open **2**, 1–13 (2021)
19. Zhang, H., Cisse, M., Dauphin, Y.N., Lopez-Paz, D.: mixup: Beyond empirical risk minimization. In: Proceedings of ICLR (2018)

Designing a Configurable Requirements Engineering Tool for Teaching

Agnese Rozenberga[1,2](✉), Marite Kirikova[2], and Janis Stirna[1]

[1] Department of Computer and Systems Sciences, Stockholm University, Kista, Sweden
{agnese.rozenberga,js}@dsv.su.se

[2] Institute of Applied Computer Systems, Riga Technical University, Kipsalas iela 6A, Riga LV-1048, Latvia
Marite.Kirikova@rtu.lv

Abstract. Requirements Engineering (RE) is among the core topics of education in Computer Science. It familiarizes students with a range of frameworks for the classification of requirements. These include frameworks that distinguish between functional and non-functional requirements, those that organize requirements into layers of abstraction (business, stakeholder, solution), practitioner-oriented taxonomies, and standards-based approaches to expressing requirements. Whilst each framework has its own distinct value, the structural differences between them have the potential to result in conceptual fragmentation within educational settings. Industrial RE tools characteristically incorporate predefined classification logic and are developed for enterprise environments. This restricts their pedagogical suitability and methodological flexibility. This paper presents a conceptual design of a RE tool for educational settings. More specifically, a conceptual model of a tool enabling the definition of alternative classification schemas at the project level while preserving conceptual consistency within a learning scenario was developed. The model also supports role-based interactions to simulate the transformation of stakeholder needs into structured solution requirements. The proposed RE tool is intended to reduce methodological rigidity in RE education by supporting structurally diverse classification approaches within a controlled and configurable environment.

Keywords: Requirements engineering education · RE tool · Requirements classification

1 Introduction

Requirements Engineering (RE) is a foundational discipline in the development of software and information systems, with a direct impact on project success. Despite its significance, teaching RE continues to present challenges. A literature review by Daun et al. [1] highlights the diversity of teaching approaches in RE and the persistent difficulties students face in applying RE concepts effectively. Similarly, Ouhbi et al. [2] observe that RE education is fragmented across various approaches and highlight the need for more

F. Zerbato et al. (Eds.): CAiSE 2026, LNBIP 587, pp. 127–134, 2026.
https://doi.org/10.1007/978-3-032-27997-2_15

structured and practice-oriented learning environments. Empirical research further indicates that students struggle with abstraction and with structuring stakeholder needs into well-defined requirements [3, 4]. Moravánszky [5] identifies ongoing challenges in RE courses, including limited practical exposure and the gap between theoretical basis and industrial practice. In addition, studies show that experiential learning and stakeholder role simulation enhances understanding of the RE processes [6, 7].

These findings suggest that current teaching approaches and industrial tools do not adequately support flexible, practice oriented RE learning. The diversity of requirements classification frameworks, including functional/non-functional distinctions [8, 9], business/stakeholder/solution hierarchies [10], and extended taxonomies, contribute to the complexity of students' learning experience. To this end the goal of this paper is to introduce a vision for an educational RE tool that supports multiple classification schemas and role-based interaction.

The RE tools can be considered as a design artifact and hence this research and development project follows the principles of design science research (DSR) [11] and specifically the DSR framework proposed by [12] focusing on the creation and study of human made artefact, specifically, a RE tool for teaching. It is intended to solve practical problems discussed in Sect. 3, thus generating contextual knowledge about how the artefact will be developed and utilized as outlined in Sect. 4. The current state of the project is that of the initial iteration. More specifically, the problem explication and initial requirements analysis phases have been completed and we are in the process of designing and developing the first version of the tool.

The rest of the paper is structured as follows. Section 2 analyses diverse requirements classification frameworks and examines their underlying conceptual assumptions. Section 3 analyzes the capabilities essential for a RE tool in an educational setting. Section 4 presents the tool design including a conceptual model of the repository of RE artifacts. Section 5 concludes the paper and outlines future work.

2 Requirements Classification Perspectives

The field of RE has developed broad knowledge of requirements classification. From the point of view of what needs to be taught in a RE course, the following five frameworks were selected (Fig. 1) to represent influential, but structurally distinct, perspectives of requirements typology:

- International standardization and attribute-based typing as defined in ISO/IEC/IEEE 29148:2018 [8] – Systems and software engineering- Life cycle processes- RE. See Fig. 1a.
- The standards-oriented requirements classification model defined in the IREB CPRE [13] Foundation level handbook. See Fig. 1b.
- The abstraction-layer hierarchy rooted in business analysis described in A Guide to the Business Analysis Body of Knowledge (BABOK) [10] published by the International Institute of Business Analysis. See Fig. 1c.
- The practitioner-oriented artifact taxonomy introduced in Karl Wiegers and Candase Hokanson [14] Software Requirements Essentials: Core Practices. Classification represented in Fig. 1d.

- The behavioral and constraint-oriented distinction presented in Ian Sommerville's [9] Software Engineering book, see Fig. 1e.

The conceptual diversity exhibited by RE theory and practice indicates that there is no uniformly recognized classification of requirements. Instead, it is subject to variation in accordance with underlying assumptions concerning abstraction, system behavior, stakeholder perspective, and documentation structure. The diversity of approaches highlights several pedagogical challenges in the context of RE education [1, 2]. Students encounter multiple classification logics across a variety of courses and materials, but when it comes to practical assignments the choice of the category is usually restricted by the choice of the tool. Moreover, if two RE or software engineering courses at the same department would like to teach different classifications, for instance, at BSc or MSc levels, then this might lead to looking for two different tools, which is inefficient. This motivates the need for a configurable RE tool for education capable of accommodating diverse classification systems within the same tool.

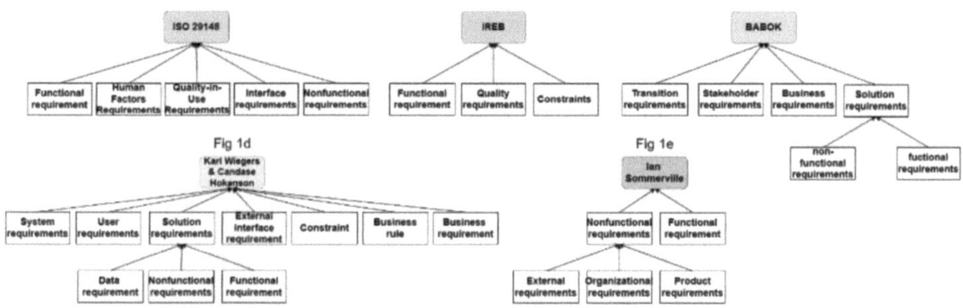

Fig. 1. Requirements classifications

3 Requirements Workshop and Analysis of Existing Tools

To better understand the challenges of teaching RE, a focused requirements workshop was conducted with five teachers of RE courses at Stockholm University and Riga Technical University. The objective of the workshop was to identify key pedagogical challenges and uncover unmet needs in current RE teaching practices.

Several recurring issues were identified. (1) Widely used professional RE tools are often financially inaccessible to universities, limiting their adoption in educational settings. In addition, many of these tools would need to be delivered in the form of pre-installed virtual machines or on a common server which is hard to manage by the teaching staff for courses with over 100 students and might not comply with tool license requirements. (2) Participants observed that when students use tools, they frequently focus on learning the tool's operational logic and functionality rather than understanding the core RE principles and methodological foundations. (3) The existence of multiple requirements classification frameworks across literature and standards was identified as a source of confusion for students, particularly when tools enforce a single predefined classification structure.

The workshop participants emphasized that effective RE education should reflect real-world practice by supporting at least two perspectives of the RE process, namely:

1. The Requirements analyst perspective, which focuses on structuring and documenting requirements correctly.
2. The Stakeholder perspective, which focuses on expressing needs, expectations, goals, and constraints from a problem domain viewpoint without necessarily adhering to formal specification structures.

The students should also be able to switch between the roles of requirements analyst and stakeholder in a course.

During the initial stages of the study as part of the problem explication phase [12], a number of widely used requirements and project management tools were examined with a view to investigating their potential application in RE courses at university level. The tools in question included ReqTest [15], Codebeamer [16], ReqView [17] and Jira with requirements management plug-ins [18]. The analysis focused on the feasibility and suitability of these resources for educational use in RE courses.

The investigation revealed several limitations from a pedagogical perspective. It is evident that a significant proportion of industrial tools are costly and designed primarily for enterprise scale project management rather than teaching and learning. The tools offer complexity and breadth of functionality that may prove overwhelming for students, thereby obscuring fundamental RE concepts. Furthermore, it is evident that these tools generally enforce predefined classification schemas, thereby reducing flexibility for exploring alternative methodological perspectives.

Existing literature also indicates that students frequently struggle with writing clear, unambiguous, and methodologically consistent requirements [3, 4]. These challenges suggest that educational tools should prioritize clarity, configurability, and conceptual transparency over advanced industrially applicable features.

In response to these findings, a configurable educational RE tool is proposed that supports multiple classification schemas and role-based interaction. By allowing teaching staff to define classification structures and assign user roles, the tool would provide a flexible learning environment that simulates industry practice while remaining accessible and pedagogically focused.

4 Requirements Classification Perspectives

In light of the workshop findings and the analysis of existing requirements classifications and RE tools, a proposal is put forward for a web-based educational RE tool designed specifically to support structured and methodologically flexible requirements learning.

4.1 Tool's Design Objectives and Requirements

In the workshop, the following tool design objectives were decided:

- Support multiple requirements classification schemas;
- Enable role-based interaction to simulate real world RE processes. The same student group should be able to act as stakeholders in one project and analysts in another;

- Focus on simplicity and educational clarity rather than industrial scale complexity;
- Avoid enforcing a single rigid methodological framework;
- Support traceability between requirements and across abstraction levels of requirements artefacts;
- Remain financially and technically accessible for academic institutions. The installation and configuration of the tool to be done with minimal resources.
- The delivery of the tool to students should be via web browser.

Unlike existing industrial tools, which are often costly, complex, and methodology-constrained, the proposed tool should be intentionally designed as a pedagogical environment. It shall allow teaching staff to configure classification schemas and requirement attributes dynamically, enabling comparison between different theoretical frameworks within a single learning environment. The tool shall support three primary roles:

- Stakeholder – defines high level needs and business-oriented requirements;
- Requirements analyst – refines stakeholder needs into structured and classified requirements;
- Administrator – configures classification schemas, requirement types and attribute structures.

Core functionalities that shall be supported by the tool include requirement creation under configurable schemas, attribute assignment and traceability relationships between requirements. Through these mechanisms, the tool should support both conceptual understanding and practical transformation processes in RE education.

4.2 A Conceptual Model of the Tool

To formally define the conceptual structure of the tool, a model illustrating its main components was developed. It defines how requirements classification schemas are defined within the tool, how requirement attributes are declared and instantiated, and how these elements are associated with user roles. See Fig. 2.

The proposed model is focused on the Requirement entity. Each Requirement is associated with exactly one RequirementType, which is defined within a specific ClassificationSchema. This design is intended to ensure conceptual consistency within a learning context, while still allowing teaching staff to select different classification frameworks across course iterations.

ClassificationSchema entity defines a set of RequirementTypes. Each RequirementType may have associated AttributeDeclarations, which define required or optional attributes. The actual values assigned to a requirement are stored as AttributeValues, thereby enabling schema configurability without altering the structural core of the system.

To facilitate industry-oriented learning, the model incorporates User and Role entities. The roles of the users, such as stakeholders or requirements analysts, determine the manner in which they interact with the requirements and, consequently, influence their responsibilities within the project. Students are organized into groups in which roles are divided, some students are designated as Requirements analysts, others as Stakeholders. This role-based structure reflects the separation of concerns observed in real world RE practice and supports the transformation of stakeholder needs into structured solution requirements.

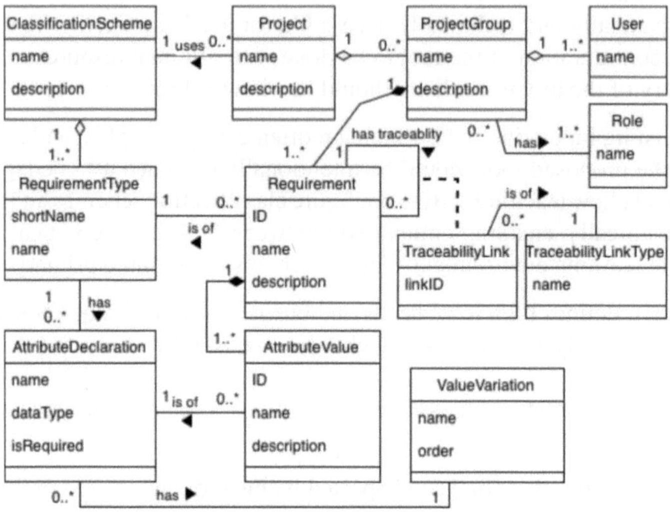

Fig. 2. A conceptual model of the RE tool prototype

Traceability link represents directed relationships between requirements of types, such as refinement, derivation, or constraint. These links facilitate the explicit modelling of abstraction levels by students, thereby enabling them to comprehend the evolution of requirements and the associated traceability.

4.3 Outline of the Tool Design

The proposed tool development is guided by core design principles derived from the previously discussed pedagogical challenges.

First, the tool enforces consistency at the project level. Only one classification schema is active within a project at any given time. This constraint prevents cognitive overload and avoids structural ambiguity for students. Different schemas may be configured across course iterations, thereby supporting methodological diversity without introducing inconsistency within a single learning scenario.

Second, the tool is structured around role-based learning. Distinct roles, such as Stakeholder and Requirements analyst, are incorporated to simulate real-world RE processes. This role separation reinforces understanding of how stakeholder needs are refined into structured requirements and highlights abstraction across multiple levels.

Finally, the tool prioritizes pedagogical simplicity. It emphasizes conceptual clarity over advanced features needed in industrial projects to avoid complexity that is unnecessary in an educational setting. The focus remains on enabling the learning of core RE principles rather than replicating comprehensive industrial tool environments.

4.4 Illustrative Scenario

To illustrate how the tool can be used in the course, a simplified description of actions is provided below. This scenario demonstrates how the tool enables explicit configuration of classification schemas.

At the beginning of the project, teaching staff members, acting in the Administrator role, define requirement types according to the chosen requirements classification scheme. For instance, types as Functional, Interface, Process and Quality requirements are created within the system. For each requirements type, the administrator configures a tailored set with attributes ensuring consistency with ISO attribute definitions [8].

During the project, students take different roles. A student acting as a Stakeholder enters a requirement describing a need or constraint. A student in the Requirements Analyst role then refines this requirement by clarifying its wording, assigning the appropriate type, specifying relevant attributes, and linking it to related system level requirements by using the traceability links of appropriate type.

Throughout the exercise, all requirements follow the configured ISO based structure. This allows students to work within a standards-aligned classification logic and to understand how requirement types and attributes are defined in practice. In a subsequent course iteration, the teaching staff may configure a different classification structure, such as a functional/non-functional model or a BABOK based hierarchy. Students can then observe how the same problem context is structured differently under alternative classification approaches.

5 Conclusions and Future Work

The classification of requirements in RE theory and practice is structurally varied. Standards based typing, abstraction layer hierarchies, behavioral distinctions and practitioner-oriented classification systems coexist without a unifying pedagogical framework. While this diversity is theoretically valuable, it introduces a degree of complexity for students who are required to navigate multiple conceptual paradigms.

The paper presented a visionary educational RE tool. Its repository for handling requirements artifacts is configurable as shown by the conceptual model that separates requirement instances from classification knowledge while maintaining project level structural consistency. The proposed approach integrates schema configurability with role-based interaction, with the objective of supporting methodological flexibility without compromising conceptual clarity.

By rethinking how requirements classification systems are represented in educational tools, this work establishes the foundation for a more adaptable and conceptually coherent approach to RE education.

Future work will focus on the implementation of a prototype and empirical classroom evaluation in order to assess the impact of schema configurability and role-based interaction on student comprehension and requirement quality. Subsequent extensions may involve the exploration of automated feedback mechanisms, including large language model (LLM) that generates feedback based on methodological sources for requirements classification frameworks as well as analytics to facilitate reflective learning.

Furthermore, the tool will also be extended towards linking requirements to candidate requirements coming from data-driven RE, as proposed in Franch et al. [19].

References

1. Daun, M., Grubb, A.M., Stenkova, V., Tenbergen, B.: A systematic literature review of requirements engineering education. Requir. Eng. **28**, 145–175 (2023)
2. Ouhbi, S., Idri, A., Fernández-Alemán, J.L., Toval, A.: Requirements engineering education: a systematic mapping study. Requir. Eng. **20**(2), 119–138 (2015)
3. Memon, R.N., Salim, S.S., Ahmad, R.: Analysis and classification of problems associated with requirements engineering education: towards an integrated view. Arab. J. Sci. Eng. **39**, 1923–1935 (2014)
4. Quintanilla Portugal, R.L., Engiel, P., Pivatelli, J., do Prado Leite, J.C.S.: Facing the challenges of teaching requirements engineering. In: Proceedings of the 38th International Conference on Software Engineering Companion (ICSE Companion), pp. 461–470. ACM (2016)
5. Moravánszky, A.: Challenges of requirements engineering education in higher education: insights from an interview study with educators in Switzerland. In: REFSQ co-Located Events 2025, CEUR Workshop Proceedings, **3959**, CEUR-WS.org (2025)
6. Otemaier, K.R., Albuquerque, R., Diniz, R., Reinehr, S., Malucelli, A.: Immersive role-playing: an experience report on a promising approach to learning requirements elicitation. In: Proceedings of the XXIII Brazilian Symposium on Software Quality (SBQS 2024), pp. 586–595. ACM, New York (2024)
7. Otemaier, K.R., Albuquerque, R., Diniz, R., Reinehr, S., Malucelli, A.: Transforming interviews into experiences: the power of immersive role playing in requirements engineering education. J. Softw. Eng. Res. Dev. **13** (2025)
8. ISO/IEC/IEEE 29148:2018: Systems and software engineering - life cycle processes - requirements engineering. International Organization for Standardization, Geneva (2018)
9. Sommerville, I.: Software Engineering, 10th edn. Pearson, Harlow (2016)
10. International Institute of Business Analysis (IIBA): A Guide to the Business Analysis Body of Knowledge (BABOK® Guide), 3rd edn. IIBA, Toronto (2015).
11. Hevner, A.R., March, S.T., Park, J., Ram, S.: Design science in information systems research. MIS Q. **28**(1), 75–105 (2004). https://doi.org/10.2307/25148625
12. Johannesson, P., Perjons, E.: An Introduction to Design Science. Springer, Cham (2014)
13. International Requirements Engineering Board (IREB): CPRE Foundation Level Handbook, version 1.2. IREB, Karlsruhe (2023)
14. Wiegers, K., Hokanson, C.: Software Requirements Essentials: Core Practices for Successful Business Analysis. Microsoft Press, Redmond (2013)
15. ReQtest: Requirements and test management tool
16. PTC: Codebeamer ALM–Application lifecycle and requirements management tool
17. ReqView: Requirements management tool
18. Rozenberga, A., Kirikova, M.: Enterprise model for requirements management: evaluation of capability gaps in Jira and marketplace applications. In: CEUR Workshop Proceedings, vol. 4171. CEUR-WS.org (2026)
19. Franch, X., Henriksson, A., Ralyté, J., Zdravkovic, J.: Data-driven agile requirements elicitation through the lenses of situational method engineering. In: Proceedings of the 29th IEEE International Requirements Engineering Conference (RE 2021). IEEE (2021)

Predictive Process Monitoring via Automated Planning

Angelo Casciani[1], Alessandra Giovannetti[1], Silvia Macagnano[1], Andrea Marrella[1(✉)], Mario Luca Bernardi[2], Marta Cimitile[3], and Fabrizio Maria Maggi[4]

[1] Sapienza University of Rome, Rome, Italy
{lastname,marrella}@diag.uniroma1.it
[2] University of Sannio, Benevento, Italy
bernardi@unisannio.it
[3] Unitelma Sapienza University, Rome, Italy
marta.cimitile@unitelma.it
[4] Free University of Bozen-Bolzano, Bolzano, Italy
maggi@inf.unibz.it

Abstract. Predictive Process Monitoring (PPM) forecasts the future behavior of ongoing business process executions to support proactive decision-making. Although state-of-the-art deep learning approaches achieve high predictive accuracy, they often act as black boxes, without explaining the execution steps that lead to a given outcome, thus limiting their applicability in scenarios requiring transparent what-if analysis. In this paper, we propose a planning-based framework for *situation prediction*, which anticipates not only whether a specific outcome is achievable but also the exact sequence of activities and data updates required to reach it. We introduce an automated pipeline that transforms event logs into PDDL planning tasks by combining process discovery with decision mining, allowing classical planners to generate compliant, goal-oriented predictions. Experiments on real-world logs show that our framework provides high solvability and predictive performance while offering transparency.

Keywords: Automated Planning · PDDL · Predictive Process Monitoring

1 Introduction and Motivation

Predictive Process Monitoring (PPM) has emerged as one of the most impactful subfields of process mining [27]. By analyzing historical *event logs* recorded by information systems, PPM techniques generate predictive models that can be queried during the ongoing execution of a business process (BP). These models aim to forecast future behavior, support proactive decision-making, and mitigate in advance operational risks.

F. Zerbato et al. (Eds.): CAiSE 2026, LNBIP 587, pp. 135–145, 2026.
https://doi.org/10.1007/978-3-032-27997-2_16

Consider a healthcare scenario in which a patient p_1 enters the hospital with suspected sepsis [12]. After the prioritization in the emergency room (*ER Sepsis Triage*) and blood tests to measure infection markers like C-reactive protein (*CRP*), doctors must decide on the next steps, such as administering intravenous antibiotics (*IV Antibiotics*) or hospitalizing p_1 in the normal care ward (*Admission NC*). By analyzing historical data from patients with similar clinical profiles, they can anticipate whether antibiotics will be prescribed or a full admission will be required. Unlike reactive BP monitoring, PPM allows for anticipating issues, and, if a high risk is predicted, doctors can proactively change the treatment path before further complications arise. Given a partial execution prefix $\alpha = \langle$*ER Sepsis Triage, CRP, Leucocytes*$\rangle$, PPM supports: (*i*) *outcome* predictions, which focus on boolean, categorical, or numerical outcomes (e.g., "*Will* p_1 *undergo antibiotics?*"); and (*ii*) *suffix* predictions, forecasting upcoming activities (e.g., "*Given* α, *will* p_1 *be admitted to the normal care and be discharged?*", resulting in the suffix $\beta = \langle$*IV Antibiotics, Admission NC, Release A*$\rangle$).

A major challenge in PPM, whose state-of-the-art technique are mainly machine learning-based, is *limited transparency* [5]. Outcome methods predict *only if* a result is achievable, but *not the sequence that produces it*, obscuring the reasoning in high-stakes scenarios. Conversely, suffix methods rely on black-box sequence matching without the causal rationale (e.g., specific clinical data) required to reach a goal, making them unsuitable for transparent what-if analyses.

In this visionary paper, we propose a paradigm shift for PPM. We argue that, to achieve transparent and actionable what-if analysis, PPM should not be treated solely as a statistical forecasting problem, but can be framed as an *Automated Planning* (AP) task based on the notion of *situation prediction.* Drawing upon the field of *reasoning about actions* [19], we define the concept of *situation* as a future state determined by the sequence of actions leading to it. In this direction, AP offers the ideal abstraction for predicting the causal effects of actions, e.g., returning a plan π that shows *how* p_1 reaches *Admission NC* given his current *CRP* levels.

AP is a branch of Artificial Intelligence (AI) that addresses the problem of generating a course of actions (i.e., a *plan*) to achieve a goal, given a description of the domain of interest and an initial state. By automatically transforming discovered BP models and decision-mining rules into standard PDDL (Planning Domain Definition Language) models [8], we can leverage off-the-shelf classical planners to synthesize future BP behaviors. Unlike neural networks, a classical planner does not guess the most likely next token, but it formally proves whether a specific target situation is reachable from the current state and returns the executable plan (i.e., the suffix) required to achieve it. We note that, in recent years, the planning community has produced a wide range of classical planners incorporating highly effective search heuristics (i.e., capable of scaling to large problems), which have been applied to tackle challenging tasks across multiple areas of Computer Science [13,14].

Through this paper, we outline the conceptual framework required to enable planning-based PPM, provide preliminary evidence of its feasibility using standard event logs, and lay out a roadmap for future research.

2 Background

PPM relies on historical data captured in *event logs*, usually represented in the IEEE *eXtensible Event Stream* (XES) standard format[1]. A log is a collection of *traces*, where each trace represents a single execution instance of a BP. Each event within a trace records an executed activity, its timestamp, and a payload of data attributes.

To formally reason about both the sequence of activities and the evolution of data payloads, we conceptualize the BP as a *Data Petri Net* (DPN) [23]. Unlike industry-standard languages like BPMN (lacking a rigorous execution semantics) or traditional Petri nets that model only the control-flow (i.e., the ordering and concurrency of activities via places, transitions, and token markings), DPNs provide an unambiguous semantics and explicitly include the data perspective, enriching transitions with *guard conditions* over data variables (thus, a transition can only fire if the control-flow marking enables it and the current data state satisfies its guard conditions). This aspect makes DPNs the ideal foundation for our *situation prediction*: the PPM task of determining not just *if* an ongoing instance (i.e., a trace prefix) will reach a specific target outcome, but exactly *what sequence* of control-flow steps and data updates is required to achieve it.

3 Related Work

PPM techniques are broadly categorized into model-based and machine learning approaches [6]. Traditional model-based methods (e.g., stochastic Petri nets) [20,28] mainly focus on time or simple suffix estimation, lacking flexible support for goal-driven predictions under complex data constraints. Conversely, deep learning (DL) models [18,26] dominate current literature due to their high accuracy but act as opaque black boxes. While recent efforts employ Large Language Models (LLMs) [16] or neuro-symbolic approaches [15] to improve interpretability, they remain data-hungry and struggle to guarantee compliance.

To address the black-box nature of DL, recent research in AI has explored the usage of LLMs that, relying on techniques like chain-of-thought prompting, can generate intermediate "reasoning traces" or step-by-step explanations alongside their predictions. However, recent literature in AP [4,10] highlighted that generating intermediate tokens should not be anthropomorphized as transparent reasoning but rather considered as probabilistic artifacts. Indeed, they documented a severe disconnect between the generated explanation and the final outcome, frequently lacking *faithfulness*: models can generate plausible and coherent explanations that are logically invalid or hallucinate constraints.

[1] IEEE Standard for XES: https://xes-standard.org/.

While it can be argued that LLMs offer flexibility in handling unstructured contexts, and that hallucinations can be mitigated by tuning generation parameters (e.g., lowering the temperature), in critical compliance-driven BPs, merely reducing the probability of an error is insufficient. This is an important limitation for PPM: as LLMs do not natively compute reachability over a defined state space, even a low-temperature model risks hallucinating a sequence of activities that violates core BP control-flow rules or data constraints. This reasoning flaw motivates our vision: true transparency and actionable predictions cannot be achieved through statistical text generation or likelihood estimations. Instead, it requires the formal synthesis of plans that are mathematically proven to be executable and compliant. To achieve this, we propose a *pure planning-based paradigm*. By automatically translating event logs into PDDL via process discovery and decision mining, we use classical planners to synthesize goal-oriented predictions, and our approach, differently from DL-based methods, our approach requires no training and guarantees that every predicted sequence is valid with respect to the process structural and data constraints.

4 A Planning-Based PPM Framework

To realize our vision of transparent PPM, we propose a framework to reduce the situation predictions to a planning task. By automatically encoding the BP control-flow and data constraints into PDDL, we can rely on off-the-shelf classical planners to synthesize sound predictions. A *classical planning task* in PDDL is specified through: a *domain*, defining the structure of the environment, and a *problem*, which describes a specific instance. A PDDL domain includes a set of *predicates*, specifying the properties and relations that can hold, and a set of *actions* Ω. An action schema $a \in \Omega$ specifies *parameters*, *preconditions* for action executability, and deterministic *effects* describing how it changes the world state. A PDDL problem complements the domain by specifying an *initial state* and a *goal condition*. The planner's objective is to find a *plan* that transitions the initial state into one satisfying the goal. In this work, we focus on *classical planning tasks* in PDDL 1.2. and Action Description Language (ADL) [17].

As illustrated in Fig. 1, our PPM approach includes two stages: the translation of a XES event log into PDDL (i.e., *model construction*) and the situation prediction performed using a classical planner (i.e., *model application*).

Model Construction. In the initial phase, the event log is processed by the Parser to capture distinct BP perspectives. First, to extract the control-flow rules, our framework supports a suite of process discovery algorithms (i.e., Inductive, Heuristics, ILP, and Alpha miners [1]). Second, we apply decision mining [21] at the model choice points to get data constraints. Specifically, for every decision point, we train a decision tree (inherently interpretable) to predict the next activity based on the available data attributes (e.g., predicting that a patient undergoes the sepsis triage if their "*CRP*" level is high). This approach naturally discretizes continuous numerical attributes into meaningful intervals (e.g., "*Leucocytes*" ≤ 12.5).

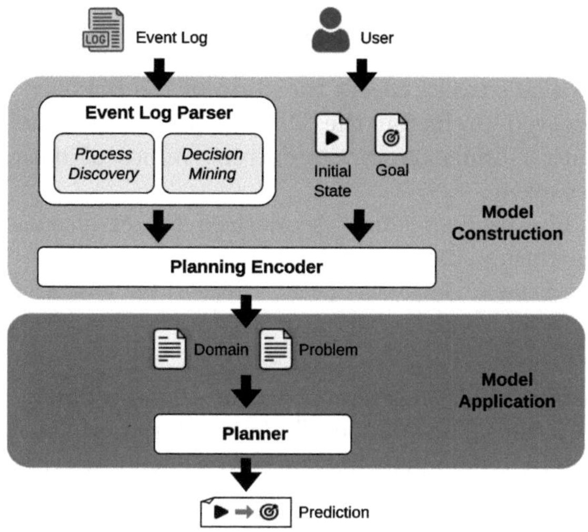

Fig. 1. Framework architecture. The XES log is converted into PDDL domain and problem files with initial states and goals, enabling the planner to generate situation predictions.

To operationalize the extracted information, the Parser produces a DPN, and the Encoder first translates its control- and data-flow into a PDDL domain.

- **Control-flow.** The DPN structure is modeled using two predicates: `(completed ?a - activity)` to track the execution history, and `(enabled ?a - activity)` to indicate that a transition is structurally executable according to the marking.
- **Data-flow.** Classical planners do not natively handle continuous numeric values. We discretize them into intervals based on the discovered decision thresholds (e.g., a guard representing $[n1, n2)$). These intervals are encoded as PDDL *constants* (e.g., `gte_n1_lt_n2`) and assigned via predicates like `(num-attr ?v - num-type)`.
- **Split Actions.** To handle activities that generate or modify data (e.g., a blood test), we adopt a *split action* encoding. We generate mutually exclusive PDDL actions for each possible data outcome (e.g., `exec_test_lte_n1` and `exec_test_gte_n1_lt_n2`). These actions share the same control-flow precondition (e.g., `(enabled test)`) but yield different data effects. The planner leverages this input-determinism to select the split action required to satisfy downstream goals.
- **Decision Rules.** The rules discovered by the decision miner are strictly enforced as *preconditions* on subsequent actions. For instance, if `next_act1` is only permitted when the test result is lower than $n1$, its PDDL definition will require both `(enabled next_act1)` and `(num-attr lte_n1)`. This mathematically guarantees that the planner cannot take branches that violate the business data rules.

Then, for each predictive query, a PDDL problem file is generated:

- **Initial State.** The `:init` reflects the state of the ongoing BP instance. We replay the observed prefix on the DPN to determine the `completed` and `enabled` activities, and extract the current values of data attributes from the prefix's last event.
- **Goal State.** The user specifies the desired target situation in the `:goal` section. The latter can be a combination of control-flow (e.g., `(completed next_act1)`) and data conditions (e.g., `(num-attr gte_n1_lt_n2)`).

Model Application. This phase requires the PDDL domain and problem for the *situation prediction*. The planner finds a solution that, starting from the initial execution prefix (which may also be empty), achieves the user-defined goal situation (e.g., *"patient discharged with leukocyte level smaller or equal than x"*). A classical planner optimizes for plan length by assuming unit costs, so it will return the shortest valid sequence of activities that transforms the initial into the goal state. Since the PDDL domain encodes the discovered DPN, the planner can not hallucinate solutions. If a solution is found, it necessarily corresponds to an executable and transparent sequence of activities and data updates that leads to the specified situation.

Implementation. For the proof-of-concept, we used the discovery algorithms provided by the PM4Py library [3] and we implemented both the Parser and the Encoder in Python. For the prediction module, i.e., the planner, we employed Fast Downward [9].

5 Illustrative Example and Preliminary Evaluation

To concretely illustrate our vision, we examine an example from the *Sepsis Cases* event log [12], which records the trajectories of patients with suspected sepsis in a hospital and presents an unstructured control-flow with multiple payload attributes that make it relevant to test the planner's predictive capabilities over data conditions.

Consider a scenario where a patient has just been admitted to the emergency room, triaged, and has undergone initial blood tests. The current trace prefix is: ⟨*ER Registration, ER Triage, ER Sepsis Triage, CRP*⟩. The clinician wants to know: *"What is the required sequence of clinical steps to ensure this patient is safely discharged, given that their current CRP level is severely high (i.e., >100 mg/L)?"*

Consider predicting a path for a registered patient, hypothesizing a scenario where he exhibits infection markers (e.g., high CRP) and reaches the sepsis triage. The initial state reflects the registration completion, while the goal enforces the target situation.

If we feed this prefix and data payload into a Long Short-Term Memory (LSTM) or Transformer-based PPM model trained on this log, it will output a probability distribution. It might predict that the next most likely activity is "Leucocytes test" (e.g., 60% probability) and that the ultimate probability of a safe discharge is low (e.g., 20%). However, the model provides no guidance on *how* to improve those odds or *what exact clinical protocol* must be followed to achieve the discharge, and if we ask an LLM to explain the neural network's prediction, it may hallucinate a plausible-sounding explanations that do not conform to the hospital's protocols.

In our planning framework, this query is formulated as a PDDL problem where:

- the *initial state* sets the DPN marking to the state immediately following the `CRP test`, and the data predicate is set to `(crp_level gte_147)`.
- the *goal* is set to `(completed Release_A)` (i.e., the standard discharge).

When invoked, the planner explores the state space defined by the discovered DPN. Rather than a probabilistic guess, and based on the decision-mining result that high CRP levels route patients toward specific interventions before discharge, it synthesizes the following sound plan, providing clinicians with a transparent, actionable, and compliant path: $\pi = \langle$`exec_Leucocytes_test`, `exec_IV_Antibiotics` (triggered because $CRP > 147$), `exec_Admission_IC`, `exec_Release_A`$\rangle$.

5.1 Preliminary Evaluation

To assess the computational feasibility and predictive ability of our framework, we conducted a preliminary evaluation using well-established event logs: (*i*) *Sepsis* [12]; (*ii*) *BPI Challenge* (BPIC) *2012 W*, representing the work items of the whole dataset [7]; and (*iii*) *BPIC 2013*, in *closed problems* (CP) and *incidents* (I) versions [24,25]. Following standard PPM protocols, we split the logs chronologically (80% for DPN discovery, 20% for testing). To test the planner, we generated incremental trace prefixes, i.e., we iteratively provided the first k events of each test trace as the observed prefix and tasked the planner with predicting the remaining sequence. We plan to adopt cross-validation techniques in future extensions to consolidate the validity of our findings further. Table 1 summarizes the results, using the Inductive Miner [11] and an optimal search strategy (i.e., A* with a blind heuristic). Note that *outcome prediction* was evaluated exclusively on the *Sepsis* log because it contains a richer set of data attributes (for clinical test results) helpful to define target data-state goals.

The preliminary outcomes validate our vision in four directions:

- Formulating PPM problems as planning tasks is highly efficient. Across all tested logs, grounding the PDDL domain and executing the state-space search took negligible time. The planner experienced zero timeouts, and when it failed to find a path, it was mainly due to the structural unsolvability of the discovered DPN.

Table 1. The preliminary results reflect the three supported predictive tasks: *situation prediction* (in terms of structural reachability, grounding overhead GT, plan length difference ΔL, and search time ST), *suffix prediction* (sequence similarity to ground-truth traces), and *outcome prediction* (solvability and similarity, evaluated *only* on the Sepsis log).

Event Log	Situation				Suffix	Outcome	
	Solv. (%)	GT (s)	ΔL	ST (s)	DL Sim. (%)	Solv. (%)	DL Sim. (%)
BPI12 A	100.0	0.06	−0.67	0.00	95.21	–	–
BPI12 W	31.0	0.30	−1.27	0.00	25.95	–	–
BPI13 CP	100.0	0.01	−1.53	0.00	90.45	–	–
BPI13 I	48.8	0.02	−0.69	0.00	95.09	–	–
Sepsis Cases	100.0	0.03	−1.60	0.01	95.94	100.0	91.4

- The situation prediction results demonstrated that the planner consistently finds the shortest valid sequence (i.e., the "*happy path*") to target situations (i.e., conjunctions of control-flow and data conditions). While this idealized trajectory may underestimate real-world inefficiencies, it shifts decision support from forecasting suboptimal human behaviors to prescribing the most efficient and compliant interventions.
- Regarding suffix prediction, the framework achieved high normalized Damerau-Levenshtein (DL) similarity to the expected historical traces in logs from which a high-fitness DPN could be reliably discovered. However, in *BPI12 W*, the similarity dropped to $\sim$ 26%, highlighting that while DL models attempt to mimic noisy behaviors, the planner synthesizes the ideal compliant path, reporting what should happen according to the discovered rules, rather than guessing what a human might do.
- When tasked with an outcome prediction in the sepsis log, i.e., querying the planner to find plans leading to a target data-flow state, the planner achieved perfect solvability, consistently finding plans that achieved the goal state.

6 Conclusion and Research Roadmap

In this paper, we introduced a PPM framework that formulates prediction as a classical AP task by integrating process discovery and decision mining. This enables *situation predictions*: transparent forecasts that determine not only if an outcome is achievable, but the exact activity sequence required to reach it. The preliminary outcomes demonstrate that formulating PPM as an AP problem is not only conceptually sound but computationally feasible. The main advantage of our planning-based approach is *transparency*. Indeed, any resulting plan can be verified via model checking [2], ensuring trustworthy decisions in high-stakes domains like healthcare. However, realizing the full potential of this vision requires addressing the following research challenges (RCs).

RC1: Beyond the Strong Completeness Assumption. Our framework, like many PPM model-based approaches, operates under the *strong completeness assumption*, assuming that the discovered DPN captures all valid behaviors. However, real-world logs are noisy, and BP executions may deviate. If a deep learning model encounters a deviating trace, it simply predicts the next most likely event or outcome. In contrast, a planner will fail to ground the initial state if the trace cannot be replayed on the DPN.

To address this matter, we plan to integrate *conformance checking* techniques into the framework. When an ongoing trace deviates from the model, an alignment algorithm could be dynamically invoked to map the noisy prefix to the closest valid marking in the DPN, which acts as the planning initial state. This integration enables the framework to robustly handle deviations without sacrificing the soundness guarantee that the prediction remains compliant with the encoded rules.

RC2: Temporal Prescriptions. While the current approach predicts the plan to reach a goal, time is an important missing dimension for real-world PPM applicability, as stakeholders often need to know not just *what* to do, but also *when* to do it (i.e., complementing the situation prediction with remaining time prediction [28]).

Our idea is to extend the framework from classical to *temporal* planning [8], to encode in PDDL also the duration of activities and the waiting times between them mined from the event log. A temporal planner could then synthesize schedules that not only sound sequences of events but also optimize for time, moving from predictive to actionable prescriptive insights, e.g., "*to ensure a safe discharge within 48 h, antibiotics must be administered immediately, and a new blood test must conclude within 4 h*".

RC3: Embedding Real Stochasticity. Our framework manages data uncertainty via "input-determinism", creating mutually exclusive, deterministic action variants for different data outcomes. While this enables classical planning and the exploration of what-if scenarios, it does not truly account for real-world BP execution stochasticity.

To tackle this, we aim to explore *probabilistic* planning (e.g., using Markov decision processes in RDDL [22]). By mining control- and data-flow probabilities, probabilistic planners produce general *policies* (rather than linear plans) that guide practitioners along the optimal path, independent of specific events or outcomes.

RC4: Operational Integration and Decision Support. We envision integrating the framework into operational BP management systems as a continuous prescriptive engine: as event streams are ingested, the planner can synthesize *intervention plans*.

Future research will explore interactive interfaces where domain experts can tweak data parameters on the fly to visualize alternative compliant paths, enabling a sound human-in-the-loop approach to decision support.

Reproducibility. The appendix, source code, and instructions for reproducibility are available at: https://github.com/angelo-casciani/xes2plan.

Acknowledgments. This work was supported by the Sapienza FOND-AIBPM, PRIN 2022 MOTOWN, and NRRP MUR PE0000013-FAIR projects. A. Casciani conducted this work while enrolled in the National Doctorate in AI run by Sapienza (CUP B53C23003500006, Mission 4 NRRP Generic Research Scholarship, Component 1).

References

1. Augusto, A., et al.: Automated discovery of process models from event logs: review and benchmark. IEEE Trans. Knowl. Data Eng. **31**(4), 686–705 (2019)
2. Baier, C., Katoen, J.P.: Principles of Model Checking. MIT Press, Cambridge (2008)
3. Berti, A.: Pm4py: a process mining library for Python. Softw. Impacts **17** (2023)
4. Bhambri, S., et al.: Interpretable traces, unexpected outcomes: investigating the disconnect in trace-based knowledge distillation. CoRR abs/2505.13792 (2025)
5. Ceravolo, P., Comuzzi, M., De Weerdt, et al.: Predictive process monitoring: concepts, challenges, and future research directions. Process Sci. **1**(1), 1–22 (2024)
6. Di Francescomarino, C., Ghidini, C.: Predictive process monitoring. In: van der Aalst, W.M.P., Carmona, J. (eds) Process Mining Handbook. LNBIP, vol. 448, pp. 320–346. Springer, Cham (2022). https://doi.org/10.1007/978-3-031-08848-3_10
7. van Dongen, B.: BPI challenge 2012 (2012). https://doi.org/10.4121/uuid:3926db30-f712-4394-aebc-75976070e91f, https://data.4tu.nl/articles/dataset/BPI_Challenge_2012/12689204/1
8. Fox, M., Long, D.: PDDL2.1: an extension to PDDL for expressing temporal planning domains. JAIR **20** (2003)
9. Helmert, M.: The fast downward planning system. J. Artif. Intell. Res. **26**, 191–246 (2006)
10. Kambhampati, S.: Stop anthropomorphizing intermediate tokens as reasoning/thinking traces! CoRR abs/2504.09762 (2025)
11. Leemans, S.J.J.: Discovering block-structured process models from event logs containing infrequent behaviour. In: BPM 2013 International Workshops (2013)
12. Mannhardt, F., Blinde, D.: Analyzing the trajectories of patients with sepsis using process mining. In: 8th International WS on Enterprise Modeling and Information Systems Architecture (EMISA), pp. 72–80 (2017)
13. Marrella, A.: Automated planning for business process management. J. Data Semant. **8**(2) (2019)
14. Marrella, A., Mecella, M.: Continuous planning for solving business process adaptivity. In: BPMDS 2025 (2011)
15. Mezini, A., Umili, E., Donadello, I., Maggi, F.M., Mancanelli, M., Patrizi, F.: Neuro-symbolic predictive process monitoring. CoRR abs/2509.00834 (2025)
16. Pasquadibisceglie, V., Appice, A., Malerba, D.: LUPIN: a LLM approach for activity suffix prediction in business process event logs. In: ICPM'24. IEEE (2024)
17. Pednault, E.P.D.: ADL: exploring the middle ground between STRIPS and the situation calculus. In: KR'89, pp. 324–332 (1989)
18. Rama-Maneiro, E., Monteagudo-Lago, P., Vidal, J.C., Lama, M.: Encoder-decoder model for suffix prediction in predictive monitoring (2022). arXiv:CoRR/2211.16106

19. Reiter, R.: Knowledge in Action. MIT Press, Cambridge (2001)
20. Rogge-Solti, A., Weske, M.: Prediction of remaining service execution time using stochastic petri nets with arbitrary firing delays. In: ICSOC'13, pp. 389–403 (2013)
21. Rozinat, A., van der Aalst, W.M.P.: Decision mining in ProM. In: BPM'06 (2006)
22. Sanner, S.: Relational dynamic influence diagram language (RDDL): language description. Unpublished MS. Australian National University **32**(27), 12 (2010)
23. Sibertin-Blanc, C.: High level petri nets with data structure. In: 6th European Workshop on Application and Theory of Petri nets, pp. 141–168 (1985)
24. Steeman, W.: BPI challenge 2013, closed problems (2013). https://doi.org/10.4121/uuid:c2c3b154-ab26-4b31-a0e8-8f2350ddac11
25. Steeman, W.: BPI challenge 2013, incidents (2013). https://doi.org/10.4121/uuid:500573e6-accc-4b0c-9576-aa5468b10cee, https://data.4tu.nl/articles/dataset/BPI_Challenge_2013_incidents/12693914/1
26. Tax, N., Verenich, I., La Rosa, M., Dumas, M.: Predictive business process monitoring with LSTM neural networks. In: Dubois, E., Pohl, K. (eds.) CAiSE 2017. LNCS, vol. 10253, pp. 477–492. Springer, Cham (2017). https://doi.org/10.1007/978-3-319-59536-8_30
27. van der Aalst, W.M.P.: Process mining: a 360 degree overview. In: van der Aalst, W.M.P., Carmona, J. (eds.) Process Mining Handbook. LNBIP, vol. 448, pp. 3–34. Springer, Cham (2022). https://doi.org/10.1007/978-3-031-08848-3_1
28. van der Aalst, W.M., Schonenberg, M.H., Song, M.: Time prediction based on process mining. Inf. Syst. **36**(2), 450–475 (2011)

CAiSE 2026 Forum – Tool Papers

MLegis: Demonstrating a Property Graph-Based Information System for Legislative Analytics

Soroush Ahrari, Anna Bernasconi(✉), Francesco Invernici, and Andrea Colombo

Dipartimento di Elettronica, Informazione e Bioingegneria, Politecnico di Milano, Milano, Italy
soroush.ahrari@mail.polimi.it,
{anna.bernasconi,francesco.invernici,andrea1.colombo}@polimi.it

Abstract. Analyzing the complexity and interconnections of legislation poses significant challenges for information systems that must manage richly structured, temporally evolving institutional data. Traditional document-centric approaches fail to adequately capture the relational and dynamic nature of regulatory ecosystems. We present **MLegis**, an information system engineered to model, manage, and analyze legislative corpora through a property graph conceptualization. The system represents laws, articles, governments, and legislatures as interconnected entities enriched with structural, temporal, and linguistic properties. This modeling approach enables expressive path-based querying, impact analysis, and longitudinal analytics over constantly updating legislation. **MLegis** adopts a layered architecture comprising a graph data layer, a GraphQL-based service layer, and an interactive frontend supporting advanced statistical analysis, readability assessment, and LLM-assisted reporting. We demonstrate the platform on the Italian legislation use case and evaluate it through a user study assessing usability, perceived utility, and learning impact. Results confirm the effectiveness of the proposed architecture in supporting knowledge-intensive analysis tasks. The proposed modeling and architectural approach is generalizable to other regulatory domains, contributing to the engineering of data-intensive legislative information systems. **Tool:** https://mlegis.eu/. **Video:** https://gmql.eu/mlegis_demo.html.

Keywords: Property Graphs · Knowledge Graphs · Legislative Information Systems · Graph Analytics · Digital Governance

1 Introduction

Legislative corpora constitute complex and continuously evolving regulatory ecosystems. Laws are not isolated documents but highly interconnected artifacts linked through citations, amendments, repeals, and temporal dependencies. Understanding this structure is essential for researchers, policymakers, and

F. Zerbato et al. (Eds.): CAiSE 2026, LNBIP 587, pp. 149–157, 2026.
https://doi.org/10.1007/978-3-032-27997-2_17

legal professionals; monitoring its evolution is crucial for evaluating the quality of legislation and identifying trends and correlations with economic analysis [14]. However, traditional systems are primarily document-centric and focus on structuring and modelling the internal content of the laws [13], rather than large-scale relational and analytical exploration.

To address this limitation, we developed `MLegis` (https://mlegis.eu), a graph-based information system that models legislative data as a property graph [3] by representing laws, articles, governments, and legislatures as interconnected entities enriched with structural, temporal, and linguistic properties. The demonstration showcases how this underlying data-centric design enables:

- Structural exploration of legal dependencies (e.g., amendments, repeals, citations),
- Longitudinal analysis of legislative production and complexity,
- Comparative evaluation across legislatures and governments,
- Integration of readability and complexity metrics and LLM-assisted reporting within a unified analytical workflow.

By leveraging a graph-based conceptual model for evolving legislative ecosystems, this demo paper introduces (i) an information architecture that operationalizes this model; ii) an integration of graph analytics and LLM-driven reporting within the structured information framework. The Italian legislative system serves as a prototype demonstration, which is empirically validated via a user study conducted to assess the platform's usability and utility by a general public of non-domain experts. `MLegis` illustrates how property graph technologies can be engineered into a coherent information system supporting knowledge-intensive analysis, digital governance transparency, and data-driven monitoring of legislative quality.

2 Model, Architecture, and Functionalities

2.1 The Legislative Property Graph

The power of `MLegis` stems from strong conceptual modeling choices at its core. Fundamental requirements for the data model include capturing temporal evolution, multi-level granularity (with potential expansion to levels of governance), inter-textual dependencies, and versioning.

We model the corpus of Italian legislation using the Property Graph model [10], paired with the Graph Query Language (GQL), recently become an ISO standard [7]. This model has been selected in [2] over RDF or relational models for its ability to combine semantics and properties in a flexible and rich schema, capturing complex, multifaceted relationships in legal data and best supporting path-based reasoning, impact analysis, and dependency propagation.

The knowledge graph schema is depicted in Fig. 1. Key entities are represented as **nodes**. A `Law` is a specific legislative act. `LawUnit` (i.e., `Article` and `Attachment`) are granular parts of a law, depending on their nature. `Legislature` and `Government` are the political entities that participated in the

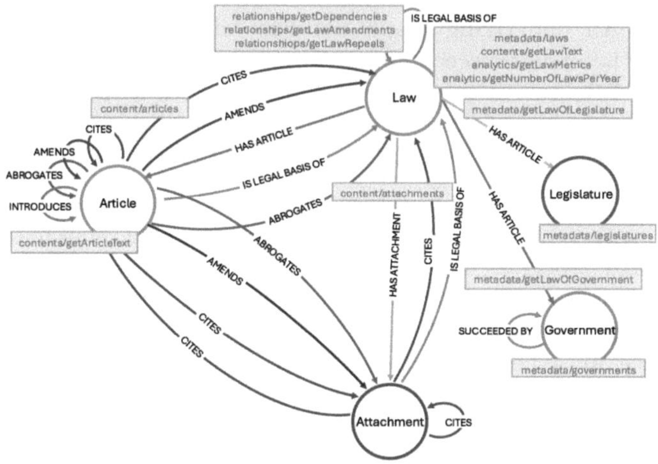

Fig. 1. Legislative Property Graph, schema, and APIs.

process of enacting the law. Relationships are modeled as directed **edges**, including `AMENDS`, `CITES`, `ABROGATES`, `IS_LEGAL_BASIS_OF`, linking `Law` or `Article` nodes, forming the core legal network. Both nodes and edges store rich metadata, as **properties**. For instance, an `Article` node stores its full text, publication date, and pre-computed linguistic metrics (e.g., Gulpease index [11], word count). An `AMENDS` edge can store the date the amendment took effect. Combining such properties through graph queries allows us to derive law versions or to compute advanced traversals that leverage both properties and links among nodes (such as computing the stock of laws in force at a certain date).

The model is currently being expanded to integrate regional and European legislative levels. In [2], an ETL pipeline was implemented to import data from unstructured data sources (e.g., Normattiva [8]); the content is transformed and enriched with NLP and LLM-based modules, then loaded onto a graph database instance (see Fig. 2, left side). The obtained graph allows us to answer complex queries that blend text analytics, relational structure, and temporal analysis, such as "*Show me the average readability score of all laws that amend Law X, grouped by the enacting government*" as well as feed smart search and reactive applications, that monitor relevant evolution of laws, such as the creation of formal *legislative voids* [3,4].

2.2 System Architecture

`MLegis` follows a three-layered architecture (Fig. 2) enabling a decoupling of the conceptual model from application services, with the possibility of extension toward additional legislative systems (to be modeled in the graph), and the prospective integration with external analytics modules in the future.

Data Layer: An underlying graph database stores the legislative property graph; we use the open-source solution provided by Memgraph [12]. The graph includes about 74k law nodes, 318k article nodes, 127k attachment nodes, 107k legal basis dependencies, 64k abrogations, 80k amendments, and 228k generic citations, with 68 governments and 20 legislatures. The content is updated daily.

Backend (API): A backend server exposes GraphQL API [5], translating frontend user requests into Cypher [6] queries that match paths on the graph, and post-processes the results. Each service exposes specific queries as illustrated in the gray boxes (overlaying the involved node/edge) in Fig. 1, including for instance the possibilities to retrieve the text of an article in force at a certain date (`contents/getArticleText`), the laws published by a specific government (`metadata/getLawOfGovernment`), the amendments of a law (`relationships/getLawAmendments`), or the counts per legislature (`analytics/getNumerOfLawsPerYear`).

Frontend: A web application renders interactive visualizations and query-building tools, including an LLM step for producing reports. Its architecture, implemented in React, has a *Client Layer*, an *Application Layer* (handled through the App Router) with APIs and Pages, and a *Service Layer* interacting directly with the API and the online Redis in-memory datastore.

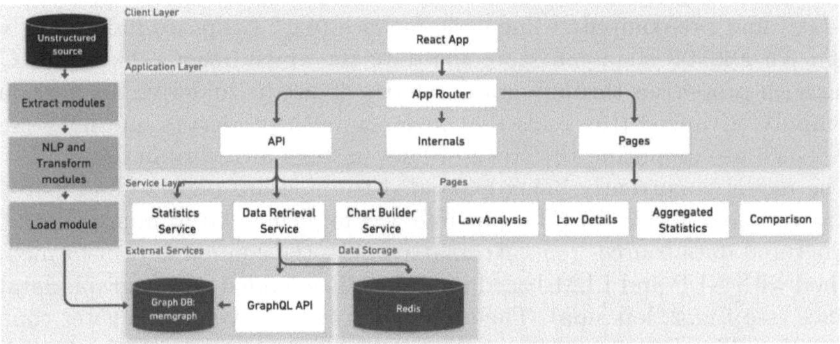

Fig. 2. System architecture of the `MLegis` platform.

2.3 Key Functionalities

The graph backend powers a rich, user-centric frontend with the following pages:

Law Analysis: Users can search for laws using several filters and receive a detailed report, including full text, metadata, and a suite of linguistic/statistical metrics (e.g., readability indices, sentence length); single laws can be clicked and analyzed in depth using the **Law Details** page. This includes an LLM-driven summarization functionality and a tool for comparing a law with other sets of laws, fetched according to user-defined features. Filters translate into combining paths and properties in the underlying Cypher statements.

Aggregated Statistics: Users can generate interactive charts. Aside from predefined visualizations, an *Advanced builder* allows us to select chart type, year/domain/legislature/government variables on the x-axis, and counts/indices on the y-axis, with different aggregation modes. Typical visualizations plot metrics (e.g., complexity, frequency of a term) over time. Underlying queries require extracting paths of arbitrary length in the graph: for instance, counting repeals per year involves (i) detecting the existence of (full) abrogation relationships that (ii) repeal all article nodes that are connected to the same law.

Comparison: Linguistic and readability metrics can be compared across governments or legislatures to evaluate and juxtapose their quality of legislation; overlapping/colored distribution charts are used, with the possibility of normalizing bins to make sample sizes statistically comparable.

3 Demonstration Scenarios

For feeding MLegis, we leverage the entire Property Graph of the Italian legislative corpus [2]. Nevertheless, the modeling methodology is transferable to other domains and the model can be adapted to other regulatory ecosystems or contribute to digital government information systems (as a preliminary test, we built the graphs of US [1] and Swiss legislative systems). Below, we overview three representative use scenarios.

Scenario 1: Single Law Analysis & Readability. The "Law Analysis" tool allows to instantly retrieve Italian laws, showcasing their pre-computed linguistic metrics. The platform assesses readability (e.g., Gulpease index) and compares its complexity to the average for that legislature. One such example can be inspected in Fig. 3A, where the Italian Constitution has been selected by using the left panel filters. The central part of the screen shows the text of the law divided by article; the right column provides the comparison context upon which the law is analyzed. The Constitution uses a considerably low number of words and sentences (w.r.t. the whole corpus distribution), with readability indices positioned around the median of the distribution. *This scenario illustrates the capability of the underlying graph model to combine structural, temporal, and linguistic properties within a unified queryable framework.*

Scenario 2: Historical Trend Analysis. The "Aggregated Statistics" module of the platform can be used to plot the (i) the law count per year; (ii) the repeal count per year; (iii) the average readability score (e.g., Gulpease) per year; and (iv) the use of gerunds per year (see Fig. 3B for reference). *These and other plots of choice of users highlight the platform's ability to support historical and political science analysis, grounded in data modelled as a graph.*

Scenario 3: Comparative Law Analysis. Users can experiment with comparing different metrics between two or more governments or legislatures (see filters set in Fig. 3C). Figure 3D shows the overlaying distributions of the Government currently run by Giorgia Meloni (since Oct 2022) and by Matteo Renzi (Feb 2014–Dec 2016). The most recent one has so far produced 653 laws, while the former produced 660. There is a significant difference in the 'Average sentence length' measure (59.5 vs 54.95), while the readability index distribution shows no clear difference. *This scenario overall demonstrates the tangible benefits of the used data and knowledge model for legislative analysis.*

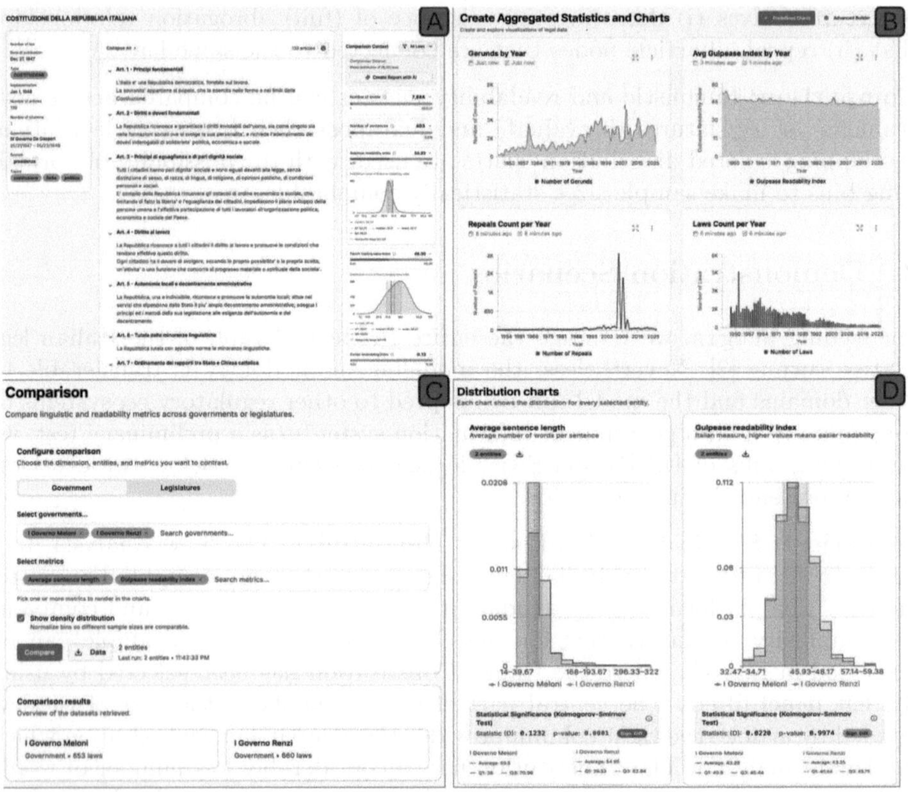

Fig. 3. Example screens illustrating the Law Details (A), the Aggregated Statistics (B), and the Comparison (C–D) functionalities.

3.1 User Study Evaluation

While the data and information quality of the knowledge graph has been discussed in [2] and the information system effectiveness as a search platform has been assessed in [4,9], here we aim to preliminarily evaluate the platform's usability, given its design.

We conducted a small user study with 21 participants, comprising 11 PhD-level students and 10 individuals from the general public, the two intended target categories for our platform (i.e., researchers and interested citizens). The study involved a set of representative tasks that utilized all functionalities of the platform, such as analyzing the quality of individual laws by producing an LLM-based report summarizing readability metrics or detecting aggregated trends in law production (i.e., identifying whether the average quality is decreasing).

Interactiveness and Ease of Use: Using standard questionnaires, we assessed the intuitiveness and integration of the website's functionalities (based on the criterion: "*The website functionalities are intuitive, easy to use, and well-integrated*") and the overall perception of convenience/difficulty in using the tool (based on the criterion: "*I found the website very inconvenient/difficult to use*").

Utility: Through task success rates and qualitative feedback, we measured how useful the various website functionalities were perceived (based on the criterion: "*The various functions of this website were useful to my purpose*").

Learning and Impact: We also evaluated the perceived speed with which users felt they could learn to use the platform (based on the criterion: "*Most people would learn to use this website very quickly*") and whether they learned something new about Italian legislation through the platform's use (based on the criterion: "*I learned something I did not know about Italian legislation*"). Finally, we included an evaluation of the perceived importance of monitoring of legislative quality using metrics (based on the criterion: "*I believe that monitoring through objective metrics of legislative quality is important*").

The user study results, summarized in Table 1, provide strong validation of the platform's core utility and relevance. Participants distinctly agreed that the functions are useful and that objective monitoring of legislative quality is important. Furthermore, the platform had a significant educational impact, as participants reported learning new information. While the overall perception of 'Intuitiveness and Integration' was positive, the lowest score was recorded for learning speed. This suggests that, while the platform's value is clear and its complexity is manageable, future efforts should focus on optimizing the initial user experience and documentation to ensure a faster and more uniform learning curve across all user profiles.

Table 1. Results based on a 5-point Likert Scale (1 = Strongly Disagree, 5 = Strongly Agree). The columns represent the mean and standard deviation for the following six criteria assessed by the participants: (i) functionalities are intuitive and well-integrated, (ii) the website is inconvenient/difficult to use (lower score indicates better result), (iii) the various website functions are useful, (iv) most people would learn to use the website quickly, (v) the participant learned something new about Italian legislation, and (vi) monitoring legislative quality via objective metrics is important.

Metric	Intuitiveness & Integration	Perceived difficulty	Utility	Learning speed	Learned information	Monitoring importance
Mean	3.90	1.86	4.48	3.67	4.14	4.48
SD	0.94	0.94	0.57	1.15	0.86	0.87

4 Conclusion

MLegis is a powerful and intuitive platform that leverages a property graph model to unlock new insights from complex legislative data.

Our main contribution is the design of a conceptual model of a graph-based data representation that enables advanced analytical services for legislative data, serving a broad audience, effectively employing graph technologies to enhance accessibility and monitoring of constantly changing legislative information. By integrating linguistic analysis, historical trends, and graph-based querying, it provides a valuable tool for researchers, policymakers, and legal professionals. The positive feedback from our user study validates this approach.

Future work includes expanding the data corpus, integrating more advanced NLP and machine learning models on the graph, and extending the comparative law features, while applying the tool paradigm to graphs of other legislations and integrations with European and regional law systems.

Acknowledgements. We thank Stefano Ceri, Luigi Guiso, Chiara Leonardi, and Claudio Michelacci for the discussions that helped shape the **MLegis** demo prototype. We acknowledge the support of the GRINS (Growing Resilient, INclusive and Sustainable) project (PE_00000018, CUP B83C22005100006), which contributed to the development of this research.

References

1. Colombo, A., Cambria, F.: LLM-assisted construction of the United States legislative graph. In: Proceedings of VLDB Workshops, vol. 2150, p. 8097 (2025)
2. Colombo, A., et al.: An LLM-assisted ETL pipeline to build a high-quality knowledge graph of the Italian legislation. Inf. Process. Manag. **62**(4), 104082 (2025)
3. Colombo, A., et al.: Legislative knowledge management with property graphs. In: Proceedings of the Workshops of the EDBT/ICDT 2025 Joint Conference, Barcelona, Spain, 25 March 2025, vol. 3946. CEUR-WS.org (2025)

4. Colombo, A.: LegisSearch: navigating legislation with graphs and large language models. Artif. Intell. Law (2025)
5. Facebook: GraphQL (2016). https://graphql.org/
6. Francis, N.: Cypher: an evolving query language for property graphs. In: Proceedings of the 2018 International Conference on Management of Data, pp. 1433–1445 (2018)
7. ISO: ISO/IEC 39075:2024 - Information technology—Database language (2024). https://doi.org/ISO/IEC39075:2024
8. Istituto Poligrafico e Zecca dello Stato: Normattiva Website (2025). https://www.normattiva.it/ricerca/avanzata
9. Invernici, F., Colombo, A., Telese, F., Bernasconi, A.: Ranked multi-label-augmented topic modeling for legislative content profiling. Appl. Sci. **16**(9), 4383 (2026)
10. Kondylakis, H., et al.: Property graph standards: state of the art & open challenges. Proc. VLDB Endow. **18**(12), 5477–5481 (2025)
11. Lucisano, P.: Gulpease: una formula per la predizione della leggibilita di testi in lingua italiana (1988)
12. Memgraph Graph Database: Memgraph Ltd (2025). https://memgraph.com/
13. Palmirani, M., Governatori, G., Rotolo, A., Tabet, S., Boley, H., Paschke, A.: LegalRuleML: XML-based rules and norms. In: Olken, F., Palmirani, M., Sottara, D. (eds.) RuleML 2011. LNCS, vol. 7018, pp. 298–312. Springer, Heidelberg (2011). https://doi.org/10.1007/978-3-642-24908-2_30
14. Ruhl, J.B., Katz, D.M.: Measuring, monitoring, and managing legal complexity. Iowa Law Rev. **101**, 191 (2015)

PerSpect: An Interactive Tool for Performance Pattern Mining

Moritz Schlegelmilch[1], Piotr Zaniewski[1], Volodymyr Diemieniev[1], Jasper Saathoff[1], Tsung-Hao Huang[1(✉)], and Gyunam Park[2]

[1] RWTH Aachen University, Aachen, Germany
{moritz.schlegelmilch,potr.zaniewski,volodymyr.diemieniev, jasper.saathoff}@rwth-aachen.de, tsunghao.huang@pads.rwth-aachen.de
[2] Eindhoven University of Technology, Eindhoven, Netherlands
g.park@tue.nl

Abstract. Complex processes can be difficult to understand from event data. Traditional process models effectively visualize control flows, but lack temporal context for performance analysis. To address this, the Performance Spectrum was introduced to map the dynamics of all steps and cases over time. However, its manual interpretation is challenging due to the overlapping patterns and noise. In this tool demonstration paper, we present PerSpect, an interactive, web-based user interface that significantly enhances the original Performance Spectrum approach. To facilitate interactive analysis, the tool automates the targeted detection of established operational behaviors (e.g., batching and FIFO), alongside advanced filtering capabilities and a side-by-side comparison function for evaluating the same segment across different process variants.

Keywords: Process Mining · Performance Spectrum · Working Patterns

1 Introduction

In continuously evolving information systems, operational processes change frequently, making it difficult to maintain a stable understanding of process behavior over time. Recent process mining research addresses these challenges by identifying change periods [8] and leveraging advances in machine learning to extract insights from event logs exhibiting multiple process variants [2,7]. Despite these advances, traditional process models discovered from event logs primarily focus on control-flow relations [1], lacking a temporal dimension. While they effectively visualize the ordering of activities and reveal deviations or bottlenecks, large real-life unstable processes often result in overly complex models that fail to capture interdependencies between cases or to convey how performance evolves over time.

To address these limitations, Denisov et al. introduced the *Performance Spectrum* [4], a visual analytics technique that adds a temporal dimension by mapping the dynamics of all steps and cases over time. By visualizing individual case

F. Zerbato et al. (Eds.): CAiSE 2026, LNBIP 587, pp. 158–166, 2026.
https://doi.org/10.1007/978-3-032-27997-2_18

trajectories between pairs of activities, the Performance Spectrum enables analysts to observe detected temporal patterns that are often hidden in traditional process models. This includes identifying behaviors such as batching, synchronization, or shifts in execution speed that may correspond to changing operating conditions present in the event log.

In this tool demonstration paper, we present PerSpect[1], a modernized, web-based version of the original *Performance Spectrum* approach, featuring enhanced functionality. While its conceptual strengths are preserved, our software enhances exploratory capabilities. First, it can detect patterns such as batching and FIFO based on user-provided parameters, enabling automated, targeted pattern identification. Furthermore, it offers a variety of filters and statistics that allow users to conduct in-depth, isolated analyses. In addition, a comparison function enables users to compare the Performance Spectrum of the same segment across different selected variants. Last but not least, an export function enables analysis of the filtered log outside of the tool.

The remainder of the paper is structured as follows. Section 2 provides background on the Performance Spectrum, while Sect. 3 outlines related tools to motivate our contribution. Section 4 presents PerSpect, covering the core workflow for interactive pattern mining and comparison. Section 5 details the system architecture and implementation. Section 6 discusses tool maturity and provides a practical use case. Finally, Sect. 7 concludes the paper and outlines future work.

2 Background

Process mining techniques analyze *event logs*, which record the execution of activities for different process instances (cases). Each event contains at least a case identifier, an activity, and a timestamp. To visualize the temporal dynamics hidden within this raw data, the *Performance Spectrum* visualizes how cases move between two successive activities over time [4] (as exemplified in Fig. 2). This visualization reveals how quickly cases progress between activities and exposes characteristic operational patterns. For a pair of activities (a, b), each occurrence where a is directly followed by b in a case is plotted as a line connecting the timestamp of a and the timestamp of b. Time is shown on the x-axis, while the two activities are placed on the y-axis.

One of the most prominent behaviors visible in the Performance Spectrum is *batch processing*, where multiple cases are handled within a short time period [10]. Prior work distinguishes three types of batching behavior [4,10]:

- **Simultaneous**: multiple cases start and finish the activity at the same time.
- **Sequential (FIFO)**: cases are processed one after another in arrival order.
- **Concurrent**: cases overlap in execution but are not strictly sequential.

[1] A public repository is available at https://github.com/moritzkschlegelmilch/PerSpect.

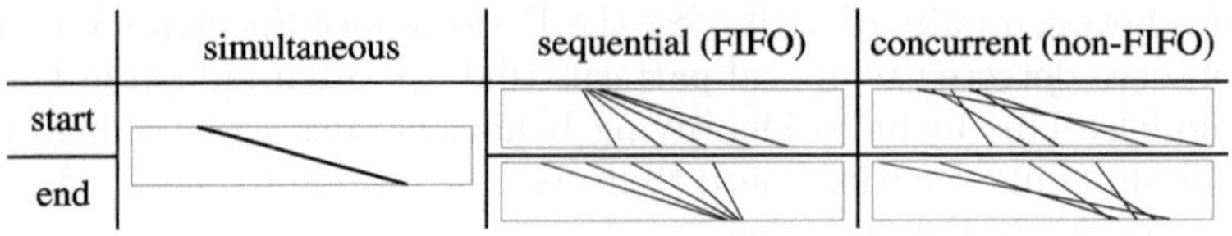

Fig. 1. Different batching patterns in the Performance Spectrum.

These batching behaviors appear as characteristic structures in the Performance Spectrum. Simultaneous batches share identical timestamps, sequential batches form ordered non-crossing lines, while concurrent batches allow overlapping and crossing lines. The aforementioned patterns are visualized in Fig. 1.

3 Related Work

To motivate our contribution, Fig. 2 illustrates an analysis performed using existing process mining tools [6,11]. The left side illustrates a directly-follows graph discovered from a real-life event log [9], while the right side presents six Performance Spectrum segments, each representing a pair of successive process steps. Notably, the segment (*Add Penalty*: *Send for Credit Collection*) exposes batching behavior that remains hidden when looking solely at the process model.

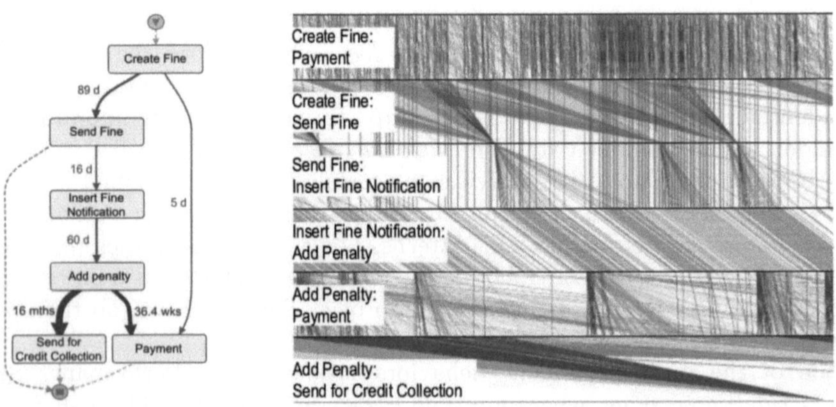

Fig. 2. Example of a process model with the corresponding performance spectrum [4].

Despite its analytical benefits, interpreting the Performance Spectrum for complex systems remains challenging due to visual clutter from overlapping patterns, noise, and irregular behavior. For example, within the (*Create Fine: Send Fine*) segment in Fig. 2, most cases exhibit a batching pattern, yet others execute the subsequent activity immediately. This entanglement makes it difficult to visually compare behaviors.

The original *Performance Spectrum Miner* [4], implemented as a ProM plug-in, demonstrated that visualizing execution flows over time uncovers phenomena like workload fluctuations, delays, batching, and synchronization effects. These insights are typically lost in traditional process models or aggregated performance metrics. This early tool provided core functional capabilities, including segment filtering, case ID selection, throughput specification, and duration classifiers. However, it treats the spectrum primarily as an end-stage visualization rather than the foundation for a structured analysis workflow, lacking the ability to export filtered event logs. Consequently, analysts are forced to manually disentangle overlapping timelines and visually interpret patterns—a task requiring significant domain expertise.

Recently, Celonis introduced a modernized iteration of the Performance Spectrum [3]. While it offers a user-friendly interface and highly configurable segment organization, extracting insights still relies on manual pattern inspection. PERSPECT bridges this gap by positioning the spectrum as the foundation of a pattern-oriented workflow. The novelty of the tool lies in seamlessly integrating automated pattern extraction directly into the visual interface, enabling users to dynamically filter, isolate, and compare specific execution behaviors on the fly. This targeted approach enables the investigation of temporal behaviors that would otherwise remain obscured in aggregated data.

4 Functionality

PERSPECT empowers analysts to interactively filter and explore temporal execution patterns, disentangling complex, overlapping behaviors such as batching and near-immediate transitions. The following paragraphs detail the core capabilities[2] of the tool.

Import and Export. To start, users are asked to upload event logs in the `.xes` (eXtensible Event Stream) format [12]. When users upload a file, the system automatically infers standard column mappings (e.g., `concept:name` for activities), though users can optionally map the essential `Case ID`, `Activity`, and `Timestamp` columns manually [1]. Once the data is uploaded, users can analyze it using the following functions. A subset of the event log, filtered for the cases in the current spectrum, can also be exported as a `.xes` file for further analysis.

Segment Picker. The Segment Picker allows users to filter the spectrum for a specific segment, which is defined as a pair of directly following activities (e.g., activity A and activity B) [4]. The starting point of a line on the spectrum corresponds to the start of the first activity (A), and the end of the line corresponds to the start of the second activity (B). The segments can be stacked to reflect the progress of the underlying process.

[2] A video introducing the main functionalities is publicly available online https://youtu.be/GhrcORMiQt4.

Filtering. The tool provides various filtering options, which are divided into two types: *Global Filters* and *Segment-specific Filters.* Global Filters affect the entire spectrum and all cases. These include:

- Variant Filter: The variants view allows the users to focus on a specific variant of the process for further analysis. Once the variants are selected, the performance spectrum will only show cases with the matching process flows.
- Date-Range Filter: Users can select a specific time period to focus on within the event log. This can be done by using a calendar popover or by dragging a time window directly onto the spectrum.
- Quartile Filter: This filter visualizes cases by duration quartiles, using color codes from light blue (fastest) to red (slowest). This filter is also part of the original tool developed in ProM [4].

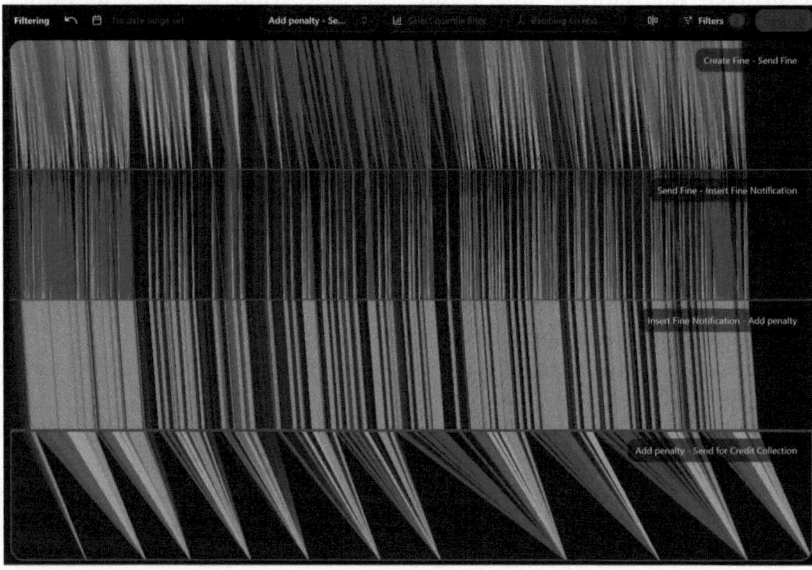

Fig. 3. An example interface of filtering by variants.

Segment-specific Filters apply only to the selected spectrum. These include:

- Batch Filters: One of the highlights of the tool is the ability to identify and extract organizational patterns from the performance spectrum, even if they are overlapping with other cases. For example, batches are sets of cases that are grouped based on their start or end time using a clustering technique. In principle, any clustering algorithm that is robust to noise can be used. In the tool, we use the DBSCAN-clustering algorithm [5] as an example to realize our pattern extraction function. Users can filter for batches that start, end, or both start and end around the same time [10]. Furthermore, users can

adjust the clustering parameters, `Epsilon` (how close the cases must be in time to belong to the same batch) and `Min-Samples` (the minimum number of cases required for a batch to be detected). Figure 4 shows an example of a segment with overlapping patterns and how different patterns are extracted and visualized separately. Notably, the tool allows setting `Epsilon` to 0 min, which enables the automated discovery of *simultaneous* batches. Lastly, the tool distinguishes between FIFO (first in, first out) and non-FIFO batching patterns.
- Interactive Filter: The interactive filter allows users to interactively select cases of interest within a segment. While the original ProM plugin merely highlighted such selections, our implementation dynamically updates all other spectra to reflect the chosen cases.

The system automatically tracks every filtering action performed by the user. This enables the user to recover a prior state of the spectrum.

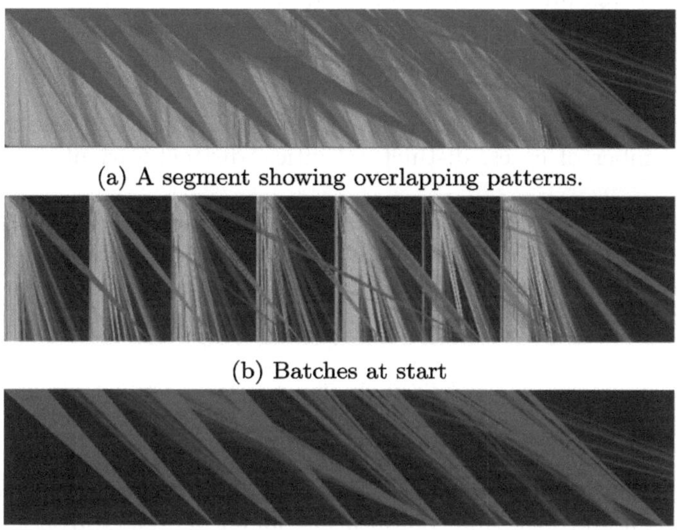

(a) A segment showing overlapping patterns.

(b) Batches at start

(c) Batches at end

Fig. 4. An example showing different patterns of the same segment.

Comparative Analysis. The tool enables direct, side-by-side comparison of filtered spectra by allowing users to create and assign meaningful names to multiple configurations. Each configuration saves the specific state of a spectrum. Users can seamlessly switch between these configurations to compare different filtered views, or easily remove them when no longer needed. To ensure readability, the viewport is designed to display a maximum of two configurations side-by-side at any given time. Figure 5 shows an example view of the comparative analysis.

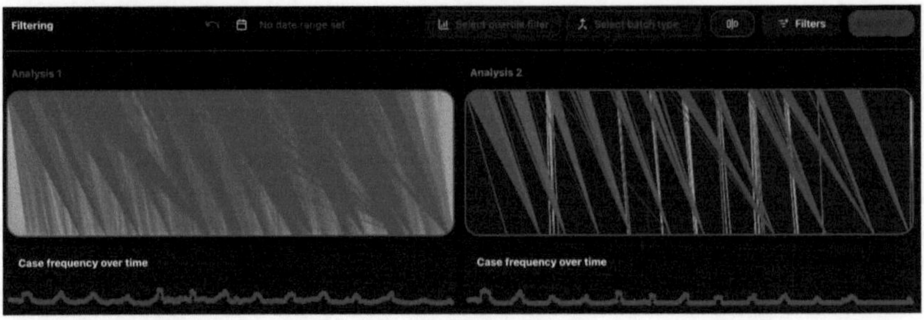

Fig. 5. An example interface of the comparative analysis.

Process and Pattern Statistics. To help analyze detected patterns, the tool provides several quantitative metrics and diagrams.

- Frequency Diagrams: Located below the Performance Spectrum, these diagrams show how frequently cases start and end over time, displaying the number of cases per time bin. Users can hover over points on the diagram for more details.
- Basic Statistics: This section provides metrics for the current selection, including the number of cases, distinct activities, distinct variants, and duration mean.
- Batch Statistics: When batch filtering is active, this section displays information such as the total number of batches, average batch size, average batch duration, average batch interval, and the percentage of cases in the entire event log that are part of a batch.

5 Architecture

The system follows a client–server architecture consisting of a backend for event log management and spectrum computation, and a web-based frontend for interactive analysis.

Backend Services and Spectrum Processing. The backend exposes a REST API implemented with FastAPI. Event logs are uploaded to the server, while metadata (name, storage path, and attribute mappings) is stored in a lightweight SQLite database managed via Alembic. For performance, loaded event logs are cached in memory using a Least Recently Used (LRU) strategy, and concurrent loading is synchronized to avoid redundant operations. Spectrum generation follows a query-based pipeline that separates global filters from segment-specific filters. Global filters (e.g., case selection, time range, segment or variant selection) determine the base spectra, after which segment-specific filters are applied. Filters are executed in a controlled order to ensure consistent results, and case sets are synchronized across spectra by intersecting case identifiers.

Frontend. The frontend is implemented as a Vue-based single-page application and introduces *configurations* as independent analysis states that can be displayed side-by-side. Each configuration maintains its own filter history and submits a unified filter payload to the backend to retrieve spectra or export the filtered event log.

6 Maturity

PerSpect is a fully documented open-source research prototype. Designed for integration into existing process mining pipelines, it supports the de facto standard `.xes` format [12] for event log import and export. The tool's maturity lies in transforming the Performance Spectrum from a purely exploratory visualization into a systematic, pattern-oriented analytical workflow. By automating the detection of temporal behaviors—such as simultaneous, FIFO and non-FIFO batching—and enabling isolated, side-by-side comparisons, PerSpect supports both academic research and practical application in analyzing event data.

Use Case Example. To demonstrate these capabilities in practice, the Road Traffic Fine Management process is used [9]. An analyst investigating delays might focus on the (*Add Penalty*: *Send for Credit Collection*) segment shown in Fig. 3. Using the Batch Filter, PerSpect reveals that over 97% of cases follow a sequential batching pattern where only 11 batches occur with an average interval of 410 d. This indicates that cases are held in a long-term backlog and cleared in massive, infrequent bursts. PerSpect provides the visual and numerical evidence to reveal these patterns, providing a level of transparency that control-flow models typically fail to capture.

7 Conclusion

We developed PerSpect to overcome the interpretation challenges caused by visual clutter, overlapping temporal patterns, and noise in complex event logs. The tool delivers a modern, web-based instantiation of the original Performance Spectrum concept. By introducing the automated algorithmic detection of organizational patterns, advanced filtering for isolated analysis, and comparative viewport configurations, PerSpect empowers analysts to uncover structural performance behaviors that typically remain hidden within aggregated metrics.

Future work will focus on expanding the filter selection to include attribute filters, capturing a broader range of execution behaviors. Additionally, we aim to integrate more advanced visual summaries to deepen insights into temporal dynamics. Finally, we plan to explore side-by-side integrations with control-flow visualizations, such as BPMN models or directly-follows graphs. By visually linking a selected spectrum segment directly to its corresponding activities within an overall process model, users will gain immediate structural context for their performance analysis.

References

1. van der Aalst, W.M.P.: Process Mining - Data Science in Action. 2nd edn. Springer, Cham (2016). https://doi.org/10.1007/978-3-662-49851-4
2. Cai, R., Zheng, C., Wang, J., Li, D., Wang, C., Li, B.: Reinforcement learning-based streaming process discovery under concept drift. In: Guizzardi, G., Santoro, F.M., Mouratidis, H., Soffer, P. (eds.) CAiSE 2024. LNCS, vol. 14663, pp. 55–70. Springer, Cham (2024). https://doi.org/10.1007/978-3-031-61057-8_4
3. Celonis SE: Performance Spectrum (2026). https://docs.celonis.com/en/performance-spectrum.html. Accessed 09 Apr 2026
4. Denisov, V., Fahland, D., van der Aalst, W.M.P.: Unbiased, fine-grained description of processes performance from event data. In: Weske, M., Montali, M., Weber, I., vom Brocke, J. (eds.) BPM 2018. LNCS, vol. 11080, pp. 139–157. Springer, Cham (2018). https://doi.org/10.1007/978-3-319-98648-7_9
5. Ester, M., Kriegel, H.P., Sander, J., Xu, X.: A density-based algorithm for discovering clusters in large spatial databases with noise. In: Proceedings of the Second International Conference on Knowledge Discovery and Data Mining. KDD'96, pp. 226–231. AAAI Press (1996). https://cdn.aaai.org/KDD/1996/KDD96-037.pdf
6. Günther, C.W., Rozinat, A.: Disco: discover your processes. In: Lohmann, N., Moser, S. (eds.) Proceedings of the Demonstration Track of the 10th International Conference on Business Process Management (BPM 2012), Tallinn, Estonia, 4 September 2012, pp. 40–44. CEUR Workshop Proceedings, CEUR-WS.org (2012). https://ceur-ws.org/Vol-940/paper8.pdf
7. Kraus, A., van der Aa, H.: Machine learning-based detection of concept drift in business processes. Process Sci. **2**(1) (2025). https://doi.org/10.1007/S44311-025-00012-W
8. Kraus, A., Elyasi, K.A., van der Aa, H.: On the use of steady-state detection for process mining: Achieving more accurate insights. In: Krogstie, J., Rinderle-Ma, S., Kappel, G., Proper, H.A. (eds.) CAiSE 2025. LNCS, vol. 15701, pp. 204–220. Springer, Cham (2025). https://doi.org/10.1007/978-3-031-94569-4_12
9. de Leoni, M.M., Mannhardt, F.: Road traffic fine management process (2015). https://doi.org/10.4121/UUID:270FD440-1057-4FB9-89A9-B699B47990F5
10. Martin, N., Swennen, M., Depaire, B., Jans, M., Caris, A., Vanhoof, K.: Retrieving batch organisation of work insights from event logs. Decis. Support Syst. **100**, 119–128 (2017). https://doi.org/10.1016/j.dss.2017.02.012, Smart Business Process Management
11. Verbeek, E., Buijs, J.C.A.M., van Dongen, B.F., van der Aalst, W.M.P.: ProM 6: the process mining toolkit. In: Rosa, M.L. (ed.) Proceedings of the Business Process Management 2010 Demonstration Track, Hoboken, NJ, USA, 14–16 September 2010. CEUR Workshop Proceedings, CEUR-WS.org (2010). https://ceur-ws.org/Vol-615/paper13.pdf
12. Verbeek, E., Buijs, J.C.A.M., van Dongen, B.F., van der Aalst, W.M.P.: XES Tools. In: Soffer, P., Proper, E. (eds.) Proceedings of the CAiSE Forum 2010, Hammamet, Tunisia, 9–11June 2010. CEUR Workshop Proceedings, CEUR-WS.org (2010). https://ceur-ws.org/Vol-592/PaperDemo07.pdf

PMDAgile: A Process-Model-Driven Tool for Agile Software Development

Cielo González Moyano(✉), Florian Six, and Jan Mendling

Humboldt-Universität zu Berlin, Berlin, Germany
{c.gonzalez.moyano,franz.florian.six,jan.mendling}@hu-berlin.de

Abstract. Agile software development is widely adopted due to its emphasis on collaboration and adaptability. At the same time, agile teams continue to face persistent and interrelated challenges in practice. Existing tool support addresses particular aspects of agile development but does not provide integrated support across these concerns. This paper introduces PMDAgile, a process-model-driven tool that integrates business process models into agile project environments. PMDAgile is designed to address three targeted challenges: requirements specification and communication, planning and prioritization, and change management. An exploratory evaluation with industry practitioners indicates positive perceptions of usefulness and ease of use, as well as support for the three targeted challenges, suggesting that integrating business process models into agile workflows may help mitigate these difficulties.

Keywords: Process Models · Business Process Models · Agile Software Development · Agile Support Tool · Agile Challenges

1 Introduction

Agile methodologies have become the dominant paradigm in contemporary software development, replacing traditional plan-driven approaches in many organizational contexts [15]. Their widespread adoption is largely attributed to their emphasis on stakeholder collaboration, incremental value delivery, and responsiveness to evolving business needs [1]. Despite these advantages, agile teams continue to face persistent and interrelated challenges, particularly in the areas of requirements communication, planning coordination, and change management [25]. As software-intensive information systems grow in scale and complexity, it is a natural step to evaluate alternatives that could address these challenges without compromising the purpose of agile methodologies.

Existing research has proposed numerous alternatives to mitigate these challenges, addressing specific agile issues (e.g., communication [11], knowledge sharing [10], and requirements [22]) or supporting particular development phases (e.g., design [18] and planning [28]). In addition, commercial platforms such as Jira [4] and Slack [26] are widely used in practice to provide tool-based support for coordination and communication. While these alternatives and tools offer

F. Zerbato et al. (Eds.): CAiSE 2026, LNBIP 587, pp. 167–175, 2026.
https://doi.org/10.1007/978-3-032-27997-2_19

valuable contributions, they generally address particular aspects of agile development rather than providing an integrated perspective. As projects increase in scale and involve multiple stakeholders, artifacts, and iterations, maintaining a shared and coherent understanding across requirements, planning activities, and evolving functionality becomes more demanding. Given the interrelated nature of agile challenges [14], addressing them in isolation may limit overall effectiveness. Therefore, more comprehensive tool-based approaches that jointly address these interrelated challenges are needed.

In this paper, we introduce Process-Model-Driven Agile (PMDAgile), a collaborative software tool that integrates business process models within agile project environments to support agile development. The use of business process models is motivated by their capabilities to facilitate communication and knowledge sharing, as well as their potential to address multiple challenges in agile development [16]. While business process models can be applied in various ways within agile software development, PMDAgile deliberately focuses on three key challenges frequently reported by practitioners [1,20,25]: (1) defining and communicating requirements and application scope among stakeholders, (2) planning and prioritizing activities, and (3) managing changes in iterative development contexts. For each of these challenges, PMDAgile operationalizes the use of business process models to provide structured support within agile methodologies. An exploratory evaluation with industry practitioners provides initial insights into the tool's usability and practical relevance. The tool is publicly available at https://d1h7fd76rse39y.cloudfront.net. For a short demonstration video, see https://youtu.be/iqUwEHTcJ-M.

The remainder of this paper is structured as follows. Section 2 introduces agile software development and its relation to business process models, and reviews existing tools supporting agile practices. Section 3 presents PMDAgile, including its goals, key features, system architecture, and user interface. Section 4 reports on the evaluation results and discusses the tool's maturity. Finally, Sect. 5 concludes the paper and outlines directions for future work.

2 Background and Related Work

Agile software development comprises approaches such as Scrum [24], Kanban [3], and ScrumBan [23], which emphasize stakeholder collaboration, incremental delivery, and responsiveness to change [5]. Although agile methods prioritize working software over documentation, structured artifacts and shared representations remain essential for coordination and communication.

Modeling plays an important role in software development by supporting analysis, design, and stakeholder communication [13]. Several proposals have explored integrating modeling practices into agile environments [2]. In particular, Gonzĺez Moyano et al. [16] identify 15 different uses of business process models in agile software development projects, highlighting their potential to address common challenges. However, this and similar work mainly discuss methodological integration and do not propose concrete tool support to operationalize these

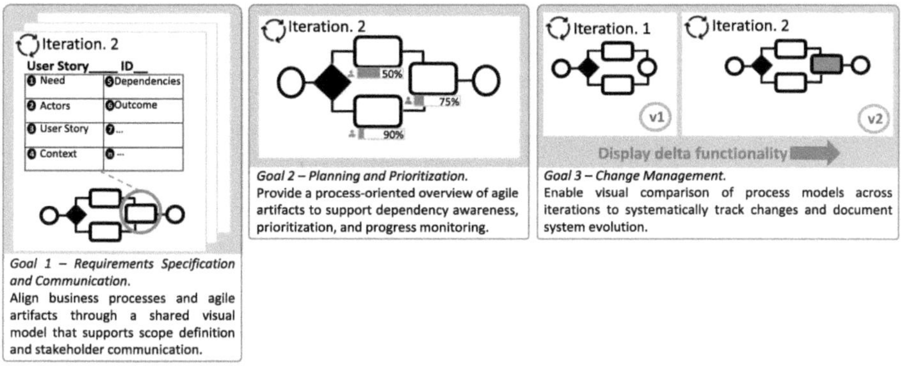

Fig. 1. Overview of the main goals of PMDA.

insights in agile project settings. Prior research has identified such tool support as necessary to mitigate recurring challenges [10].

Although such tool support remains limited, some tool-based efforts have begun to address this gap. Floruț and Buchmann [8] propose a modeling tool that extends BPMN and UML with agile-specific concepts to support requirements management. While this approach strengthens structural traceability between requirements and process artifacts, it does not address the use of business process models to support other aspects of agile software development, such as planning coordination and iteration-based evolution.

More broadly, existing tool support for agile software development can be categorized into research prototypes and commercial platforms. Research-oriented tools typically address specific development activities, such as collaborative system design [18], planning and task coordination [28], or requirements elicitation and knowledge sharing [12]. While these tools provide valuable support, they generally focus on isolated aspects of agile work. Commercial platforms such as Jira [4] and Slack [26] are widely used in practice to facilitate coordination and communication [17]. Although flexible and extensible, these tools are primarily general-purpose and are not specifically designed to integrate business process modeling as part of agile development practices.

Overall, despite the potential of business process models in agile contexts, comprehensive tool support that systematically integrates them as collaborative artifacts within agile project environments remains underexplored.

3 Process-Model-Driven Agile

This section introduces PMDAgile by presenting its design goals, core features, and system architecture.

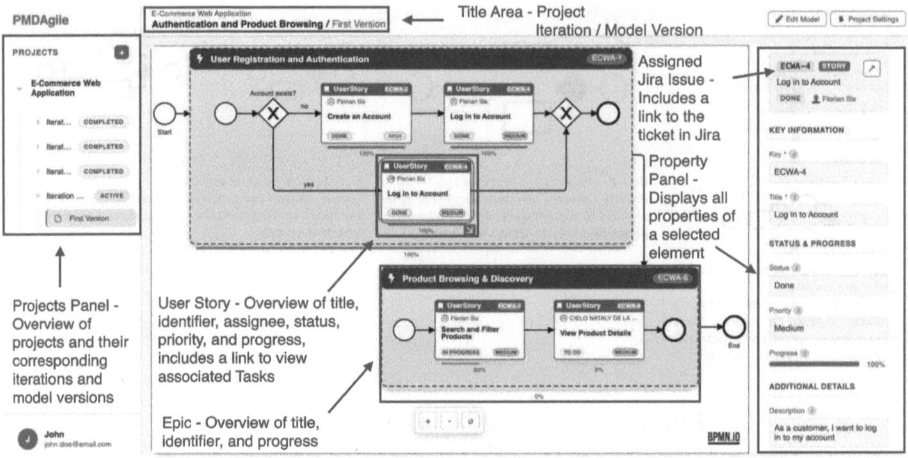

Fig. 2. PMDAgile user interface.

3.1 Design Goals

PMDAgile aims to support agile software development by addressing three interrelated challenges: requirements specification and communication, planning and prioritization, and change management (see Fig. 1). Each of the following goals directly corresponds to one of these challenges.

Goal 1 – Requirements Specification and Communication. Agile projects are characterized by evolving requirements and continuous stakeholder interaction. Misunderstandings regarding scope, priorities, or responsibilities may lead to inconsistencies and ineffective decision-making. PMDAgile addresses this challenge by integrating business process models with agile artifacts (e.g., user stories), enabling requirements to be defined and discussed within the context of the underlying business process. This shared visual representation supports alignment between business and technical perspectives and clarifies responsibilities across actors.

Goal 2 – Planning and Prioritization. Agile backlogs often lack an explicit representation of dependencies and their relation to business processes. PMDAgile enhances planning by linking agile artifacts to process activities and enriching them with iteration- and progress-related information (e.g., status, assignee, completion percentage). This integrated view provides a process-oriented overview of project status, supporting prioritization decisions and improving coordination.

Goal 3 – Change Management. Iterative development requires systematic handling of changes across iterations. PMDAgile supports change management by enabling visual comparison of process models across iterations. This allows teams to identify additions, modifications, and removals of process elements, thereby documenting system evolution and facilitating informed decision-making.

3.2 Features

The key features of PMDAgile and their relation to the previously defined goals are presented below. Figure 2 illustrates the main interface of the tool.

The interface is structured into three main areas. The *Projects Panel* on the left provides an overview of created projects and lists all completed and active iterations. The central *Modeling Canvas* enables users to create and visualize business process models associated with selected projects and their iterations. On the right-hand side, the *Property Panel* displays detailed information about the currently selected element, allowing users to inspect and manage linked agile artifacts directly within the process model. The example shown in Fig. 2 presents the business processes related to functionalities for an e-commerce web application. These functionalities are specifically focused on authentication and product browsing.

BPMN Modeler. At its core, the tool provides an interactive BPMN modeling canvas that supports standard BPMN constructs and editing functionalities. PMDAgile adopts a representational mapping in which BPMN elements are used to model agile artifacts: BPMN tasks represent agile tasks, collapsed subprocesses represent user stories, and expanded subprocesses represent epics. These elements are enriched with agile-specific metadata (e.g., status, priority, assignee) retrieved from Jira, enabling agile work items to be contextualized within their underlying business processes. This mapping allows backlog items to be interpreted within the process flow by different stakeholders, making dependencies and execution order explicit, thereby contributing in particular to Goal 1 and Goal 2.

Model Comparison. To support Goal 3, PMDAgile enables comparison of BPMN models across iterations. Models are presented in a side-by-side view, where additions, removals, and modifications of process elements are visually highlighted, while unchanged elements are de-emphasized. A structured summary complements the visual comparison by listing all detected changes, facilitating systematic tracking of process evolution.

Integration with External Project Management System. To support Goal 1 and Goal 2 in particular, PMDAgile integrates with Jira [4], enabling users to connect existing projects and import agile artifacts (i.e., epics, user stories, and tasks) into the modeling environment. Linked elements are automatically synchronized to ensure consistency between Jira and the corresponding business process models.

Collaboration. PMDAgile supports shared project access, enabling multiple users to collaboratively create and maintain process models within a common workspace. This feature directly supports Goal 1.

3.3 Architecture

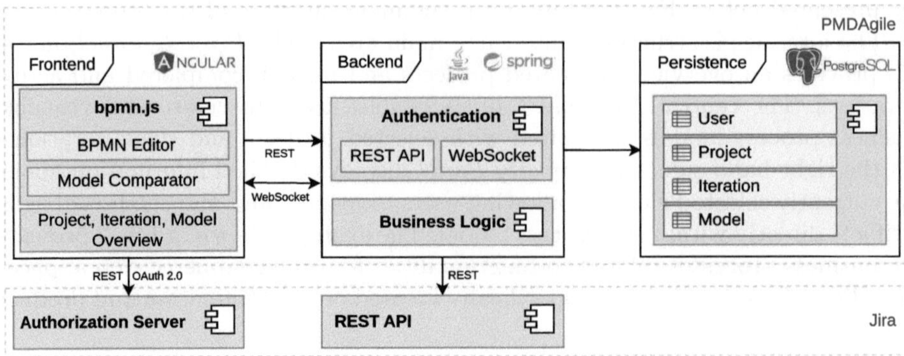

Fig. 3. PMDAgile architecture.

The overall architecture of the system is illustrated in Fig. 3. The tool follows a layered architecture comprising three main layers: the *frontend layer*, the *backend layer*, and the *persistence layer*. The frontend layer is implemented using Angular [9] and is responsible for user interaction and visualization. It provides core views, including a project, iteration, and model overview, as well as a dedicated BPMN editor implemented using bpmn.js [6], allowing users to create and modify BPMN-based process models. In addition, the frontend includes a model comparison component that supports the inspection of different model versions across iterations. Furthermore, the frontend acts as an OAuth 2.0 client when integrating with Jira. It communicates with the Jira Authorization Server to initiate the authorization process and obtain an authorization code. This code is passed to the backend, enabling the secure retrieval of an access token for subsequent API interactions on behalf of the authenticated user. Communication with the backend is primarily realized through RESTful APIs for standard operations, while WebSockets are used to allow collaborative interaction on shared resources. The backend layer, implemented using Java [19] and Spring Boot [27], encapsulates the application's core logic and coordination functionality. It exposes REST endpoints and handles authentication and authorization. A dedicated service layer contains the business logic related to project management, iteration handling, and the creation and modification of BPMN models. The persistence layer employs a PostgreSQL [21] database, which is accessed exclusively through the backend. It follows a repository-based design, providing separate repositories for users, projects, iterations, and BPMN models.

4 Maturity

To obtain preliminary insights into the practical relevance and usability of PMDAgile, we conducted an exploratory evaluation with ten experienced industry practitioners representing six professional roles: two product managers, one project manager, two software architects, two technical leaders, two software developers, and one business analyst. Participants were introduced to the tool, engaged in hands-on interaction, and completed a structured questionnaire based on the Technology Acceptance Model (TAM) [7], enriched with additional items aligned with the three framework goals and complemented by open-ended questions. Descriptive statistics indicate positive perceptions regarding both perceived usefulness (M = 5.98, SD = 0.73) and perceived ease of use (M = 6.13, SD = 0.52) on a 7-point Likert scale (1 = Strongly Disagree, 7 = Strongly Agree). Several participants mentioned that they appreciated that PMDAgile is not overwhelming in terms of functionality or complexity and that it focuses on the needs of different roles.

With respect to the specific goals, participants reported strong agreement that PMDAgile supports communication of requirements across team members (M = 6.3, SD = 0.64), planning and prioritization (M = 6.1, SD = 0.83), and facilitates adaptation to project changes (M = 5.7, SD = 0.78). Practitioners particularly appreciated the visual integration of agile artifacts within business process models, highlighting the clarity it provides for understanding task dependencies and communicating project status. Additionally, participants emphasized the value of using standard process notation to present project progress in a way that is understandable to business stakeholders. Scalability emerged as a potential limitation in large projects, prompting suggestions for improved abstraction mechanisms to support epic-level visualization.

5 Conclusion and Future Work

In this paper, we introduced PMDAgile, a process-model-driven tool that aims to address three critical challenges in agile software development projects: defining and communicating requirements, planning and prioritizing activities, and managing changes. An exploratory evaluation with ten industry practitioners indicates positive perceptions of usability and practical relevance. The results suggest that leveraging business process models within agile environments represents a viable direction for addressing interconnected agile challenges. Future work includes conducting a more extensive evaluation with a larger number of practitioners and a field study, expanding the scope of addressed agile challenges, and improving scalability through enhanced abstraction mechanisms for large and complex projects.

Acknowledgement. The research of the authors was supported by the Einstein Foundation Berlin under grant EPP-2019-524, the German Federal Ministry of Research, Technology and Space under grant 16DII143, and the Deutsche Forschungsgemeinschaft under grants 496119880 (VisualMine) and 531115272 (ProImpact).

References

1. Agile: The 17th state of agile report (2023). https://stateofagile.com/

2. Alfraihi, H., Lano, K.: The integration of agile development and model driven development. In: Proceedings of MODELSWARD 2017, pp. 451–458 (2017)
3. Anderson, D., Carmichael, A.: Essential Kanban Condensed. Blue Hole Press (2016)
4. Atlassian: Jira (2024). https://www.atlassian.com/
5. Beck, K., et al.: Manifesto for agile software development (2001). https://agilemanifesto.org/. Accessed 8 Mar 2021
6. Camunda Services GmbH: bpmn.js – a BPMN 2.0 rendering and editing toolkit for the web (2024). https://bpmn.io/toolkit/bpmn-js/. Accessed 21 Feb 2026
7. Davis, F.D.: Perceived usefulness, perceived ease of use, and user acceptance of information technology. MIS Q. **13**(3), 319–340 (1989)
8. Floruţ, C., Buchmann, R.A.: Modeling tool for managing requirements and backlogs in agile software development. In: CEUR Workshop Proceedings, vol. 312 (2022)
9. Google LLC: Angular: one framework. Mobile & desktop (2024). https://angular.io/. Accessed 21 Feb 2026
10. Jiménez, M., Piattini, M., Vizcaíno, A.: Challenges and improvements in distributed software development: a systematic review. Adv. Softw. Eng. (2009)
11. Korkala, M., Maurer, F.: Waste identification as the means for improving communication in globally distributed agile software development. J. Syst. Softw. **95**, 122–140 (2014)
12. Lohmann, S., Riechert, T., Auer, S.: Collaborative development of knowledge bases in distributed requirements elicitation. Softw. Eng., 22–28 (2008)
13. Malinova, M., Mendling, J.: Cognitive diagram understanding and task performance in systems analysis and design. MIS Q. **45**(4), 2101–2158 (2021)
14. Meckenstock, J.N.: Shedding light on the dark side-a systematic literature review of the issues in agile software development methodology use. J. Sys. Soft. **211**, 111966 (2024)
15. Mishra, A., Alzoubi, Y.I.: Structured software development versus agile software development: a comparative analysis. Int. J. Syst. Assur. Eng. Manag. **14**(4), 1504–1522 (2023)
16. Moyano, C.G., Pufahl, L., Weber, I., Mendling, J.: Uses of business process modeling in agile software development projects. Inf. Softw. Technol. **152**, 107028 (2022)
17. Naik, N., Jenkins, P., Newell, D.: Learning agile scrum methodology using the groupware tool TRELLO through collaborative working. In: CISIS-2019, pp. 343–355. Springer (2020). https://doi.org/10.1007/978-3-030-22354-0_31
18. Nicolaescu, P., Rosenstengel, M., Derntl, M., Klamma, R., Jarke, M.: Near real-time collaborative modeling for view-based web information systems engineering. Inf. Syst. **74**, 23–39 (2018)
19. Oracle corporation: Java platform, standard edition documentation. Oracle corporation (2024). https://docs.oracle.com/en/java/javase/. Accessed 27 Feb 2026
20. Petre, M.: UML in practice. In: 35th ICSE, pp. 722–731. IEEE (2013)
21. PostgreSQL global development group: PostgreSQL: the world's most advanced open source relational database (2024). https://www.postgresql.org/. Accessed 21 Feb 2026
22. Rasheed, A., et al.: Requirement engineering challenges in agile software development. Math. Probl. Eng. **2021**, 1–18 (2021)
23. Reddy, A.: The Scrumban [R] Evolution: Getting the Most Out of Agile, Scrum, and Lean Kanban. Addison-Wesley Professional (2015)
24. Schwaber, K., Beedle, M.: Agile Software Development with Scrum, vol. 1. Prentice Hall Upper Saddle River (2002)

25. Shameem, M., Kumar, R.R., Kumar, C., Chandra, B., Khan, A.A.: Prioritizing challenges of agile process in distributed software development environment using analytic hierarchy process. J. Softw.: Evol. Process **30**(11), e1979 (2018)
26. Technologies, S.: slack (2024). https://slack.com
27. VMware, Inc.: Spring boot reference documentation. VMware, Inc. (2024). https://docs.spring.io/spring-boot/docs/current/reference/html/. Accessed 27 Feb 2026
28. Wang, X., Maurer, F.: TabletopAagilePlanner: a tabletop-based project planning tool for agile software development teams. In: IEEE International Workshop Horizontal Interactive Human-Comput. Syst., 121–128 (2008) IEEE

D3SD: A Web-based Tool for Data Service Design in Cyber-Physical Production Networks

Ada Bagozi, Devis Bianchini, Valeria De Antonellis, Massimiliano Garda(✉), Michele Melchiori, and Anisa Rula

Department of Information Engineering, University of Brescia, Via Branze 38, 25123 Brescia, Italy
{ada.bagozi,devis.bianchini,valeria.deantonellis,massimiliano.garda, michele.melchiori,anisa.rula}@unibs.it

Abstract. Designing data services in Cyber-Physical Production Networks (CPPN) involves managing service composition across organisational boundaries, supporting both vertical and horizontal integration, while ensuring data sovereignty, access control, and regulatory compliance. In this paper, we present D3SD (Three-layer Data Services Designer), a web-based tool for designing data services using a three-layered service model that distinguishes between different levels of the production network. D3SD provides process designers in CPPN with a BPMN-based graphical environment for modelling atomic data services that operate on data within individual supply chain actors. It also supports their composition at the smart factory and supply chain levels by leveraging a variant of the Process-to-Services (P2S) approach to suggest groupings of atomic data services that maximise internal cohesion while minimising coupling between aggregations. To ensure privacy-by-design and data sovereignty, the tool integrates Role-Based Access Control (RBAC) and GDPR responsibilities directly into the design process. We demonstrate D3SD through a multi-actor supply chain scenario derived from an industrial use case in a research project.

Keywords: Service-oriented architectures · Service modelling · Internet of Services · Internet of Production · Cyber-Physical Production Networks

1 Introduction

Industrial systems are progressively evolving into interconnected, data-driven ecosystems that span multiple autonomous actors across organisational and supply chain boundaries, enabling both vertical and horizontal integration [8]. These ecosystems, known as Cyber-Physical Production Networks (CPPN), rely on data exchange for coordination, monitoring, and optimisation across networks of heterogeneous Cyber-Physical Production Systems (CPPS), i.e., factory-level

F. Zerbato et al. (Eds.): CAiSE 2026, LNBIP 587, pp. 176–184, 2026.
https://doi.org/10.1007/978-3-032-27997-2_20

Cyber-Physical Systems [3]. As the scale and complexity of these environments increase, service-oriented approaches have emerged as a key enabler of modular and interoperable architectures. In particular, paradigms such as the Internet of Services (IoS) foster the encapsulation of data access, processing, and sharing functionalities into modular services, giving rise to concepts such as *Big Service* [6], which emphasises flexible composition of services across multiple organisational layers. While service-oriented approaches facilitate interoperability, composing services across actors with different roles, responsibilities, and data ownership increases complexity, and requires careful management of access control, data sovereignty, and GDPR compliance constraints.

To address these issues, we proposed in [1] a three-layered data service model, distinguishing between: (i) *atomic services* that operate on data within individual actors, (ii) *CPPS services* that aggregate atomic services within a single factory, and (iii) *CPPN services* that coordinate services across multiple actors in the supply chain. This layered approach supports modular and scalable service design, grounding service composition in actor boundaries and the associated access control and governance constraints. Enabling process designers to fully benefit from this model, however, requires adequate tool support.

In this paper, we present D3SD (Three-layer Data Services Designer), a web-based tool that supports process designers in CPPN by providing a BPMN-based graphical environment for modelling atomic data services at the actor level and composing them at the smart factory and supply chain levels. The main contributions of D3SD are: (i) a BPMN-based graphical environment for modelling atomic data services grounded in actor-level data operations; (ii) the automated identification of CPPS and CPPN service aggregations through a variant of the Process-to-Services (P2S) approach [2], which suggests groupings of atomic data services that maximise internal cohesion while minimising inter-aggregation coupling, combined with human-in-the-loop interactive refinement; and (iii) the integration of privacy-by-design principles, including RBAC policies and GDPR role assignments, directly at design time. As discussed in Sect. 6, these aspects are not jointly addressed by existing BPMN extensions or BPMS platforms. The applicability of D3SD has been demonstrated within the scope of a multi-actor supply chain case study based on a research project, focusing on the production of highly customisable deep-sea valves[1]. While D3SD builds upon well-established concepts from service-oriented modelling (e.g., the P2S approach), it is explicitly tailored to the structural and organisational characteristics of production networks, using a three-layered service model and integrated RBAC/GDPR governance with domain-aware aggregation and consistency rules to provide methodological and technological support beyond generic tools, addressing the coordination challenges of intertwined production networks.

The remainder of the paper is organised as follows. Section 2 presents an overview of the three-layered data service model for CPPN. Section 3 describes the main functionalities of the D3SD tool. Section 4 introduces the demonstra-

[1] FISVAL Project ("Integrated and sustainable Supply Chain for the production of Smart Valves", funded by Lombardy Region - Italy, 2019-2021).

tion scenario. Section 5 discusses the maturity of the tool. Section 6 reviews related work and positions our tool among existing solutions. Finally, Sect. 7 concludes the paper and outlines future development directions.

2 A Three-Layered Data Service Model for CPPN

In the following, we present the three-layered data service model we proposed in [1]. The model is intended to address the complexity of data service management in CPPN, while aligning with the goals of vertical and horizontal integration in smart factory ecosystems, taking into account role-based data access policies as well as data sovereignty and privacy issues.

Atomic services. Represent atomic activities on data from the perspective of each individual actor. These services encompass operations such as accessing data from the field and from Enterprise Information Systems, or from other actors (*Collect* services); sharing specific information with other actors (*Dispatch* services); monitoring or processing data internally (e.g., filtering, transformation, storage) for implementing flexible data pipelines such as anomaly detection or quality assessment (*Process&Monitor* services); and visualising data for internal purposes (*Display* services). Atomic services facilitate modular design, allowing for efficient reuse in diverse compositions.

CPPS services. Represent composite services that (recursively) aggregate services within the borders of a single factory. These services serve the specific business roles of individual actors of the production network, offering flexibility, while managing access policies. They facilitate resilience and adaptability within the CPPS, the latter being associated with the production lines of each actor.

CPPN services. Represent a composition of other services (either atomic or CPPS services) from multiple actors across the entire supply chain and in intertwined supply chains. On the one hand, CPPS services align with data governance best practices that are specific to each individual actor, ensuring that internal data management is secure and compliant with legal regulations (since they implement complex functionalities based only on data owned by individual actors). On the other hand, CPPN services are designed to adapt to the evolving data processing requirements at the supply chain level, where the partnership of actors (e.g., suppliers) and the customers' requirements may change over time.

3 Main Functionalities of the Tool

Figure 1 illustrates an overview of the modules of D3SD. The tool is accessible via a standard web browser and has been developed using Django, a Python-based web framework, following a modular architecture. The frontend integrates a BPMN 2.0 graphical editor based on the `bpmn-js` library, which serves as the primary entry point for the design process. Designers model supply chain data flows as BPMN diagrams, where tasks represent fine-grained data operations that can be promoted to atomic services and aggregated into composite services, either within a single actor or across multiple actors in the supply chain. In

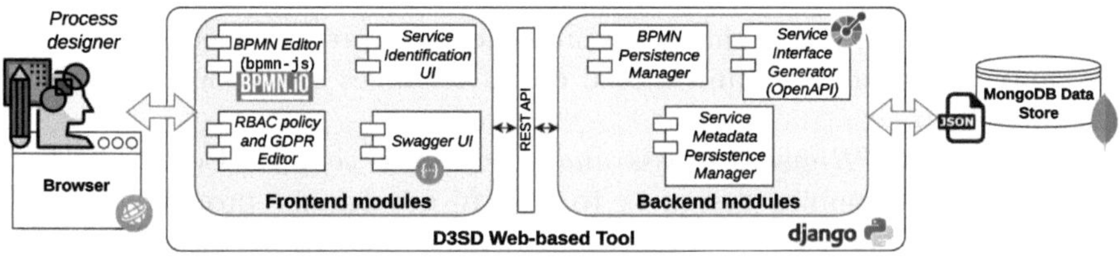

Fig. 1. Overview of D3SD frontend and backend modules.

D3SD, each BPMN pool represents a separate organisational actor, while lanes within a pool can be used to organise internal responsibilities. This ensures that atomic services are defined at the actor level and that CPPS groupings correctly reflect intra-actor boundaries. The backend provides RESTful APIs to support the service design operations and uses a MongoDB document-oriented repository to store BPMN diagrams and OpenAPI-compliant service interfaces in JSON format. The latter are automatically generated by the tool from the service metadata specified at design time and act as contracts for subsequent implementation. In the following, we explain the main functionalities of D3SD (denoted as F1-F2).

(F1) Atomic Data Services Definition. The design process starts with the modelling of a BPMN diagram, in which each task represents a fine-grained data operation. For each task, the designer specifies a set of baseline properties, including service name and type, invocation method, and endpoint URL, as well as the associated inputs and outputs, representing respectively the parameters required for invocation and the data produced upon execution. Through this specification, each task is promoted to an atomic data service, conceived as a self-contained, RESTful-invocable unit that can be exposed and consumed within the supply chain context.

(F2) CPPS and CPPN Services Identification and Definition. Once atomic services are defined, D3SD supports the identification of meaningful aggregations that can be exposed as composite services. Building on the atomic services defined in F1, candidate groupings are derived through a variant of the P2S approach, adapted to the three-layered service model, which analyses the underlying BPMN control- and data-flow dependencies to maximise internal cohesion while minimising coupling between aggregations. With respect to the original P2S formulation, the variant introduces a flow-connectivity penalty that discourages merging services not directly or transitively connected in the BPMN sequence flow, ensuring that service boundaries reflect actual execution dependencies across actors. Designers can interactively explore, compare, and manually revise alternative groupings as needed, retaining full control over final decisions through a human-in-the-loop approach that combines automated guidance with expert judgement. The organisational boundaries encoded in the BPMN model determine the nature of each aggregation. Groupings that involve services within the same pool (i.e., operated by a single actor) are classified as CPPS services, capturing the internal process logic and data responsibilities of an individual factory. Conversely, groupings that span multiple pools are classified as CPPN services, representing inter-organisational data exchanges and coordination across the supply chain.

• *RBAC- and GDPR-aware access and governance policies.* Beyond technical properties, D3SD enables designers to specify governance properties (namely RBAC policies and GDPR responsibilities) for composite services, taking into account both the abstraction level of the service and the organisational boundaries of the involved actors. In particular, for CPPN services, designers can specify GDPR roles (e.g., data controller, data processor) for each actor, directly linking service compositions to data governance obligations. To support this process, D3SD implements consistency rules that automatically derive initial RBAC settings and GDPR assignments when services are aggregated. For example, when a CPPN service is composed of atomic or CPPS services owned by different actors, the tool propagates RBAC permissions specified in the component services as a starting point, which designers can then review and adjust.

4 Demonstration Scenario

In this section, we introduce a demonstration scenario that has been used to showcase how D3SD supports the design of services in CPPN following the three-layered data service model presented in Sect. 2. The scenario focuses on an industrial case study concerning the production of highly customisable deep-sea valves, involving multiple actors operating in intertwined supply chains. The BPMN collaboration diagram shown in Figure 2 within the tool GUI represents interactions among a *Customer*, a *Production Leader*, a *Forging Process Supplier*, and a *Mechanical Parts Supplier*, with a focus on production planning and monitoring processes (the BPMN source diagram is available in `.bpmn` format in the `examples` folder within the GitLab repository of D3SD, see Sect. 5).

(1) Atomic Data Services Definition. The process designer defines BPMN tasks corresponding to data-related operations. Each task is then mapped to an atomic service by specifying a concrete interface specification, including service name and type, invocation method, endpoint URL, and input/output parameters. As a result, 27 atomic services were designed.

(2) CPPS and CPPN Services Identification and Definition. Atomic services were then aggregated into higher-level services following actor boundaries. Leveraging the P2S-based identification approach described in Sect. 3, the designer was able to interactively explore and compare alternative aggregation strategies before choosing the most suitable configuration. Within the Production Leader pool, six atomic services were ultimately grouped into two CPPS services, corresponding to internal production planning and quality management subprocesses. At the highest abstraction level, services were composed across different actors to obtain two CPPN services, representing production scheduling (Figure 2, left side of the top BPMN diagram) and production monitoring (Figure 2, right side of the top BPMN diagram) at the supply chain level. These CPPN services coordinate the Production Leader and the external suppliers,

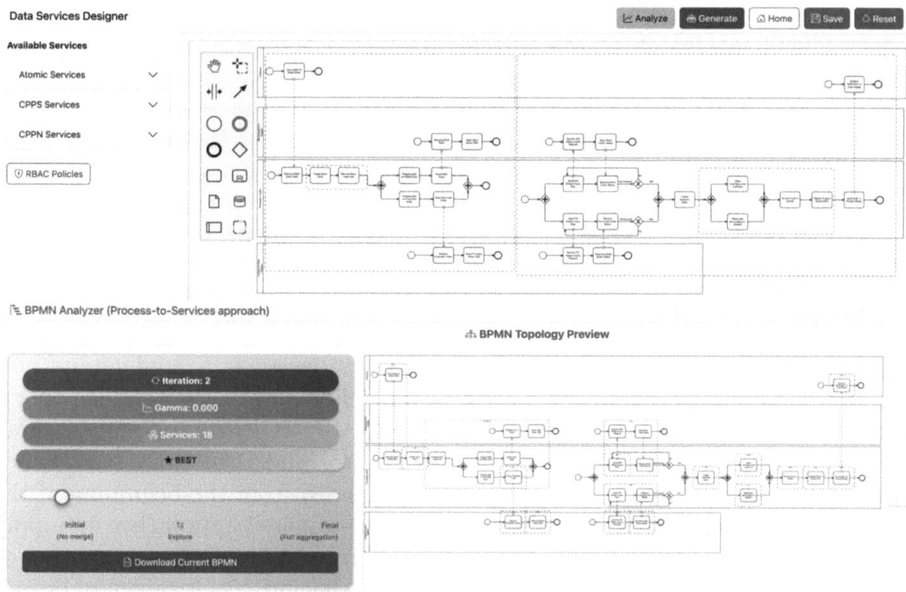

Fig. 2. D3SD tool GUI. BPMN diagram for the data services in the demonstration scenario (top). Service identification panel for the P2S approach (bottom).

capturing end-to-end data flows across organisational boundaries. This layered classification ensures that the resulting service architecture faithfully reflects both intra-factory responsibilities and inter-organisational coordination needs across the supply chain. Finally, access control and data governance constraints were defined for each service. For CPPS services, invocation permissions were restricted to the owning actor, while CPPN services were associated with RBAC policies specifying which actors are authorised to invoke each component service (e.g., in the scope of the `Production Scheduling` CPPN service, the Customer cannot invoke the `Send Purchase Order` service). In addition, GDPR responsibilities were assigned to CPPN service actors to ensure inter-organisational coordination complies with data sovereignty and regulatory constraints (e.g., for the `Production Scheduling` CPPN service, the Production Leader is a Data Controller, suppliers act as Data Controllers or Processors depending on context, the Customer is a Data Subject).

5 Maturity

D3SD has been implemented as a research-oriented, web-based prototype designed to support the systematic modelling of data services in CPPN. Its initial validation was carried out through illustrative use cases in the deep-sea valves domain, the primary industrial scenario for which the tool was conceived. Additional experiments were conducted in the agri-food and healthcare sectors, which, although not CPPN in the strict sense, present comparable challenges: multi-actor supply chains with heterogeneous data ownership boundaries, dynamic partner relationships, and stringent inter-organisational governance requirements. The applicability of D3SD to these sectors confirms that such challenges (and the three-layered service model designed to address them) characterise a broader class of production-like networks for which general-purpose service design tools remain inadequate. The source code of D3SD, and a video showcasing the tool, are available at https://gitlab.com/dbwis/d3sd-tool.

6 Related Work

Designing data services in CPPN requires process designers to understand how data flows within and across actor boundaries, define atomic-level service operations, and consistently aggregate them at the factory (CPPS) and supply chain (CPPN) levels, while ensuring that access control and regulatory compliance requirements arising from data sharing are addressed from the beginning of the design process. As analysed in [1], existing service-oriented approaches in Supply Chain 4.0 primarily focus on deployment concerns (e.g., fog/edge computing or IT/production integration) rather than on data sharing. They typically do not guide designers in extracting services from process models or composing them across CPPN layers, increasing the risk of inconsistent or non-compliant service designs. D3SD strives to bridge this gap by providing a unified platform for data-oriented service design, aggregation, and governance, effectively linking the three-layered data service model with concrete tool support for designers.

Several BPMN extensions have partially addressed modelling challenges in Smart Manufacturing by enriching process models with Cyber-Physical System semantics. Authors in [7] introduced RBPMN, a role-based extension capturing interactions among human, digital, and physical entities in smart factory processes. The work in [5] proposed an extension for inter-organisational business process governance incorporating data governance and accountability across collaborative networks. Authors in [4] presented BPMNE4IoT, a comprehensive framework for modelling, executing, and monitoring IoT-driven business processes, addressing both design-time modelling and runtime execution. However, none of these extensions adopts a layered data service model distinguishing atomic, CPPS, and CPPN services, or integrates GDPR role assignments and RBAC policies.

Business Process Management Systems (BPMS) such as Camunda, Flowable, and Activiti offer mature environments for modelling and executing BPMN workflows. However, they operate primarily as runtime engines focused on orchestrating process execution, and offer no native support for identifying services from process models. Moreover, their scope does not extend to managing data sharing across organisational boundaries or incorporating data sovereignty requirements and GDPR responsibilities into the modelling phase. Consequently, while they provide robust workflow execution, they leave unaddressed the governance, access-control, and cross-actor data management concerns that are central in multi-actor production networks.

7 Conclusions and Future Work

In this paper, we presented D3SD, a web-based tool that implements a three-layered data service model for CPPN. The tool supports process designers in: (i) extracting atomic services from BPMN tasks; (ii) aggregating them into CPPS and CPPN services through a variant of the P2S approach for automated cohesion/coupling analysis in a human-in-the-loop setting; and (iii) fostering privacy-by-design via RBAC and GDPR role assignments at design time. Validation on a multi-actor industrial case study, complemented by experiments in the agri-food and healthcare domains, confirms the versatility of D3SD and its ability to adapt to diverse production contexts. These evaluations show that D3SD can support data service design across sectors with different regulatory, organisational, and interoperability requirements, demonstrating robustness and generalisability.

Executable Workflows Generation. We plan to extend D3SD with the capability to generate executable workflows from service definitions. In this direction, a preliminary module has already been developed, although its full integration into D3SD is still in progress. We conceive workflow generation as a programmatic process, grounded in translation rules that map BPMN constructs to orchestration primitives, preserving semantics while ensuring transparency and controllability. The target execution environment is Laravel Workflow (now Durable Workflow), a PHP library that provides a flexible and declarative framework for managing state machines and workflow logic, and that integrates naturally with typical web-based service stacks. Grounding the translation in this framework bridges the gap between the design-time activities supported by the tool and their runtime execution. The translation strategy is defined as follows. Each BPMN actor is mapped to an independent Laravel project, preserving organisational boundaries. CPPN services become the main workflows coordinating the overall process, while CPPS services are implemented as child workflows (invoked via the `ChildWorkflowStub` class). Atomic services are translated into three coordinated components: (i) an Activity for asynchronous orchestration (via the `ActivityStub` class); (ii) a Service class encapsulating business logic; (iii) a Controller exposing the corresponding REST endpoint. Message flows are realised through HTTP communication between actors, using *webhooks* to start remote workflows and *signals* for asynchronous synchronisation. Control-flow constructs are mapped to native orchestration primitives, with parallel gateways (implemented through `ActivityStub::all()`) and exclusive gateways (handled via conditional waiting mechanisms such as `Workflow::await()`), ensuring semantic alignment with the original BPMN model. To streamline the translation effort, Large Language Models (LLMs) will be employed to suggest code templates and assist in resolving modelling ambiguities. Their role is intentionally supportive: LLM-based suggestions complement, rather than replace, the deterministic, rule-driven translation core, preserving human oversight.

Acknowledgements. The authors thank Engs. A. Bino, F. Mio, and R. Santicoli for their contributions to the development and testing of D3SD during their Master's theses at the University of Brescia, Dept. of Information Engineering.

References

1. Bagozi, A., Bianchini, D., Garda, M., Melchiori, M., Rula, A.: A multi-layered data service model for cyber-physical production networks. J. Ind. Inf. Integr., 101043 (2025)
2. Bianchini, D., Cappiello, C., De Antonellis, V., Pernici, B.: Service identification in interorganizational process design. IEEE Trans. Serv. Comput. **7**(2), 265–278 (2013)
3. Hawkins, M.: Cyber-physical production networks, internet of things-enabled sustainability, and smart factory performance in industry 4.0-based manufacturing systems. Manage. Finan. Markets **16**(2), 73–83 (2021)
4. Kirikkayis, Y., Gallik, F., Winter, M., Reichert, M.: BPMNE4IoT: a framework for modeling, executing and monitoring IotTdriven processes. Future Internet **15**(3), 90 (2023)
5. Ribeiro, V., Barata, J., da Cunha, P.R.: Modeling inter-organizational business process governance in the age of collaborative networks. Electron. Mark. **34**(1), 51 (2024)
6. Shi, H., Xu, H., Xu, X., Wang, Z.: How big service and internet of services drive business innovation and transformation. In: International Conference on Advanced Information Systems Engineering (CAiSE), pp. 517–532 (2022)
7. Skouti, T., Seiger, R., Furrer, F.J., Strahringer, S.: RBPMN: the value of roles for business process modeling. Softw. Syst. Model. **23**(6), 1375–1406 (2024)
8. Tseng, M.L., Tran, T.P.T., Ha, H.M., Bui, T.D., Lim, M.K.: Sustainable industrial and operation engineering trends and challenges Toward Industry 4.0: a data driven analysis. J. Ind. Prod. Eng. **38**(8), 581–598 (2021)

KARIBDIS - A Knowledge-Graph-Based Business Process Management System for Semantically Explainable Process Execution Support

Leon Bein(✉) and Luise Pufahl

School of Computation, Information, and Technology, Technical University of Munich, Heilbronn, Germany
Leon.Bein@tum.de, Luise.Pufahl@tum.de

Abstract. To realize their vision, Intelligent Business Process Management Systems (BPMS) need to be able to reason upon and provide explanations grounded in complex domain knowledge. *Knowledge Graph* (KG) technologies have been identified as potential key building block to achieve this, by providing means to formalize, maintain, and reason upon domain knowledge. However, research into the design of KG-based BPMS is sparse. This paper presents KARIBDIS, a prototype implementation of a KG-based BPMS. KARIBDIS allows extracting diverse process knowledge from various sources and importing and integrating it in its internal KG. Further, it enables explainable decision support during process execution, grounded in the imported knowledge. We showcase the functionalities and architecture of the prototype and demonstrate its utility using a reality-inspired example process.

Keywords: Business Process Automation · Knowledge Graphs · Knowledge-intensive Processes

1 Introduction

The *Business Process Management (BPM)* discipline is concerned with supporting the design, execution, monitoring, and improvement of an organization's business processes [8,19]. To this end, *Business Process Management Systems (BPMS)* are employed to support the execution of business processes by determining, prioritizing, and assigning tasks, managing handovers, and handling errors [8,18]. While traditional BPMSs simply follow imperative models to drive process execution, the growing complexity of organizational decision-making and the need to support less structured processes that strongly depend on expert domain knowledge motivate extending the scope and applicability of such systems, from simply orchestrating tasks to providing comprehensive decision support and optimization [5,13]. In turn, increasing data availability through digitization, as well as recent advances in Artificial Intelligence (AI)

F. Zerbato et al. (Eds.): CAiSE 2026, LNBIP 587, pp. 185–193, 2026.
https://doi.org/10.1007/978-3-032-27997-2_21

research, have facilitated the rise of a new kind of *intelligent* or *AI-augmented* BPMS, promising to enable a more autonomous and adaptive orchestration of business processes [7,18].

To adequately support domain-knowledge-driven decision-making in processes, e.g., deciding the next best steps or resources to assign, systems need to be able to reason upon and consequently internally represent said knowledge. Further, to allow process participants to trust and act upon, but also to challenge and improve, system recommendations and decisions, the systems need to provide explanations [7,9]. These explanations need to be *interpretably grounded in the domain knowledge* (or *semantically explainable* [16][1]) so that users can assess whether a system's reasoning is sound or not [6,17].

To enable, i.a., such semantically explainable execution support, *Knowledge Graph* (KG) technologies have been pointed out as a promising building block for intelligent BPMSs [1,2,4,7]. Knowledge graphs can be defined as data graphs that encode knowledge of a domain and formalize its semantics [11], promising to be a powerful tool to integrate and formalize the diverse knowledge aspects of complex business processes.

However, so far, practical research on harnessing KGs for BPMS design is sparse. In this paper, we provide a detailed demonstration of the KARIBDIS[2] prototype of a KG-based BPMS that builds upon a knowledge graph as internal knowledge base. KARIBDIS highlights the possibilities of KG-BPMSs by providing baseline implementations to (i) extract process knowledge from sources such as texts, event logs, and existing domain ontologies, (ii) integrate the extracted knowledge into a unified process knowledge graph, and (iii) use the encoded knowledge to execute business processes and provide simple semantically explainable decision support, concretizing visions of previous works [2–4]. In the remainder of this paper, we describe the features of KARIBDIS in more detail and demonstrate its utility using a reality-inspired example case.

2 Tool Description

The *KARIBDIS* prototype is publicly available as a Python-based web application through GitHub[3]. For this paper, we refer to version 1.1 of the prototype. It builds around the W3C standard *Resource Descriptor Framework (RDF)*[4] and surrounding standards and technologies, which operationalize a triple-based approach to encoding knowledge graphs. Its architecture is informed by general BPMS architectures proposed in literature (cf. [8,19]) as well as an abstract proposal from [2]. Figure 1 gives an overview of the prototype architecture and key technologies used.

[1] As opposed to *mechanistic explainability* often considered for explainable AI, which is more useful to system researchers and engineers [12].

[2] As an acronym for "Knowledge-Augmented Reasoning for Intelligent Business Decision and Intelligence Support".

[3] https://github.com/INSM-TUM/karibdis.

[4] https://www.w3.org/RDF/.

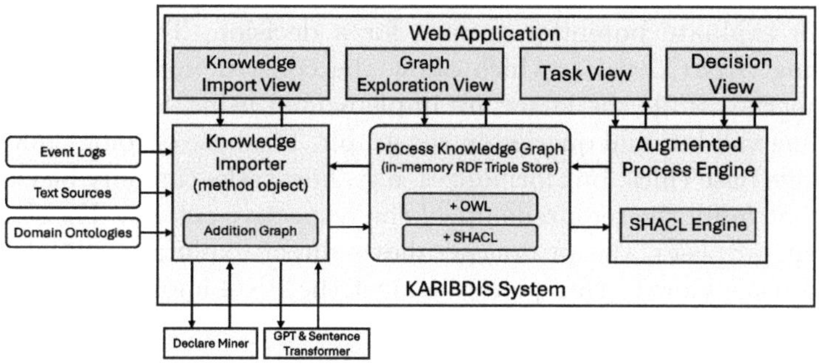

Fig. 1. KARIBIDS prototype architecture with key technologies (concretized from [2]).

The system is composed of (i) a process knowledge graph, (ii) knowledge importers, (iii) a KG-based process engine, as well as (iv) a GUI that is divided into various views. In the following, we describe the components and their relationships in more detail.

2.1 Process Knowledge Graph and Graph Exploration View

The *Process Knowledge Graph* (PKG) is a single knowledge graph that integratively encodes the different process knowledge dimensions into one data structure, including domain-specific concepts relevant for process execution, allowing them to be uniformly managed and reasoned upon (cp. [2]). The PKG is implemented as an in-memory RDF triple store using the RDFLib Python library[5]. It encodes ontological knowledge using the W3C *Web Ontology Language (OWL)*[6], and rules for driving process execution and providing decision support are encoded using the W3C *Shapes Constraint Language (SHACL)*[7].

To allow for basic process execution and to provide a framework for connecting domain-specific concepts with process management knowledge, the PKG is pre-filled with a *base process knowledge ontology*. The KARIBDIS base ontology defines classes for activities, tasks (i.e., activity instances), cases, resources, roles, and process values. Through activities and their direct dependencies, expressed as Declare-Condec [15], the ontology encodes control-flow process knowledge. Through resources, roles, and their relations, as well as through requirements of activities for performing resources, the ontology encodes organizational process knowledge. The ontology allows logging process executions through task and case nodes, as well as attributes relating to relevant lifecycle transitions (derived from [19]), such as `startedAt` for tasks.

For process rules and constraints, the prototype encodes *deductive rules*, which infer true facts from present knowledge, and *decision support rules*, which

5 https://github.com/RDFLib/rdflib.
6 https://www.w3.org/TR/owl2-rdf-based-semantics/.
7 https://www.w3.org/TR/shacl/.

constrain or evaluate potential options for a decision. The former are implemented using *SHACL rules*, which allow the construction of new facts based on graph queries, while the latter are implemented using *SHACL shapes*, which allow defining validational queries on the graph. The base ontology does not provide extensive base rules, but formalizes, e.g., how tasks can only be executed by resources that fulfill the requirements of the respective activity. For research and development purposes, the prototype allows direct exploration of the PKG by providing a basic view to run queries against the PKG and visualize the results.

2.2 Knowledge Importers and Knowledge Import View

Knowledge Importers are responsible for supporting users in encoding process knowledge into the system. The importers closely collaborate with the *Knowledge Import View* component, which brings human input and validation into the extraction and import process. Together, the components extend the classical role of process modeling tools, allowing more general knowledge input. The importers follow a four-step pipeline of extraction, alignment, validation & adaptation, and application: Process knowledge is first extracted from the various sources and brought into a structured form (a set of triples to be added). So far, KARIBDIS supports event logs, text sources, and existing domain ontologies, for each of which dedicated extraction methods have been developed. After extraction, the structured knowledge to be loaded can be aligned with ontological knowledge already present in the system by identifying and merging duplicate nodes and edges. To do so, KARIBDIS uses an NLP-based approach adapted from [10], which identifies duplication candidates but ultimately lets users decide. Finally, the system enables human validation and adaptation by presenting the knowledge update to be performed and allowing it to be freely edited.

2.3 Augmented Process Engine and Decision and Task Views

The *Augmented Process Engine* (APE) acts like a conventional process engine in that it orchestrates active cases and tasks, resource allocations, and automated task executions, and reacts to events from users and external sources. However, instead of conventional process models, the APE uses the general process semantics and specific domain semantics encoded in the PKG in order to do so, extending the approach from [3]. The APE interacts with users through the decision and task views, which display decisions to make and tasks to complete, respectively.

Like conventional process engines, the APE follows an event-centric approach. Central to this approach are knowledge update events, which can be triggered, e.g., by users opening new cases, making decisions, or completing tasks. On a knowledge update, deductive rules are reevaluated to derive all new facts (i.e., triples) that can be deduced from the new state of knowledge, in turn potentially triggering subsequent knowledge update events. After no more knowledge updates are triggered, the engine checks for open decisions, which in the prototype relate to either deciding next activities to perform or resources to allocate, derived from respective queries on the PKG.

For an open decision, all possible options are evaluated using the decision support rules. Every rule thereby contributes to potentially every option (i) a domain-grounded natural language reasoning for why to (not) choose the option, for human interpretation, as well as (ii) a numerical score for machine interpretation. The decision view then presents the respective options for human decision-making, prioritizing by total score, and highlighting for every option the aggregated reasoning for and against choosing it. Once a decision is made by the user, a respective knowledge update is triggered.

3 Demonstration

In the following, we demonstrate the usage of KARIBDIS on a reality-inspired example process for treating patients with sepsis in a hospital to show its utility. A video version of this demonstration, as well as the necessary material, can be found through the KARIBDIS repository.

3.1 Example Process

The process is derived from the *Sepsis Cases Event Log* [14], real-world observations of such a process from a Dutch hospital. Figure 2 models the key execution paths derived from the event log:

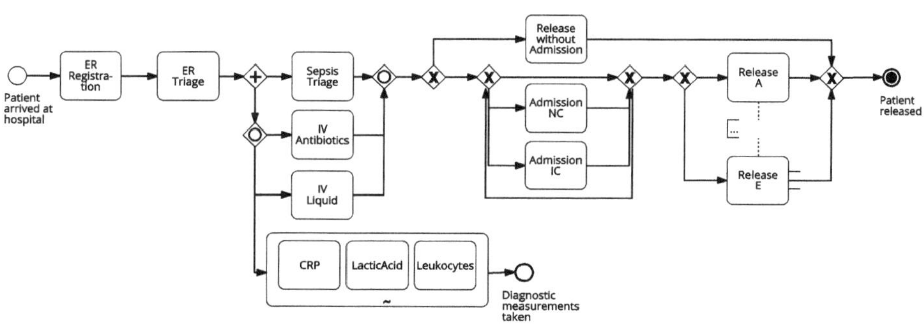

Fig. 2. Sepsis treatment process as considered in this paper, based on [14].

The process starts with a patient's *Emergency Room (ER) Registration*, followed first by a general *ER Triage*, and then a specific *ER Sepsis Triage* for patients with suspicion of sepsis. Before admission to a care ward, intravenous (IV) infusions of *Antibiotics*, *Liquid*, or both may be administered. Further, at any time after ER Triage, measurements of the biomarkers *C-Reactive Protein (CRP)*, *Lactic Acid*, and *Leukocytes* may be taken in any order and any number of times. After Sepsis Triage, patients can be either sent for *Admission to the Normal Care (NC)* ward, *Admission to the Intensive Care (IC)* ward, or *Released without Admission*, if their symptoms are mild enough. During treatment in one of the two wards, transfer is possible in case of severity changes. Finally, patients are *Released* from the wards and hospital, annotated with variants *A* to *E*. This process is driven by medical expert knowledge. For instance, the diagnosis of Sepsis can be subsumed under the fulfillment of at least two of four so-called SIRS criteria, and, for the purpose of demonstration, we assume that patients with medical risks should be transferred to the IC.

3.2 Demonstration Case

For medical processes such as the sepsis treatment process, knowledge sources include texts, such as clinical guidelines and expert inputs, event logs, such as the Sepsis Cases event log, and existing ontologies, such as the Sepon sepsis ontology[8] and the Mondo general disease ontology[9]. As an example, we can import knowledge from the sepsis event log, the Sepon and Mondo ontologies, as well as manually collected expert statements about the process. For each source, a distinct import procedure needs to be performed. For example, from the event log, i.a., activities and resources, but also collectible measurements such as the leukocyte count can be extracted in KARIBDIS. For alignment, e.g., the duplication of the leukocyte count as a process value as well as a biomarker can be detected, and respective nodes connected. During validation, a user might notice, e.g., that a textual rule was incorrectly formalized, and correct the mistake.

Let us now assume that all of the above knowledge has been loaded, and consider a concrete decision in a concrete case execution. Suppose a patient arrives at the hospital with severe symptoms and a high-risk clinical history in the form of high age and diabetes. After the patient has passed the three triage activities and their health characteristics have been recorded, a decision has to be made whether to admit the patient to the normal or intensive care unit.

Figure 3 shows parts of how such a case would be represented in the KARIBDIS process knowledge graph. The excerpt shows how common process management knowledge, e.g., tasks, activities, and cases, is formalized as a graph and integrated with domain-specific concepts such as diseases and their relationships.

The figure also highlights how deductive rules infer new edges from existing knowledge: Assuming that the black nodes and edges, i.e., collected case characteristics and performed tasks, are known, first the abnormality of the measured leukocytes, and then diagnoses for sepsis and leukocytosis can be inferred.

Then, when evaluating where to send the patient, this information is considered by the decision support rules. For instance, the diagnosis of sepsis (inferred from collected triage information) is used to recommend admission in general, while the diagnoses of diabetes and leukocytosis contribute in favor of admission to the IC, through the domain knowledge that they induce a high risk of organ

[8] https://bioportal.bioontology.org/ontologies/SEPON.
[9] https://bioportal.bioontology.org/ontologies/MONDO/.

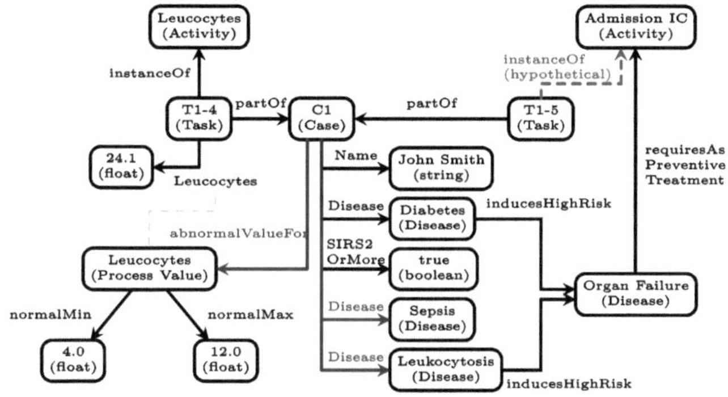

Fig. 3. PKG excerpt with reasoning knowledge for IC transfer. Green denotes deduced edges, while orange marks the decision option under evaluation. I.a., the single SIRS criteria were abstracted from. (Color figure online)

failure, which in turn requires preventive action. In contrast, the triage activities are negatively assessed, as they should only be executed once and have already been. Figure 4 displays a screenshot of the decision UI for this case, showcasing how the system consequently recommends admitting the patient to the IC, but ultimately leaves the decision to the user.

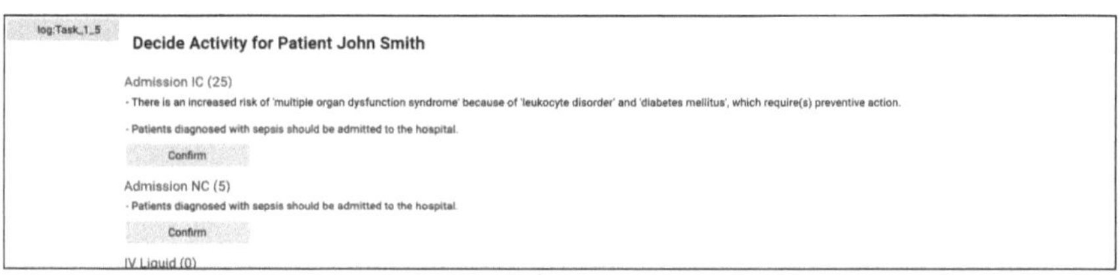

Fig. 4. Screenshot of decision interface showcasing explanation for admission to IC. Interface shows highest highest-ranked options with scores and reasoning.

4 Conclusion

In this paper, we have presented KARIBDIS, a prototype knowledge-graph-based BPMS. KARIBDIS provides proof-of-concept implementations for extracting different process knowledge aspects from sources such as event logs, texts, and ontologies and importing and integrating it in its internal KG. It enables basic explainable decision support during process execution, grounded in the imported knowledge. This paper contributes to the investigation and realization of AI-augmented BPMS that utilize knowledge graph technologies. While KARIBDIS provides only prototypical implementations, it showcases the general feasibility and utility of such systems. As such, it can serve as a foundation for further practical research into KG-based BPMS, allowing to delve deeper on each of the three sub-challenges of process knowledge extraction, encoding, and reasoning.

Acknowledgments. We thank our student assistant, Shreyansh Jha, for supporting the implementation of KARIBDIS.

Disclosure of Interests. The authors have no competing interests to declare that are relevant to the content of this article

References

1. Beheshti, A., et al.: ProcessGPT: transforming business process management with generative artificial intelligence. In: 2023 IEEE International Conference on Web Services (ICWS), IEEE, Chicago, IL, USA (2023)
2. Bein, L.: Knowledge graph reasoning for intelligent and explainable business process technologies. In: BPM 2025 Doctoral Consortium. CEUR Workshop Proceedings, vol. 4032. CEUR-WS.org (2025)
3. Bein, L., Martin, N., Pufahl, L.: KRAFT – a knowledge-graph-based resource allocation framework. In: Business Process Management: Responsible BPM Forum, Process Technology Forum, Educators Forum. Springer, Cham (2026). https://doi.org/10.1007/978-3-032-02936-2_11
4. Bein, L., Pufahl, L.: Knowledge Graphs: A Key Technology for Explainable Knowledge-Aware Process Automation? In: Business Process Management Workshops, vol. 534, Springer, Cham (2025). https://doi.org/10.1007/978-3-031-78666-2_2
5. Ciccio, D., Marrella, C., Russo, A., A.: Knowledge-intensive processes: characteristics, requirements and analysis of contemporary approaches. J. Data Semant. **4**(1) (2015)
6. Doran, D., Schulz, SC., Besold, TR.: What does explainable AI really mean? A new conceptualization of perspectives. In: 1st International Workshop on Comprehensibility and Explanation in AI and ML 2017 at (AI*IA 2017). CEUR Workshop Proceedings, vol. 2071. CEUR-WS.org (2017)
7. Dumas, M., et al.: AI-augmented business process management systems: a research manifesto. ACM Trans. Manage. Inf. Syst. **14**(1) (2023)
8. Dumas, M., La Rosa, M., Mendling, J., Reijers, H.A.: Fundamentals of Business Process Management. Springer, Berlin, Heidelberg (2018). https://doi.org/10.1007/978-3-642-33143-5.pdf
9. Fettke, P., Fournier, F., Limonad, L., Metzger, A., Rinderle-Ma, S., Weber, B.: XABPs: towards eXplainable autonomous business processes (2025)
10. Hertling, S., Paulheim, H.: OLaLa: ontology matching with large language models. In: Proceedings of the 12th Knowledge Capture Conference 2023, ACM, Pensacola FL USA (2023)
11. Hogan, A., et al.: Knowledge Graphs, Synthesis Lectures on Data, Semantics, and Knowledge, vol. 54. Springer, Cham (2022)
12. Kästner, L., Crook, B.: Explaining AI through mechanistic interpretability. Eur. J. Philos. Sci. **14**(4) (2024)
13. Kir, H., Erdogan, N.: A knowledge-intensive adaptive business process management framework. Inf. Syst. **95** (2021)

14. Mannhardt, F., Blinde, D.: Analyzing the trajectories of patients with sepsis using process mining. RADAR+EMISA 2017 (2017)
15. Pesic, M., Van Der Aalst, W.M.P.: A Declarative Approach for Flexible Business Processes Management. In: Business Process Management Workshops, vol. 4103. Springer, Berlin, Heidelberg (2006). https://doi.org/10.1007/11837862_18
16. Sander, J., Kuwertz, A.: Supplementing machine learning with knowledge models towards semantic explainable AI. In: Advances in Intelligent Systems and Computing, Springer, Cham (2021). https://doi.org/10.1007/978-3-030-74009-2_1
17. Tiddi, I., Schlobach, S.: Knowledge graphs as tools for explainable machine learning: a survey. Artif. Intell. **302** (2022)
18. Vu, H., Leopold, H., van der Aa, H.: What is business process automation anyway? In: 56th Hawaii International Conference on System Sciences (HICSS 2023). ScholarSpace (2023)
19. Weske, M.: Business Process Management: Concepts, Languages. Architectures, 3rd edn. Springer, Berlin, Heidelberg (2019). https://doi.org/10.1007/978-3-658-41584-6

FIDES: A Neuro-Symbolic Conversational Tool for Faithful Production Process Intelligence

Angelo Casciani[1(✉)], Fabrizio Italia[1], Livia Lestingi[2], Matteo Marinacci[1], Andrea Marrella[1], and Andrea Matta[2]

[1] Sapienza University of Rome, Rome, Italy
{casciani,marinacci,marrella}@diag.uniroma1.it and italia.2143104@studenti.uniroma1.it
[2] Polytechnic University of Milan, Milan, Italy
{livia.lestingi,andrea.matta}@polimi.it

Abstract. Modern production systems demand timely diagnostic and prognostic insights, yet the complexity of existing process intelligence (PI) tools creates a high technical barrier even for domain experts. This paper presents FIDES, a conversational neuro-symbolic tool designed to enable access to these analysis engines via natural language. Unlike approaches uniquely based on Large Language Models (LLMs) that often hallucinate operational results, FIDES implements a sound routing architecture: it uses LLMs strictly for understanding and translating the user's intent into machine-readable encodings, while delegating the orchestration to a domain-independent automated planner. The planner autonomously decomposes complex queries and routes them to the appropriate PI engines, ensuring rigorous results. We demonstrate the tool's maturity and usability through a lab-scale manufacturing case study, highlighting how its web-based interface enables non-technical users to perform faithful multi-perspective analysis of production processes.

Keywords: Production system · Large Language Model · Simulation · Formal Verification · Process Mining · Process Intelligence

1 Introduction and Problem Description

With the advent of Industry 4.0, production systems are experiencing an important digital transformation. Internet-of-Things devices now generate vast amounts of *production data*, enabling the creation of *digital models* that reflect manufacturing activities throughout their lifecycle [15]. Manufacturing companies aim to leverage this data to augment human expertise, fostering a collaborative environment where decision-making is faster, more accurate, and informed [2].

F. Zerbato et al. (Eds.): CAiSE 2026, LNBIP 587, pp. 194–203, 2026.
https://doi.org/10.1007/978-3-032-27997-2_22

However, achieving this goal is hindered by significant barriers. Current process intelligence (PI) tools (e.g., for simulation, verification, process mining) operate in silos and require highly skilled users to configure them and interpret raw outputs. Most domain experts (e.g., plant managers) lack the technical expertise to interact with these tools effectively. Consequently, decision-making often relies on manual data selection, which is time-consuming, error-prone, and limited to single-perspective analyses, increasing the risk of sub-optimal decisions [10].

Furthermore, the inadequacy of classical information systems engineering paradigms in managing the volatility of modern digital ecosystems calls for new methodologies and tools [16]. Sudden machine breakdowns, urgent order injections, and fluctuating resource availability demonstrate this volatility in the manufacturing domain [7]. Traditional PI systems rely on static dashboards and rigid workflows designed for stable requirements [16]. When a change occurs, the engineering effort required to reconfigure a simulation model or verify a new property is often too time-consuming to support real-time decision-making.

To address these challenges, we previously introduced a conceptual conversational framework for production systems [6]. In this paper, we extend that work with a concrete implementation by presenting FIDES, a neuro-symbolic conversational tool for PI designed to understand the user's intent, translate it into machine-readable instructions, and orchestrate PI tools. In particular, FIDES adopts an *"LLM-as-formalizer"* approach [20] from the ground up. Our architectural philosophy draws a direct analogy to the *dual-process theory* proposed by Kahneman [9]. We treat the Large Language Model (LLM) strictly as a *"system 1"* translator to handle the ambiguity of natural language. Conversely, we treat the PI engines as *"system 2"* components for the sound computation of rigorous results.

Unlike our initial work, FIDES features a user-friendly graphical user interface (GUI) and introduces a novel *sound routing mechanism* to orchestrate this duality. By replacing rigid graphical controls with a neuro-symbolic conversational interface, we enable domain experts to query the underlying digital models via natural language. While LLMs are good at language processing and translation, they are unreliable planners [17]. To prevent the "system 1" LLM from hallucinating operational outcomes, FIDES integrates a "system 2" Artificial Intelligence (AI) planner, ensuring that complex user requests are decomposed into a sound sequence of operations before being delegated to the appropriate PI engines, specifically a *simulation*, a *formal verification*, and a *process mining* module.

The tool is designed for *non-technical users* who need *actionable* insights without having deep technical knowledge of the PI engines [13]. A typical scenario involves a plant manager asking: "*What is the impact of station A failure on waiting times for producing x pieces?*" FIDES autonomously finds a sequence of actions needed to compute the requested information and routes the encoded tasks to the simulation engine. Then, it returns a faithful natural language answer, abstracting away the underlying results from the engine.

The novelty of this demonstration lies in this modular, *neuro-symbolic* software architecture. By combining the linguistic flexibility of LLMs with the reliability of formal solvers, we address the reasoning limitation of LLMs, ensuring that the chat interface does not compromise the validity of the results. We demonstrate the tool's maturity through a lab-scale case study within the MOTOWN project[1], highlighting its reliability and usability.

The rest of the paper is organized as follows. Section 2 discusses related work. Section 3 describes the software architecture, Sect. 4 presents the demonstration scenario, and Sect. 5 assesses the maturity of the tool. Finally, Sect. 6 reports the tool's current limitations and Sect. 7 concludes the paper.

2 Related Work

The application of LLMs in production systems is a rapidly growing field. Recent tools have integrated LLMs to automate simulation parameterization [22], optimize energy efficiency [21], or serve as interfaces for digital twins [18].

In the context of LLMs for automated planning, existing solutions generally fall into two categories [20]. *LLM-as-planner* approaches use the LLM directly to generate plans, suffering from hallucinations and failing to account for operational constraints [17], which is unacceptable in safety-critical industrial settings. Conversely, *LLM-as-formalizer* techniques couple LLMs with specific solvers (e.g., uniquely for heat treatment [19] or for verification [3]). However, these lack a unified orchestrator capable of handling composed PI requests that require multi-perspective analysis, such as combining process mining (for process discovery) with simulation (for what-if analysis).

FIDES differentiates itself by adopting an *LLM-as-formalizer* architecture [20]. Unlike purely LLM-based tools, we do not ask the LLM to solve the problem, but we use it strictly as a "system 1" translator to convert the natural language user's intent into formal encodings. A sound, domain-independent planner, acting as "system 2", then decomposes these queries and routes them to the appropriate PI engine. This hybrid approach ensures that the flexibility of natural language is backed by the sound guarantees of formal solvers, supporting reliability and usability.

3 Tool and Software Architecture

The architecture of FIDES follows a *modular*, *two-tier* design divided into *frontend* and *backend*, as illustrated in Fig. 1, and it is implemented in Python (`v3.11`), ensuring interoperability between the components. The starting point for the tool is an event log in XES format capturing the historical execution traces of the production system, grounding the analysis in empirical data [1]. To facilitate reproducibility and deployment, the entire tool is containerized using Docker[2].

[1] MOTOWN project: http://www.open.diag.uniroma1.it/project_detail/28097.

[2] Docker documentation: https://www.docker.com/.

Frontend. The entry point for the user is the Web-based GUI, built using the Gradio[3] library, which provides a responsive chat UI suitable for prototyping and demonstration. This interface enables non-technical stakeholders, such as plant managers, to input natural language queries (e.g., *"simulate the production of 200 pieces assuming a breakdown on station A"*). The frontend also handles the visualization of the answer, presenting both textual summaries of the PI tasks execution and artifacts (e.g., process model discovered from an event log of the production process) returned by the backend.

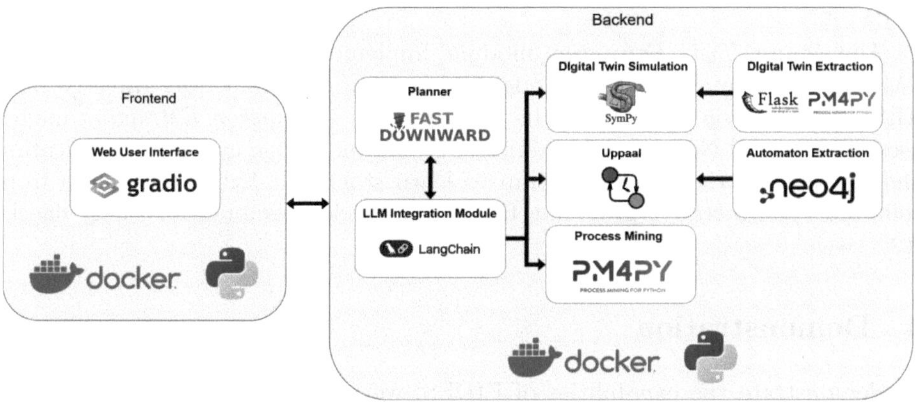

Fig. 1. High-level software architecture of the FIDES.

Backend. The core of the tool, responsible for the "neuro-symbolic" routing, encompasses two main components. The *LLM Integration Module* acts as the semantic parser, and it is implemented with LangChain[4], supporting both local and API-based language models. Instead of answering the user directly, it translates the natural language intent into a formal goal specification. Simple requests are routed directly to the appropriate PI engine. Conversely, requests composed of multiple goals are formalized as *Planning Domain Definition Language* (PDDL) problems and dispatched to a domain-independent *planner*, ensuring the system does not hallucinate execution outcomes. For this, we employ Fast Downward [8], which receives the goals and generates a sound plan that defines which engines are required to solve the problem (e.g., *discover model → verify property → run simulation*).

The backend also hosts the specialized PI engines that perform the actual analysis tasks. As the input of FIDES is the raw event log in XES, the architecture integrates two extraction components to derive up-to-date digital models directly from execution data, ensuring they accurately reflect the current state

[3] Gradio documentation: https://www.gradio.app/.

[4] LangChain documentation: https://www.langchain.com/.

of the production system. The PI tools then operate either on these extracted artifacts or directly on the event log.

In particular, the *Process Mining* module uses PM4Py to parse logs and perform process discovery, conformance checking, variant analysis, and filtering. The *Simulation* engine, built using SimPy[5], runs discrete event simulations to compute performance metrics (e.g., throughput, waiting times) based on the parametrized digital twin and the scenarios configured by the orchestrator according to the user's request. Finally, the verification module uses UPPAAL [11] for checking safety properties in Timed Computation Tree Logic (TCTL) (e.g., deadlock freedom) against the extracted Probabilistic Timed Automata (PTA) [5].

The *Digital Twin Extraction* module, implemented as a Flask service, uses PM4Py[6] to compute process model and simulation parameters directly from XES event logs via split miner [4]. Similarly, the *Automaton Extraction* engine uses Python and Neo4j[7] to maintain a system knowledge graph for verification and implements the L^*_{sha} algorithm to learn stochastic hybrid automata from collected system traces, providing the formal models required for safety checks [12].

4 Demonstration

To demonstrate the capabilities of FIDES, we utilize a lab-scale reproduction of a real-world manufacturing line, i.e., the *Lego factory* developed within the MOTOWN project. The physical twin (see Fig. 2) consists of multiple processing stations connected by conveyor belts and its execution is captured in a XES event log. A common operational challenge in this setting is managing the *trade-off* between *throughput* and *safety* (e.g., deadlock freedom) when production targets change. In this scenario, let us assume a plant manager who needs to validate a production batch of 20 units but, importantly, they must first ensure that the current configuration of the line is safe from stalling.

Figure 3 shows an interaction with the GUI, which proceeds as follows.

Step 1: Natural Language Request. The user inputs a multi-objective query into the chat interface: *"Verify if the production process is deadlock-free and tell me how much time is needed to produce 20 pieces."* This request is challenging as it requires a safety check (which needs verification from UPPAAL) and a quantitative performance estimation (via simulation by the digital twin module).

Step 2: Neuro-Symbolic Orchestration. Instead of attempting to answer directly, the LLM Integration Module parses the intent and forwards the generated PDDL problem to the Fast Downward planner. The planner analyzes the

[5] SimPy documentation: https://simpy.readthedocs.io.

[6] PM4Py documentation: https://processintelligence.solutions/pm4py.

[7] Neo4j documentation: https://neo4j.com/docs/.

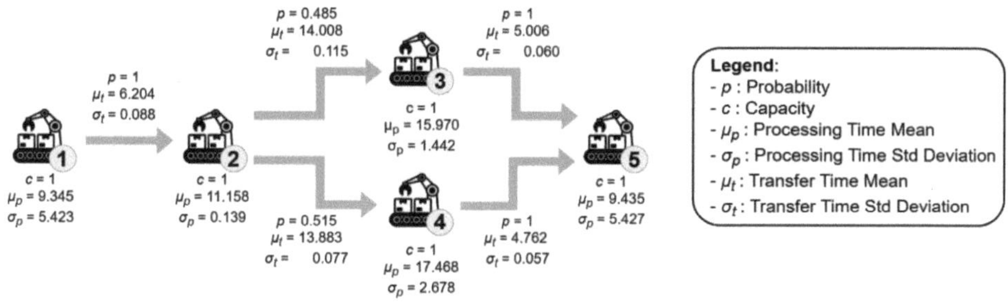

Fig. 2. The LEGO factory annotated with the corresponding simulation parameters extracted from the event log. Time-related parameters are in seconds (s).

request and generates a sound two-step execution plan, including the deadlock check and the simulation of the production of 20 units.

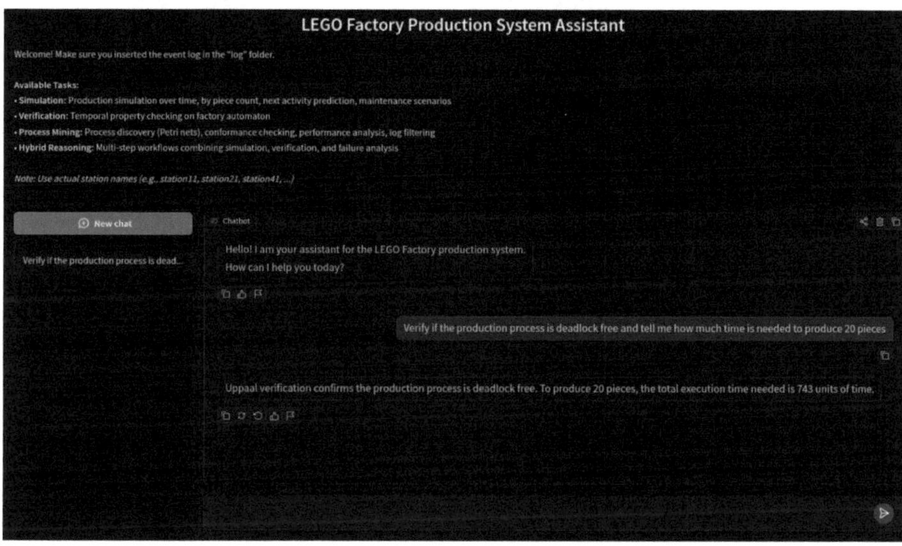

Fig. 3. Demonstration of the FIDES user interface.

Step 3: Execution and Artifact Generation. Next, FIDES executes the plan sequentially. First, UPPAAL checks for the absence of a deadlock against the PTA and returns a result (e.g., *"property satisfied"*). Then, the simulation module initializes the digital twin with the specified parameters (20 pieces in this case) and runs the discrete event simulation, returning a value (e.g., 45 min).

Step 4: Response Generation. Ultimately, the LLM aggregates the raw outputs from both engines, constructing a natural language response that contextualizes the technical results for the user, as shown in the chat window in Fig. 3.

5 Maturity and Availability

Maturity. FIDES is currently a research prototype at *Technology Readiness Level* (TRL) 4, i.e., a technology validated in a laboratory environment [14], developed within the MOTOWN national research project. The system is built upon mature, industry-standard libraries and tools, including SimPy, UPPAAL, PM4Py, and Fast Downward.

To validate the requests orchestration, we conducted a *quantitative evaluation* assessing the tool's ability to route and encode requests across varying complexity levels, ranging from simple simulation tasks to hybrid optimization. The results for a representative subset of models are summarized in Table 1. Our benchmarks confirm that the orchestration layer achieves near-perfect routing accuracy ($\geq 98\%$) when employing state-of-the-art proprietary models (e.g., `gpt-5.1` or `gemini-2.5-flash`). While open-weight models like `mistral-nemo` show promise in encoding specific queries, smaller models occasionally report hallucinated execution results instead of responding with the required encoding. This explicitly justifies the need for a tool like FIDES, which uses the LLM solely for translation and offloads the task execution to deterministic PI engines.

Furthermore, our experiments indicate that medium-sized open-source models perform reliably on atomic encoding tasks, suggesting that the tool can support a privacy-preserving mixed deployment. Organizations can use a powerful LLM for the routing logic while delegating data-sensitive schema encoding to local models. This is a critical advantage for manufacturing domains, as it allows them to maintain full control over their production data and mitigate the risks associated with external API calls.

Table 1. Few-shot accuracy over five runs for *routing* (R) and encoding of *simulation* (SI), *verification* (V), *process mining* (PM), *structural information* (ST), and *hybrid* (H) tasks.

Model	*R*	*SI*	*V*	*PM*	*ST*	*H*
llama-3.2-1b	0.21	0.48	0.02	0.52	0.81	0.08
llama-3-8b	0.70	0.79	0.78	1.00	0.98	0.52
mistral-nemo	0.91	0.92	0.72	1.00	1.00	0.63
gemini-2.5-flash	**0.99**	0.99	**0.99**	**1.00**	0.92	0.95
gpt-5.1	0.98	**1.00**	0.90	**1.00**	**1.00**	**0.99**

Moreover, a group of academics and graduate students assessed the conversational tool with respect to usability. Their feedback highlighted the system's ability to correctly interpret requests even when they were not perfectly formalized, suggesting that the natural language interface can lower the PI barrier to entry compared to configuring traditional dashboards.

Availability. The tool is released as an open-source project to foster collaboration and transparency. The source code is available on GitHub at: https://github.com/angelo-casciani/FIDES. A video demonstration showcasing the tool in the Lego factory use case is available at: https://youtu.be/bZUNWQW07bc.

6 Limitations and Threats to Validity

While FIDES lowers the barrier to entry for PI, it is not a universal solution, and its effectiveness is bounded by several limitations. First, regarding *reliability and traceability*, the multi-hop neuro-symbolic architecture introduces several layers of abstraction. While the planner guarantees that the orchestration is *syntactically* valid and logically sound, ensuring *semantic* alignment with the user's goal remains challenging. As natural language is inherently ambiguous, the LLM might interpret the request in a way that does not completely align with the user's true intent. Furthermore, abstracting the PI engine complexity away from the user naturally reduces traceability: the human receives an answer but cannot easily verify the intermediate encodings, a challenge already common to many commercial PI platforms. Additionally, the sensitivity of the final PI results to minor variations in the user's initial prompt formulation requires further investigation.

Second, regarding *system requirements and scope*, the tool currently requires substantial manual engineering to define the planning domain in PDDL and the specific preconditions and effects for each integrated PI tool. As a result, FIDES is effective at orchestrating a bounded set of pre-configured tools but cannot yet automatically integrate unseen engines out-of-the-box.

Finally, we acknowledge *threats to validity* deriving from the rapid evolution of LLMs, which could alter the performance baselines. To mitigate this, our preliminary evaluation considered both proprietary and open-source models, demonstrating that the architectural benefits hold regardless of the underlying LLM. To address the inherent stochasticity of LLMs, we averaged performance over five runs and provided the employed prompts to ensure reproducibility.

7 Conclusion

This paper presented FIDES, a conversational tool based on neuro-symbolic AI technologies that democratizes access to faithful production PI. By bridging the gap between natural language and sound PI engines, we empower non-technical users to perform multi-perspective analysis tasks, from process mining and production simulations to safety verifications, without needing to master the specific syntax of each tool. Aligning with Kahneman's dual-process theory, the main innovation of our architecture is the use of an automated planner as a *"system 2"* component for sound routing of requests encompassing the invocation of multiple PI engines, mitigating the risk of LLM (i.e., *"system 1"*) hallucinations in critical decision-making for production processes.

Future work will focus on enhancing the framework's autonomy, extensibility, and usability. To improve autonomy, we aim to implement a self-correcting feedback loop in which the LLM uses error messages from the PI tools to iteratively refine its translations without human intervention. To support extensibility, we plan to automate the formalization of the planning domain by automatically extracting the preconditions and effects of new PI engines, avoiding the current manual PDDL encoding. Regarding validation, we will move beyond the lab-scale case study to test the tool against large-scale industrial logs, identifying potential bottlenecks in the orchestration layer. Finally, we intend to develop a low-code graphical interface to enhance accessibility, featuring pre-structured question patterns to assist users with limited technical backgrounds in formulating semantically unambiguous queries.

Acknowledgments. This work was supported by the Sapienza project FOND-AIBPM, the PRIN 2022 project MOTOWN, the PNRR MUR project PE0000013-FAIR, and the EU Horizon Europe Research and Innovation Programme under Grant 101092021 (AutoTwin). Angelo Casciani conducted this research while enrolled in the Italian National Doctorate in Artificial Intelligence run by Sapienza University of Rome (CUP B53C23003500006, Mission 4 NRRP Generic Research Scholarship, Component 1). Matteo Marinacci is supported by Thales Alenia Space and Regione Lazio, through the fellowship 35752-22066DP000000040-A0627S0030 *Utilizzo dell'Intelligenza Artificiale a supporto della progettazione e qualifica del prodotto spaziale.*

References

1. Acampora, G., Vitiello, A., Stefano, B.N.D., van der Aalst, W.M.P., Günther, C.W., Verbeek, E.: IEEE 1849: the XES standard. IEEE Comput. Intell. Mag. **12**(2), 4–8 (2017)
2. Agostinelli, S., et al.: A context-aware framework to support decision-making in production planning. In: CAiSE 2024, pp. 248–264 (2024)
3. Arora, D., Kambhampati, S.: Learning and leveraging verifiers to improve planning capabilities of pre-trained language models. CoRR **abs/2305.17077** (2023)
4. Augusto, A., Carmona, J., Verbeek, E.: Advanced process discovery techniques. In: Process Mining Handbook, LNBIP, vol. 448, pp. 76–107. Springer (2022)
5. Beauquier, D.: On probabilistic timed automata. Theoret. Comput. Sci. **292**(1), 65–84 (2003)
6. Casciani, A., Lestingi, L., Marrella, A., Matta, A.: A conversational framework for faithful multi-perspective analysis of production systems. In: CAiSE 2025. LNCS, vol. 15701, pp. 163–181. Springer (2025)
7. Frigerio, N., Tan, B., Matta, A.: Simultaneous control of multiple machines for energy efficiency: a simulation-based approach. Int. J. Prod. Res. **62**(3), 933–948 (2024)

8. Helmert, M.: The fast downward planning system. J. Artif. Intell. Res. **26**, 191–246 (2006)
9. Kahneman, D.: Thinking, Fast and Slow. Penguin, London (2012)
10. Keskin, Z., et al.: LLM-enhanced human-machine interaction for adaptive decision-making in dynamic manufacturing process environments. IEEE Access **13**, 44650–44661 (2025)
11. Larsen, K.G., Pettersson, P., Yi, W.: UPPAAL in a nutshell. Int. J. Softw. Tools Technol. Transf. **1**(1–2), 134–152 (1997)
12. Lestingi, L., Sbrolli, C., Scarmozzino, P., Romeo, G., Bersani, M.M., Rossi, M.: Formal modeling and verification of multi-robot interactive scenarios in service settings. In: FormaliSE@ICSE 2022, pp. 80–90. ACM (2022)
13. Liu, M.X., Liu, F., Fiannaca, A.J., Koo, T., Dixon, L., Terry, M., Cai, C.J.: "We Need Structured Output": towards User-centered Constraints on Large Language Model Output. In: Ext. Abstracts of the CHI Conf. on Human Factors in Computing Systems, pp. 10:1–10:9. ACM (2024)
14. Mankins, J.C.: Technology readiness levels (1995)
15. Negri, E., Berardi, S., Fumagalli, L., Macchi, M.: MES-integrated digital twin frameworks. J. Manuf. Syst. **56**, 58–71 (2020)
16. Porra, J., Hirschheim, R., Land, F., Lyytinen, K.: Seventy years of information systems development methodologies from early business computing to the agile era: a two-part history. Part 1: From pre to early ISD methodology era: the emergence of ISD methodologies and their golden era (1880–1980). J. Inf. Technol. **40**(4), 441–469 (2025)
17. Stechly, K., Valmeekam, K., Kambhampati, S.: On the self-verification limitations of large language models on reasoning and planning tasks. In: ICLR 2025. OpenReview.net (2025)
18. Sun, Y., Zhang, Q., Bao, J., Lu, Y., Liu, S.: Empowering digital twins with large language models for global temporal feature learning. J. Manuf. Syst. **74**, 83–99 (2024)
19. Sun, Y., et al.: Development of an intelligent design and simulation aid system for heat treatment processes based on LLM. Mater. Des. **248**, 113506 (2024)
20. Tantakoun, M., Muise, C., Zhu, X.: LLMs as planning formalizers: a survey for leveraging large language models to construct automated planning models. In: Findings of the ACL 2025, pp. 25167–25188. ACL (2025)
21. Wang, Z., Qin, H.: Intelligent industrial production process automatic regulation system based on LLM agents. In: AIEA 2024, pp. 133–137. IEEE (2024)
22. Xia, Y., Dittler, D., Jazdi, N., Chen, H., Weyrich, M.: LLM experiments with simulation: large language model multi-agent system for simulation model parametrization in digital twins. In: ETFA 2024, pp. 1–4 (2024)

CONFETTY: A Tool for Enforcement and Data Confidentiality on Blockchain-Based Processes

Michele Kryston[1(✉)], Edoardo Marangone[2], Alessandro Marcelletti[3], and Claudio Di Ciccio[1]

[1] Utrecht University, Utrecht, The Netherlands
{m.kryston,c.diciccio}@uu.nl
[2] Sapienza University of Rome, Rome, Italy
edoardo.marangone@uniroma1.it
[3] University of Camerino, Camerino, Italy
alessand.marcelletti@unicam.it

Abstract. Blockchain technology enforces the security, robustness, and traceability of operations of Process-Aware Information Systems (PAISs). In particular, transparency ensures that all data is publicly available, fostering trust among participants in the system. Although this is a crucial property to enable notarization and auditing, it hinders the adoption of blockchain in scenarios where confidentiality is required, as sensitive data is handled. Current solutions rely on cryptographic techniques or consortium blockchains, hindering the enforcement capabilities of smart contracts and the public verifiability of transactions. This work presents the CONFETTY open-source web application, a platform for public-blockchain based process execution that preserves data confidentiality and operational transparency. We use smart contracts to enact, enforce, and store public interactions, while we adopt attribute-based encryption techniques for fine-grained access to confidential information. This approach effectively balances the transparency inherent in public blockchains with the enforcement of the business logic.

Keywords: Business Process Management · Blockchain · Multi-Authority Attribute Based Encryption · InterPlanetary File System

1 Introduction

Public permissionless blockchains enable new forms of trustworthy Process-Aware Information Systems (PAISs) and inter-organizational collaborations [16], thanks to their ensemble of characteristics. Distributed ledgers and consensus protocols underpin a shared, tamper-proof repository where multiple parties can store data without a central authority. Cryptographic primitives provide security guarantees and support accountability for recorded actions. Smart contracts

F. Zerbato et al. (Eds.): CAiSE 2026, LNBIP 587, pp. 204–212, 2026.
https://doi.org/10.1007/978-3-032-27997-2_23

are programs deployed and executed within the blockchain environment, which encode and automatically enforce business logic. In this environment, transparency is crucial since both on-chain data and the operations performed by smart contracts are visible and verifiable by everyone.

Collaborative process execution and monitoring require properties such as business logic enforcement and transparency [6]. However, in many blockchain-based approaches, exchanged data is publicly accessible, making their adoption impractical when confidentiality is essential. Therefore, finding an appropriate balance between transparency and confidentiality is fundamental in domains that handle sensitive information. Existing solutions typically address this issue in two main ways. On the one hand, private permissioned blockchains are used to restrict data visibility. While effective at hiding data, this approach reduces transparency for external auditors and often relies on strong security assumptions about the consortium system. On the other hand, cryptographic techniques enable fine-grained access control, so that only authorized parties can read the data [9,13,14]. Despite their benefits, their integration with process management systems is limited or non-existent.

To overcome this issue, we present the tool implementation of CONFidentiality EnforcemenT TransparencY (CONFETTY) [15], an approach and an architecture for blockchain-based process enactment that preserves the confidentiality of exchanged information while keeping public enforcement and transparency of process execution. In particular, we encode the business process logic of the interactions between parties in smart contracts, and we rely on Multi-Authority Attribute-Based Encryption (MA-ABE) [2] to provide fine-grained access control over activity payloads and information artifacts, ensuring that only authorized parties can access sensitive data.

The remainder of the paper is organized as follows. Section 2 presents the technologies of the framework, while Sect. 3 introduces a running example. In Sect. 4, we present CONFETTY's features by depicting its application in the running example. Section 5 evaluates the maturity of the framework. In Sect. 6, we review related work. Finally, Sect. 7 concludes the paper and proposes directions for future research and development.

2 Background

Before explaining CONFETTY, we discuss its conceptual pillars in this section.

A **blockchain** is a distributed append-only ledger that records transactions, namely asset transfers among accounts, in a tamper-proof manner. Transactions are organized into blocks that contain a set of entries (among other things) and a cryptographic hash that links each block to its predecessor, forming a chain. Most blockchains (e.g., Ethereum) support the execution of smart contracts, namely programs executed in a decentralized manner via virtual machines (e.g., the Ethereum Virtual Machine, EVM) [20].

Performing a transaction incurs a cost on the invoker. This cost depends on the complexity of the on-chain operation and the size of the exchanged data.

Therefore, users may employ additional technologies, such as distributed hash-table tamper-proof storage systems, to deal with large amounts of data. In this way, only a low-cost unique link to that file is saved on-chain. An example of such technology is **InterPlanetary File System (IPFS)** [1], a peer-to-peer network for decentralized data storage that provides access to resources via a unique content-addressed, tamper-proof locator.

Attribute-Based Encryption (ABE) is a public-key encryption scheme that links encrypted data with decryption keys via attributes . Such a scheme can be used to fine-grain access to data stored on IPFS for specific users. Typically, one authority generates decryption keys, introducing a single point of failure. Multi-Authority Attribute-Based Encryption (MA-ABE) [2] is a variant of ABE that removes this issue by improving decentralization. In the Ciphertext-Policy version of MA-ABE (MA-CPABE) [11], users are associated with attributes, and data is encrypted using logical formulas (policies) created upon such attributes.

3 Running Example

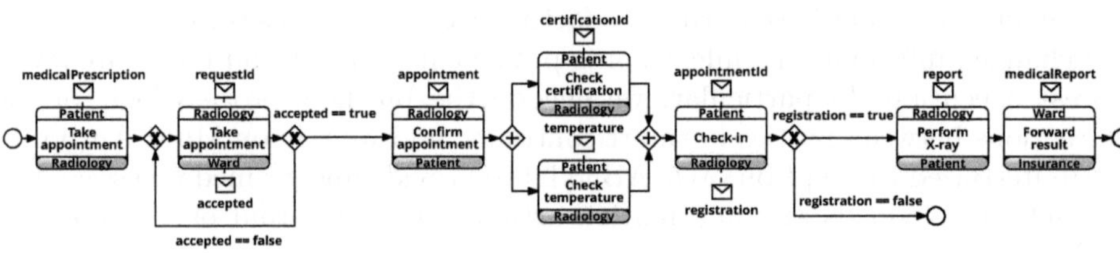

Fig. 1. BPMN choreography diagram of an X-ray diagnostic analysis [5].

Figure 1 illustrates an example in the healthcare domain inspired by [5] that we will use throughout the paper to provide a clear description of CONFETTY. First, the patient presents the medical prescription and asks for an appointment. Then, the radiology department checks the ward's availability, and the appointment is confirmed if a date is available. Otherwise, a new tentative date is proposed. Once the patient's registration details are collected, the patient's temperature and vaccination certificate are verified. A radiology clerk subsequently evaluates whether the appointment can be confirmed. If so, the X-ray exam is performed, and the results, along with a final report, are delivered to the patient. Finally, an insurance agency receives the patient's results and may access the medical report to activate compensatory actions under the subscribed contract (e.g., the reimbursement of medical bills). In addition to the participants shown in the choreography of Fig. 1, we assume the presence of the local Ministry of Health's inspector. Although not directly involved in the execution, the inspector must retain full access to the exchanged information for auditing purposes even after the process instance completes.

4 Innovation and Features

CONFETTY is the first implemented platform enabling public-blockchain based process execution with fine-grained access control mechanisms to safeguard confidential data exchanges. Figure 2 diagrammatically depicts its architecture and functionalities. In this section, we explain them and illustrate the implemented prototype at work with the example described in Sect. 3.

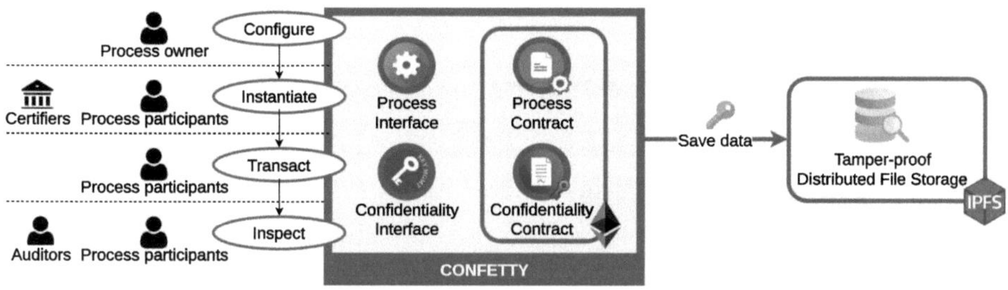

Fig. 2. An overview of the CONFETTY architecture and functionalities.

CONFETTY relies on two external infrastructures used as architectural buttresses: *(i)* A **Programmable Blockchain Platform** (in our implementation, Ethereum), *(ii)* and a **Tamper-proof Distributed File Storage** (here, IPFS). The former maintains the public state storing transactions and runs smart contracts that implement and execute the process logic. The latter (which we will henceforth refer to as Distributed FS for brevity) stores the encrypted data.

CONFETTY is comprised of four main components. *(i)* The **Process Interface** handles all the participants' operations that are related to the process. It acts as an interface to the blockchain, abstracting from the technical implementation and exposing functionality to users. *(ii)* The **Process Contract** is a smart contract that manages the process instances and their execution. It elaborates and manages all process specifications and their public states. *(iii)* The **Confidentiality Interface**, built upon MA-ABE, is responsible for handling participants' authorizations and operations involving confidential data. It operates as a façade towards the blockchain to store access grants, distributes decryption keys to the users, and handles the storage and retrieval of encrypted data. *(iv)* The **Confidentiality Contract** is a smart contract that notarizes the authorizations over confidential data, and their writing and access operations.

CONFETTY provides four main functionalities. Figure 3 shows the graphical user interface designed to support the first two: *Configure* and *Instantiate*. *(i)* The **Configure** functionality allows process owners to specify the process to run on-chain. The process owner sends the process specification files to the Process Interface, which elaborates the inputs and stores the behavioral and business logic on-chain. Then, the Process Interface composes the access policies for the confidential data. The process owner can revise these policies by adding custom roles that are not expected active parties in the process but need access to data (e.g., the Ministry of Health). Once policies are confirmed, they are sent to the Confidentiality Interface, which stores them in the Distributed FS and saves the generated locator on-chain.

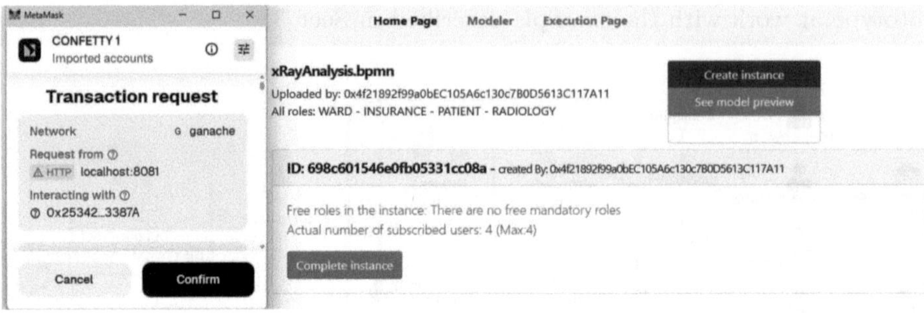

Fig. 3. Kick-start of the process instance setting its public state on-chain.

(ii) The **Instantiate** functionality allows users to authenticate themselves as participants in the process, specifying their role via the Process Interface. Certifiers attest to authentication and confirm the user's self-declared roles. The Process Interface merges the newly received information with the process data acquired in the Configure functionality. Thereupon, a selected participant kick-starts a new process instance via the Process Interface, thereby initializing the instance's public state by sending a transaction.

Figure 4 shows CONFETTY's graphical user interface for the *Transact* and *Inspect* functionalities. *(iii)* The **Transact** functionality allows process participants to exchange information at runtime, in the form of both public and confidential data. Public data is directly stored on-chain, becoming publicly available and usable for control-flow decisions. A user sends execution data to the Process Interface, which invokes the Process Contract to request a state update and forwards the execution data. This step also advances the process, updating the expected next elements and participants. To handle confidential information, the Process Interface receives and forwards the data to the Confidentiality Interface, which retrieves the policy from the Distributed FS and uses it to encrypt the data via MA-ABE, ensuring that only authorized participants can access it. Then, the Confidentiality Interface stores the encrypted data in the Distributed FS, its locator in the Confidentiality Contract, and notarizes the operation on-chain.

(iv) The **Inspect** functionality allows participants and auditors to access data. Public data can be freely retrieved, while confidential data is restricted to authorized users only. In the latter case, the user requests a decryption key via the Confidentiality Interface. Then, the Confidentiality Interface forwards the request to the Confidentiality Contract, which notarizes it on the Distributed

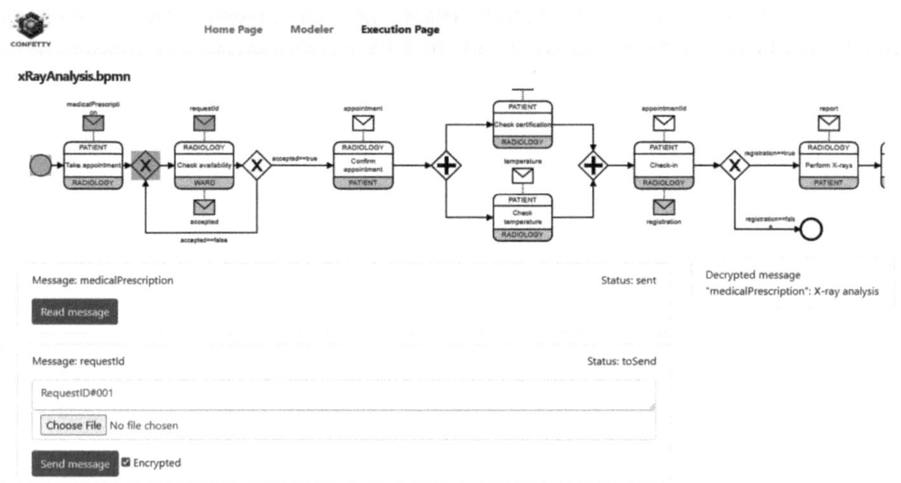

Fig. 4. CONFETTY interface showing examples of message send and read.

Ledger for traceability. The Confidentiality Interface generates an attribute-based key (or *a-b key* for short) for the user who requested it. The a-b key, as the name suggests, encodes the user's attribute as per the ABE scheme. Once the user receives the a-b key, they can invoke the Confidentiality Interface to read the confidential data. Then, the Confidentiality Interface retrieves the encrypted data from the Distributed FS and forwards it to the user. Only if the user's attributes satisfy the policy specified during data encryption can the user's a-b key decrypt the confidential data.

A Note on Decryption Keys. We remark that an a-b key is associated with the individual user. The same key will be used to access all messages. In our example, consider a user who holds the attributes characterizing them as a `WARD` in the context of the case `PID476948`. Their a-b key can decrypt the requestId for that case, but not the appointment. The a-b key of a `PATIENT` user participating in the same case (`PID476948`) can decrypt the appointment instead, but not the requestId. Notice that an `INSPECTOR` from the Ministry of Health, instead, can use their unique a-b key to access all the aforementioned documents regardless of the related process instance. Since their individual key is the sole instrument for users to access a document, the Confidentiality Interface does not need to generate a different decryption key for every document and give the same copy to multiple users (which would be necessary with symmetric encryption [10]), nor create numerous copies of the same document for different decryption keys (one per user, if an asymmetric encryption scheme was employed [9]). Therefore, our approach saves unnecessary data replications and key distributions, while ensuring integrity. Also, as the key stays with the users, and the documents are stored and notarized on tamper-proof external infrastructures (the Distributed

FS and the Programmable Blockchain Platform, respectively), the information remains available even in case the CONFETTY system stops functioning.

5 Maturity

An Apache Tomcat 9 application server[1] hosts the Process Interface and the Confidentiality Interface, implemented with JDK 13 and Python 3.6.9, respectively. Users interact with the server via the TLS protocol. Go-ipfs v. 0.7 operates as the Distributed Tamper-proof File Storage.(See footnote 1) Sepolia and Ganache(See footnote 1) serve as Programmable Blockchain Platforms, the former as a test environment and the latter as a local RPC. Both are connected to the Process and Confidentiality Interfaces through Web3.js v. 1.10.0 (see Footnote 1). Smart contracts are executed on the Ethereum Virtual Machine (EVM) and are written in Solidity v. 0.8.17.

We developed an initial prototype of CONFETTY to experimentally evaluate the performance of our approach [15], built upon the workflow management engine of ChorChain [3] and the data encryption/decryption mechanisms of MARTSIA [8]. Compared to that preliminary release, this version of the CONFETTY tool comes packaged in a Docker container to enable its deployment and execution on a local machine. Also, it offers a refined graphical interface for users to interact with its functionalities. Results from literature-based processes and synthetic tests (varying the number of process participants, the choreography model size, the number of gateways, and the message payload size) show that off-chain execution time grows linearly and remains orders of magnitude smaller than the average Ethereum block time. Therefore, the tool imposes little to no overhead on the bandwidth for infrastructural information. Regarding costs, they are comparable to or lower than those of state-of-the-art tools, although the latter only permit users to send process messages in clear. Experimental evidence is reported in the aforementioned paper [15], alongside a discussion of the framework's robustness to cyberattacks with a threat model analysis.

The source code and Wiki, offering a step-by-step tutorial on system setup and operation, are publicly available at https://github.com/Process-in-Chains/CONFETTY. To watch a video showcasing the tool, visit https://youtu.be/lj529HyqsbQ.

6 Related Work

Lately, several solutions have been developed for (1) blockchain-based process automation and (2) preserving data confidentiality using cryptographic techniques. To automate collaborative processes (1), approaches including Caterpillar [12], Lorikeet [19], and the aforementioned ChorChain [4], have shown that

[1] Apache Tomcat: https://tomcat.apache.org/; go-ipfs (now Kubo): https://github.com/ipfs/kubo; Sepolia: https://sepolia.dev/; Ganache: https://archive.trufflesuite.com/ganache/; Web3.js: https://web3js.readthedocs.io/en/v1.10.0/. Accessed: April 10, 2026.

blockchain-based solutions can strengthen trust among participants in multi-party collaborations and support monitoring and auditing [18]. They advance the integration of blockchain technology with process management, leveraging the security and traceability guarantees offered by distributed ledgers. However, they mainly address the control-flow perspective and do not provide mechanisms for secure, fine-grained access control to share data stored on public platforms. To cater for data confidentiality on blockchain (2), encryption techniques have been leveraged. B-Box [17], CAKE [14], LU-MAABE-OD [7] and the aforesaid MARTSIA [13] combine IPFS, ABE, and blockchain technology to this end, similarly to our approach. Although they address secure access control on blockchains, these solutions lack integration with process management systems. CONFETTY is the first solution addressing both the above challenges.

7 Conclusion and Future Work

In this work, we introduced CONFETTY, a platform for public-blockchain based process execution that combines transparency and public enforcement of the workflows while preserving secrecy of confidential data flows. Process data for enforcement and auditability purposes is maintained on-chain as a public state, whose evolution is handled by smart contracts implementing the process control-flow and data-flow logic. We guarantee data confidentiality through the cryptographic scheme of MA-ABE. In CONFETTY, data is encrypted, and access is granted only to authorized parties based on user attributes used to define access policies, which are bound to users' decryption keys. Future work includes a field study to evaluate usability and adoption with real-world stakeholders. Further directions are the full decentralization of both architecture and governance and the design of mechanisms for automated decision support via computation over encrypted data.

Acknowledgments. This work was partly funded by projects Health-e-Data and BRIE, funded by the EU-NGEU under the Cyber 4.0 NRRP MIMIT programme, and ASGARD, funded by Sapienza University of Rome under grant RG123188B3F7414.

References

1. Benet, J.: IPFS - content addressed, versioned, P2P file system. CoRR **abs/1407.3561** (2014)
2. Chase, M.: Multi-authority attribute based encryption. In: Vadhan, S.P. (ed.) TCC 2007. LNCS, vol. 4392, pp. 515–534. Springer, Heidelberg (2007). https://doi.org/10.1007/978-3-540-70936-7_28
3. Corradini, F., Marcelletti, A., Morichetta, A., Polini, A., Re, B., Tiezzi, F.: ChorChain: a model-driven framework for choreography-based systems using blockchain. In: ITBPM@BPM, pp. 26–32 (2021)
4. Corradini, F., Marcelletti, A., Morichetta, A., Polini, A., Re, B., Tiezzi, F.: Engineering trustable and auditable choreography-based systems using blockchain. ACM Trans. Manage. Inf. Syst **13**(3) (2022)

5. Corradini, F., Marcelletti, A., Morichetta, A., Polini, A., Re, B., Tiezzi, F.: A flexible approach to multi-party business process execution on blockchain. Fut. Gen. Comp. Syst. **147**, 219–234 (2023)
6. Di Ciccio, C., Meroni, G., Plebani, P.: On the adoption of blockchain for business process monitoring. SoSyM **21**(3), 915–937 (2022)
7. Hong, L., Zhang, K., Gong, J., Qian, H.: A practical and efficient blockchain-assisted attribute-based encryption scheme for access control and data sharing. Secur. Commun. Netw. **2022**(1), 4978802 (2022)
8. Kryston, M., Marangone, E., Di Ciccio, C.: MARTSIA: a tool for confidential data exchange via public blockchain. In: CAiSE Forum, pp. 173–180 (2025)
9. Köpke, J., Meroni, G., Salnitri, M.: Designing secure business processes for blockchains with SecBPMN2BC. Future Gener. Comput. Syst. **141**, 382–398 (2023)
10. Lin, C., He, D., Zeadally, S., Huang, X., Liu, Z.: Blockchain-based data sharing system for sensing-as-a-service in smart cities. ACM Trans. Internet Techn. **21**(2), 40:1–40:21 (2021)
11. Liu, Z., Jiang, Z.L., Wang, X., Wu, Y., Yiu, S.: Multi-authority ciphertext policy attribute-based encryption scheme on ideal lattices. ISPA/IUCC/BDCloud/SocialCom/SustainCom pp. 1003–1008 (2018)
12. López-Pintado, O., García-Bañuelos, L., Dumas, M., Weber, I., Ponomarev, A.: Caterpillar: a business process execution engine on the Ethereum blockchain. Softw. Pract. Exper. **49**(7), 1162–1193 (2019)
13. Marangone, E., Di Ciccio, C., Friolo, D., Nemmi, E.N., Venturi, D., Weber, I.: MARTSIA: enabling data confidentiality for blockchain-based process execution. In: EDOC. pp. 58–76 (2023)
14. Marangone, E., Di Ciccio, C., Weber, I.: Fine-grained data access control for collaborative process execution on blockchain. In: BPM Blockchain and RPA Forum, pp. 51–67. Springer (2022)
15. Marcelletti, A., Marangone, E., Kryston, M., Di Ciccio, C.: Balancing confidentiality and transparency for blockchain-based process-aware information systems. In: BPM Forum, pp. 238–255 (2026)
16. Mendling, J., Weber, I., van der Aalst, W.M., et al.: Blockchains for business process management - challenges and opportunities. ACM Trans. Manag. Inf. Syst. **9**(1), 4:1–4:16 (2018)
17. Pham, V.D., Tran, C.T., Nguyen, T.: B-box - a decentralized storage system using IPFS, attributed-based encryption, and blockchain. In: RIVF. pp. 1–6 (2020)
18. Stiehle, F., Weber, I.: Blockchain for business process enactment: a taxonomy and systematic literature review. In: BPM Blockchain and RPA Forum. LNBIP, vol. 459, pp. 5–20. Springer (2022)
19. Tran, A.B., Lu, Q., Weber, I.: Lorikeet: a model-driven engineering tool for blockchain-based business process execution and asset management. In: BPM Demos, pp. 56–60. Springer (2018)
20. Wood, G.: Ethereum: a secure decentralised generalised transaction ledger (2014)

CAiSE 2026 Doctoral Consortium - Process Mining: Supporting Analysis and Use in Practice

Interactive Context-Aware Navigation of Process Models

Zahra Ahmadi(✉)

Research Centre for Information Systems Engineering (LIRIS), KU Leuven, Warmoesberg 26, 1000 Brussels, Belgium
zahra.ahmadi@kuleuven.be

Abstract. Process mining enables the discovery of process models from event data. However, traditional process discovery approaches often ignore contextual information or process attributes that may strongly influence real-world process behavior. This PhD research proposes a novel contextualized process discovery approach that exploits key contextual information to improve process analysis. The main idea is to use the information to enrich or abstract the discovered process model. On the one hand, the information can be used to specialize activities, resulting in contextualized process models that make context-dependent behaviors explicit. On the other hand, they can be used to group or abstract behaviours, which details may hinder process analysis. An important challenge is to find the right level of detail/abstraction that helps to answer a specific research question, i.e., finding the right trade-off between model complexity and interpretability. To support the selection and comparison of contextualized and generalized process models, the PhD also designs complexity-aware metrics to be considered within the contextualized process mining approach, including entropy-based metrics. Additionally, the PhD aims to develop tool support for interactive, context-aware process discovery that allows navigation through contextualization via zoom in/out functionality.

Keywords: Contextualization · Generalization · Context-aware Process Discovery

1 Introduction

Process mining (PM) techniques are widely used to discover, analyze, and improve processes based on event data [1]. By discovering process models from event logs, PM enables analysts to get insights into how processes are actually executed in practice. However, many existing discovery approaches in PM focus on control-flow behavior and treat events as context-independent, overlooking the influence of contextual information such as environmental conditions or user characteristics.

In real-world processes, context variables play a critical role in shaping process behavior. To get more accurate and meaningful process discovery results,

F. Zerbato et al. (Eds.): CAiSE 2026, LNBIP 587, pp. 215–223, 2026.
https://doi.org/10.1007/978-3-032-27997-2_24

contextualization emerges as a powerful way to use information about the real-world environment in which a process occurs [11]. Additionally, it may be that process executions are recorded in a level of detail that hinders the discovery of the underlying process. While several techniques have been proposed for considering contextual information into process models [8,9,13,16], most approaches do not directly integrate this information into the control flow of discovered models. Hence, analysts often struggle to interpret the models to navigate flexibly between detailed and abstract process views.

This PhD research focuses on process discovery, aiming to enable context-aware navigation across different abstraction levels of process models. Context variables are used to (i) specialize activities and uncover context-dependent behavior, allowing analysts to zoom in on specific patterns and (ii) generalize detailed activity executions, enabling analysts to zoom out and obtain high-level views of complex processes. For example, in an order handling process, an activity such as "Process order" may be executed differently depending on context variables such as order type, customer priority, or delivery urgency. A detailed model that shows all these variations may become complex and difficult to interpret, or a simplified model that ignores these differences may hide important behavioral patterns. Therefore, analysts need the ability to flexibly move between detailed, context-aware views and higher-level process models depending on the analysis objective.

The research investigates contextualized process discovery techniques that systematically integrate context variables into process discovery. This includes creating specialization activity hierarchies and complexity-aware guidance mechanisms that balance detail and understandability. Additionally, the research aims to develop a tool that supports an interactive way, moving beyond traditional frequency-based process discovery tools.

The proposed approaches will be evaluated using real-world datasets from different domains, including animal behavior analysis, human behavior monitoring, industrial processes, and healthcare. Through this work, the PhD aims to provide both methodological foundations and practical support for more interpretable, explainable, and flexible process analysis. While the current focus is on contextualized specialization to zoom in on process behavior, future work will also explore context-driven generalization to support zooming out and achieving high-level process views.

2 Research Problem and Research Questions

2.1 Research Problem

Context variables, including personal, social, task-related, environmental, and spatio-temporal information [11], play a crucial role in shaping process behavior. However, current process discovery techniques offer limited support for incorporating context variables into process model discovery. Most existing approaches either ignore this information or treat it as supplementary information, rather than integrating it directly into the structure of the discovered process model.

One approach for incorporating context variables is activity relabeling, where activities are refined based on the values of contextual variables [4]. However, this approach can rapidly increase the number of distinct activities in the model, leading to increased complexity and reduced interpretability. This highlights a fundamental trade-off between providing contextual detail and maintaining model understandability. Conversely, when analysts require a high-level perspective on highly variable processes, such as those in healthcare or human behavior analysis, existing techniques may struggle to find an interpretable underlying process.

This reveals a fundamental limitation in current process discovery techniques: the absence of mechanisms for flexible, context-aware navigation across different abstraction levels of process models. Analysts need support not only to zoom into detailed, context-specific behaviors, but also to abstract away from complexity and obtain meaningful high-level process views, all while being guided by considerations of complexity and interpretability. The central challenge addressed in this PhD research is therefore: How can context variables be used to support bidirectional navigation in process discovery (zooming in and out) across abstraction levels of process models, while maintaining an appropriate balance between model complexity and understandability?

2.2 Research Questions

To address this problem, the following research questions are defined:

- RQ1- Contextualized Specialization (zooming in): How can context variables be systematically used to discover contextualized process models that reveal context-dependent behavior?
- RQ2- Context-Driven Generalization (zooming out): How can context variables be used to generalize detailed activity executions and obtain higher-level process models that support global understanding of highly variable processes?
- RQ3- Complexity and Interpretability: How does context-based specialization and generalization affect process model complexity and understandability, and how can this trade-off be quantified?
- RQ4- Tool Support and Interaction: How can tool support be designed to enable interactive, context-aware zooming in and zooming out of process models?

These research questions aim to provide both methodological contributions and practical guidance for applying contextualized process discovery in real-world scenarios. Figure 1 shows the overview of this research.

3 Related Work

This section offers an extensive review of previous research on contextualization process discovery techniques. Context is defined as "any information that can be used to characterize the situation of an entity", where an entity may refer to persons, places, or objects relevant to a user application [10]. In the domain of PM, several studies emphasize the importance of context for improving analysis

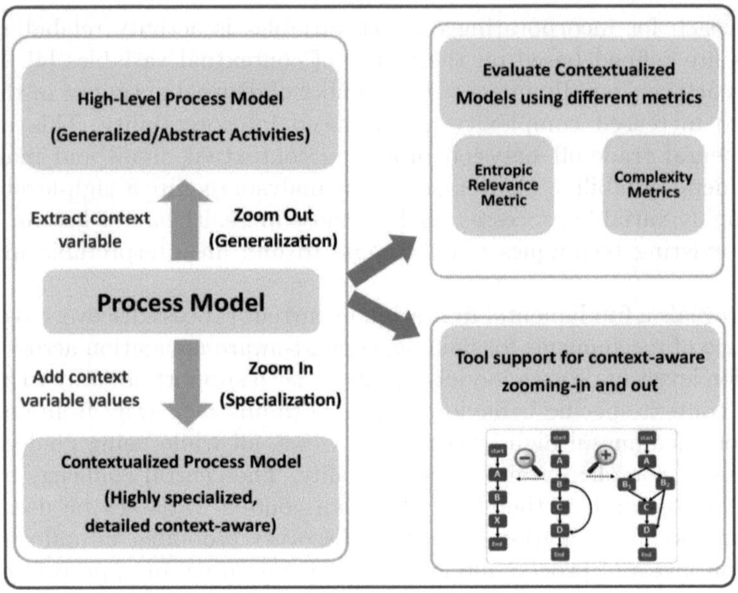

Fig. 1. Overview of the PhD research vision.

quality and interpretability. The authors in [2] stress the relevance of considering the context of events in business process analysis and incorporating context-specific event data to enrich PM and enhance analysis accuracy. Similarly, the work in [11] aims to improve the quality of eventâĂŞactivity mappings by considering contextual information, proposing a framework with different context dimensions: personal and social, task, environmental, and spatial-temporal, to address scenarios involving low-level events. Another context classification system is introduced in [9] for use in process monitoring and prediction. In this research, particular attention is given to the task dimension, which captures the specific details and circumstances surrounding the execution of a task within a business process, including task rules, goals, causality, history, application, and properties.

Some studies have further incorporated context into PM techniques. For example, [12] proposes the Guided Process Discovery method, which groups low-level events based on behavioral activity patterns while capturing domain knowledge about the relationship between high-level activities and low-level events. The framework introduced in [14] focuses on context-aware PM by automatically capturing contextual information from business process execution environments to enhance process flexibility. In [17], a framework is proposed for generating label refinements based on the time attribute of events. The CAP3 approach presented in [13] leverages context-specific domain knowledge and expert input to identify relevant contextual information. Furthermore, [16] introduces a technique that integrates control-flow and data perspectives into a single approach by expanding inductive process discovery, prioritizing context data over control flow. The TROPIC approach in [8] exploits contextual information through a multi-perspective trace clustering technique that considers control flow, trace attribute data, and time-series sensor data.

Although prior research has not fully explored the use of contextual information for deriving process insights, this PhD research uses context variables to develop a new process discovery approach that flexibly exploits contextual information through activity specialization hierarchies. The proposed research aims to contribute to understanding and optimizing processes at different levels of granularity.

4 Research Approach and Work Completed So Far

4.1 Contextualized Activity Specialization Hierarchy Approach

This research [4] proposes an approach for contextualized process discovery based on hierarchical activity relabeling. The key idea is that activities in an event log can be relabeled according to selected context variables, allowing the same activity to be represented differently under different contextual values. To structure this process, activity hierarchy specializations are used, where each level of the hierarchy corresponds to a specific degree of contextualization, enabling the generation of multiple contextualized event logs and consequently the mining of their corresponding process models. This hierarchical structure supports incremental refinement and allows analysts to granulate the process by progressively incorporating additional contextual information. Hence, the approach enables the exploration of how context variables influence process behavior while retaining control over model complexity. Figure 2 illustrates an example of a hierarchical tree for the *Eating* activity from analyzing the bees' behaviour experiment. At the first level, the activity is specialized according to two values for the flower content: *treated* and *untreated*. At the second level, each node from the first level is further specialized based on two flower color values, *yellow* and *blue*.

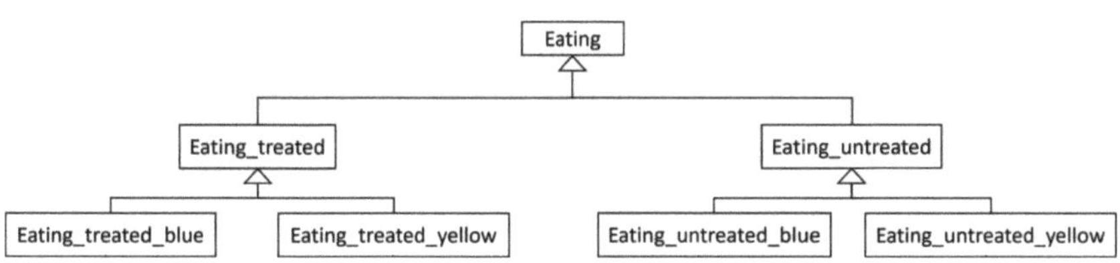

Fig. 2. An example of a hierarchical tree for Eating activity. (Color figure online)

This concept was operationalized in the CARPI (Contextualized Activity hieRarchies for Process dIscovery) method in [5], which provides a structured, multi-phase approach to selecting relevant activities, identifying contextual variables by providing different approaches to minimize the values of context variables, constructing specialization hierarchies, and discovering contextualized process models. Figure 3 shows the steps of the CARPI approach. The approach consists of both automated and manual steps. Some steps are supported by algorithmic techniques, such as clustering techniques in 2.3 or process discovery methods in 4.2; other steps, such as the selection of relevant context variables in 2.2 or the selection of specialization level in 4.1, rely on expert knowledge to ensure meaningful and domain-relevant results.

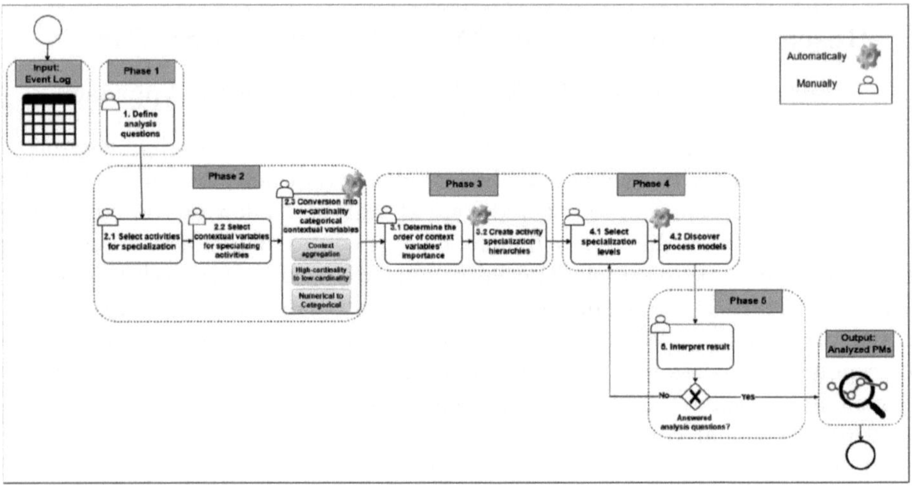

Fig. 3. The proposed CARPI approach.

CARPI has been applied to multiple real-world datasets to evaluate its effectiveness. The first case study uses a bee behavior dataset, where context variables describe different environmental and situational conditions [3]. The second case study focuses on human behavior in a smart home environment, where context variables capture aspects of daily routines and living conditions [15]. The resulting contextualized process models reveal differences in behavior across contextual situations, supporting a more fine-grained understanding of daily activities [7]. In addition, the approach has been evaluated in an industrial manufacturing setting, demonstrating its applicability beyond behavioral datasets [5]. The results show that incorporating context variables through activity relabeling significantly improves the interpretability of process behavior. At the same time, the experiments highlight the risk of increased complexity when too many context variables are applied simultaneously.

4.2 Balancing Complexity and Interpretability with ContextER

To address the complexity introduced by contextualization, we propose ContextER, an entropy-based approach that automatically evaluates and selects appropriate specialization levels [6]. ContextER uses Entropic Relevance to quantify behavioral unpredictability and identify models that offer the best trade-off between complexity and informativeness. This work shows how complexity metrics can be used not only for evaluation, but also as decision-support tools during contextualized process discovery. Current work focuses on refining this metric and exploring additional complexity-related measures that can be used to compare contextualized models.

5 Ongoing and Future Work

The ongoing and future works of this PhD focus on improving the evaluation metric as a decision tool for guiding experts into the best contextualized model, introducing a context-driven generalization approach to abstract the process model, and developing a tool that can support zooming in/out of the process model based on the context information.

5.1 Evaluation Metric as a Decision Tool

In addition to the entropy-based metric explored so far, ongoing work focuses on extending and comparing a set of complexity and interpretability metrics for contextualized process models. This includes investigating behavioral complexity metrics, which capture unpredictability in execution behavior, as well as structural complexity metrics, which reflect the structural properties of models. The goal of this work is to create a composed metric that can be used as a decision-support tool to assist experts in selecting process models at the appropriate abstraction level.

5.2 Context-Driven Generalization (Zooming Out)

While the completed work focuses primarily on zooming into processes, the next phase of this PhD will investigate the opposite direction: process generalization. In many real-world domains, such as healthcare, event logs often show a very high degree of variability, and they have fine-grained activity labels, where applying traditional process discovery techniques leads to extremely detailed and complex models. To address this challenge, future work will investigate generalization, in which detailed activity labels are abstracted into more general ones. Instead of refining activities using context, this approach aims to zoom out by grouping detailed activity executions based on shared contextual characteristics. For example, in healthcare datasets where the same medical action may be recorded under different labels, contextual variables such as medical speciality, treatment category, or patient condition can be used to generalize activities and obtain a higher-level view of the process. This allows analysts to switch between detailed and abstract representations depending on their goal. Together, contextualized specialization and context-driven generalization enable a bidirectional navigation mechanism across different abstraction levels of process models.

5.3 Tool Support for Context-Aware Zooming In and Out

In [7], we proposed the use of different visualizations for process models by defining several KPIs and representing specialized activities using different colors. In addition, the frequency of activities and transitions was visualized through variations in node size and the thickness of arrows within the process model. A further key objective of this PhD is to develop a tool that enables interactive navigation between different abstraction levels. Current discovery tools rely on frequency-based and control-flow-based criteria, such as filtering infrequent behavior or simplifying transitions, and they do not consider context variables and therefore only provide limited support for explaining why certain behavior occurs. The designed tool will introduce a context-aware interaction concept, allowing users to inject context variables into the model to specialize activities, abstract activities by grouping context values to generalize behavior and compare models using complexity and interpretability metrics. By integrating contextual information directly into model construction and exploration, it will support more meaningful and explainable process analysis.

Acknowledgments. This research was supported by the Flemish fund for scientific research (FWO) with grant number G0B6922N.

References

1. der Aalst, V., Mining, W.P.: Discovery, Conformance and Enhancement of Business Processes, vol. 136. Springer, Heidelberg (2011)
2. van der Aalst, W., Dustdar, S.: Process mining put into context. IEEE Internet Comput. **16**(1), 82–86 (2012)
3. Ahmadi, Z., Bertrand, Y., Pozo Romero, M.I., Serral, E.: Analysing the foraging behaviour of bees using process mining: a case study. In: International Conference on Process Mining, pp. 5–18. Springer (2023)
4. Ahmadi, Z., De Weerdt, J., Serral Asensio, E.: A novel contextualization method for process discovery using activity specialization hierarchies. In: International Conference on Business Process Modeling, Development and Support, pp. 143–155. Springer (2024)
5. Ahmadi, Z., De Weerdt, J., Serral Asensio, E.: Context-driven process discovery: enhancing process flow interpretability with contextualized activity hierarchies: Z. ahmadi et al. Software and Systems Modeling, pp. 1–20 (2025)
6. Ahmadi, Z., De Weerdt, J., Serral Assension, E.: Contexter: an entropy-based contextualized process discovery approach to balance interpretability and complexity. In: IFIP Working Conference on The Practice of Enterprise Modeling, pp. 245–259. Springer (2025)

7. Ahmadi, Z., Shirali, M., De Weerdt, J., Serral, E.: Context-enriched process discovery from IoT data sources for human behavioral monitoring. In: IFIP Working Conference on The Practice of Enterprise Modeling, pp. 209–226. Springer (2025)
8. Bertrand, Y., De Weerdt, J., Serral, E.: A novel multi-perspective trace clustering technique for IoT-enhanced processes: a case study in smart manufacturing. In: BPM 2023, pp. 395–412. Springer (2023)
9. Brunk, J.: Structuring business process context information for process monitoring and prediction. In: IEEE 22nd CBI, vol. 1, pp. 39–48. IEEE (2020)
10. Dey, A.K.: Understanding and using context. Pers. Ubiquit. Comput. **5**, 4–7 (2001)
11. Koschmider, A., Mannhardt, F., Heuser, T.: On the contextualization of event-activity mappings. In: Daniel, F., Sheng, Q.Z., Motahari, H. (eds.) BPM 2018. LNBIP, vol. 342, pp. 445–457. Springer, Cham (2019). https://doi.org/10.1007/978-3-030-11641-5_35
12. Mannhardt, F., de Leoni, M., Reijers, H.A., van der Aalst, W.M., Toussaint, P.J.: Guided process discovery-a pattern-based approach. IS **76**, 1–18 (2018)
13. Márquez-Chamorro, A.E., Revoredo, K., Resinas, M., Del-Rio-Ortega, A., Santoro, F.M., Ruiz-Cortes, A.: Context-aware process performance indicator prediction. IEEE Access **8**, 222050–222063 (2020)
14. Mounira, Z., Mahmoud, B.: Context-aware process mining framework for business process flexibility. In: Proceedings of the 12th IIWAS, pp. 421–426 (2010)
15. Rad, M.F., Roudposhti, K.K., Khoobkar, M.H., Shirali, M., Ahmadi, Z., Fernández-Llatas, C.: DAMMI: daily activities in a psychologically annotated multi-modal IoT dataset (2024). arXiv:2410.04152 arXiv preprint
16. Shraga, R., Gal, A., Schumacher, D., Senderovich, A., Weidlich, M.: Inductive context-aware process discovery. In: 2019 ICPM, pp. 33–40. IEEE (2019)
17. Tax, N., Alasgarov, E., Sidorova, N., Haakma, R.: On generation of time-based label refinements (2016). arXiv:1609.03333 arXiv preprint

Supporting Hypothesis Testing in Object-Centric Process Mining: An AI Scaffold to Surface Hidden Analytical Failures

Antolin Claude(✉)

ESCP Business School, Heubnerweg 8-10, 14059 Berlin, Germany
aclaude@escp.eu

Abstract. Hypothesis-testing behavior drives finding quality in process mining, yet failures in hypothesis testing often remain hidden from the analyst. Object-centric process mining (OCPM) amplifies this challenge by requiring analysts to test hypotheses across object types. This dissertation designs and evaluates an AI scaffold that detects hidden analytical failures during OCPM analysis and surfaces them through reflective prompting. The scaffold interacts with PM engines through standardized protocols such as the Model Context Protocol (MCP), enabling structured observation of the analyst's reasoning. WP 1 observes how analysts with varying PM backgrounds work with object-centric event logs, identifying failure modes and expertise-differentiated patterns. WP 2 translates findings into a scaffold that detects failures algorithmically and surfaces them through reflective prompts. WP 3 evaluates using a 2×2 between-subjects design (PM background $\times$ scaffold condition). Contributions include: the first empirical study of hypothesis-testing behavior in OCPM; design principles for failure-detecting scaffolds; and evidence on how expertise shapes scaffold effects.

Keywords: Object-Centric Process Mining · Hypothesis Testing · Analytical Scaffolding · AI–PM Interaction · Design Science

1 Problem and Motivation

An analyst opens an object-centric event log: orders, customers, items, employees, packages, products. Something is wrong with order completion times, but the source may lie in item characteristics, packaging schedules, or employee assignments. Without a strategy for testing findings across object types, she focuses on what she recognizes, reports something locally plausible, and misses the actual cause. Could the interaction with the tool have led to finding the root cause? If yes, would an AI layer support or be detrimental to the process of process mining? How does that answer vary across PM expertise levels?

Hidden Hypothesis-Testing Failures. In case-centric PM, Zerbato et al. [43] show that hypothesis-testing steps associate with finding quality ($\rho = 0.52$,

F. Zerbato et al. (Eds.): CAiSE 2026, LNBIP 587, pp. 224–235, 2026.
https://doi.org/10.1007/978-3-032-27997-2_25

$p < 0.001$); earlier work [42] provides initial insights into exploratory PM practices that motivated this finding. Yet these failures remain hidden from the analyst who commits them. Sorokina et al. [34] explain the mechanism: confirming observations suppress the signal for further testing (Prediction-Error Minimization). Zimmermann et al. [44] document 23 case-centric analyst challenges; analysis focus failures are among the most consequential. Arnott [6] establishes that such cognitive biases systematically affect decision support system use. Whether these phenomena manifest in OCPM has not been studied (to the best of the author's knowledge).

OCPM Amplification. Object-centric event logs [9] link each event to multiple objects simultaneously, enabling analytical questions impossible in flat PM [1,2]. Van der Aalst [3] argues that OCPM provides the grounding AI requires for operational improvement; yet cross-object exploration remains underexplored [10]. OCPM creates a more complex hypothesis space: an analyst must test findings not only within an object type but across object types. When analysts remain within orders without checking items, packages, or employees, the case-centric confirmation mechanism (or lack thereof) still operates. Furthermore, the multi-object structure offers no inherent signal that cross-type checking was omitted.

AI–PM Interaction as Intervention Layer. The Model Context Protocol (MCP) [23] standardizes how AI agents interact with analytical engines through typed tool calls. PM-specific MCP servers [28] are one emerging instance, exposing process discovery, bottleneck analysis, variant analysis, and correlation tools. Such protocol layers make every analytical operation observable and instrumentable as a timestamped event. For this dissertation, standardized AI–PM protocols provide both the technical substrate for the scaffold and the theoretical lens: the question is how AI-mediated interaction with PM tools can surface hidden failures in real time.

Target Population. This dissertation addresses PM analysts working under resource-constrained conditions: those lacking routine access to a PM expert peer, domain specialist, or dedicated team that could challenge or verify findings during analysis. Such analysts are increasingly common as organizations adopt OCPM tools without building specialist teams [7,15,32].

AI-Mediated Visibility and the Reliance Constraint. One response to invisible analytical failures is AI support that surfaces them. Hettrich et al. [22] show that AI-assisted novices in project planning perform comparably to unassisted professionals: AI can bridge the expertise gap. Yet this carries a reliance calibration problem. Dogru and Krämer [14] demonstrate that expertise shapes AI reliance: higher expertise promotes self-reliance and may cause under-engagement with AI advice; lower expertise corresponds to higher AI trust and potential over-reliance. Sun et al. [36] confirm that experts find scaffolding tedious and may disengage [38]. Schaffer et al. [31] show that users with higher familiarity trust AI more but adhere less: explanations help only low-familiarity users. Fill and Muñoz Cádiz [17] warn that GenAI may de-skill practitioners who become dependent on AI outputs. The design challenge is therefore to make invisible failures visible, but in a way that calibrates reliance appropriately across expertise levels and preserves the reasoning effort required for skill development.

Research Goal and MRQ. Following Johannesson and Perjons [25]: *Design and develop an AI scaffold that detects hidden hypothesis-testing failures during OCPM analysis and surfaces them through reflective prompting, and evaluate whether it improves finding quality while calibrating reliance appropriately across expertise levels.*
MRQ: What hypothesis-testing failures do analysts exhibit when working with OCPM data, how do these failures differ across expertise levels, and can a scaffold that detects and surfaces these failures through AI–PM interaction improve analysis quality while avoiding over-reliance in novices and under-engagement in experts?

2 Related Work and Positioning

OCPM and GenAI in PM. Berti and van der Aalst [9] define OCEL and the OC-DFG; PM4Py [11] supports OCEL 2.0. Emerging GenAI–PM work optimizes system outputs: Jessen et al. [24] use LLMs for conversational querying; Barbieri et al. [8] develop natural language interfaces; Buss et al. [13] extract OCEL from text; Amling et al. [4] verbalize process explanations; Kourani et al. [27] leverage LLMs for modeling. These optimize outputs rather than analyst reasoning. This dissertation targets the reasoning process itself.

AI–PM Interaction Through Standardized Protocols. The MCP [23] standardizes AI agent tool invocation. PM MCP servers [28] expose analytics through typed calls. This has two consequences: every analytical operation becomes a machine-readable behavioral event, and the scaffold's Failure Detector can reason over tool call sequences at the semantic level of analytical operations.

Behavioral PM Research. Prior work establishes the hypothesis-testing–quality link [43] and documents exploratory practices [42]. Sorokina et al. [34] explain the cognitive mechanism (PEM4PPM); Van Suetendael et al. [35] catalog 26 behavioral patterns; Zimmermann et al. [44] identify 23 challenges; Ammann et al. [5] examine how PM users act, think, and feel. All findings concern case-centric PM; their extension to OCPM is theoretically motivated but empirically open.

Context and Sense-Making. Grisold et al. [20] develop a context framework for PM sense-making. Franzoi et al. [18] extend this into a Process Mining Context Taxonomy (process-immediate, organization-internal, organization-external), evaluated with 20 PM experts. Their user study reveals that experts requested structured, question-driven guidance and reported that the taxonomy expanded the search space for explanations and could reduce biases, confirming that even experienced analysts benefit from structured prompting during sense-making. Franzoi et al. address *what* contextual factors to consider; this dissertation addresses *how* the analyst's hypothesis-testing process can be monitored and supported in real time.

Expertise Gap and Appropriate Reliance. Hettrich et al. [22] demonstrate through a 2×2 factorial design that AI assistance elevates novice performance to the level of unassisted professionals, effectively bridging the expertise gap. Dogru and Krämer [14] operationalize appropriate reliance through Relative Positive AI Reliance (RAIR) and Relative Positive Self-Reliance (RSR), showing that expertise shapes reliance patterns. Narechania et al. [29] show that AI guidance produces nuanced effects depending on analysis stage. These findings inform the evaluation design: the scaffold must bridge the gap for novices without inducing over-reliance, while providing value to experts without causing under-engagement.

Scaffolding Foundations. This dissertation frames OCPM analysis as an Information Problem Solving (IPS) task [41]. Boetje et al. [12] synthesize 69 studies into seven IPS design principles; Principles 6–7 (process support during the task; just-in-time feedback) ground the scaffold's intervention logic. VanLehn [39] shows Socratic step-level interaction matches human tutoring effectiveness.

Positioning. This dissertation is the first to: (1) observe hypothesis-testing behavior empirically in OCPM; (2) design a scaffold that detects failures through protocol-mediated behavioral traces and surfaces them via reflective prompting; (3) evaluate how expertise shapes scaffold effects on finding quality and reliance calibration.

3 Research Design

Three work packages enact the five DSR activities [25] (Table 1). An observation platform, built before WP 1, provides the shared foundation: a protocol-mediated OCPM environment where all analytical operations are executed as typed tool calls against PM4Py OCEL 2.0 [11] and recorded as timestamped events in a decision log. WP 1 uses it without scaffold; WP 2 adds the scaffold layer; WP 3 evaluates the full system.

SQ1 (WP 1): What hypothesis-testing failures do analysts exhibit in OCPM, how do they differ across expertise levels, and what do they imply for scaffold design?

SQ2 (WP 2): How should the scaffold detect and surface hidden failures in protocol-mediated analytical interactions while calibrating reliance across expertise levels?

SQ3 (WP 3): Do scaffolded novices approach unscaffolded expert performance, and do experts benefit from scaffolding without under-engaging?

4 WP 1: Observing OCPM Analytical Practice

WP 1 characterizes what happens when analysts of varying expertise work with object-centric event logs, focusing on what hypothesis-testing failures they commit and which remain hidden. This is the first empirical study of hypothesis-

Table 1. Work packages enacting the five DSR activities [25].

WP	DSR Activity	Method	Participants	Knowledge
1	Explicate problem	Think-aloud + interview	Novices + experienced	Descriptive
2	Define req.; Design; Demonstrate	Expert walkthroughs + prototype sessions	PM researchers + students	Prescriptive
3	Evaluate artefact	2×2 between-subjects + transfer task	Novices + experienced	Descriptive + Explanatory

testing behavior in OCPM, with findings feeding directly into WP 2 scaffold design.

Following Zerbato et al.'s [43] approach in case-centric PM, n = 16–24 analysts work individually on an analytical task using the Order Management OCEL 2.0 dataset [26] in the observation platform, verbalizing their reasoning. Approximately half have substantive PM background (experienced practitioners or advanced PM students), half are PM novices. This stratification enables comparison of analytical failures and reliance patterns across expertise levels. No scaffold is active. Participants analyze the order-management process to identify what drives variation in order completion times. The task can be approached within a single object type but is more fully answered by examining relationships across object types (e.g., whether item characteristics or packaging schedules explain order delays). It is open-ended by design: WP 1 observes what analysts actually do, not what they should do.

The platform records every analytical operation as a typed, timestamped event: which tool was called (bottleneck analysis, correlation, variant retrieval, etc.), with which parameters (object types, filters, metrics), and in what sequence. Think-aloud provides concurrent reasoning data. A short post-task interview probes moments of difficulty or premature closure using selected decision-log timestamps.

Two researchers code inference steps, distinguishing testing across object types (HTEST-cross) from remaining within one type (HTEST-single). Tool call sequences provide direct evidence: an analyst who queries bottlenecks filtered to orders but never queries items or packages exhibits a measurable single-type pattern. Finding quality is rated by two raters (Cohen's κ). Hybrid thematic analysis [16] combines deductive codes from prior PM behavioral research with inductive codes for OCPM-specific patterns. Reliance patterns (premature closure, external attribution, self-correction) are coded following Dogru and Krämer's [14] framework.

WP 1 produces descriptive knowledge: the first characterization of hypothesis-testing failures in OCPM (including which failures analysts remain unaware of) and how these differ across expertise levels; expertise-differentiated requirements for WP 2 scaffold design; and behavioral baselines for WP 3 comparison.

5 WP 2: Designing and Demonstrating the Scaffold

WP 2 translates WP 1's empirical findings into a scaffold through iterative development and formative evaluation [33]. All WP 2 participants are distinct from WP 1 and WP 3.

Functional, structural, and environmental requirements [25] emerge from WP 1: which failure modes to target at which expertise level, at what threshold, and what analytical state the LLM must encode. Context-sensitivity is essential: following Grisold et al. [20] and Franzoi et al. [18], the scaffold must attend to the analyst's current analytical state, including which object types have been queried and which contextual dimensions explored, not merely trigger on generic patterns.

Architecture

Two components are added to the observation platform (Fig. 1):

Failure Detector (rule-based; thresholds from WP 1): monitors the tool call log for behavioral signatures of hidden failures. Because every analytical operation is a typed call, detection rules operate at the semantic level, e.g., extended sequences of bottleneck or variant queries filtered to a single object type without cross-type operations, correlation calls that confirm an initial finding without testing alternatives, or claims about object relationships without edge-metric calls that would verify them.

Reflective Prompt Generator: LLM conditioned on the analyst's current state [10] (object types queried, filters active, tools invoked, metrics examined) generates a question that surfaces the hidden failure, e.g., "You have examined order bottlenecks; what might correlation analysis on item attributes reveal about this pattern?" or "What alternative explanation have you ruled out?" The reflective format (questions not answers) is grounded in VanLehn [39]: the reasoning effort produces the learning. This design also addresses over-reliance: rather than providing answers that novices might accept uncritically [30], the scaffold surfaces the failure while requiring the analyst to resolve it.

Observation Platform (built before WP 1)

Analyst Interface	Protocol-Mediated	Decision Log
natural language +	PM Tool Layer	typed + timestamped
direct manipulation	(PM4Py OCEL 2.0)	tool calls

Scaffold Layer (designed in WP 2, specifications from WP 1)

Failure Detector	Reflective Prompt Generator
rules over tool call sequences	LLM + analytical state → question

Fig. 1. Architecture. The protocol-mediated tool layer makes behavioral traces machine-readable. WP 3: scaffold active (ON) or silent (OFF).

Design Principles

Four DPs as prescriptive knowledge [19,37], grounded in IPS, scaffolding, and AI–PM interaction research:

DP1 Authentic OCPM Task (Boetje P1 [12]): real OCEL 2.0 data with genuine relational complexity, ensuring that cross-object hypothesis testing is both possible and necessary.

DP2 Reflective Failure Surfacing (VanLehn [39]; Boetje P6–7): at detected failure, surface the hidden state by asking a question specific to the analyst's context; never provide the answer, preserving the reasoning effort that produces skill development.

DP3 Protocol-Mediated Behavioral Logging (Boetje P4–7): every analytical operation logged as a typed tool call, making the analyst's behavioral trajectory machine-readable for real-time failure detection.

DP4 Context-Sensitive Detection (Franzoi et al. [18]; Grisold et al. [20]): failure detection considers which object types have been queried and which contextual dimensions explored, rather than triggering on isolated events.

Formative Evaluation

Expert walkthroughs ($n = 4–6$, ex ante) review architecture and sample prompts [33]. Prototype use sessions ($n = 6–8$, ex post) with PM students drive refinement of thresholds and prompt templates before WP 3.

6 WP 3: Evaluating the Scaffold

WP 3 determines whether the scaffold improves finding quality while calibrating reliance appropriately across expertise levels, and whether any benefit persists to a transfer task.

A 2×2 between-subjects factorial design (Table 2), following Hettrich et al. [22]: $n = 80–120$ ($n \geq 20$ per cell), recruited primarily from practitioner networks; where practitioner access is limited, master's students and early practitioners serve as controlled proxies. An optional third condition, AI-ANSWER (LLM provides direct answers rather than reflective questions), may be included to isolate the reflective mechanism from generic AI assistance.

Table 2. WP 3 experimental conditions (2×2 between-subjects).

	Scaffold-OFF	Scaffold-ON
PM Novice	Baseline novice	Bridging effect? Over-reliance?
PM Experienced	Expert baseline	Expert benefit? Under-engagement?

Main task (Session 1): Order Management OCEL 2.0; scaffold active for Scaffold-ON conditions. Transfer task (Session 2, four weeks later): different OCEL 2.0 dataset; scaffold inactive for all, testing whether scaffolded participants developed hypothesis-testing habits that persist without support.

Following Hettrich et al. [22] and Dogru and Krämer [14], primary measures are: finding quality, HTEST-cross ratio, and RAIR/RSR. Secondary measures include task time, NASA-TLX [21], tool call diversity (distinct object types queried, distinct tool types used), and post-task interviews.

Hypotheses

H1: Scaffold-ON novices outperform Scaffold-OFF novices on finding quality (bridging effect).

H2: Scaffold-ON novices approach Scaffold-OFF expert performance (expertise gap reduction).

H3: Scaffold-ON novices show higher RAIR than RSR (appropriate positive AI reliance, not over-reliance on incorrect prompts).

H4: Scaffold-ON experts show higher RSR than RAIR (appropriate self-reliance, not under-engagement).

H5: Transfer task performance is higher for participants who were scaffolded in Session 1 (habit formation).

Analysis. Two-way ANOVA (PM background × scaffold condition) for main effects and interaction; planned contrasts for specific hypotheses; regression analysis with NASA-TLX as mediator. Tool call logs provide process-level behavioral metrics (tool diversity, cross-type query ratio) as additional dependent variables. A subsequent field deployment in 2–3 organizations could assess further validity [40].

7 Expected Contributions and Current Status

Contributions. *Descriptive*: Empirical characterization of hypothesis-testing failures in OCPM and their variation across expertise levels. *Prescriptive*: Design principles for scaffolds that detect hidden failures through AI–PM interaction traces and surface them through reflective prompting. *Explanatory*: Evidence on how expertise shapes scaffold effects on finding quality and reliance.

Theoretical Contribution. Extends behavioral PM research [43,44] to OC-PM and contributes to AI–PM interaction research [3,23] by studying how protocol-mediated scaffolding shapes analytical reasoning; advances expertise gap research [14,22] with expertise-differentiated scaffold effects.

Current Status and Risks. Early-stage proposal; empirical work has not yet begun. All elements are open to refinement. Risks include limited access to experienced participants, difficulty detecting some failures from tool call logs alone, and limited generalizability of controlled results.

Feedback Sought. This proposal is in an initial phase and any feedback is welcome, particularly on scope, the 2×2 design, the WP balance, and the AI–PM protocol framing.

Acknowledgments. The author thanks Prof. Dr. Bick for supervision and feedback.

Disclosure of Interests. The author has no competing interests to declare.

Use of Generative AI. Grammarly was used for linguistic editing. All scientific content is the author's responsibility.

References

1. Aalst, W.: Object-centric process mining: unraveling the fabric of real processes. Mathematics **11**, 2691 (2023). https://doi.org/10.3390/math11122691
2. Aalst, W., Berti, A.: Discovering object-centric petri nets (2020). https://doi.org/10.48550/arXiv.2010.02047
3. van der Aalst, W.M.P.: No AI without PI! Object-centric process mining as the enabler for generative, predictive, and prescriptive artificial intelligence (2025). https://arxiv.org/abs/2508.00116
4. Amling, J., Slany, E., Dormagen, C., Kretschmann, M., Scheele, S.: Bridging the Interpretability Gap in Process Mining: A Comprehensive Approach Combining Explainable Clustering and Generative AI, pp. 78–103 (2025). https://doi.org/10.1007/978-3-032-08324-1_4
5. Ammann, J., Lohoff, L., Wurm, B., Hess, T.: How do process mining users act, think, and feel? Bus. Inf. Syst. Eng., 1–23 (2025). https://doi.org/10.1007/s12599-025-00931-9
6. Arnott, D.: Cognitive biases and decision support systems development: a design science approach. Inf. Syst. J. **16**, 55–78 (2006). https://doi.org/10.1111/j.1365-2575.2006.00208.x
7. Badakhshan, P., Wurm, B., Grisold, T., Geyer-Klingeberg, J., Mendling, J., Brocke, J.v.: Creating business value with process mining. J. Strateg. Inf. Syst. **31**, 2023 (2022). https://doi.org/10.1016/j.jsis.2022.101745
8. Barbieri, L., Madeira, E., Stroeh, K., Aalst, W.: Towards a Natural Language Conversational Interface for Process Mining, pp. 268–280 (2022). https://doi.org/10.1007/978-3-030-98581-3_20
9. Berti, A., Aalst, W.: OC-PM: analyzing object-centric event logs and process models. Int. J. Softw. Tools Technol. Transf. **25**, 1–17 (2022). https://doi.org/10.1007/s10009-022-00668-w
10. Berti, A., Park, G., Rafiei, M., Aalst, W.: A generic approach to extract object-centric event data from databases supporting SAP ERP. J. Intell. Inf. Syst. **61**, 1–23 (2023). https://doi.org/10.1007/s10844-023-00799-9
11. Berti, A., van Zelst, S., Schuster, D.: PM4Py: a process mining library for Python. Softw. Impacts **17**, 100556 (2023). https://doi.org/10.1016/j.simpa.2023.100556. https://www.sciencedirect.com/science/article/pii/S2665963823000933
12. Boetje, J., Sichterman, B., Ginkel, S.V., Smakman, M., Versendaal, J.: Design principles for developing information problem solving competence in higher education: a systematic review and meta-analysis. Rev. Educ. Res., 00346543251338057 (2025). https://doi.org/10.3102/00346543251338057
13. Buss, A., Kecht, C., Kratsch, W., Röglinger, M., Sadeghianasl, S., Wynn, M.T.: Process mining between the lines: extracting object-centric event logs from textual data. Inf. Syst. **140**, 102713 (2026). https://www.sciencedirect.com/science/article/pii/S030643792600027X
14. Ömer Dogru, E., Krämer, N.C.: Investigating appropriate reliance on AI-based decision support systems: the role of expertise, trust, and self-confidence. J. Decis. Syst. **34**(1), 2593251 (2025). https://doi.org/10.1080/12460125.2025.2593251
15. Eggert, M., Dyong, J.: Applying process mining in small and medium sized IT Enterprises – Challenges and Guidelines, pp. 125–142 (2022). https://doi.org/10.1007/978-3-031-16103-2_11
16. Fereday, J., Muir-Cochrane, E.: Demonstrating rigor using thematic analysis: a hybrid approach of inductive and deductive coding and theme development. Int. J. Qual. Methods **5**, 1–11 (2006). https://doi.org/10.1177/160940690600500107

17. Fill, H.G., Cádiz, J.M.: De-skilling and up-skilling in times of generative AI: implications for education in computer science. VSH-AEU-Bulletin **1**(1), 37–40 (2026). https://www.unifr.ch/inf/digits/assets/public/files/research/papers/Fill_Munoz-Cadiz_2026_VSH-AEU_Bulletin_2026-01_Artificial%20Intelligence_Print%20Version.pdf
18. Franzoi, S., Hartl, S., Grisold, T., van der Aa, H., Mendling, J., Brocke, J.v.: Explaining process dynamics: a process mining context taxonomy for sense-making. Process Sci. **2** (2025). https://doi.org/10.1007/s44311-025-00008-6
19. Gregor, S., Chandra Kruse, L., Seidel, S.: The anatomy of a design principle. J. Assoc. Inf. Syst. **21**(11), 1622–1652 (2020). https://doi.org/10.17705/1jais.00649
20. Grisold, T., Aa, H., Franzoi, S., Hartl, S., Mendling, J., Brocke, J.: A context framework for sense-making of process mining results. In: Lu, X., Pufahl, L., Song, M. (eds.) 6th International Conference on Process Mining, ICPM 2024, Kgs. Lyngby, Denmark, 14–18 October 2024, pp. 57–64. IEEE (2024). https://doi.org/10.1109/ICPM63005.2024.10680665. Publisher Copyright: 2024 IEEE
21. Hart, S.G., Staveland, L.E.: Development of NASA-TLX (task load index): results of empirical and theoretical research. In: Hancock, P.A., Meshkati, N. (eds.) Human Mental Workload, Advances in Psychology, vol. 52, pp. 139–183. North-Holland (1988). https://doi.org/10.1016/S0166-4115(08)62386-9, https://www.sciencedirect.com/science/article/pii/S0166411508623869
22. Hettrich, B., Krings, N., Kock, A.: Bridging the expertise gap: the role of generative AI in supporting project planning tasks for novices and professionals. Creat. Innov. Manag. **34** (2025). https://doi.org/10.1111/caim.70002
23. Hou, X., Zhao, Y., Wang, S., Wang, H.: Model context protocol (MCP): landscape, security threats, and future research directions. ACM Trans. Softw. Eng. Methodol. (2026, just Accepted). https://doi.org/10.1145/3796519
24. Jessen, U., Sroka, M., Fahland, D.: Chit-chat or deep talk: prompt engineering for process mining (2023). https://arxiv.org/abs/2307.09909
25. Johannesson, P., Perjons, E.: An Introduction to Design Science (2021). https://doi.org/10.1007/978-3-030-78132-3
26. Knopp, B., van der Aalst, W.M.: Order management object-centric event log in OCEL 2.0 standard (2026). https://doi.org/10.5281/zenodo.18373906
27. Kourani, H., et al.: Leveraging large language models for business process modeling. Softw. Syst. Model. (2025). https://doi.org/10.1007/s10270-025-01318-w
28. MicrosoftDocs Contributors: Process mining model context protocol (MCP) server reference (preview) (2026). https://github.com/MicrosoftDocs/power-automate-docs/blob/main/articles/process-mining-mcp-server-reference.md. Microsoft Power Automate documentation. Accessed 1 Apr 2026
29. Narechania, A., Endert, A., Sinha, A.: Guidance source matters: how guidance from AI, expert, or a group of analysts impacts visual data preparation and analysis, pp. 789–809 (2025). https://doi.org/10.1145/3708359.3712166
30. Pitts, G., Rani, N., Mildort, W.: Trust and reliance on AI in education: AI literacy and need for cognition as moderators (2026). https://doi.org/10.48550/arXiv.2604.01114
31. Schaffer, J., O'Donovan, J., Michaelis, J., Raglin, A., Höllerer, T.: I can do better than your AI: expertise and explanations. In: Proceedings of the 24th International Conference on Intelligent User Interfaces, IUI 2019, pp. 240–251. Association for Computing Machinery, New York (2019). https://doi.org/10.1145/3301275.3302308

32. Shamasbi, S.M., Looy, A.V., Weber, B., Röglinger, M.: A typological theory of roles in process mining: conceptualising competencies through text mining of job vacancy data. Enterp. Inf. Syst. **19**(11), 2521389 (2025). https://doi.org/10.1080/17517575.2025.2521389
33. Sonnenberg, C., Brocke, J.v.: Evaluations in the science of the artificial – reconsidering the build-evaluate pattern in design science research, vol. 7286, pp. 381–397 (2012). https://doi.org/10.1007/978-3-642-29863-9_28
34. Sorokina, E., Soffer, P., Hadar, I., Leron, U., Zerbato, F., Weber, B.: PEM4PPM: a cognitive perspective on the process of process mining. In: Business Process Management: 21st International Conference, BPM 2023, Utrecht, The Netherlands, 11–15 September 2023, Proceedings, pp. 465–481. Springer, Heidelberg (2023). https://doi.org/10.1007/978-3-031-41620-0_27
35. Suetendael, J., Depaire, B., Jans, M., Martin, N.: Understanding the behavior of process mining analysts: a catalogue of exploratory process mining behaviors. Process Sci. **2**, 1–27 (2025). https://doi.org/10.1007/s44311-025-00021-9
36. Sun, L., Liu, Y., Joseph, G., Yu, Z., Zhu, H., Dow, S.P.: Comparing experts and novices for AI data work: insights on allocating human intelligence to design a conversational agent. In: Proceedings of the AAAI Conference on Human Computation and Crowdsourcing, vol. 10, no. 1, pp. 195–206 (2022). https://doi.org/10.1609/hcomp.v10i1.21999. https://ojs.aaai.org/index.php/HCOMP/article/view/21999
37. Säfström, A.I., Lithner, J.: Promoting validity of design principles for teaching through educational design research. Math. Think. Learn., 1–20 (2025). https://doi.org/10.1080/10986065.2025.2595712
38. Tie, J., et al.: "Should i give up now?" investigating LLM pitfalls in software engineering. ACM Trans. Softw. Eng. Methodol. (2026).https://doi.org/10.1145/3801972
39. Vanlehn, K.: The relative effectiveness of human tutoring, intelligent tutoring systems, and other tutoring systems. Educ. Psychol. **46**(10), 197–221 (2011). https://doi.org/10.1080/00461520.2011.611369
40. Volkoff, O., Strong, D.: Critical realism and affordances: theorizing it-associated organizational change processes. MIS Q. Manage. Inf. Syst. **37**, 819–834 (2013). https://doi.org/10.25300/MISQ/2013/37.3.07
41. Walraven, A., Brand-Gruwel, S., Boshuizen, H.: Information-problem solving: a review of problems students encounter and instructional solutions. Comput. Hum. Behav. **24**, 623–648 (2008). https://doi.org/10.1016/j.chb.2007.01.030
42. Zerbato, F., Soffer, P., Weber, B.: Initial insights into exploratory process mining practices. In: Polyvyanyy, A., Wynn, M.T., Van Looy, A., Reichert, M. (eds.) BPM 2021. LNBIP, vol. 427, pp. 145–161. Springer, Cham (2021). https://doi.org/10.1007/978-3-030-85440-9_9
43. Zerbato, F., Zimmermann, L., Vrotsou, K., Weber, B.: From analysis to findings: how do process mining analysts discover results? Inf. Syst. **135**, 102596 (2026). https://doi.org/10.1016/j.is.2025.102596. https://www.sciencedirect.com/science/article/pii/S0306437925000808
44. Zimmermann, L., Zerbato, F., Weber, B.: What makes life for process mining analysts difficult? A reflection of challenges. Softw. Syst. Model. **23**, 1345–1373 (2023). https://doi.org/10.1007/s10270-023-01134-0

The Impact of Process Mining Archetypes on Business Process Performance

Angela Sekulovska(✉)

School of Economics and Business, University of Ljubljana, Ljubljana, Slovenia
angela.sekulovska@ef.uni-lj.si

Abstract. Process mining has emerged as an important data-driven approach for analyzing and improving business processes based on event log data. Although the field has traditionally focused on technical issues, growing evidence suggests that organizational and managerial factors play a critical role in shaping process mining adoption and outcomes. Recent studies have introduced maturity models and taxonomies of process mining setups, yet it remains unclear whether recurring combinations of these characteristics form distinct archetypes and how such archetypes relate to business process performance. This dissertation addresses this gap by investigating how process mining setups are structured in organizations, which archetypes can be identified, and how these archetypes differ in terms of business process performance. The study follows an exploratory sequential mixed-methods design: a qualitative phase of multiple case studies and semi-structured interviews will identify relevant setup dimensions and derive empirically grounded archetypes, followed by a survey-based quantitative phase examining recurring configurations and their relationship with business process performance. The research is currently in its early qualitative stage, with the first case organization identified and interview preparation underway. The dissertation contributes a configurational understanding of process mining adoption and its implications for business process performance.

Keywords: Process mining · Business process management · Maturity · Archetypes · Configurations · Business process performance

1 Introduction

Since its introduction in the early 1990s, Business Process Management (BPM) has become a well-established discipline defined as a structured approach to coordinating and managing work activities to deliver consistent results and identify improvement opportunities [12]. With the rise of digital transformation initiatives, BPM has returned to the forefront for organizations seeking to remain competitive in rapidly changing markets [16,21]. At the intersection of process science and data science, process mining has emerged as a discipline that includes techniques designed to extract, visualize, and analyze large volumes of process-related data captured in event logs [2]. Event logs contain digital traces consisting

F. Zerbato et al. (Eds.): CAiSE 2026, LNBIP 587, pp. 236–244, 2026.
https://doi.org/10.1007/978-3-032-27997-2_26

of an activity, a timestamp and a unique identifier, created when employees use information systems while performing their work [1]. Unlike traditional "to-be" modeling, process mining offers organizations an evidence-based approach to discovering their "as-is" processes as they actually occur in practice [8].

Process mining adoption is widespread across healthcare, supply chain, audit, and manufacturing, delivering benefits such as increased process awareness, automation opportunities, cost reductions, enhanced compliance, and greater customer satisfaction [19,29]. The process mining software market is projected to grow from $3.66 billion in 2025 to $42.69 billion in 2032 at a compound annual growth rate of 42% [17], and about 74% of companies in a recent Deloitte study reported actively using or planning to use process mining [9].

Despite this growing interest, most research on process mining has focused on technical issues such as algorithm development, while organizational and managerial implications have been largely overlooked [6,19]. This dissertation addresses this gap by investigating how process mining setups are structured, which archetypes exist, and how these archetypes differ in terms of business process performance.

2 Related Work

To address the gap between technical and organizational perspectives, [6] proposed a five-level research framework that divides process mining analysis into technical, individual, team, organizational, and ecosystem levels, prompting new research on actual process mining use in organizations. Furthermore, [19] identified four key adoption challenges: business case calculation, process selection, implementation, and ongoing use, and emphasized the need for organizational alignment, data governance, and cultural adaptation. The way process mining facilitates process awareness is further shaped by the governance approach: bottom-up versus top-down implementation can affect both perceived value and actual outcomes [13]. Based on this, recent studies have examined how organizations derive business value from process mining [4], identified critical success factors in process, customer, financial and innovation dimensions [23], and investigated the types of user and required competencies of process mining [3,22].

To address related challenges, [5] developed the Process Mining Maturity Model (P3M) across five dimensions: organization, data foundation, people's knowledge, scope of process mining activity, and governance, to help organizations increase process mining readiness. They assumed that maturity archetypes exist and called for future research on transformation paths to improve process mining initiatives. Building on this, [20] introduced the Holistic Process Mining Maturity Model (HP3M) with seven dimensions: technology, pipeline, data, people, culture, governance, and strategic alignment, identifying strategic alignment as critical for integrating process mining into organizational goals. However, they acknowledged that HP3M requires adaptation to fit each organization's specific context, suggesting that maturity may depend on organizational and industry-specific factors. [24] developed a taxonomy for characterizing organizational process mining setups, highlighting variation in structural and governance arrangements, and called for future research to empirically derive archetypes linking specific configurations to business process performance outcomes.

Beyond technical and maturity challenges, organizations have also struggled with the organizational setup of process mining itself [25]. Evidence indicates that establishing a Center of Excellence (CoE) as the main unit responsible for process mining is a key accelerator for organization-wide adoption [29]. Typically, organizations start with a proof of concept on a selected process, run pilot projects, and gradually expand process mining to other core processes to achieve end-to-end visibility [9]. The underlying assumption is that each organization has adopted process mining in a way that fits its specific context, resulting in high variability among setups [24]. However, from a holistic perspective, certain adoption dimensions are likely to occur together, forming configurations or archetypes [27]. Archetypes are context-specific configurations derived from organizational dimensions such as strategy, structure, processes, size, and culture [31]. For example, one archetype might be characterized by a centralized CoE, top-down management support, and an organization-wide scope of process mining, while another might reflect a bottom-up, IT-driven initiative with limited process scope and no formal governance structure.

Based on the above, there is a clear research gap: to the best of my knowledge, no empirical research has examined whether specific combinations of process mining maturity dimensions [5,20] and organizational characteristics [24] form recurring archetypes of process mining setups. Similar studies have used configurational theory as the main theoretical lens [10,33], which explains outcomes by considering how different organizational elements combine rather than examining individual factors in isolation [27]. Based on the principle of equifinality, different configurations can lead to similar outcomes [15]. The purpose of my dissertation is therefore to understand how different process mining setup archetypes impact business process performance.

3 Research Questions

Considering the issues outlined above and within the specific context of process mining setup archetypes, the following research questions will be posed:

RQ1: How Are Process Mining Setups Structured in Organizations?

- The aim is to explore and map the different ways that organizations structure and employ process mining in practice, drawing from existing literature (taxonomy, maturity models, adoption studies) and multiple case studies to assess which setup dimensions are relevant.
- To achieve that, I will draw from existing literature (taxonomy, maturity models, adoption studies) and conduct multiple-case studies to assess which setup dimensions are relevant in practice.

RQ2: Which Archetypes of Process Mining Setups Exist in Organizations?

- The aim is to identify recurring combinations of characteristics forming different archetypes across organizations, using qualitative coding, cross-case comparison, and survey-based validation through Qualitative Comparative Analysis (QCA).
- To achieve that, I will use qualitative coding and cross-case comparison, and later validate patterns through a survey (e.g., Qualitative Comparative Analysis (QCA)).

RQ3: What Are the Differences in Business Process Performance Between Process Mining Archetypes?

- The aim is to evaluate how different process mining archetypes influence business process performance (e.g. efficiency, compliance, innovation, customer value) and determine whether distinct configurations lead to varying performance levels, using QCA on survey data.
- To achieve that, I will use the survey data to measure and compare business process performance across archetypes (e.g., QCA).

The three research questions follow a progressive logic, moving from exploration to configuration to evaluation. RQ1 establishes an overview of process mining setups through literature and qualitative case study insights. RQ2 develops a survey instrument based on qualitative findings to identify recurring archetypes. RQ3 evaluates performance differences across archetypes. This stepwise approach captures the variety of process mining adoption practices, reveals structural patterns, and evaluates organizational implications.

4 Research Design and Methods

The research will use a mixed methods approach and follow an exploratory sequential research design, with the qualitative phase first, followed by a quantitative phase. Exploratory sequential designs first seek to understand the phenomenon being studied by gathering qualitative insights, which are then used to design and adjust appropriate measures and assessments to fit the context of a specific population [7], in the context of this research, organizations that have adopted process mining. An exploratory sequential design is appropriate for this research context for several reasons. The field of process mining has been predominantly technical, focusing mainly on algorithmic developments, while organizational aspects have only recently begun to receive attention. Therefore, we can argue that the field is under-theorized. The few existing studies address topics such as adoption challenges [25,32], critical success factors [23], maturity models [5,20], organizational characteristics [24], and user [3] and team roles [22], resulting in a scattered stream of research perspectives.

In this context, we can assume that relying solely on quantitative measures adapted from related fields would not be rigorous enough and may even be methodologically weak. This is especially true because process mining is considered a unique category within the broader field of business intelligence and analytics (BIA) tools, as it acts as an"x-ray" that reveals processes and behavior [4]. Unlike other BIA tools, the adoption of PM typically involves cross-functional collaboration between IT and various business stakeholders [19], which can complicate the transfer of constructs and measures from similar fields. In addition, scholars have highlighted the disparity between the views of academics and practitioners on challenges associated with process mining adoption [25], and stress that future research inquiries need to develop theories in close collaboration with practice [6,19].

To address this, the qualitative phase will use a multiple case study design [14,34], focusing on organizations that have adopted process mining. Access to case organizations will be gained through existing professional networks, leveraging industry connections to identify suitable cases. Semi-structured interviews with key stakeholders (e.g., process mining consultants, CoE leads, process owners, CIOs/CDOs) will serve as the main data source, supplemented by secondary data (e.g., documentation, reports, news, blog posts) where available. Cases will be sampled across industries, sizes, and maturity levels to capture a range of organizational setups. The data will be analyzed abductively, combining within- and cross-case analysis [28], with the aim of deriving empirically grounded archetypes of process mining setups.

In the quantitative phase, I will develop a survey targeting organizations that have adopted process mining. While clustering can be used to derive archetypes, it requires a sufficiently large sample to ensure solution stability [30], which may be challenging for process mining adopters, as there are no publicly available statistics on the number of organizations that have implemented this technology. In contrast, QCA is explicitly designed for small to medium samples [18], making it a more suitable approach for the proposed dissertation. Its inductive approach has been recommended for novel domains lacking established theories, as it builds propositions from the bottom up through iterative empirical analysis and within-case interpretation [11]. This makes QCA particularly appropriate for process mining studies, where adoption outcomes result from complex interdependencies, and configurational theorizing can capture equifinality [26].

5 Preliminary Results

The research is currently in the qualitative phase. The first case organization has been identified and access is being established. This organization is a large multinational enterprise that has been using process mining across multiple business processes and has established a dedicated Center of Excellence for process mining. Initial conversations with stakeholders suggest that the governance model and the degree of strategic alignment between the process mining initiative and broader organizational goals are particularly influential dimensions of the process mining setup. Interview protocols are being finalized and data collection is planned to commence shortly. Additional case organizations are being identified to ensure diversity in industry, size, and process mining maturity level, as required by the theoretical sampling strategy. These early findings will inform the refinement of the conceptual framework for process mining setup dimensions prior to cross-case analysis.

6 Expected Contributions

The expected results of my research will be a structured and empirically grounded understanding of how organizations set up and use process mining. Using a mixed-method research design, the study will first map the various ways PM is organized in practice by drawing on multiple case studies across industries, company sizes, and maturity levels. Then it will identify recurring combinations of organizational characteristics, that is, the archetypes of process mining adoption. Finally, these archetypes will be linked to business process performance outcomes (such as compliance, innovation, efficiency, and customer value) to provide insights into whether and how different organizational setups influence business process performance.

Therefore, this research is expected to yield both theoretical and practical contributions. Theoretically, it will extend the process mining literature by moving beyond technical developments to focus on the organizational aspects of PM adoption. It will contribute to the broader field of BPM by applying configurational theory and extending the principle of equifinality [15] to the context of the adoption of process mining. The research will also provide the first empirically grounded identification of archetypes of process mining setups by integrating and advancing existing frameworks such as taxonomies [24] and maturity models [5,20]. Finally, it will deepen the theoretical understanding of how different process mining configurations affect business process performance and outputs, contributing to the ongoing discussion on the organizational value of PM [6].

From a practical perspective, the findings of this research will provide practitioners with evidence-based archetypes of PM setups derived from real organizational practices. These archetypes can serve as templates or reference models that organizations can use when designing and refining their own PM initiatives. Rather than adopting a one-size-fits-all approach, managers will be able to tailor their PM setups to their specific requirements, such as processes, industries, or maturity levels. Similarly, the archetypes could enable organizations to benchmark their existing PM arrangements against empirically identified patterns. By comparing their current setups with the archetypes, organizations can better understand their current position and identify opportunities for reconfiguration.

Acknowledgments. The author acknowledge the financial support of the Slovenian Research and Innovation Agency (grant no. P2-0037).

Disclosure of Interests. The author has no competing interests to declare that are relevant to the content of this article.

References

1. van der Aalst, W.M.: Process Mining. Springer (2011). https://doi.org/10.1007/978-3-642-19345-3
2. van der Aalst, W.M.P.: Process Mining Handbook. Lecture Notes in Business Information Processing, Springer (2022). https://doi.org/10.1007/978-3-031-08848-3
3. Ammann, J., Lohoff, L., Wurm, B., Hess, T.: How do process mining users act, think, and feel? Bus. Inf. Syst. Eng. (2025). https://doi.org/10.1007/s12599-025-00931-9
4. Badakhshan, P., Wurm, B., Grisold, T., Geyer-Klingeberg, J., Mendling, J., Vom Brocke, J.: Creating business value with process mining. J. Strateg. Inf. Syst. **31**(4), 101745 (2022)
5. Brock, J., Brennig, K., Löhr, B., Bartelheimer, C., von Enzberg, S., Dumitrescu, R.: Improving process mining maturity - from intentions to actions. Bus. Inf. Syst. Eng. **66**(5), 585–605 (2024). https://doi.org/10.1007/s12599-024-00882-7
6. vom Brocke, J., Jans, M., Mendling, J., Reijers, H.A.: A five-level framework for research on process mining. Bus. Inf. Syst. Eng. **63**(5), 483–490 (2021). https://doi.org/10.1007/s12599-021-00718-8
7. Cresswell, J.W.: A Concise Introduction to Mixed Methods Research, SAGE Publications (2023)
8. Davenport, T.H., Spanyi, A.: What process mining is, and why companies should do it. Harvard Bus. Rev. (2019). https://hbr.org/2019/04/what-process-mining-is-and-why-companies-should-do-it
9. Deloitte: Global Deloitte Process Mining Study (2025). https://www.deloitte.com/de/de/services/consulting-financial/research/global-process-mining-survey.html (2025)
10. Depino-Besada, N.I., Sartal, A., León-Mateos, F., Llach, J.: Exploring the relationships between digital transformation, organizational slack and business performance: a configurational approach. Bus. Process. Manag. J. **31**(2), 416–442 (2024). https://doi.org/10.1108/bpmj-02-2024-0084
11. Di Paola, N., Chari, S., Iannacci, F., Kraus, S.: Configurational theory in business and management research: status quo and guidelines for the application of qualitative comparative analysis (QCA). Technol. Forecast. Soc. Chang. **211**, 123907 (2025). https://doi.org/10.1016/j.techfore.2024.123907
12. Dumas, M., La Rosa, M., Mendling, J., Reijers, H.A.: Fundamentals of Business Process Management. Springer Berlin Heidelberg (2018). https://doi.org/10.1007/978-3-662-56509-4_9
13. Eggers, J., Hein, A., Böhm, M., Krcmar, H.: No longer out of sight, no longer out of mind? how organizations engage with process mining-induced transparency to achieve increased process awareness. Bus. Inf. Syst. Eng. **63**(5), 491–510 (2021). https://doi.org/10.1007/s12599-021-00715-x
14. Eisenhardt, K.M.: Building theories from case study research. Acad. Manag. Rev. **14**(4), 532–550 (1989)
15. El Sawy, O.A., Malhotra, A., Park, Y., Pavlou, P.A.: Seeking the configurations of digital ecodynamics: it takes three to tango. Inf. Syst. Res. **21**(4), 835–848 (2010). https://doi.org/10.1287/isre.1100.0326
16. Fischer, M., Imgrund, F., Janiesch, C., Winkelmann, A.: Strategy archetypes for digital transformation: defining meta objectives using business process management. Inf. Manag. **57**(5), 103262 (2020). https://doi.org/10.1016/j.im.2019.103262

17. Fortune Business Insights: Process Mining Software Market Size: Global Report [2032]. https://www.fortunebusinessinsights.com/process-mining-software-market-104792 (2025)
18. Greckhamer, T., Furnari, S., Fiss, P.C., Aguilera, R.V.: Studying configurations with qualitative comparative analysis: best practices in strategy and organization research. Strateg. Organ. **16**(4), 482–495 (2018). https://doi.org/10.1177/1476127018786487
19. Grisold, T., Mendling, J., Otto, M., vom Brocke, J.: Adoption, use and management of process mining in practice. Bus. Process. Manag. J. **27**(2), 369–387 (2020). https://doi.org/10.1108/bpmj-03-2020-0112
20. Hijriani, A., Comuzzi, M.: Developing and evaluating HP3M: the holistic process mining maturity model. Enterprise Inf. Syst. (2025). https://doi.org/10.1080/17517575.2025.2567696
21. Kerpedzhiev, G.D., König, U.M., Röglinger, M., Rosemann, M.: An exploration into future business process management capabilities in view of digitalization. Bus. Inf. Syst. Eng. **63**(2), 83–96 (2020). https://doi.org/10.1007/s12599-020-00637-0
22. Maleki Shamasbi, S., Van Looy, A., Weber, B., Röglinger, M.: A typological theory of roles in process mining: conceptualising competencies through text mining of job vacancy data. Enterprise Inf. Syst. (2025). https://doi.org/10.1080/17517575.2025.2521389
23. Mamudu, A., Bandara, W., Wynn, M.T., Leemans, S.J.: Process mining success factors and their interrelationships. Bus. Inf. Syst. Eng. (2024). https://doi.org/10.1007/s12599-024-00860-z
24. Marcus, L., Schmid, S.J., Friedrich, F., Röglinger, M., Grindemann, P.: Navigating the landscape of organizational process mining setups. Bus. Inf. Syst. Eng. (2024). https://doi.org/10.1007/s12599-024-00908-0
25. Martin, N., et al.: Opportunities and challenges for process mining in organizations: results of a Delphi study. Bus. Inf. Syst. Eng. **63**(5), 511–527 (2021). https://doi.org/10.1007/s12599-021-00720-0
26. Mattke, J., Maier, C., Weitzel, T., Gerow, J.E., Thatcher, J.B.: Qualitative comparative analysis (QCA) in information systems research: Status quo, guidelines, and future directions. Commun. Assoc. Inf. Syst. **50**, 208–240 (2022). https://doi.org/10.17705/1cais.05008
27. Meyer, A.D., Tsui, A.S., Hinings, C.R.: Configurational approaches to organizational analysis. Acad. Manag. J. **36**(6), 1175–1195 (1993). https://doi.org/10.2307/256809
28. Paré, G.: Investigating information systems with positivist case research. Commun. Assoc. Inf. Syst. **13** (2004). https://doi.org/10.17705/1cais.01318
29. Reinkemeyer, L.: Process Intelligence in Action: Taking Process Mining to the Next Level, Springer (2024)
30. Rutterford, C., Copas, A., Eldridge, S.: Methods for sample size determination in cluster randomized trials. Int. J. Epidemiol. **44**(3), 1051–1067 (2015). https://doi.org/10.1093/ije/dyv113
31. Short, J.C., Payne, G.T., Ketchen, D.J.: Research on organizational configurations: past accomplishments and future challenges. J. Manag. **34**(6), 1053–1079 (2008). https://doi.org/10.1177/0149206308324324
32. Syed, R., Leemans, S.J., Eden, R., Buijs, J.A.: Process mining adoption: a technology continuity versus discontinuity perspective. In: International Conference on Business Process Management, pp. 229–245. Springer (2020)

33. Van Looy, A., Trkman, P., Clarysse, E.: A configuration taxonomy of business process orientation. Bus. Inf. Syst. Eng. **64**(2), 133–147 (2021). https://doi.org/10.1007/s12599-021-00700-4
34. Yin, R.K., Campbell, D.T.: Case Study Research and Applications: Design and Methods, SAGE Publications (2018)

CAiSE 2026 Doctoral Consortium - Requirements Engineering

Engineering Temporal Requirements

Franziska S. Hollauf(✉)

Department of Informatics-Systems, University of Klagenfurt, Klagenfurt, Austria
franziska.hollauf@aau.at

Abstract. Temporal requirements concern time-related aspects of information systems, such as deadlines, durations, and minimum and maximum time spans between events. Having collected a set of such temporal requirements, we need mechanisms to verify that they are not in conflict with each other, i.e., that they are temporally correct, as a conflict, for example, could lead to missing a deadline when the information system is executed. Several approaches for detecting conflicts among temporal constraints have been developed, based on temporal constraint networks as a representation model. But to date, none of the current approaches incorporates earlier knowledge about the uncertainty of an activity's duration. This dissertation closes this gap through three major contributions. First, we will introduce a new checking approach for agile controllability, the recently introduced notion of temporal correctness, which includes earlier available information about uncertain durations. Second, we will develop an algorithm for checking agile controllability for weak contingent activities in polynomial time. Third, we will develop a modeling tool for engineers of temporal requirements that leverages the new notion of agile controllability. Overall, this research develops an agile controllability-based approach to verify temporal correctness for a broader class of temporal constraint networks than dynamic controllability, the currently prevailing temporal correctness notion, can handle.

Keywords: Temporal Requirements · Temporal Correctness · Temporal Constraint Networks

1 Introduction

Temporal aspects can be found in various application areas of information systems (ISs), such as requirements engineering [4], business processes [9], service composition [14], constraint-based planning [13], or legal smart contracts [11]. Temporal aspects, in the form of requirements or constraints, cover the duration of activities, deadlines, and minimum and maximum time spans between events, and the temporal sequence of tasks. We refer to them as *temporal requirements.*

The process of creating ISs begins with the elicitation, documentation, and analysis of requirements, including temporal requirements [10]. Temporal requirements can either be fixed or controlled by engineers [4]: For example,

F. Zerbato et al. (Eds.): CAiSE 2026, LNBIP 587, pp. 247–255, 2026.
https://doi.org/10.1007/978-3-032-27997-2_27

requirements mandated by law must be adhered to, whereas requirements stated by management or by contract with another party are negotiable.

Adequate representation of temporal requirements is therefore a necessity for requirement models. Having a model of a system with temporal requirements, the question arises of whether these requirements are conflicting during execution [6]: Will the execution of a model instance lead to violations of present temporal constraints during the execution of an IS? For example, if a business process misses a deadline, this time failure may cost the company money and its good reputation. Requirements engineers thus need means to analyze conflicts to ensure that systems can be built in accordance with all these requirements and still run in production without causing time failure. Specifically, they must ensure that the elaborated temporal constraints, whether given by law or negotiated, can be met without violations at runtime.

Thus, a critical need for engineers of temporal requirements is, first, an adequate representation of temporal requirements as a foundation for correctness checking. Second, there is a need for checking algorithms for temporal correctness at the early requirements analysis stage to ensure compliance with temporal requirements at runtime, i.e., the absence of temporal constraint violations. Third, a tool that combines modeling and checking of temporal constraints to support engineers in elaborating temporal requirements.

This thesis aims to meet these needs while overcoming the limitations of current state-of-the-art approaches in the area of temporal constraint networks (see Sect. 2). Hence, this research introduces an agile-controllability-based approach that enables temporal correctness verification for a broader class of temporal constraint networks than dynamic controllability, the currently prevailing temporal correctness notion, can verify.

2 State-of-The-Art

For representing temporal requirements, several approaches exist: graphical representations with modeling notations, descriptions in natural language, or formal specifications like general constraint languages or temporal logic [4,8]. Keet and Berman [8] conclude in their research that graphical models are preferred by modelers over temporal logic. Based on the same observation, Eder et al. [4] presented how temporal requirements can be modeled and the temporal correctness verified with the help of temporal constraint networks. In *temporal constraint networks* (TCNs), nodes represent timepoints, and edges represent inequalities that capture temporal constraints between them. Specific types of TCNs and notions of temporal correctness were defined for different purposes. TCN types and correctness notions relevant to this work are explained below, using a running example of an ordering process and highlighting the remaining challenges.

The simplest type of TCNs are *Simple Temporal Networks* (STNs), which are entirely under the control of an agent [3]. For example, the time required to order furniture in a web shop, with the constraint that the reserved goods must be purchased within 15 min, is entirely under the customer's control.

Satisfiability is, thus, an adequate notion for temporal correctness [3]. Satisfiability demands that one valid scenario, i.e., assignment of fixed values to the timepoints of a TCN, exists that satisfies all temporal constraints. It can be checked with the help of shortest-path algorithms [2]. In the ordering example, any duration below 15 min would constitute a valid scenario, while exceeding 15 min would result in a constraint violation.

As a next step in the ordering example, one would have to wait for the delivery of the furniture, which is beyond one's control and hence has an uncertain duration. Such contingent events, i.e., non-controllable and associated with an uncertain task duration, require a new type of TCN. The *Simple Temporal Network with Uncertainty* (STNU) extends the STNs with the possible representation of contingent durations [1,13]. Contingent durations are now represented as two timepoints, the contingent event and its activation point, which are restricted by two constraints representing this contingent activity's minimum and maximum duration.

Dynamic controllability is the most studied notion of temporal correctness for STNUs. Based on the fact that a contingent activity's duration is only known when it completes, it requires a scenario in which later timepoints (greater assigned values) may depend on earlier timepoints (smaller assigned values) but not vice versa, and that such a scenario must be valid for all possible contingent durations [4,15]. The two main approaches for checking whether STNUs are dynamically controllable are Morris-Muscettola (MM) [13] and the Relax-Upper-Lower-system (RUL) by Cairo and Rizzi [1], which are based on constraint propagation rules.

Extending the ordering example, consider that the web shop states that the exact delivery date will be communicated within one week after submitting the order. Thus, scheduling the task of requesting a home office day on the delivery date, two days prior, is feasible. Modeling this example as an STNU and checking its temporal correctness would lead to a negative result. In this case, dynamic controllability is too restrictive. Thus, a new type of TCN with a new notion of temporal correctness was recently proposed by Posenato et al. [15]: The *Simple Temporal Network with Uncertainty and Oracles* (STNUO) is an STNU with additional timepoint nodes, called oracles, that present the timepoints at which the duration of other timepoints will be revealed. The new notion of temporal correctness for STNUOs is *agile controllability.* It allows timepoints to depend not only on earlier timepoints but also on those known earlier.

Two key challenges, however, remain from the current algorithm for checking whether STNUOs are agilely controllable proposed by Posenato et al. [15]. The first key challenge (C1) is overcoming the limitation of high memory consumption by this checking algorithm. It is based on the MM-system [13] and uses an exponential breadth-first search algorithm without backtracking, at the cost of higher memory usage. The second key challenge (C2) is tool support for engineers designing agile controllable networks with respect to engineering oracles, as the proposed tool by Posenato et al. [15] lacks this support. Engineering oracles covers, for instance, deciding whether an oracle could resolve a constraint violation or when such an oracle would have to happen. This dissertation aims to address these shortcomings and contribute to the fields of temporal constraint networks and the engineering of temporal requirements.

3 Research Questions and Contributions

Challenge C1 concerns the approach by Posenato et al. [15]: They propose an exponential algorithm based on the propagation rules by MM [13] with high memory usage, which limits the size of STNUOs and the amount of used oracles that this approach can handle. Thus, the first research question (RQ), goal (G), and artifact (A) are the following:

RQ1 How to design an algorithm checking STNUOs for agile controllability with less memory consumption than the approach by Posenato et al. [15]?
G1 Develop an algorithm based on the constraint propagation RUL-system [1] for checking agile controllability that provides better scalability in terms of the input size of the STNUOs than the approach of Posenato et al. [15].
A1 A RUL-based algorithm for checking agile controllability with better scalability in terms of the input size of the STNUOs than the approach of Posenato et al. [15].

Aiming for a sound and complete algorithm for checking agile controllability in general raises the question of whether, for a specific subset of STNUOs, an algorithm checking these special STNUOs in polynomial time is theoretically possible. A possible subset for this aim would be networks with weak contingent activities. If a contingent activity is an activity whose duration is only known when it is completed, a weak contingent activity is then an activity whose duration is revealed at its activation timepoint. Thus, the subset relation is that for STNUOs, we may know about contingent durations prior to their finish, but for weak contingent durations, this optional prior knowledge is fixed to its activation timepoint.

There are various use cases where activities are weakly contingent. For example, consider that driving to a destination takes 1 to 2 h, depending on traffic. When you start driving, a navigation system will calculate the exact driving time based on current traffic conditions. Hence, the drive's duration is known at the start and not only when one arrives at the destination.

These considerations lead to the following second research question, goal, and artifact:

RQ2 How to design an algorithm that checks networks with weak contingent activities for agile controllability in polynomial time?
G2 Design a representation for temporal constraint networks with weak contingent timepoints and develop a sound and complete algorithm that decides at design time in polynomial time whether a temporal constraint network with weak contingent timepoints is agilely controllable.

A2 A data-structure for temporal constraint networks with weak contingent timepoints and a sound and complete algorithm for deciding at design time in polynomial time whether a temporal constraint network with weak contingent timepoints is agilely controllable.

The third aim of this dissertation is to support requirement engineers and modelers in the process of elaborating correct (agilely controllable) temporal requirements or temporal constraint networks using a design tool, as described in key challenge C2. Thus, the third research question, goal, and artifact are the following:

RQ3 Which capabilities does a modeling tool need to support temporal requirement engineers in the process of designing agilely controllable networks?
G3 Design and implement a modeling tool based on the approach by Lubas et al. [12] that provides algorithms for (incrementally) designing agilely controllable networks.
A3 A tool for engineering temporal requirements, offering especially algorithms for (incrementally) designing agilely controllable networks.

4 Methodology

This work follows the Design Science methodology proposed by Wieringa [16]. As the nature of this PhD research are design problems, it follows the design cycle with its three phases: problem investigation, treatment design, and treatment validation. The word treatment refers, in this case, to the artifact designed to treat the design problem.

In the first phase, we investigate the problem by analyzing the state-of-the-art literature (see Sect. 2). The identified design problems are then formulated as goals (G1-3) and as research questions (RQ1-3), considering the formulation suggestions proposed by Wieringa [16] (see Sect. 3). As the overall goal of this PhD thesis is to design a tool for engineering temporal requirements, offering algorithms for designing agilely controllable networks that overcome the limitations of current-state-of-the-art TCN approaches, the artifacts A1 and A2 can be seen as supporting goals toward achieving artifact A3.

The methods used for treatment design and validation differ depending on the individual artifact. Hence, this section presents, for each design problem (RQ1-3), the research methods used to design the artifact and the methods for artifact validation.

4.1 Agile Controllability for Simple Temporal Networks with Uncertainty and Oracles

To answer RQ1, we plan to define a formal model for an STNUO by extending the definition of STNUs with oracles as additional timepoints, each being linked by a function with a contingent timepoint. Consequently, we will extend the constraint propagation rules, the RUL-system, by Cairo and Rizzi [1] to consider oracles. Further, a formal definition of agile controllability and a backtracking depth-search algorithm based on these extended propagation rules for checking agile controllability will be designed. A proof-of-concept prototype will be implemented, on which we will run experiments measuring execution time to demonstrate the feasibility and scalability of our approach across different network sizes, varying numbers of oracles, and varying numbers of contingent links.

4.2 Agile Controllability for Weak Contingent Activities

To answer RQ2, we plan to define a formal model for representing a network with weak contingent activities as a special type of STNUOs, called STNU^{w}s. Based on this, we will design a sound and complete algorithm for checking agile controllability for weak contingent activities in polynomial time. The main idea for the algorithm is transforming the given problem into a known, already solved problem:

1. We will define a transformation from STNU^{w}s to STNUs and vice versa.
2. We will take advantage of the characteristic proven by Cairo and Rizzi [1] that an STNU is still dynamically controllable under the RUL-propagation system if the contingent duration is revealed at any time between the activation timepoint plus the minimum, respectively, maximum possible duration of the contingent link.
3. We will formally prove the correctness of this transformation by proving that the transformation preserves the characteristic of agile, respectively, dynamic controllability, as we proved based on 2. that for this specific case, the two characteristics are equivalent.
4. This will allow us to apply the algorithms for DC-checking in polynomial time for checking agile controllability of weak contingent networks.

To demonstrate the approach's feasibility, performance, and scalability, we will again implement a prototype and run experiments to measure its runtime. The approach will further explore which types of STNUOs can be transformed into networks with weak contingent activities (STNU^{w}s).

4.3 Tool Support for Agile Controllability

To answer RQ3, we will build on the capabilities of an existing tool [12] and extend them with our results from RQ1 and RQ2. Key features of such a temporal process designer will be:

1. Checking whether a designed process model is admissible under the following notions of temporal correctness: satisfiability, dynamic controllability, and agile controllability (STNUO or STNU^{w}s).
2. Identifying the conflicting constraints that lead to a violation, depending on the temporal correctness notion.

3. Supporting the incremental design, i.e., adding and deleting constraints, by instantaneously checking for conflicts for the various notions of correctness.
4. Computing the strictest temporal constraints between events for agile controllability, which can be added without causing a violation.
5. Checking whether an oracle could solve a conflict.
6. Computing when an oracle must happen so that it can contribute to an admissible process.

To demonstrate the approach's feasibility, performance, and scalability, we will run experiments measuring the run times of each tool feature.

5 Status Quo and Preliminary Results

This Ph.D. project is in its 3rd of 4 years. The answer to RQ1 is already established: In a first approach, we defined a formal model for an STNUO and extended the constraint propagation RUL-system [1] to consider oracles. We further provided a formal definition of agile controllability. Based on these extended propagation rules, we designed an algorithm using a depth-first backtracking search. We implemented a proof-of-concept prototype and conducted experiments to measure execution time, demonstrating the feasibility of our approach. The experiments revealed that our approach is comparable to the one presented in [15], as example networks in typical problem sizes in many application areas were run within 3 s. These first results were published in [5].

This first attempt, however, did not consider the possibility that a controller may use the oracle of a contingent activity to schedule its activation timepoint. Consider the example scenario of an engine repair. Depending on the extent of the damage, the repair takes 1 to 4 days. The duration of the repair can typically be determined in an assessment before the repair activity. This information allows scheduling the start of repairs so they can be completed on a specific date. Therefore, we extended the propagation rules and our proposed algorithm for checking agile controllability. The prototype was adapted, and its performance and scalability were analyzed in several experiments. These extensions and a formal proof are presented in [7].

For RQ2, we are currently writing a paper on our approach to agile controllability for weak contingent activities. Based on the results from RQ1 and RQ2, the next step is to develop tool support for modelers and requirements engineers (RQ3).

6 Conclusion

Means for engineering temporal requirements, such as data structures, algorithms, and design tools, are essential across many application areas in Information Systems Engineering. Temporal constraint networks provide engineers a formal model with an easy-to-understand visual representation for expressing temporal requirements. As the state-of-the-art approaches are limited by high memory usage and incomplete support for engineering agilely controllable networks, this dissertation project aims at addressing these challenges by contributing adequate representation for STNUs with oracles (STNUOs), respectively with weak contingent activities (STNU^ws), algorithms for checking agile controllability for STNUOs and STNU^ws, and a design tool for engineers designing agile controllable networks.

Acknowledgments. This research work is supervised by Prof. Johann Eder (Johann.Eder@aau.at) and Prof. Dragi Kimovski (Dragi.Kimovski@aau.at) at the University of Klagenfurt. Many thanks to them for their ongoing support throughout my Ph.D. research.

Declaration on Generative AI. During the preparation of this work, the author used Grammarly to: grammar and spelling check, paraphrase, and reword. After using this tool, the author reviewed and edited the content as needed and takes full responsibility for the publication's content.

References

1. Cairo, M., Rizzi, R.: Dynamic controllability of simple temporal networks with uncertainty: simple rules and fast real-time execution. Theoret. Comput. Sci. **797**, 2–16 (2019). https://doi.org/10.1016/j.tcs.2018.11.005
2. Cormen, T.H., Leiserson, C.E., Rivest, R.L., Stein, C.: Introduction to Algorithms. The MIT Press, 3rd edn. (2009). https://mitpress.mit.edu/9780262533058/introduction-to-algorithms
3. Dechter, R., Meiri, I., Pearl, J.: Temporal constraint networks. Artif. Intell. **49**(1–3), 61–95 (1991). https://doi.org/10.1016/0004-3702(91)90006-6
4. Eder, J., Franceschetti, M., Lubas, J.: Time and processes: towards engineering temporal requirements. In: Fill, H.G., et al. (eds.) Proceedings of the 16th ICSOFT 2021. vol. 1, pp. 9–16. SciTePress (2021). https://doi.org/10.5220/0010625400090016
5. Eder, J., Posenato, R., Combi, C., Franceschetti, M., Hollauf, F.S.: Agile controllability of simple temporal networks with uncertainty and oracles. In: Sala, P., et al. (eds.) 31st Int. Symposium on TIME 2024. LIPIcs, vol. 318, pp. 4:1–4:16. Leibniz-Zentrum für Informatik, Germany (2024). https://doi.org/10.4230/LIPIcs.TIME.2024.4
6. Hashmi, M., Governatori, G., Lam, H.-P., Wynn, M.T.: Are we done with business process compliance: state of the art and challenges ahead. Knowl. Inf. Syst. **57**(1), 79–133 (2018). https://doi.org/10.1007/s10115-017-1142-1
7. Hollauf, F.S., Posenato, R., Combi, C., Eder, J.: Modeling oracles in simple temporal networks with uncertainty. Inf. Comput. **307**, 105382 (2025). https://doi.org/10.1016/J.IC.2025.105382
8. Keet, C.M., Berman, S.: Determining the preferred representation of temporal constraints in conceptual models. In: Mayr, H.C., et al. (eds.) 36th Int. Conf. ER, pp. 437–450. Springer (2017). https://doi.org/10.1007/978-3-319-69904-2_33

9. Lanz, A., Posenato, R., Combi, C., Reichert, M.: Simple temporal networks with partially shrinkable uncertainty. In: Loiseau, S. (ed.) Proceedings of the 6th Int. Conf. ICAART 2015, vol. 2, pp. 370–381. SciTePress (2015). https://doi.org/10.5220/0005200903700381
10. Laplante, P.A., Kassab, M.: Requirements Engineering for Software and Systems (4th ed.). Auerbach Publications (2022). https://doi.org/10.1201/9781003129509
11. Lubas, J., Eder, J.: A time-aware model for legal smart contracts. In: van der Aa, H., et al. (eds.) Enterprise, Business-Process and Information Systems Modeling. LNBIP, vol. 479, pp. 121–135. Springer (2023). https://doi.org/10.1007/978-3-031-34241-7_9
12. Lubas, J., Franceschetti, M., Eder, J.: Resolving conflicts in process models with temporal constraints. In: Link, S., et al. (eds.) Proceedings of the ER Forum and PhD Symposium 2022. CEUR Workshop Proceedings, vol. 3211 (2022). https://ceur-ws.org/Vol-3211/CR_103.pdf
13. Morris, P.H., Muscettola, N.: Temporal dynamic controllability revisited. In: 20th National Conf. AAAI 2005, pp. 1193–1198 (2005). https://cdn.aaai.org/AAAI/2005/AAAI05-189.pdf
14. Pichler, H., Wenger, M., Eder, J.: Composing time-aware web service orchestrations. In: van Eck, P., et al. (eds.) CAiSE. LNCS, vol. 5565, pp. 349–363. Springer (2009). https://doi.org/10.1007/978-3-642-02144-2_29
15. Posenato, R., Franceschetti, M., Combi, C., Eder, J.: Introducing agile controllability in temporal business processes. In: van der Aa, H., et al. (eds.) 25th Int. Conf. BPMDS, and 29th Int. Conf. EMMSAD 2024. LNBIP, vol. 511, pp. 87–99. Springer (2024). https://doi.org/10.1007/978-3-031-61007-3_8
16. Wieringa, R.J.: Design Science Methodology for Information Systems and Software Engineering. Springer (2014). https://doi.org/10.1007/978-3-662-43839-8

Beyond the User–Product Relationship: Extending the Scope of UX Evaluation

Jessica Kollmorgen[1,2(✉)]

[1] University of Seville, Seville, Spain
[2] University of Applied Sciences Emden/Leer, Emden/Leer, Germany
jessica.kollmorgen@ux-researchgroup.com

Abstract. User experience (UX) evaluation is widely used to assess interactive systems and support design decisions in information system engineering. Existing approaches describe UX as an effect emerging from user-product interaction and operationalize it through standardized measurement instruments. However, empirical observations suggest that UX results do not solely reflect product-related qualities but depend on evaluation prerequisites such as user needs and contextual conditions not explicitly considered in current approaches, indicating persistent interpretability limitations across diverse usage situations.

This doctoral research addresses the limited scope of current UX evaluation by developing an extension that explicitly incorporates user- and context-related evaluation prerequisites. It investigates how these prerequisites shape the assessment of UX factors, what UX results represent under varying circumstances, and how structural characteristics of evaluation approaches influence result interpretability.

Methodologically, the research follows the Design Science Research Methodology, grounding iterative scope development in three empirical study types: exploratory studies identify evaluation prerequisites from the user perspective, structural studies examine their relationship to existing UX measurement approaches, and explanatory studies analyze their impact on UX evaluation results in practice. The expected contribution is an empirically grounded extension of UX evaluation scope that explicates the conditions under which results can be meaningfully interpreted. By making evaluation prerequisites explicit, this research strengthens the methodological foundations of UX assessment and supports more reliable evaluation of interactive information systems.

Keywords: User Experience · UX Evaluation · User Needs · Context of Use · Design Science Research

1 Introduction and Problem Motivation

User experience (UX) [1] has become an established perspective for evaluating interactive systems and their impact on users. In information system engineering, UX measurements are increasingly used to inform design decisions and to assess

F. Zerbato et al. (Eds.): CAiSE 2026, LNBIP 587, pp. 256–266, 2026.
https://doi.org/10.1007/978-3-032-27997-2_28

system quality in use. To support systematic evaluation, various UX evaluation methods have been proposed, including qualitative techniques [2], behavioral measures [3], and standardized questionnaires such as UEQ+ [4], AttrakDiff [5], and UMUX [6].

Among these, questionnaire-based instruments are widely used because they operationalize UX through predefined factors and enable efficient and comparable assessments. In particular, modular approaches such as UEQ+ allow tailoring factor sets to specific evaluation contexts [4].

This stands in contrast to the broader scope of UX described in established definitions. According to ISO 9241–210 [1], user experience results not only from system properties but also from users' internal states and the context of use, including users, goals, tasks, and environmental conditions. Similarly, UX research emphasizes that experience emerges from goal-oriented interaction embedded in a specific context [7,8].

However, existing UX evaluation approaches primarily assess how product-related factors influence the user experience [9]. As a result, UX evaluation in practice implicitly focuses on the effects of the userproduct interaction while only indirectly accounting for contextual and user-related prerequisites. Typical examples of such product-oriented UX factors include *Efficiency*, *Perspicuity*, and *Dependability* as defined in UEQ+ [4]. These factors capture perceived qualities of the interactive system itself. However, they do not explicitly account for whether users' goals, needs, or situational conditions enable a meaningful assessment of these qualities in the first place.

Despite this broader scope, research on UX evaluation has primarily focused on defining UX factors [10–12] and establishing reliable measurement instruments [4,13]. In contrast, limited insight exists into the conditions under which these UX factors can be meaningfully interpreted [14,15].

Another interpretation challenge arises from differing uses of the term user needs. In usability engineering, user needs are defined as requirements that enable users to achieve intended outcomes within a specific context of use [16]. In UX research, the term typically refers to psychological drivers of experience [17]. UX evaluation approaches rarely distinguish between these meanings, which complicates the interpretation of UX factor assessments.

Against this background, this doctoral research addresses the limited scope of current UX evaluation. It extends this scope by explicitly incorporating user- and context-related prerequisites that shape how UX evaluations are formed and interpreted. The goal is to clarify when UX factors can be meaningfully assessed and what UX evaluation results indicate, thereby improving their use for decision-making in information system engineering. In practice, UX evaluation results are often used to inform design decisions and compare alternative system solutions. However, if these results are interpreted without considering underlying user needs and contextual conditions, they may lead to misleading conclusions about system quality. By extending the scope of UX evaluation, this research aims to support more reliable decision-making in the design and assessment of interactive information systems.

2 Related and Preliminary Work

This section situates the identified scope problem of UX evaluation within existing research. First, related literature is reviewed to show that UX factors and evaluation prerequisites have largely been studied separately. Subsequently, preliminary studies from this doctoral research are summarized, providing empirical indications of this separation in practice.

2.1 Related Work

Existing research has addressed different perspectives relevant to UX evaluation, but these perspectives have been investigated without explicit consideration of their implications for the scope of UX evaluation.

Research on user needs has shown that experience is shaped by the extent to which interaction fulfills underlying prerequisites, understood as psychological drivers influencing perceived satisfaction and emotional responses [17]. Hassenzahl et al. [14] provided empirical evidence showing that positive experiences arise when interactive systems support the fulfillment of fundamental psychological needs such as autonomy, competence, and relatedness. Kölln et al. [15] further showed, based on a mixed-methods study, that users interpret and assess UX factors differently depending on their goals, environments, and interaction settings.

Research on the context of use has shown that UX emerges and is evaluated under specific contextual conditions. Lallemand and Koenig [2] demonstrated through a scale-development study that contextual factors constitute an independent dimension influencing UX, identifying multiple context dimensions including physical, social, task, and internal context. Klein et al. [8] further showed, in a mixed-methods study on voice user interfaces, that variations in usage situations such as environment, task demands, and social setting influence how users interpret and evaluate UX factors.

Research on the validity of UX evaluation instruments has primarily focused on defining UX factors and establishing their psychometric properties. Schrepp and Thomaschewski [4] developed and validated the UEQ+, demonstrating that predefined UX factors can be reliably operationalized using standardized scale structures. Kollmorgen et al. [18] provide further guidance on the selection and interpretation of UX questionnaires within the UEQ family. Subsequent studies validated additional UX scales across different domains, including Trust [10], Comprehensibility of Voice User Interfaces [11,13], and Social Acceptance [12]. While these studies show that UX factors can be measured reliably and integrated into stable factor structures, they provide limited insight into their content validity in evaluation practice. In particular, they do not examine whether users can meaningfully assess these factors under varying user needs and contextual conditions, or what UX ratings actually represent in such situations.

This missing integration between evaluation prerequisites and UX factor assessment constitutes the starting point for the preliminary studies presented in the following section.

2.2 Preliminary Work

The preliminary studies conducted in this doctoral research provide empirical evidence for the limited scope of current UX evaluation approaches. Collectively, they demonstrate that UX assessments are shaped by user- and context-related prerequisites that are not explicitly represented in existing evaluation instruments.

Two exploratory studies examined how UX evaluations are formed from the users' perspective without relying on predefined factor structures. A Critical Incident Technique study [19] collected and qualitatively analyzed experience reports from more than 150 participants describing particularly positive or negative interaction episodes with digital systems. Thematic coding revealed that UX judgments are grounded in goal-oriented interaction situations and shaped by contextual conditions and perceived need fulfillment. Recurring constructs such as *Nostalgia* or *Self-Improvement* indicate that UX evaluations emerge from situational experience formation rather than isolated product characteristics. A subsequent Repertory Grid study [20] with over 60 participants elicited user-generated constructs through structured triad comparisons and qualitative categorization. Participants relied on highly individualized criteria that frequently did not correspond to predefined UX factors, such as *Mental Demand* or *Personal Initiative*. This suggests that standardized assessments capture only part of the experiential dimensions users actually employ when forming evaluations.

Two further studies investigated how such characteristics affect the application of standardized UX evaluation instruments. A quantitative validation study [21] with 290 participants applied exploratory and confirmatory factor analyses alongside reliability measures to newly introduced UEQ+ social scales. The results confirmed satisfactory psychometric properties, demonstrating that additional UX factors can be reliably operationalized within existing measurement frameworks. However, a subsequent importance study with 600 participants across six product categories revealed substantial inconsistencies in practical applicability. Relationships between UX factor ratings and global evaluation measures were examined using regression-based approaches and KPI analysis [9]. Participants frequently reported difficulties in assessing certain social UX factors, and several scales showed unstable factor loadings in applied contexts. These findings indicate that even theoretically sound UX factors may not be interpretable when relevant user- or context-related prerequisites are not fulfilled.

Taken together, these findings show that UX factors, user needs, and contextual conditions have each been studied, but largely in isolation. Existing approaches provide reliable measurements of predefined factors, yet integrated models that explicitly account for how these elements jointly shape evaluation outcomes are missing. From a practical perspective, UX results cannot always be directly used for decision-making if certain factors cannot be meaningfully assessed in a given context, creating a risk of misinterpretation or overgeneralization. This missing integration constitutes the central research gap addressed in this doctoral research.

3 Research Approach

To address the identified scope limitations of current UX evaluation approaches, this research follows a design-oriented approach that combines conceptual development with empirical investigation. The goal is to systematically extend the scope of UX evaluation beyond the traditional focus on userproduct interaction.

Specifically, this doctoral research examines how user needs and contextual conditions influence the assessment and interpretation of UX factors in practice. These evaluation prerequisites are currently not explicitly represented in existing UX evaluation approaches, despite their recognized role in experience formation.

3.1 Research Objective and Research Questions

Rather than proposing a new evaluation instrument, this research focuses on extending the scope of UX evaluation itself by explicitly incorporating user- and context-related prerequisites that shape how UX factors are interpreted in practice. This leads to the following main objective:

Develop a (comprehensive and empirically grounded) extension of the scope of UX evaluation by systematically integrating user needs, product interaction, and contextual social-environmental factors (including AI-driven dynamics) to improve the interpretability and meaningfulness of UX evaluation results.

Based on this overarching objective, the following research questions guide the dissertation:

- ***RQ1: How do user needs influence the meaningful assessment of UX factors?***
  This question addresses a missing link between research on psychological user needs, which explains how experiences emerge [14,17], and UX evaluation approaches that do not consider evaluation prerequisites. Preliminary findings from exploratory studies [19,20] indicate that UX judgments are shaped by goal-oriented interaction situations, suggesting that user needs influence whether UX factors can be meaningfully assessed.
- ***RQ2: What do UX evaluation results actually represent under varying usage conditions?***
  This question responds to the observation that UX validity research focuses on psychometric properties rather than on what UX factor ratings actually represent under varying conditions [4,12]. Preliminary studies on social UX factors (see Sect. 2.2) showed that theoretically sound scales can still produce ambiguous results when evaluation prerequisites are not fulfilled.
- ***RQ3: How do the structural representation and formulation of UX factors influence the interpretability of UX evaluation results?***
  This question responds to the observation that prior research has focused on structuring UX into measurable factors [4,5], rather than on how these structures affect the interpretability of UX results. Preliminary findings (see Sect. 2.2) suggest that product-centered formulations can constrain meaningful assessment when underlying goals or needs are not addressed.

Together, these research questions address how UX evaluation can be extended beyond a purely product-centered perspective. By systematically investigating evaluation prerequisites within a design science research framework, this work provides a structured basis for interpreting UX evaluation results in the engineering and assessment of interactive information systems.

In the longer term, this research aims to provide a foundation for developing measurement approaches that operationalize this extended scope of UX evaluation. While existing instruments focus on predefined UX factors, the proposed scope extension is intended to enable a more holistic assessment of UX. However, as the relevant influences and their relationships are not yet sufficiently understood, the development of such measurement instrument (i.e., the artifact) is considered a subsequent step building on the conceptual results of this research.

3.2 Methodological Basis

This research follows the Design Science Research Methodology (DSRM) [22], which provides a structured process for addressing identified problems through the iterative design and evaluation of artifacts.

In this work, the design science artifact is an empirically grounded extension of the scope of UX evaluation that explicitly incorporates user- and context-related prerequisites influencing the assessment of UX factors.

The DSRM steps are directly mapped to the research objective and subsequent research questions (see Fig. 1). *Step 1: Identify problem & motivation* is grounded in empirical inconsistencies observed in UX scale application across different usage contexts (see Sect. 2).

Step 2: Define objectives of a solution focuses on clarifying the role of user needs, UX factors, and contextual conditions as prerequisites of UX evaluation (see Sect. 3.1).

Step 3: Design & development focuses on structuring how these prerequisites relate to UX factors within an extended evaluation scope. In design science research, such structuring artifacts are used to make implicit relationships explicit and to support understanding of complex evaluation phenomena [23, 24]. Thus, qualitative and quantitative analyses of UX factors are used to identify where existing instruments fail to provide meaningful assessments. Based on these insights, the artifact will be a measurement instrument that specifies which aspects must be represented in a holistic UX evaluation and how they relate to each other.

Step 4: Demonstration and *Step 5: Evaluation* examine whether this scope extension improves the interpretability of UX evaluation results in empirical settings. The artifacts are evaluated in DSR by assessing their explanatory power and their usefulness for understanding the problem domain [25].

Overall, DSRM provides the methodological basis for systematically developing and empirically grounding an extension of the scope of UX evaluation. The following section describes how this process is operationalized through complementary empirical study types.

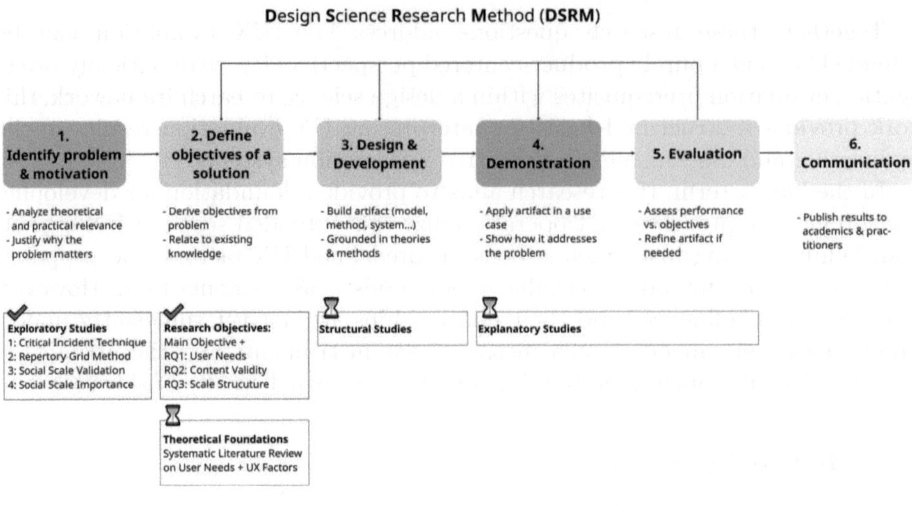

Fig. 1. Design Science Research Methodology [22] applied to this doctoral research. The figure illustrates the main research steps and their iterative nature as well as the current and planned phases of the work.

3.3 Methodology

To operationalize the DSRM process, this research follows an iterative empirical strategy consisting of exploratory, structural, and explanatory studies (see Fig. 1). Such staged research designs are commonly used to progressively build, formalize, and test understanding of complex phenomena [26].

In *Step 1*, the initial interpretability problem is addressed by investigating how UX evaluations are formed from the user's perspective. Using mixed-method approaches, including the Critical Incident Technique and the Repertory Grid Method (see Sect. 2.2), the exploratory studies identified user- and context-related prerequisites such as goals, situational conditions, and evaluation criteria that shape UX factor assessments. These approaches are particularly suited to uncovering experience formation processes that cannot be captured through predefined measurement constructs [14].

In *Step 3*, the *structural studies* examine how the prerequisites identified in *Step 1* relate to existing UX evaluation approaches. Quantitative validation approaches are applied to analyze content validity and structural properties of UX scales. Such analyses are necessary for determining whether measurement constructs adequately represent the phenomena they intend to capture [27]. In this doctoral research, the structural studies serve to reveal limitations in the applicability and interpretability of UX scales across usage contexts.

In *Step 4* and *Step 5*, the *explanatory studies* investigate how variations in evaluation prerequisites influence the interpretation of UX factors in practice. By systematically examining how selected user needs and contextual conditions affect UX ratings, these studies test the explanatory power of the conceptual artifact. In design science research, such empirical evaluation is used to assess whether an artifact improves understanding of the problem domain [25].

Overall, this combination of exploratory, structural, and explanatory studies enables a stepwise investigation of the identified scope problem: first by uncovering evaluation prerequisites, then by relating them to existing UX factors, and finally by examining how they influence the interpretability of UX evaluation results in practice. Across these study types, the results are iteratively integrated into the artifact, progressively refining the extended scope of UX evaluation and its underlying structure.

4 Discussion and Outlook

The preliminary findings highlight a fundamental challenge for UX evaluation: the interpretability of UX results cannot be fully understood without considering the conditions under which they are formed. Existing approaches provide standardized factor assessments but offer limited guidance on how results should be interpreted in relation to users' goals, situational contexts, and interaction conditions (see Sect. 2). Established approaches predominantly assess the effects of user-product interaction, while user- and context-related prerequisites remain implicit. It therefore often remains unclear whether UX evaluations reflect system qualities, situational constraints, or the fulfillment of underlying user needs. For practitioners, making these prerequisites explicit can help avoid misinterpretation of UX scores and support more informed design decisions under specific usage conditions.

A key challenge for future research lies in systematically integrating these prerequisites into UX evaluation, clarifying how user needs, contextual conditions, and interaction situations shape the formation and interpretation of UX factors. The ongoing doctoral research addresses this by progressively extending the scope of UX evaluation. The expected contribution is a clearer foundation for interpreting UX results and, in the longer term, the basis for a measurement instrument that captures what is necessary to produce meaningful and interpretable assessments of interactive information systems.

The ongoing doctoral research addresses these challenges by progressively extending the scope of UX evaluation to explicitly incorporate user- and context-related prerequisites. The expected contribution is a clearer foundation for interpreting UX evaluation results, enabling a more differentiated understanding of what UX assessments indicate in practice and supporting more informed use of UX data in the design and evaluation of interactive information systems. In the longer term, the proposed scope extension provides the basis for developing a measurement instrument that enables a more holistic assessment of UX. By clarifying how user needs and contextual conditions shape UX evaluation, this work defines what such an instrument must capture to produce meaningful and interpretable results.

Acknowledgments. This research was supported by the EQUAVEL project PID2022-137646OB-C31, funded by MICIU/AEI/10.13039/501100011033 and by ERDF, EU.

Disclosure of Interests. The authors have no competing interests to declare that are relevant to the content of this article.

References

1. International Organization for Standardization: ISO 9241–210:2019(en) Ergonomics of human-system interaction – Part 210: Human-centred design for interactive systems (2019). https://www.iso.org/obp/ui/#iso:std:iso:9241:-210:ed-2:v1:en. Accessed 20 Feb 2026
2. Lallemand, C., Koenig, V.: Measuring the contextual dimension of user experience: development of the user experience context scale (UXCS). In: Proceedings of the 11th Nordic Conference on Human-Computer Interaction (NordiCHI '20), article 55, pp. 1–13. ACM, New York (2020). https://doi.org/10.1145/3419249.3420156
3. Tullis, T., Albert, W.: Measuring the User Experience: Collecting, Analyzing, and Presenting Usability Metrics, 2nd edn. Morgan Kaufmann, Oxford (2013). https://doi.org/10.1016/C2011-0-00016-9
4. Schrepp, M., Thomaschewski, J.: Design and validation of a framework for the creation of user experience questionnaires. Int. J. Int. Multimedia Artif. Intell. **5**(7), 88–95 (2019). https://doi.org/10.9781/ijimai.2019.06.006
5. Hassenzahl, M., Burmester, M., Koller, F.: AttrakDiff: Ein Fragebogen zur Messung wahrgenommener hedonischer und pragmatischer Qualität. In: Szwillus, G., Ziegler, J. (eds.) Mensch & Computer 2003: Interaktion in Bewegung, pp. 187–196. Teubner, Stuttgart (2003)
6. Lewis, J.R.: The system usability scale: past, present, and future. Int. J. Hum. Comput. Int. **34**(7), 577–590 (2018). https://doi.org/10.1080/10447318.2018.1455307
7. Hassenzahl, M.: Experience Design: Technology for All the Right Reasons. Morgan & Claypool Publishers, San Rafael, CA (2010)
8. Klein, A.M., Deutschländer, J., Kölln, K., Rauschenberger, M., Escalona, M.J.: Exploring the context of use for voice user interfaces: toward context-dependent user experience quality testing. J. Softw. Evolution Process **36**(7), e2618 (2024). https://doi.org/10.1002/smr.2618
9. Hinderks, A., Schrepp, M., Domínguez Mayo, F.J., Escalona, M.J., Thomaschewski, J.: Developing a UX KPI based on the user experience questionnaire. Comput. Stand. Interfaces **65**, 38–44 (2019). https://doi.org/10.1016/j.csi.2019.01.007
10. Hinderks, A., Schrepp, M., Rauschenberger, M., Thomaschewski, J.: Reconstruction and validation of the UX factor trust for the user experience questionnaire plus (UEQ+). In: Proceedings of the 19th International Conference on Web Information Systems and Technologies (WEBIST 2023), pp. 319–329 (2023). https://doi.org/10.25968/opus-3146
11. Klein, A.M., Hinderks, A., Schrepp, M., Thomaschewski, J.: Construction of UEQ+ scales for voice quality: measuring user experience quality of voice interaction. In: Proceedings of Mensch und Computer 2020 (MuC '20), pp. 1–5. ACM, New York (2020). https://doi.org/10.1145/3404983.3410003

12. Mortazavi, E., Doyon-Poulin, P., Imbeau, D., Robert, J.-M.: Development and validation of four social scales for the UX evaluation of interactive products. Int. J. Hum. Comput. Int. **40**(20), 6608–6621 (2024). https://doi.org/10.1080/10447318.2023.2258026
13. Klein, A.M., Kollmorgen, J., Hinderks, A., Schrepp, M., Rauschenberger, M., Escalona, M.J.: Validation of the UEQ+ scales for voice quality. Comput. Stand. Int. **93**, 103971 (2025). https://doi.org/10.1016/j.csi.2024.103971
14. Hassenzahl, M., Diefenbach, S., Göritz, A.: Needs, affect, and interactive products - facets of user experience. Interact. Comput. **22**(5), 353–362 (2010). https://doi.org/10.1016/j.intcom.2010.04.002
15. Kölln, K., Deutschländer, J., Klein, A.M., Rauschenberger, M., Winter, D.: Identifying user experience aspects for voice user interfaces with intensive users. In: Proceedings of the 18th International Conference on Web Information Systems and Technologies (WEBIST 2022), pp. 385–393. SciTePress (2022). https://doi.org/10.5220/0011383300003318
16. International Organization for Standardization: ISO/IEC 25064:2013 Systems and software engineering - Systems and software Quality Requirements and Evaluation (SQuaRE) - Common Industry Format (CIF) for usability: User needs report. ISO, Geneva (2013)
17. Sheldon, K.M., Elliot, A.J., Kim, Y., Kasser, T.: What is satisfying about satisfying events? testing 10 candidate psychological needs. J. Pers. Soc. Psychol. **80**(2), 325–339 (2001). https://doi.org/10.1037/0022-3514.80.2.325
18. Kollmorgen, J., Hinderks, A., Thomaschewski, J.: Selecting the appropriate user experience questionnaire and guidance for interpretation: the UEQ family. Int. J. Int. Multimedia Artif. Intell. **9**(4), 126–139 (2025). https://doi.org/10.9781/ijimai.2024.08.005
19. Kollmorgen, J., Turhan, Y., Escalona, M.J., Thomaschewski, J.: Influence of UX factors on user behavior: the critical incident technique. In: Proceedings of the 21st International Conference on Web Information Systems and Technologies (WEBIST 2025), vol. 1, pp. 121–132. SciTePress (2025). https://doi.org/10.5220/0013669600003985
20. Kollmorgen, J., Hinderks, A., Escalona, M.J., Thomaschewski, J.: Identification of cross-product experience factors. In: Schrepp, M. (ed.) Design, User Experience, and Usability, pp. 391–408. Springer Nature Switzerland, Cham (2025). https://doi.org/10.1007/978-3-031-93224-3_25
21. Kollmorgen, J., Hinderks, A., Escalona, M.J., Thomaschewski, J.: Protocol for validation of the UEQ+ social factors. ResearchGate preprint (2025). https://doi.org/10.13140/RG.2.2.30881.26729
22. Peffers, K., Tuunanen, T., Rothenberger, M.A., Chatterjee, S.: A design science research methodology for information systems research. J. Manag. Inf. Syst. **24**(3), 45–77 (2007)
23. Hevner, A.R., March, S.T., Park, J., Ram, S.: Design science in information systems research. Manag. Inf. Syst. Q. **28**(1), 75–106 (2004). https://doi.org/10.2307/25148625
24. Wand, Y., Weber, R.: Research commentary: information systems and conceptual modeling – a research agenda. Inf. Syst. Res. **13**(4), 363–376 (2002)
25. Gregor, S., Hevner, A.R.: Positioning and presenting design science research for maximum impact. Manag. Inf. Syst. Q. **37**(2), 337–355 (2013). https://doi.org/10.25300/MISQ/2013/37.2.01

26. Edmondson, A.C., McManus, S.E.: Methodological fit in management field research. Acad. Manag. Rev. **32**(4), 1155–1179 (2007). https://doi.org/10.5465/amr.2007.26586086
27. MacKenzie, S.B., Podsakoff, P.M., Podsakoff, N.P.: Construct measurement and validation procedures in MIS and behavioral research: integrating new and existing techniques. Manag. Inf. Syst. Q. **35**(2), 293–334 (2011). https://doi.org/10.2307/23044045

CAiSE 2026 Doctoral Consortium - Data Foundation for Information System Engineering

A Modernization Decision Framework for Legacy Information Systems

Ada Slupczynski(✉)

Research Group Software Construction, RWTH Aachen University, Aachen, Germany
slupczynski@swc.rwth-aachen.de

Abstract. Modernizing legacy information systems remains challenging due to fragmented knowledge, unclear decision factors, and intuitive rather than systematic approaches. This mid-stage doctoral research addresses these challenges by integrating technical, architectural, and organizational knowledge to support evidence-based modernization decisions. The research contributes: (1) a modernization knowledge ontology synthesizing findings across modernization, EA debt, change management, and compliance; (2) a factor catalog derived through systematic literature review; (3) a decision-making process extending the Renaissance framework with multi-domain considerations; and (4) a proof-of-concept LLM-supported architecture for operationalizing accumulated modernization knowledge in practice. Preliminary results include a terminology hierarchy and synonym inventory, a factor catalog under expert validation, a process with quality gates and feedback loops, and an initial RAG-based tool architecture. This work aims to enable more transparent, quantifiable, and explainable modernization decisions.

Keywords: Modernization · Information Systems · Legacy Systems · Enterprise Architecture · EA Debt

1 Introduction

Modernizing legacy information systems (hereafter referred to as *legacy systems* for brevity) remains a persistent challenge in Information Systems Engineering, particularly for organizations that rely on large, business-critical systems [8]. Such systems typically exhibit high levels of accumulated technical and enterprise architecture debt, which increases maintenance costs and complexity while hindering the organization's ability to adapt to evolving business requirements. As these systems continue to age, knowledge gaps emerge as experts leave or retire, while documentation is usually incomplete, inaccurate, or technically outdated [17]. Despite the availability of numerous modernization methods in scientific literature, identifying a suitable approach for a given legacy system remains challenging due to the lack of standardized decision support [15].

Prior research on modernization has predominantly focused on a technical perspective and existing processes remain largely technical in scope, with

F. Zerbato et al. (Eds.): CAiSE 2026, LNBIP 587, pp. 269–277, 2026.
https://doi.org/10.1007/978-3-032-27997-2_29

recent work only beginning to consider business and organizational perspectives [8,17]. However, the decision of whether and how to modernize is still often driven by technology trends rather than systematic factor-based assessment [5]. This reflects a significant research gap: while individual modernization methods, case studies, and experience reports are well documented, the accumulated knowledge is not structured or operationalized to guide organizational decision-making [2,4].

This doctoral thesis addresses this gap by investigating how modernization decision-making can be systematically supported through the integration of technical, architectural, and organizational knowledge. The research contributes four design artifacts: (1) a modernization knowledge ontology synthesizing findings across multiple areas of concern, (2) an identification and systematization of factors influencing modernization decisions, (3) a process or framework enabling quantifiable and explainable modernization decisions, and (4) a proof-of-concept LLM-supported architecture for evidence-based modernization planning and method selection in practice.

The remainder of this paper presents the problem statement and research questions (Sect. 2), related work (Sect. 3), research methodology (Sect. 4), preliminary results (Sect. 5), and conclusions (Sect. 6).

2 Problem Statement and Research Questions

In our prior study [17], 21 experts (developers, software architects, system architects, and testers) from a large software development organization were interviewed over a ten-month period, revealing three recurring issues: unclear or extensive modernization goals leading to partial outcomes, unavailable or incomplete documentation causing expert misalignment, and framing modernization too narrowly as a technical effort. While the single-organization scope is a limitation, the subsequent exploratory literature review confirmed and broadened these challenges. Based on these findings, four challenges were identified:

- **C1 - Fragmented understanding.** Modernization spans many areas of concern (e.g. technical/EA debt, definitions, methods, change management, compliance) with no unified synthesis.
- **C2 - Unknown decision factors.** Organizations lack clarity on which factors should inform modernization decisions across organizational, technical, and governance domains.
- **C3 - Intuitive decisions.** Modernization decisions rely on intuition rather than structured, quantifiable reasoning.
- **C4 - Knowledge not utilized.** Even when knowledge is gathered, there is no architecture or tool support for applying it in practice.

Each challenge is addressed by a corresponding research question:

RQ1 (C1): *What kind of integration of technical, architectural, and organizational knowledge is necessary to support prudent modernization decisions?*

RQ2 (C2): *Which factors influence modernization decision-making across organizational, technical, and governance domains?*
RQ3 (C3): *What properties must a decision-making process satisfy to enable structured and explainable modernization decisions?*
RQ4 (C4): *What tool architecture would operationalize the modernization knowledge to enable evidence-based modernization decisions?*

3 Related Work

Following Khadka et al. [8], modernization is "the process of evolving existing software systems when traditional maintenance practices can no longer achieve the desired system properties". While Khadka et al. focus on four methods, this work adopts the broader 7Rs taxonomy [1,5]: Retire, Retain, Rehost, Replatform, Redesign, Replace, and Rewrite. The 7Rs provide finer granularity and cover the full decision space - distinguishing Rehost and Replatform and including Retire and Retain. Beyond method classification, the boundaries between modernization and related concepts (e.g., maintenance, reengineering) remain blurred due to inconsistent terminology [14], which further motivates the need for a unified knowledge ontology.

Empirical evidence from both earlier studies [15] and more recent case studies [5] suggests that modernization decisions remain predominantly based on intuition, lacking a systematic assessment of decision factors. Existing studies [3,7,10] treat factors as independent checklists, ignoring interdependencies. Recent work [2,4] identifies process definition as a research opportunity, yet most processes focus only on method selection. Warren & Ransom [18] propose a process model but focus primarily on technical considerations, while previous studies [8,17] show that framing modernization too narrowly as a technical task leads to organizational problems.

In summary, existing research lacks: (1) a comprehensive synthesis across modernization domains, (2) factor catalogs with interdependencies, (3) factor-aware decision processes, and (4) practical tool support.

4 Research Method

The research follows Design Science Research (DSR) [6], an appropriate paradigm for producing prescriptive, evaluated artifacts addressing real-world organizational problems. Each step builds on the results of the previous one, progressing from understanding the problem domain to producing actionable decision support.

In the first step, **semi-structured interviews** (N = 21, over 10 months) [17] with practitioners from a large software development organization identified the four challenges described in Sect. 2. Then, an iterative **exploratory literature review** produced a *modernization knowledge ontology* covering terminology, technical/EA debt, stakeholder engagement, compliance, decision making, and methods classification.

Based on identified knowledge gaps, a **systematic literature review (SLR)** [11,12], supervised as a Master's thesis and extended by the author, yielded a *catalog of 70 factors* with interdependencies across business and technical categories. A **two-part expert questionnaire** was designed for validation: Part 1 (completed, N = 14) confirmed the factors and added industry-specific ones; Part 2 (in progress) will assess interdependencies, impact, and prioritization. A second SLR on modernization methods produced a *classification of 62 justifications and 10 needs* (under review) grouped into 10 method properties. Both SLRs followed established guidelines [9]; the first searched ACM, dblp, IEEE, Inspec, and Scopus, and the second IEEE, ScienceDirect, Scopus, Springer Link, and IET Digital Library.

Synthesizing the knowledge ontology, factor catalog, and method classification, a *7-phase decision-making process* was designed by extending the Renaissance [18] process with Prudence Evaluation Process (PEP) [16] and with the multi-domain knowledge gathered in the preceding steps, to guide organizations through evidence-based modernization planning. Finally, to make this accumulated knowledge practically accessible, we propose an *LLM-supported tool architecture* using Retrieval-Augmented Generation (RAG), intended as a decision assistant that surfaces relevant factors, methods, and risks.

The four design artifacts constitute the modernization decision framework: the knowledge ontology (addressing RQ1) provides foundational understanding; the factor catalog (addressing RQ2) identifies what to consider; the decision process (addressing RQ3) structures evidence-based planning; and the LLM-supported tool (addressing RQ4) operationalizes accumulated knowledge in practice. The research questions, employed methods, and intended artifacts are illustrated in Fig. 1. Each artifact is evaluated empirically: the knowledge ontology via expert interviews (Q3 2026); the factor catalog via expert questionnaire (N = 14); the decision process via expert walkthroughs with retrospective scenarios (Q4 2026, addressing RQ3); and the LLM prototype via scenario-based practitioner assessment of decision quality and explainability (Q1 2027, addressing RQ4).

5 Preliminary Results

5.1 Modernization Knowledge Ontology

The proposed modernization knowledge ontology synthesizes findings across multiple domains: modernization terminology, technical/EA debt, change management, stakeholder engagement, and compliance. Key preliminary results include clarification of terminology to reduce practitioner confusion (challenge C1).

Terminology Model. Literature analysis revealed inconsistent use of modernization terms (e.g., *digitalization*, *maintenance*, *reengineering*) [14] and activity descriptors (*technique*, *approach*, *method*). Our five-level preliminary conceptual

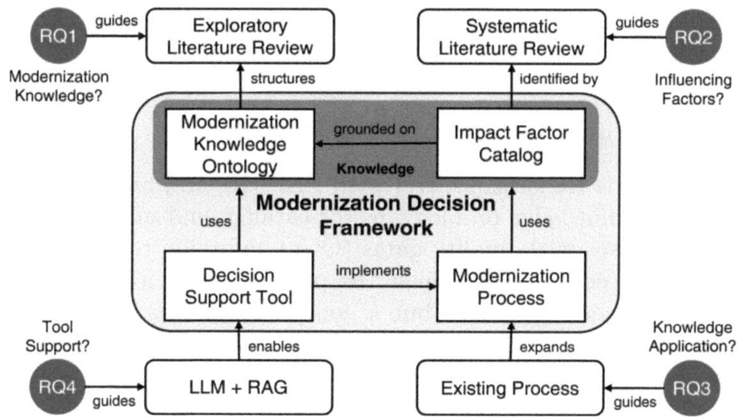

Fig. 1. Overview of the research questions, employed methods, and intended results.

model distinguishes: (1) Modernization approach (umbrella term), (2) Modernization strategy (big bang vs. iterative), (3) Modernization method (7Rs taxonomy), (4) Modernization technique (specific implementation, e.g., wrapping for Retain), and (5) Modernization task (fine-granular activities).

Method Synonyms. Modernization methods are used interchangeably in the literature. An initial synonym inventory maps common aliases to each of the 7Rs (e.g., Retain → Encapsulation/Wrap; Replatform → Containerization; Redesign → Refactor/Rearchitect).

Beyond terminology, the ontology covers: (1) *technical and EA debt*, where accumulated debt across code, architecture, and enterprise levels creates interdependencies that single-perspective assessments miss; (2) *change management*, where resistance and insufficient stakeholder involvement cause failures even when technical execution succeeds [13]; and (3) *compliance* requirements (e.g., DORA, NIS2) that increasingly constrain modernization options. The ontology's coverage and terminological consistency will be validated via expert interviews (Q3 2026).

5.2 Modernization Factors

The SLR identified 70 factors with interdependencies across six factor categories: Business, Organizational, Project Management, Maintenance, System Characteristics, and Business Effects. Unlike prior work [3,7] treating factors as independent checklists, our catalog captures relations between factors. For example, Business Strategy drives Modernization Projects, which are constrained by the complexity of Legacy Systems and Technical Debt. This relational structure reveals that addressing technical factors alone is insufficient; business and organizational factors must be considered simultaneously. Preliminary validation ($N = 14$) confirmed the factors and identified additional industry-specific ones.

Ongoing validation (Part 2) will further assess interdependency accuracy and factor prioritization.

5.3 Modernization Decision-Making Process

The process expands Renaissance [18] with PEP [16] and multi-domain considerations from the knowledge ontology, factor catalog, and method classification. It comprises 7 phases with quality gates (QGs) enforcing readiness before progression (Fig. 2). Feedback loops make the process inherently cyclical: modernization is never a one-time effort but a continuous cycle. Documentation and communication are cross-cutting concerns active throughout all phases. Key differentiators include: (1) separation of strategic and operational planning, (2) multi-domain scope beyond purely technical concerns, and (3) multiple feedback loops enabling iteration. Evaluation via expert walkthroughs with retrospective scenarios (Q4 2026) will assess whether quality gates and feedback loops improve decision traceability.

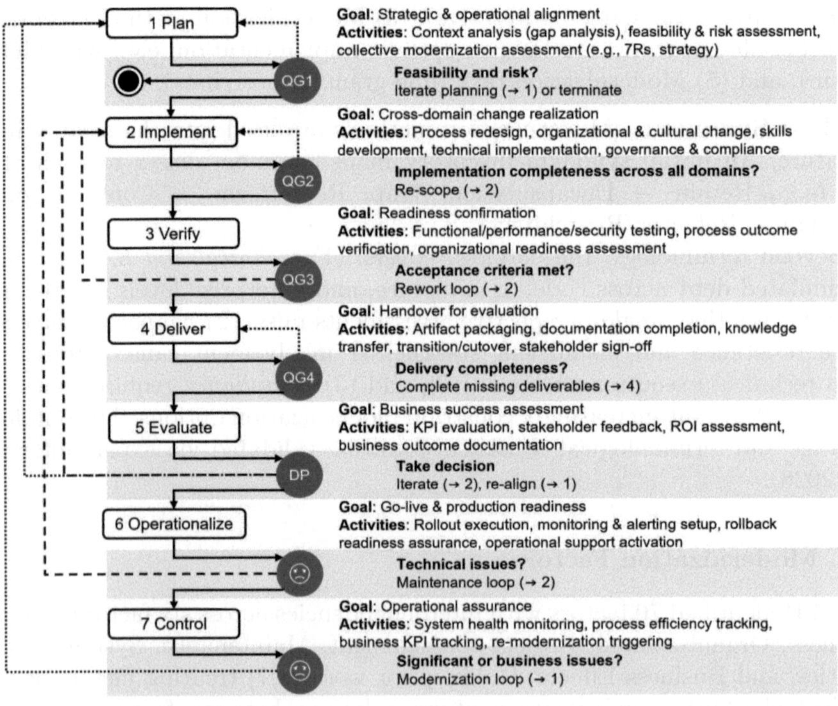

Fig. 2. Simplified modernization decision-making process (QG - Quality Gate, DP - Decision Point).

5.4 Modernization Decision Tool Support

The planned proof-of-concept RAG-based LLM tool is intended to operationalize accumulated knowledge by retrieving relevant factors, querying EA/Technical Debt repositories, and synthesizing knowledge for decision support.

Experts interact with the tool conversationally, providing system characteristics, architectural context, and relevant documentation; the tool retrieves applicable factors and methods accordingly. It is designed to augment rather than replace expert judgment: for example, given a legacy banking system migration, it would surface relevant factors (e.g., Technical Debt, Compliance), suggest applicable methods, and highlight risks from similar cases. An initial architecture has been designed; prototype evaluation (Q1 2027) will measure recommendation relevance, decision traceability, and explainability.

6 Conclusion and Future Work

This doctoral research develops four design artifacts (a modernization knowledge ontology, factor catalog, decision-making process, and LLM-supported tool) to enable systematic, evidence-based modernization decisions. While preliminary results have been presented, several planned evaluation steps remain.

The remaining work proceeds in four phases: (1) expert questionnaire Part 2 to assess factor interdependencies, impact, and prioritization (Q2 2026); (2) ontology validation via expert interviews (Q3 2026); (3) expert walkthroughs with retrospective scenarios to evaluate the decision process (Q4 2026); and (4) scenario-based practitioner evaluation of the RAG-based LLM prototype (Q1 2027). Expected thesis completion is Q2 2027.

Key discussion points include: evaluation criteria for the LLM tool beyond retrieval accuracy, strategies for cross-organization process validation, and the appropriate granularity for factor interdependency modeling.

Declaration of competing interests. The authors have no competing interests to declare that are relevant to the content of this article.

Declaration of AI-assisted technologies in the writing process. In the preparation of this manuscript, LLMs were used with the sole purpose of language improvement. All contributions belong to the authors. After using this tool/service, the authors reviewed and edited the content as needed and take full responsibility for the content of the published article.

References

1. Amazon Web Services: 6 Strategies for Migrating Applications to the Cloud | Amazon Web Services. Accessed on: 28-05-2023 (2016). https://aws.amazon.com/de/blogs/enterprise-strategy/6-strategies-for-migrating-applications-to-the-cloud/

2. Assunção, W.K.G., Marchezan, L., Arkoh, L., Egyed, A., Ramler, R.: Contemporary software modernization: strategies, driving forces, and research opportunities. ACM Trans. Softw. Eng. Methodol. **34**(5), 1–35 (2025)
3. Brandtberg, R.: Re-engineering strategies for legacy software systems. Helsinki: University of Helsinki, pp. 1–2 (2020)
4. Chaima, M., Sofiane, A., Assia, B.: Modernizing legacy it systems: methods, challenges, and strategic insights. In: 2024 1st International Conference on Innovative and Intelligent Information Technologies (IC3IT), pp. 1–6. IEEE (2024)
5. Hayretci, H.E., Aydemir, F.B.: A multi case study on legacy system migration in the banking industry. In: La Rosa, M., Sadiq, S., Teniente, E. (eds.) CAiSE 2021. LNCS, vol. 12751, pp. 536–550. Springer, Cham (2021). https://doi.org/10.1007/978-3-030-79382-1_32
6. Hevner, A.R., March, S.T., Park, J., Ram, S.: Design science in information systems research. MIS Q. **28**(1), 75–106 (2004)
7. Kankaanpää, I., Tiihonen, P., Ahonen, J., Koskinen, J., Tilus, T., Sivula, H.: Legacy system evolution-a comparative study of modernisation and replacement initiation factors (2007)
8. Khadka, R., Batlajery, B.V., Saeidi, A.M., Jansen, S., Hage, J.: How do professionals perceive legacy systems and software modernization? In: Jalote, P., Briand, L., van der Hoek, A. (eds.) Proceedings of the 36th International Conference on Software Engineering, pp. 36–47. ACM, New York, NY, USA (2014). https://doi.org/10.1145/2568225.2568318
9. Kitchenham, B.: Guidelines for performing Systematic Literature Reviews in software engineering, eBSE Technical Report EBSE-2007-01 (2007)
10. Langbauer, E.: Factors influencing the legacy system modernization strategy/author ING. Emanuel langbauer, BSC (2019)
11. Pazova, A.: Factors Involved in Modernization Decision Making. Master's thesis, RWTH Aachen University, unpublished, planned to be published in 2026 (2024). https://doi.org/10.18154/RWTH-2026-03190
12. Pazova, A.: Factors involved in modernization decision making. In: 27. Workshop Software-Reengineering und-Evolution WSRE 2025, p. 15 (2025)
13. Ponnusamy, S., Eswararaj, D.: Navigating the modernization of legacy applications and data: effective strategies and best practices. Asian J. Res. Comput. Sci. **16**(4), 239–256 (2023)
14. Saarelainen, M., Hotti, V.: Different notions lead difficulties of making information system modernization decisions. In: The Fourth International Conference on Digital Information Processing and Communications (ICDIPC2014), SDIWC, pp. 43–52. (2014)
15. Saarelainen, M.M., et al.: Software modernization and replacement decision making in industry: a qualitative study. In: Proceedings of the 10th International Conference on Evaluation and Assessment in Software Engineering, pp. 12–21. Electronic Workshops in Computing, BCS Learning & Development (2006). https://doi.org/10.14236/ewic/EASE2006.3
16. Slupczynski, A., Alexander, P., Lichter, H.: Defining and evaluating prudence and recklessness of enterprise architecture debt. In: Filipe, J., Śmiałek, M., Brodsky, A., Hammoudi, S. (eds.) Enterprise Information Systems, pp. 237–261. Springer Nature Switzerland, Cham (2024)

17. Slupczynski, A., Lichter, H.: Challenges and impact factors on modernization projects - results of an industry study (2025). https://dl.gi.de/handle/20.500.12116/46588
18. Warren, I., Ransom, J.: Renaissance: a method to support software system evolution, pp. 415–420 (2002). https://doi.org/10.1109/CMPSAC.2002.1045037

Object-Centric Event Data: Conceptualization, Extraction and Querying

Hosna Hooshyar(✉)

Free University of Bozen-Bolzano, Bozen-Bolzano, Italy
Hosna.Hooshyar@student.unibz.it

Abstract. *Object-centric process mining (OCPM)* addresses the limitations of case-centric process mining by allowing events to relate to multiple objects of different types and by capturing object-to-object relationships. However, the practical adoption of OCPM is still hindered by three challenges: (1) conceptualizing *object-centric event data (OCED)* in a standardized way that is semantically precise and interoperable across tools, (2) investigating how OCED can be extracted from legacy information systems according to this model, including the assumptions and trade-offs involved, and (3) identifying the requirements and principles for querying OCED in a way that respects its unflattened structure. This PhD research tackles these challenges by developing an ontology-based conceptual model for object-centric event data grounded in unified foundational ontologies, investigating how ontology-based data access can support the extraction of OCED from existing information systems, and defining the semantic requirements and design principles for querying OCED. Preliminary results include an initial UFO-based metamodel that addresses limitations of current object-centric event data representations, including the current OCED Core Model, capturing object relationships, event-to-event relations, and the temporal evolution of object attributes and relations.

Keywords: Object-Centric Event Data · Object-centric process mining · Event Log Format · Event Log Extraction · Querying

1 Introduction

Process science is a multidisciplinary field that integrates insights from information technology and management sciences to analyze, enhance, and manage operational processes [3]. Within this paradigm, process mining focuses on delivering fact-based and actionable outcomes to support continuous improvement of organizations [4]. Event data (or event logs) consist of sets of events retrieved from databases that depict the execution of processes [7]. Traditional process mining techniques assume that each event log captures the life-cycle of a single

F. Zerbato et al. (Eds.): CAiSE 2026, LNBIP 587, pp. 278–286, 2026.
https://doi.org/10.1007/978-3-032-27997-2_30

object, known as *case*. Consequently, every event in the log is linked to exactly one case, and different objects are analyzed in isolation [25].

However, real-world information systems often present a more complex reality: objects frequently interact with one another, and events may be associated with multiple objects of varying types [6]. To analyze real-world event data under case-centric presumptions one must select a specific case identifier, and flatten the data [14]. This flattening step alters the integrity of event logs and introduces several issues, including loss of events, convergence, and divergence [6].

To address these challenges, *object-centric process mining (OCPM)* has been proposed. Unlike traditional approaches, where each event is linked to a single case, OCPM allows an event to be associated with multiple objects of different types. It also acknowledges that objects can participate in numerous events, and recognizes Object-to-Object (O2O) relationships [2].

The foundation of any process mining technique is its event log, as process mining is enabled by the digital footprint of recorded events [4]. This makes OCED a critical component of OCPM. However, working with event data originating from heterogeneous information systems requires a precise conceptualization and a standardized representation of OCED to ensure unambiguous interpretation and interoperability between tools and systems [13]. In addition, practical adoption depends on methods to extract OCED from diverse legacy information systems and on querying techniques that allow users to retrieve insights from object-centric data, since existing querying approaches are no longer directly applicable [23].

This PhD research aims to address these challenges by (1) developing a conceptual model for OCED that overcomes limitations of existing representations, (2) investigating how object-centric event data can be extracted from legacy information systems according to this model, and (3) designing querying methods compatible with the unflattened nature of OCED, enabling users to query object-centric data effectively.

The rest of the paper is organized as follows. Section 2 reviews the work most closely related to the conceptualization, extraction, and querying of OCED. Section 3 presents preliminary results, introducing our metamodel. Section 4 outlines the research plan, and Sect. 5 concludes and discusses future perspectives.

2 Related Work

Van der Aalst et al. present one of the first studies on object-centricity by introducing the Object-Centric Behavioral Constraint model and defining an object-centric event log as a set of process events in which multiple object types interact, events reference multiple objects and objects participate in multiple events [5].

2.1 Conceptualization

[18] introduced OCEL V1, dealing with events, objects, their attributes, and many-to-many *Event-to-Object relations (E2O)*. However, it does not account for

Event-to-Event relations (E2E), O2O, dynamic attributes, or any characteristics of E2O. OCEL V1 was extended by [19] into *Data-aware OCEL (DOCEL)*, supporting attributes with multiple simultaneous values, and dynamic attribute values. The OCEL V1 was extended to OCEL V2 [8], in which object attributes can be dynamic, supporting time-varying attributes without explicitly anchoring them to events. E2O and O2O relations can now include a qualifier, however, events continue to be atomic, E2E relations are still not supported, and O2O are still modelled as static. *Event-Knowledge Graphs (EKGs)* were introduced to provide a graph-structured representation of OCEDs [16]. An EKG supports many-to-many E2O, (static) O2O and incorporates E2E to express directly-follows dependencies between events. Later on, Fahland et al. proposed a core metamodel[1] for OCED, depicted in Fig. 1 [17]. This metamodel represents the simplest structure (based on the number of concepts and relations) for object-centric event data that the OCED working group was able to identify.

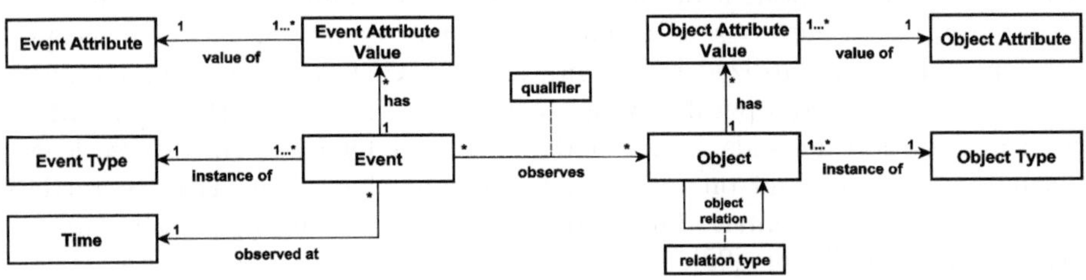

Fig. 1. OCED Core Model proposed by Fahland et al. [17]

2.2 Extraction

Case-centric event log extraction relies on identifying relevant entities and selecting one as the case [16]. This requirement highlights why this approach is unsuitable for OCED: it forces the log to be centered around a single case. Accordingly, several works shift to richer extraction.

Fahland derives an EKG from a multi-entity event table by creating event nodes, identifying entities, and adding directly-follows relations between events linked to the same entity [16]. OnProm toolkit supports semi-automatic extraction from legacy systems using *Ontology-Based Data Access (OBDA)* method. OnProm V1 targets XES, while OnProm V2 adds OCEL [12,28]. Although the authors report linear scalability, the approach is limited to relational databases and requires substantial manual modeling effort. Berti et al. extract OCEL logs from SAP ERP by building a graph of relations from a manually selected master table and mapping tables to primitive events, which are then automatically

[1] For simplicity, this model will be referred to as the *Core Model* throughout the remainder of this work.

translated into an OCEL; however, the approach is SAP-specific and depends on master-table selection [9,10].

Swevels et al. transform legacy data into OCED by adapting the event knowledge graph model and formalizing OCED as a property-graph schema with a two-layer base ontology [16,26]. Miri et al. [24] propose **OCPM^2**, a generalized OCED extraction methodology extending PM^2 [17]; a case study shows feasibility but also limitations, especially in capturing accurate E2O relationships. Wei et al. introduce **Dirigo**, which extracts OCEL V2-compliant logs and captures the temporal dimension of O2O [27].

2.3 Querying

To date, the development of process querying methods remains largely fragmented. Numerous languages and systems have been designed independently, often without coordination or integration across efforts [1]. In comparison, the querying of OCED is even less mature and remains underexplored. Only a limited number of approaches have explicitly addressed querying in object-centric settings. Two notable approaches to querying OCED that have been explored in the literature are: (1) Esser and Fahland model multi-dimensional event data as a labeled property graph and show that retrieval and aggregation queries can be expressed in Cypher [15]; (2) Küsters and Van der Aalst propose *Object-Centric Process Querying* (OCPQ), a nested object-centric query approach with a graphical tool, supporting tasks such as constraint checking and filtering over an OCEL V2-inspired data model [23].

3 Preliminary Results

From the conceptualization perspective, the project aimed to develop a metamodel for object-centric event data that can be used to analyze and compare existing representations, including the current OCED Core Model (shown in Fig. 1). These limitations include event atomicity, the absence of explicit E2E, limited semantic, ambiguous representation of certain notions (e.g., O2O), and the static treatment of object relationships.

This work adopts an ontology-based approach to conceptualize OCED, motivated by two primary factors. Firstly, business process modeling predominantly focuses on entities resembling events and, in contrast, the (structural) conceptual modeling discipline focuses on object-like entities [21]. An ontology-based approach can effectively capture and balance both object-oriented and event-oriented perspectives. Secondly, traditional conceptual modeling techniques often lack precise semantic specifications for their underlying model terminology, leading to inconsistent interpretations and applications of knowledge.

To address the mentioned limitations, we adopted a theoretical framework specifically designed to model events, objects, their properties, and relations. This framework is based on a subset of the *Unified Foundational Ontology (UFO)* [20], namely the UFO-B [22]. We focused on a specific subset of UFO-B, called

gUFO[2] a gentle, lightweight, OWL-based ontology, engineered to facilitate the application of UFO-B in diverse domains, including Semantic Web technologies. Our ontology-based metamodel is depicted in Fig. 2.

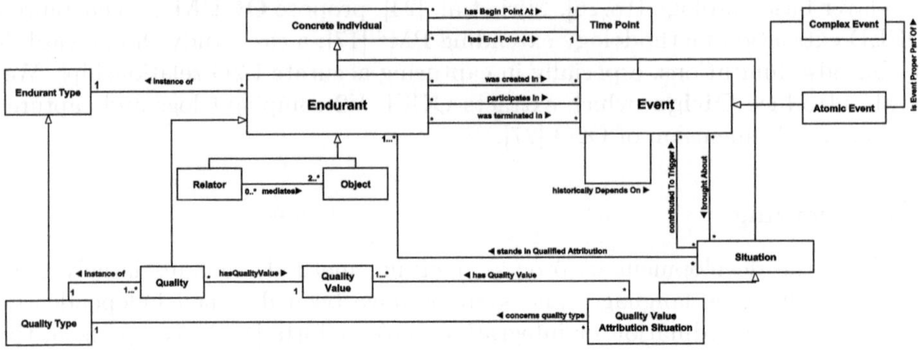

Fig. 2. Proposed gUFO-based metamodel for OCED

4 Research Plan

Considering the initial results on the conceptualization aspect of the project, at this stage, the main focus is on the extraction. However, two parallel lines of research will be followed too: the evaluation of metamodel and querying.

4.1 OCED: Conceptualization

Unambiguity and expressiveness are two important properties of OCED [17]. To evaluate the proposed metamodel with respect to these dimensions, we employ Alloy to formally model a series of real-world examples using the Core Model, OCEL 2.0, and the proposed metamodel. The resulting formalizations are then compared to assess whether the proposed metamodel provides improvements in terms of clarity and expressive power.

4.2 OCED: Extraction

On the data extraction side, the objective is to extract OCED from legacy information systems. Most existing approaches are designed to work with specific types of input data (e.g., data in ERP format, case-centric event logs) and targets a particular OCED format (e.g., OCEL V1, EKG). These approaches also operate under certain assumptions about the maturity level of the input data. The development of the OCED extraction methodology will be guided by the following research questions:

[2] https://nemo-ufes.github.io/gufo/.

- **RQ.1:** Which assumptions about source data and domain knowledge are necessary for faithful OCED extraction, and to what extent can these assumptions be relaxed or automated?"
- **RQ.2:** What trade-offs arise between source-independence, automation effort, extraction quality, and performance when extracting OCED from heterogeneous systems?
- **RQ.3:** What requirements must an extraction model satisfy to capture all information necessary for constructing OCED, including dynamic object attributes and relations, from legacy information systems?
- **RQ.4:** Which metrics best evaluate OCED extraction quality and effort, and how do alternative extraction approaches perform under these metrics?

The foundation of our extraction method is *Ontology-Based Data Access (OBDA)* [11], which offers several advantages: it relies on logical formalisms with well-understood semantics and computational properties, and it allows data to remain in its original sources rather than requiring migration. Adopting this method, our ontology-driven conceptualization can serve as the final framework for OCED extraction. Xiong et al. detailed how they employed OBDA to extract OCED from relational databases based on OCEL V1 [28]. As a first step, we use their approach as a baseline to identify which assumptions, semantic commitments, and limitations must be revised for OCED extraction under our metamodel. The authors first selected a subset of tables from a dataset and modeled the underlying information system as $I = \langle R, D \rangle$, where R is the relational schema and D the set of data instances. They then defined a domain ontology T together with a mapping M to construct a VKG over I. The mapping M links I to T and consists of mapping assertions pairing (1) a SQL query over I (**Source**) with (2) a triple template over T (**Target**).

Next, the VKG is aligned with an event ontology E by annotating classes in T with elements of E. This is the point where our OCED metamodel is instantiated, since E provides the vocabulary for the event-log concepts and relations required by the standard. Finally, once annotations are completed, OnProm generates an updated VKG specification, along with a derived mapping M' and the event ontology E. As a result, the original information system I is exposed as a VKG expressed in the vocabulary of the event standard.

4.3 OCED: Querying

In the first step, we will use the OCPQ approach introduced by [23] as a baseline to assess which querying requirements are already supported and which remain open for ontology-based OCED representations. Although their definition of OCED is inspired by OCEL V2, the authors state that their querying method is independent of any specific OCED model. This makes it well-suited for integration with our ontology-based metamodel. At the same time, we plan to incorporate a set of requirements for querying OCED, as identified by Esser and Fahland [15], which focus on structural and behavioral aspects of multi-dimensional event data.

5 Conclusion

This PhD project targets the challenges that currently limit the adoption of object-centric process mining: an unambiguous conceptualization of OCED, reliable extraction from heterogeneous legacy systems, and querying capabilities that match the many-to-many relations of the data. Building on preliminary work, we adopt an ontology-based approach grounded in gUFO to strengthen the semantics of key notions (events, objects, attributes, and relations) and to better represent object-to-object and event-to-event associations as well as changes over time. Next steps focus on (1) implementing and evaluating an OBDA-driven extraction methodology across multiple data sources and domains with dedicated quality metrics (e.g., completeness of object attributes and relations), and (2) developing a querying approach that satisfies structural/behavioral requirements while remaining usable for stakeholders with different levels of technical expertise. The resulting extraction pipeline, and querying method, are intended to improve interoperability, reduce information loss, and enable more effective analysis of real-world, object-centric processes[3].

References

1. Process querying methods. Process Querying Methods (2022). https://api.semanticscholar.org/CorpusID:248385546
2. van der Aalst, W.M.P.: Academic Perspective: How Object-Centric Process Mining Helps to Unleash Predictive and Generative AI, pp. 219–232. Springer Nature Switzerland, Cham (2024). https://doi.org/10.1007/978-3-031-61343-2_22. https://doi.org/10.1007/978-3-031-61343-2_22
3. van der Aalst, W.M.: Data science in action (2016). https://api.semanticscholar.org/CorpusID:63302911
4. van der Aalst, W.M.: Object-centric process mining: dealing with divergence and convergence in event data. In: IEEE International Conference on Software Engineering and Formal Methods (2019). https://api.semanticscholar.org/CorpusID:202158060
5. van der Aalst, W.M., Li, G., Montali, M.: Object-centric behavioral constraints. ArXiv abs/1703.05740 (2017). https://api.semanticscholar.org/CorpusID:1251806
6. Adams, J.N., Park, G., Levich, S., Schuster, D., van der Aalst, W.M.: A framework for extracting and encoding features from object-centric event data. ArXiv abs/2209.01219 (2022). https://api.semanticscholar.org/CorpusID:252089617
7. Berti, A., van der Aalst, W.M.: Oc-pm: analyzing object-centric event logs and process models. Int. J. Softw. Tools Technol. Transfer **25**, 1–17 (2022). https://api.semanticscholar.org/CorpusID:252383512
8. Berti, A., et al.: OCEL (object-centric event log) 2.0 specification. ArXiv abs/2403.01975 (2024). https://api.semanticscholar.org/CorpusID:268247880

[3] During the preparation of this work, the author used ChatGPT in order to: Improve writing style, Grammar and spelling check, Paraphrase and reword. After using this tool/service, the author reviewed and edited the content as needed and take full responsibility for the publication's content.

9. Berti, A., Park, G., Rafiei, M., van der Aalst, W.M.P.: A generic approach to extract object-centric event data from databases supporting SAP ERP. J. Intell. Inf. Syst. **61**, 835–857 (2023). https://api.semanticscholar.org/CorpusID:259756855
10. Berti, A., Park, G., Rafiei, M., van der Aalst, W.M.: An event data extraction approach from sap erp for process mining. In: ICPM Workshops (2021), https://api.semanticscholar.org/CorpusID:238419098
11. Calvanese, D.: Ontology-based data access: from theory to practice (2012). https://api.semanticscholar.org/CorpusID:263695587
12. Calvanese, D., KALAYCI, T.E., Montali, M., Santoso, A.: The ONPROM toolchain for extracting business process logs using ontology-based data access. In: International Conference on Business Process Management (2017). https://api.semanticscholar.org/CorpusID:473692
13. van Dongen, B.F., van der Aalst, W.M.: A meta model for process mining data. In: EMOI-INTEROP (2005). https://api.semanticscholar.org/CorpusID:1358231
14. Esser, S., Fahland, D.: Storing and querying multi-dimensional process event logs using graph databases. In: Business Process Management Workshops (2019). https://api.semanticscholar.org/CorpusID:208004690
15. Esser, S., Fahland, D.: Multi-dimensional event data in graph databases. J. Data Seman. **10**, 109–141 (2020). https://api.semanticscholar.org/CorpusID:219124021
16. Fahland, D.: Process mining over multiple behavioral dimensions with event knowledge graphs. In: Process Mining Handbook (2022). https://api.semanticscholar.org/CorpusID:250095403
17. Fahland, D., et al.: Towards a simple and extensible standard for object-centric event data (oced) - core model, design space, and lessons learned. ArXiv abs/2410.14495 (2024). https://api.semanticscholar.org/CorpusID:273482617
18. Ghahfarokhi, A.F., Park, G., Berti, A., van der Aalst, W.M.: OCEL: a standard for object-centric event logs. In: Symposium on Advances in Databases and Information Systems (2021). https://api.semanticscholar.org/CorpusID:236992634
19. Goossens, A., Smedt, J.D., Vanthienen, J., van der Aalst, W.M.: Enhancing data-awareness of object-centric event logs. In: ICPM Workshops (2022). https://api.semanticscholar.org/CorpusID:254275413
20. Guizzardi, G., Benevides, A.B., Fonseca, C.M., Porello, D., Almeida, J.P.A., Sales, T.P.: UFO: unified foundational ontology. Appl. Ontology 17, 167–210 (2021). https://api.semanticscholar.org/CorpusID:244875087
21. Guizzardi, G., Guarino, N., Almeida, J., Almeida, A.: Ontological considerations about the representation of events and endurants in business models (2016). https://doi.org/10.1007/978-3-319-45348-4_2
22. Guizzardi, G., Wagner, G., de Almeida Falbo, R., Guizzardi, R., Almeida, J.P.A.: Towards ontological foundations for the conceptual modeling of events. In: International Conference on Conceptual Modeling (2013). https://api.semanticscholar.org/CorpusID:9223003
23. Küsters, A., van der Aalst, W.M.P.: Ocpq: Object-centric process querying and constraints. In: Research Challenges in Information Science (2025). https://api.semanticscholar.org/CorpusID:279124199
24. Miri, N.Y., Khayatbashi, S., Zdravkovic, J., Jalali, A.: Ocpm2: extending the process mining methodology for object-centric event data extraction. ArXiv abs/2503.10735 (2025). https://api.semanticscholar.org/CorpusID:277043345
25. Rebmann, A., Rehse, J.R., van der Aa, H.: Uncovering object-centric data in classical event logs for the automated transformation from XES to OCEL. In:

International Conference on Business Process Management (2022). https://api.semanticscholar.org/CorpusID:251438879
26. Swevels, A., Fahland, D., Montali, M.: Implementing object-centric event data models in event knowledge graphs. In: ICPM Workshops (2023). https://api.semanticscholar.org/CorpusID:269147669
27. Wei, J., Ouyang, C., ter Hofstede, A., Wang, Y., Huang, L.: Dirigo: a method to extract event logs for object-centric processes. ArXiv abs/2411.07490 (2024). https://api.semanticscholar.org/CorpusID:273969909
28. Xiong, J., Xiao, G., Tahir, Kalayci, T.E., Montali, M., Gu, Z., Calvanese, D.: A virtual knowledge graph based approach for object-centric event logs extraction. In: ICPM Workshops (2022). https://api.semanticscholar.org/CorpusID:253101054

Integrating Geospatial Data Into Business Process Management

Vito Chan(✉)

Humboldt-Universität zu Berlin, Unter den Linden 6, 10117 Berlin, Germany
vito.chan@hu-berlin.de

Abstract. Business Process Management (BPM) traditionally focuses on digitally mediated processes supported by Process-Aware Information Systems (PAIS). While effective in capturing control-flow events, current approaches provide limited visibility into processes unfolding within physical environments. Geospatial data, capturing real-world phenomena, is a promising tool to bridge this gap. However, existing BPM methods offer limited support for leveraging such spatio-temporal data. This research investigates how geospatial data can be integrated into BPM to bridge the gap between digital process traces and physical execution. To achieve this overarching goal, we define three objectives: (1) integrate geospatial data into PAIS to capture events and the physical execution of processes, (2) represent geospatial information in event logs while preserving spatial and temporal characteristics, and (3) embed geospatially enriched event data into process mining techniques to enable spatially-aware discovery, conformance checking, and analysis. Following an algorithm engineering methodology, this research develops artifacts to establish structured design knowledge and define a solution space for geospatially enabled BPM of real-world processes.

Keywords: Process-Aware Information Systems · Geospatial Data · Business Process Management

1 Introduction

Business Process Management (BPM) is an interdisciplinary field that integrates information technology and management science to develop methods and knowledge for understanding, managing, and improving operational processes [10,22]. At the core of BPM, Process-Aware Information Systems (PAIS) serve as a crucial component that supports the management, execution, and monitoring of operational processes [9]. By providing these functionalities, PAIS are central to capturing information about events, activities, and decisions within a process [21]. Through this information, they provide the foundation to obtain insights into operational processes and to facilitate process improvement using process mining techniques [22]. While traditional BPM approaches have been effective for processes that are digitally supported or computer-mediated, the technological and operational landscape is rapidly evolving.

F. Zerbato et al. (Eds.): CAiSE 2026, LNBIP 587, pp. 287–294, 2026.
https://doi.org/10.1007/978-3-032-27997-2_31

Over the past decade, rapid technological progress and large-scale production have made Internet of Things (IoT) devices, sensor networks, and connected mobile technologies both more powerful and more affordable. Unlike traditional PAIS that primarily capture digitally mediated interactions involving humans and software systems [22], these technologies enable the observation of physical objects and environmental conditions. Examples include air pressure measurements recorded onboard an aircraft, photographic records collected at road intersections, or Global Positioning System (GPS) traces captured through smartphones. Because such systems are often inherently location-aware, the data they generate is typically geospatial.

We define geospatial data as data linked to a spatial reference, where the associated attributes may describe real-world phenomena or identifiable entities. By capturing raw physical phenomena from the real world, geospatial data offers the potential to bridge the gap between information systems and physical operations, revealing processes that were previously unrecorded [13]. If we picture a fast-food restaurant, the order management system may record when an order is placed, started, completed, and served. By integrating sensors and indoor positioning technologies, it becomes possible to observe when and where specific subprocesses take place, such as cooking the patty, assembling the burger, or preparing the fries. This opens opportunities for understanding and managing real-world processes with a level of granularity and contextual awareness that was previously unattainable.

Despite the potential of geospatial data, current PAIS offer limited support for leveraging geospatial data effectively, and existing approaches exhibit critical shortcomings. Location information within current PAIS often undergoes significant abstraction in both spatial and temporal dimensions. Doing so imposes a predefined structure that may be biased and may constrain analytical depth. Currently, geospatial data is predominantly used for basic performance evaluation, task assignment, or modeling of constraints and conditions, while the potential for deriving deeper process insights remains largely unexplored.

This research project aims to address this gap by integrating geospatial data into BPM, thereby enhancing process insights and effective process management. This integration is realized through three design directions: (1) integrate geospatial data into PAIS to capture events and the physical execution of processes, (2) represent geospatial information in event logs while preserving spatial and temporal characteristics, and (3) embed geospatially enriched event data into process mining techniques.

The remainder of this paper is structured as follows. Section 2 provides the background and motivation of this research project. Section 3 defines the research goal. Section 4 reports current results. Section 5 presents the work in progress. Section 6 summarizes and concludes this paper.

2 Background

The early forms of PAIS can be traced back to Workflow Management Systems, which were designed primarily to capture the execution of digitally mediated tasks and interactions [22]. Although PAIS has since evolved into a broader class of systems, it retains a strong focus on the control-flow aspect and provides limited visibility into physical execution and the environment of processes. These constraints undermine the effectiveness of process management and the modeling of complex process behavior, particularly for domains where processes are inherently spatial, such as logistics and supply chain systems.

In BPM, context-aware approaches have addressed the integration of contextual information in process-aware systems and analysis [2,4,6,11,14]. Prior work has explored capturing various contextual dimensions, which also include spatial and environmental attributes [2,4,6,11,14]. However, these approaches exhibit critical shortcomings. Due to the limited support for location information, location information is typically treated as categorical attributes and often undergoes significant abstraction in both spatial and temporal dimensions. Spatial abstraction involves aggregation into higher-level representations, such as regions, transport routes, or proximities. Temporal dynamics, on the other hand, are often discretized, capturing positions only during events or stops, such as package departures and arrivals at logistics facilities, which omits the continuous trajectory between locations. Although abstraction may improve interpretability by reducing data complexity, it risks information loss and potential bias toward predefined structures, constraining the depth of analysis. Additionally, it can obscure explicit spatial relationships, limiting advanced spatial analysis and spatial operations.

While some approaches, namely location-aware, environment-aware, and geo-enabled systems, have explicitly addressed the geospatial aspect [3,5,8,12,18–20, 23–25], they focus primarily on the static locations at discrete time points [3,12, 18,19,23–25], thereby imposing similar constraints as context-aware frameworks. Only a limited number of studies have investigated the integration of Geographic Information Systems (GIS) to retain full spatio-temporal granularity [5,24]. As a result, geospatial data is predominantly used for basic performance evaluation [3, 20], task assignment [12,20], or modeling of constraints and conditions [3,5,8, 18,20,23–25], while the potential for deriving deeper process insights remains largely unexplored.

Another relevant direction in the literature concerns the use of IoT sensor data for process analysis [1,7,15]. These studies investigate process understanding using data from local IoT sensors, yet location information was not utilized. While location information may be enriched into the event data, the representation of complex spatial features typically remains highly abstracted, thereby omitting explicit spatial relationships. Additionally, although IoT represents a significant source of geospatial data, other types of geospatial data, such as census data, satellite data, and georeferenced social media data, are not yet considered.

3 Research Goal

This research project investigates how geospatial data can be incorporated into BPM to bridge the gap between digital process traces and physical process execution and to enhance process analysis (Fig. 1). Based on the three design directions introduced in Sect. 1, the following research questions are formulated:

RQ1: How can geospatial data be incorporated into Process-Aware Information Systems to capture physical process execution and events?
RQ2: How can geospatial data be represented within event logs while preserving its spatio-temporal characteristics?
RQ3: How can geospatially enriched process data be incorporated into process mining techniques to enhance process discovery and analytical capabilities?

This research project follows an algorithm engineering methodology [16]. Research questions are addressed through the design, development, and evaluation of artifacts to establish a structured solution space for geospatially enabled process management.

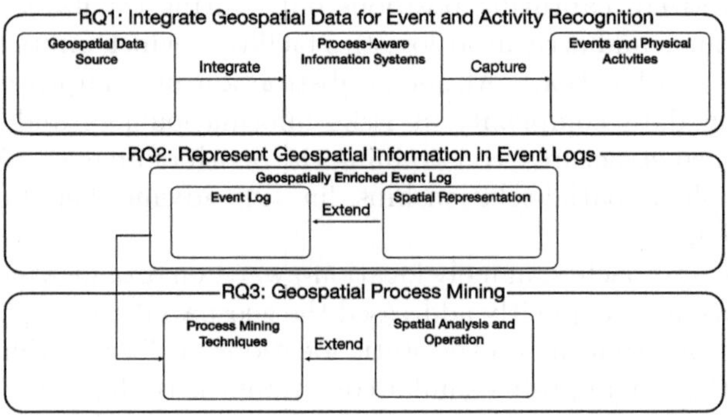

Fig. 1. Three-step framework for integrating geospatial data into BPM, covering data capture, spatio-temporal event log representation, and spatially aware process analysis.

4 Current Result: Monitoring Land-Centric Business Processes Using Remote Sensing and Satellite Data

This journal submission, currently under review, addresses **RQ1** and constitutes the first artifact. As an initial step, we identified a class of processes that cannot be readily captured by traditional information systems, which we refer to as land-centric processes. These processes are centered on land as the focal entity and are characterized by activities carried out predominantly outside PAIS, making them particularly challenging to monitor and manage with conventional PAIS.

While such activities are typically not recorded in PAIS, they often produce continuous and observable transformations of the land surface, which can be observed through remote sensing data, a form of geospatial data. We conceptualize these transformations as process-relevant state changes that enable the inference of underlying process execution. Leveraging remote sensing data, we develop a framework for integrating remote sensing data into process monitoring. By identifying relevant state transitions, the framework enables the inference of corresponding process events, thereby bridging the gap between physical operations and digital process traces.

To evaluate the feasibility of the framework, we implemented a prototype artifact in the domain of agricultural monitoring, focusing on the seed-to-harvest lifecycle as a representative land-centric process. The artifact integrates satellite imagery and survey data from the United States National Aeronautics and Space Administration (NASA) and the United States Department of Agriculture (USDA) to monitor farming processes across 506 farm patches between 2008 and 2022. The evaluation shows that crop development states can be identified from satellite observations and translated into inferred process events.

This work establishes a proof-of-concept for leveraging remote sensing data in BPM and provides initial design knowledge regarding the use of geospatial data for event inference. Additionally, this work contributes to providing new event logs of real-world processes to the community.

5 Work in Progress: Transforming Football Data Into Object-Centric Event Logs with Spatial Context Information

The current stage of the research focuses on **RQ2**, which concerns the representation of geospatial data within event logs. Existing event log standards and meta-models provide limited support for geospatial data, particularly when dealing with high spatio-temporal granularity and complex spatial relationships. This limitation becomes evident in scenarios such as team sports, where continuous player trajectories and dynamic interactions shape process behavior.

As a preliminary step, we investigated how geospatial data can be incorporated into existing event log meta-models using a real-world football dataset from Metrica Sports [17]. The dataset combines spatial trajectory data of players with a traditional event log capturing match events such as goals, substitutions, and penalty cards. While location markers can be included as simple attributes in existing event log formats, this approach fails to capture the full spatial dynamic and environmental context of events or to capture relationships between moving objects. To address this limitation, we leverage object-centric process mining and develop an object-centric modeling framework in which spatial entities, such as field regions, are treated as an object class. By modeling location as an object class, the framework enables a structured representation of spatial context within the process model while retaining spatial relationships between locations. Building on the spatially enriched object-centric event log, we further developed visualizations that project process instances onto a spatial map, thereby enabling a spatial perspective on process execution. The preliminary results have been presented at the BPM Workshop in 2025.

Despite these advances, the proposed framework still requires spatial abstraction, and challenges remain in formally modeling implicit spatial relationships between locations and objects. This sets a goal of the current research. The objective is to design a geospatial extension to the eXtensible Event Stream (XES) standard that enables the structured representation of geospatial information, including dynamic geometries, such as trajectories and spatial zones, and heterogeneous locational references, thereby supporting spatial analysis and operations. This conceptual extension will constitute the primary artifact of this phase and provide the foundation for address **RQ3**. Building on the geospatially extended event log, the next step involves integrating spatial reasoning and operations into process mining techniques, enabling spatially-aware discovery and analysis. This includes identifying spatial patterns and trajectories in process execution, detecting deviations from expected locations or routes, and analyzing location-based variations in process behavior. By embedding spatial relationships into process mining algorithms and visualizations, this research aims to bridge digital process traces with their physical execution context and uncover insights that remain hidden in traditional control-flow-based analysis.

6 Conclusion

This research project aims to conceptualize the integration of geospatial data into BPM to bridge the gap between digital process traces and physical process execution, while enhancing process analysis. Across three phases, the project addresses limitations in current Process-Aware Information Systems and process mining techniques, developing artifacts that generate design knowledge on: (1) the integration of geospatial data into PAIS to capture events and physical execution of processes, (2) the representation of geospatial information in event logs while preserving spatial and temporal characteristics, and (3) the embedding of geospatially enriched event data into process mining techniques to enable spatially aware discovery, conformance checking, and analysis. Together, these artifacts establish a structured framework for geospatially enabled process management, providing both methodological guidance and practical tools for analyzing processes in their real-world spatial context, thereby enabling deeper process insights and more effective process management.

Acknowledgments. This work was supervised by Jan Mendling and Stephan Fahrenkrog-Petersen. Vito Chan reports financial support provided by Federal Ministry of Research, Technology and Space.

Declaration on Generative AI. During the preparation of this work, the author used ChatGPT in order to: Grammar and spelling check, Paraphrase and reword. After using these tools/services, the author reviewed and edited the content as needed and takes full responsibility for the publication's content.

Disclosure of Interests. The authors have no competing interests to declare that are relevant to the content of this article.

References

1. Ahmadi, Z., Bertrand, Y., Pozo Romero, M.I., Serral, E.: Analysing the foraging behaviour of bees using process mining: a case study. ICPM, pp. 5–18. Springer (2023)
2. Ahmadi, Z., De Weerdt, J., Serral Asensio, E.: Context-driven process discovery: enhancing process flow interpretability with contextualized activity hierarchies. SoSyM (2025)
3. Behkamal, B., et al.: Geo-Enabled Business Process Modeling (2022)
4. Bertrand, Y., De Weerdt, J., Serral, E.: A novel multi-perspective trace clustering technique for IoT-enhanced processes: a case study in smart manufacturing. In: BPM, pp. 395–412. Springer, Cham (2023)
5. Blank, P., Maurer, M., Siebenhofer, M., Rogge-Solti, A., Schonig, S.: Location-Aware Path Alignment in Process Mining. In: 2016 IEEE 20th International Enterprise Distributed Object Computing Workshop (EDOCW), pp. 1–8 (2016)
6. Brunk, J.: Structuring business process context information for process monitoring and prediction. IEEE 22nd CBI **1**, 39–48 (2020)
7. Brzychczy, E., Żuber, A., van der Aalst, W.: Process mining of mining processes: analyzing longwall coal excavation using event data. TSMC-Syst. (2024)
8. Corradini, F., Mozzoni, L., Piccioni, J., Re, B., Rossi, L., Tiezzi, F.: Modeling, formalizing, and animating environment-aware bpmn collaborations. In: BPM, pp. 106–125. Springer, Cham (2026)
9. Dumas, M., Aalst, W.M.v.d., Hofstede, A.H.t.: Process-Aware Information Systems: Bridging People and Software Through Process Technology. John Wiley & Sons (2005)
10. Dumas, M., La Rosa, M., Mendling, J., Reijers, H.A.: Introduction to business process management. In: Fundamentals of Business Process Management, pp. 1–33. Springer (2018)
11. Dörndorfer, J., Seel, C.: A Framework to Model and Implement Mobile Context-Aware Business Applications, pp. 23–38. (2018)
12. Fernandez-Llatas, C., Lizondo, A., Monton, E., Benedi, J.M., Traver, V.: Process mining methodology for health process tracking using real-time indoor location systems. Sensors **15**(12), 29821–29840 (2015)
13. Janiesch, C., et al.: The internet-of-things meets business process management: a manifesto. IEEE SMC Mag. **6**(4), 34–44 (2020)
14. Koschmider, A., Mannhardt, F., Heuser, T.: On the contextualization of event-activity mappings. In: BPM Workshops, pp. 445–457. Springer, Cham (2019)
15. Lepsien, A., Bosselmann, J., Melfsen, A., Koschmider, A.: Process mining on video data. In: ZEUS. CEUR-WS.org (2022)
16. Mendling, J., Leopold, H., Meyerhenke, H., Depaire, B.: Methodology of algorithm engineering. ACM Comput. Surv. **58**(4), 1–38 (2026)
17. MetricaSports: metricasports/sample-data: Metrica sports sample data (2021). https://github.com/metrica-sports/sample-data. Accessed: 06-10-2025
18. Poss, L., Dietz, L., Schönig, S.: LABPMN: Location-Aware Business Process Modeling and Notation. In: CoopIS, pp. 198–216. Springer, Cham (2024)
19. Poss, L., Schönig, S.: Location-aware business process modeling and execution. SoSyM **24**(1), 37–67 (2025)
20. Tchemeube, R.B., Amyot, D., Mouttham, A.: Location-aware business process management for real-time monitoring of a cardiac care process, pp. 230–244 (2013)

21. Van Der Aalst, W.: Process mining: overview and opportunities. ACM TMIS **3**(2), 1–17 (2012)
22. Van Der Aalst, W.M.: Process-aware information systems: design, enactment, and analysis. In: WECSE, pp. 2221–2233. Wiley, 1 edn (2009)
23. Zhu, X., Recker, J., Zhu, G., Maria Santoro, F.: Exploring location-dependency in process modeling. BPMJ **20**(6), 794–815 (2014)
24. Zhu, X., Vanden Broucke, S., Zhu, G., Vanthienen, J., Baesens, B.: Enabling flexible location-aware business process modeling and execution. DSS **83**, 1–9 (2016)
25. Zhu, X., Zhu, G., Baesens, B.: Towards location-aware process modeling and execution, pp. 186–197 (2014)

Author Index

F. Zerbato et al. (Eds.): CAiSE 2026, LNBIP 587, pp. 295–296, 2026.
https://doi.org/10.1007/978-3-032-27997-2

MIX
Papier aus verantwortungsvollen Quellen
Paper from responsible sources
FSC® C105338

If you have any concerns about our products,
you can contact us on
ProductSafety@springernature.com

In case Publisher is established outside the EU,
the EU authorized representative is:
Springer Nature Customer Service Center GmbH
Europaplatz 3, 69115 Heidelberg, Germany

Printed by Libri Plureos GmbH
in Hamburg, Germany